A GOOD BIRTH, A SAFE BIRTH

"The book is terrific. Rarely do two authors of such understanding and commitment collaborate to produce such a work. There must be dozens of general information books available on childbirth, but this one stands entirely alone as the most thoroughly presented, most personally practical and most timely of all. . . . If only there was a way for every mother to read it."

—David Stewart, Ph.D.
Medical Statistician and Executive
Director, NAPSAC International

"It delivers a long overdue message to the medical field about the nature of the birth process as seen from center stage. My congratulations."

—Norman Cousins, author of
Anatomy of an Illness

"Diana Korte and Robert Scaer have done a superb job. They show that what women want is also best for their babies. They help us understand doctors, nurses, and hospitals, and give practical, effective strategies for having a good, safe birth. This is a book I can recommend wholeheartedly and with enthusiasm. It says it all!"

—Lynn Moen, President
Birth and Life Bookstores

"A warm-hearted, level-headed, and devastatingly well-documented look at the way the medical world makes life miserable for women in childbirth. . . . Korte and Scaer tell you what to do to protect yourself *and* your baby from the unwarranted interferences customary in most hospitals. . . . From now on I'm giving *A Good Birth, A Safe Birth* to all my pregnant friends."

—Karen Pryor, author of
Nursing Your Baby

A GOOD BIRTH, A SAFE BIRTH

"The chronic obstetrical crisis that has been building for several centuries is now reaching an acute stage. The year 1984 is the right time to publish such a book."

—Michel Odent, M.D., author of
Birth Reborn

"The information presented in this well-written, thought-provoking book could make a fundamental positive change in the emotional quality of the birth for both mother and father. I was especially intrigued by the idea of having present at the labor and birth, in addition to the father, a female doula (someone to care for the mother and father and be their advocate with doctors and nurses) and a monitrice (a private obstetrical nurse)."

—Lucy Waletzky, M.D.
Clinical Assistant Professor of
Psychiatry and Obstetrics and Gynecology
Georgetown University Hospital
Washington D.C.

"*A Good Birth, A Safe Birth* should help mothers open up discussions with everyone involved in their births—the best way to begin planning for one of the most important days in your life and your baby's."

—Gail Sforza Brewer, author of
*The Brewer Medical Diet for Normal
and High-Risk Pregnancy*

"Women have the right to enjoy the full pleasure potential of their own bodies that comes through their unique gifts of birthing, breastfeeding and mothering. This clear and interesting book is full of useful suggestions about how to make childbearing a really good experience."

—Niles Newton, Ph.D.
Professor of Behavioral Sciences
Northwestern University Medical School

A GOOD BIRTH, A SAFE BIRTH

"I strongly recommend this well written and researched book for parents who wish to be informed enough to join the professionals in the decision-making process for their own infant's birth."

—Marshall Klaus, M.D.
author of *Parent-Infant Bonding*
Professor and Chairman,
Department of Pediatrics
Michigan State University

"The book everyone's been waiting for. I wish I could give it to every pregnant woman."

—Barbara Seaman, author of
Women and the Crisis in Sex Hormones
Co-Founder, National Women's Health Network

"A marvelous teaching tool for childbirth educators written without fear or hostility. It helps put to rest many of the myths and mysteries surrounding birth."

—Rhondda Evans Hartman, R.N., M.A.
Bradley Childbirth Instructor

"Physicians truly concerned with the well-being of mothers and their infants should read this book, because it so deeply reflects the heart of women and their justifiable resistance to hospital-based obstetric care."

—Doris Haire, President
American Foundation for
Maternal and Child Health

A GOOD BIRTH, A SAFE BIRTH

Diana Korte and
Roberta Scaer

Bantam Books
Toronto ▪ New York ▪ London ▪ Sydney

A GOOD BIRTH, A SAFE BIRTH

A Bantam Book / March 1984

Book design by Renée Gelman.

Cover photograph by Mimi Cotter

Library of Congress Cataloging in Publication Data

Korte, Diana.
  A good birth, a safe birth.

  Bibliography: p. 300
  Includes index.
  1. Childbirth.   2. Childbirth—Psychological aspects.
  3. Pregnant women—Family relationships.   4. Hospitals,
  Gynecologic and obstetric.   I. Scaer, Roberta.   II. Title.
RG652.K67 1984   618.2   83-20008
ISBN 0-553-34068-9 (pbk.)

Published simultaneously in the United States and Canada

Bantam Books are published by Bantam Books, Inc. Its trademark, consisting of the words "Bantam Books" and the portrayal of a rooster, is Registered in the United States Patent and Trademark Office and in other countries. Marca Registrada. Bantam Books, Inc., 666 Fifth Avenue, New York, New York 10103.

PRINTED IN THE UNITED STATES OF AMERICA

FG   0   9   8   7   6   5   4   3   2   1

With affection, to all the women we know in La Leche League who helped us toward the good births, breastfeeding, and mothering of our children.

CONTENTS

ACKNOWLEDGMENTS

We're both grateful to our husbands, Gene Korte and Bob Scaer, and all eight of our children—Kathy, Mike, Andy, and Amanda Scaer . . . and Neil, Drew, Aren, and Juliana Korte. They encouraged us, while putting up with our joint, all-consuming passion to write this book.

Many others helped, too. Mary Ann Fitzharris, our Boulder editor, not only cleaned up our copy before we submitted it but kept encouragement flowing. We're grateful for the advice and feedback our manuscript readers gave us: Renee Chalfant-Bednark, Darleen Eide, Donna Ewy, Pat and Michael Fritsch, Jan Graham Lippitt, Pam Novotny, Barbara Pfeifle, Karen Pryor, Judy Sanders, and David Stewart, among others.

Local March of Dimes Director Becky Messina was invaluable. She launched the M.O.M. Survey with financial support from the Northern Colorado chapter of the March of Dimes. We thank the forty-two volunteers who helped us with the Boulder survey. Our special appreciation goes to Shannon Pope in Wenatchee, Washington, and The COMA Committee (Bobbi Seabolt, DeSales Beling, Linda Levy, Mary T. Maher, Linda Schummers, Susan M. Treanor, and Cheryl E. Wood) in Baltimore, Maryland, for sharing their survey results and enthusiasm with us. Thanks also go to the thousands of women who participated in all three surveys and others who responded to us in workshops or told of their concerns in phone calls and letters.

We can't forget Boulder's Community Hospital—its administrators, doctors, nurses, and trustees who worked with us and other consumers to give women the maternity care they want. The process was often heated, but the job was well done and something for all of us to be proud of. Special thanks to Patrick Cussen, then director of nursing at Community Hospital, who guided the maternity-care changes through the morass of hospital bureaucracy.

Dozens of health professionals provided us with interviews and copies of research findings. Many are cited throughout the book, and others are listed in the references. A special nod goes to those who didn't agree with us but cooperated anyway. We must give credit to those matchless sources of information David and Lee Stewart, the directors of the National Association of Parents and Professionals for Safe Alternatives in Childbirth (NAPSAC), and Madeleine Shearer, editor of the journal *Birth*.

The following are our major influences and forerunners, listed alphabetically: American Society for Psychoprophylaxsis in Obstetrics

(ASPO), Suzanne Arms, Robert Bradley, Adelle Davis, Donna Ewy, Ina May Gaskin, Doris Haire, Rhondda Hartman, International Childbirth Education Association (ICEA), Marjorie Karmel, Sheila Kitzinger, John Kennell, Marshall Klaus, La Leche League International, Ashley Montagu, Niles Newton, and Karen Pryor.

And, finally, special mention goes to Toni Burbank, our Bantam editor, who gave us the freedom to write the book that we knew had never been written before, and to our agent, Lynn Seligman, who believed in us.

A GOOD BIRTH,
A SAFE BIRTH

INTRODUCTION

The two trends in hospital childbirth today move simultaneously in opposing directions. One is the growing number of hospitals providing homelike accommodations to couples. (Emphasis: Birth is a human event, a family affair, with no drugs or other intervention.) The other is high-technology childbirth. (Emphasis: Birth is scientific, with electronic fetal monitor, IV, labor induction, analgesia, anesthesia, or cesarean operation.)

Which trend is growing the fastest? Most births finish with one, usually several, high-tech interventions. Cesarean births are now more common (20 percent of all births) than are totally drug-free hospital births (less than 10 percent). For all the talk about bonding, almost all babies are still separated from their mothers most of the time in the hospital. In spite of the now-frequent presence of fathers at births, few women are completely satisfied with their hospital experience.

Are you surprised? Did you think that due to the vast number of media reports about midwives, homelike hospital birth rooms, and the saturation of Lamaze education that women are satisfied with their births and getting the options they want? Our surveys say many are not. We think you can, however, get what you want. That's why we wrote this book for you.

- We give you a sometimes startling summary of medical research regarding childbirth today—as well as a first-ever report of what 2,000 women say they want in hospital births.
- We show you why what many women label the "good" birth is also the "safe" birth for you and your baby.
- We describe the appropriate use of high-tech childbirth interventions based on scientific data, not myth.
- And, most importantly, we tell you how to get the birth you want, step by step, by finding and working with Dr. Right; why and how to hospital-shop; and what you need to know about nurses to get good care once you're in the hospital.

Each of us has spent nearly twenty years working as consumer advocates in the fields of childbirth and breastfeeding. We know there is still widespread discontent with traditional maternity care. The idea for this book began with our Boulder M.O.M. (Maternity Options for Mothers) Survey, which was financially supported by our local March of Dimes (director Becky Messina) a half dozen years ago. It was then that Boulder's Community Hospital (the only one in town with an ob unit) announced that they were going to build a new obstetrical wing.

First, we found out what women wanted through our survey. Then we learned by trial and error how to persuade the hospital not only to change their policies for maternity patients, but to incorporate what women want into hospital blueprints. (See "How to Be a Changemaker.")

The M.O.M. Survey was the first ever done on preferences in maternity care. Our survey results, spread by the media, inundated us with requests for information and help. Two more surveys were finished. Shannon Pope (The Mothers Survey) in blue-collar Wenatchee, Washington, and Bobbi Seabolt (Committee on Maternal Alternatives) in East Coast metropolitan Baltimore both read about our survey in *McCall's* magazine. Inspired to do their own surveys, their results duplicated ours. With voices strong, more than 2,000 women agreed on what's important to them when they have a baby. Details of all three surveys can be found in the Appendix.

Both of us were veteran speakers at La Leche League and childbirth education conferences. Drawing on our experience in counseling women, we began to give workshops on how to negotiate with doctors. Time after time women in the audience wanted to know the how-to's about making maternity changes in hospitals or giving birth the way they wanted.

The comments of these women were crucial in guiding the writing of this book. Women were never satisfied with just knowing the facts about birth. They wanted to know practical tips: "What can I do so that *that* doesn't happen to me?" or "Where do I go, and how do I get that option for me?"

On the way to getting the birth options you want, you need to know the important differences between a health-care consumer and a patient. A consumer uses a service; a patient accepts what's given to her. A consumer requires information to make a choice; a patient does not have a choice. A consumer feels responsibility for her own health; a patient believes her health depends on what the doctor does. A consumer investigates options; a patient doesn't know she has any. Do you see yourself as a health-care consumer or as a patient? If you're like most people, you want to be a health-care consumer, a person who takes responsibility and makes choices. A pregnant woman is a consumer for two—herself and her baby. She pays for a doctor's service (his skills*) to give her prenatal and birth care that assists her in staying healthy and in having a healthy baby.

If you're the average person, you spend less than one tenth of one percent of your lifetime in direct contact with a member of the medical profession. The rest of the time you're on your own. You already are acting as your own health-care supervisor. You may as well make informed choices while you're at it.

Unlike many health professionals, we don't think research information should be withheld from you. Or that some knowledge is too dangerous for you to know. Or that when it comes to questionable procedures, you should simply trust your doctor.

We know that there are women who don't want to be informed, who want to leave their health in their doctor's hands. However, our work with women has convinced us that, given the choice, most women want to participate in their health care. What they usually lack in order to do that is information.

Where do you as a woman get your information? According to one study, nine out of ten women consider their doctor a "very important" source. That's likely to be true for you, too. And maybe that's why so many women don't get the birth experience they want. Here's why:

■ Many women are vague about the kind of birth experience they would like to have until after the baby is born. (All 2,000 women in the consumer surveys had at least one child.) Women pregnant with a first baby aren't sure about what to expect because they are not given full information by childbirth educators, doctors, or hospitals. Many of today's first-time mothers echo Dian G. Smith's sentiments in a magazine article regarding her childbirth education when she said: "We practiced our puffing and blowing conscientiously, and having mastered these, we figured the hard part was over." But it wasn't.

■ Most doctors don't believe it is their responsibility to ask your opinion or offer explanations of every procedure, or to give you a list of possible options from which to choose. And hospitals are doctor centered, not consumer oriented. Hospitals usually provide what doctors call for.

■ Some women may know what they want but not how to get it. Women are not told how to negotiate or even that they need to. We give you such information, in contrast to books that just give you childbirth

*A NOTE ON GENDER: Although one of four medical students today is a woman, nine out of ten practicing physicians are men. Going with what is, we have used masculine pronouns to refer to doctors throughout.

preparation techniques or that attack many contemporary childbirth practices without telling you what to do about them.

This book provides information about options other women want and about the seldom discussed sexual pleasures of pregnancy, birth, and breastfeeding. Birth attendants (midwife and doctor) and places of birth (hospital, birth center, and home) are compared. We present a demystified view of doctors and nurses so that you understand why they do what they do. From pubic shaves to cesareans to newborn jaundice phototherapy, the risks and benefits of modern American childbirth interventions are discussed. And as your best guarantee of having a normal vaginal birth once you're in the hospital, we suggest that in addition to having your husband with you, you have a doula (a special helper) and a monitrice (your personal ob nurse).

This book can help you, whether you're having your first baby and you're wondering where to start, or if this is a later baby and you are more certain about what you do and don't want.

If you're pregnant now, you probably feel vulnerable in every way— and that's normal. That's why we want to give you the information you need to get the birth you want *before* you're laboring in the hospital.

If you believe you must follow all of our suggestions and do everything at once, you may feel overwhelmed. Don't. We encourage you to take only what works for you from this book, to do what you find manageable. It is not our intent to make value judgments for you.

Though research in this book represents the most up-to-date findings at the time of this writing, we know some information will need revising before the ink has a chance to dry. Nothing could be more helpful in preparing future editions than comments, questions, and criticisms from readers. If you wish to contribute, the Appendix has a questionnaire that we encourage you to complete and mail to us.

It's been a long, intense odyssey. We've been close collaborators, co-authors all the way, with our names listed alphabetically. Now our work is done. Linking arms and hearts with you, this book is born, our gift to you, our sisters, daughters, and daughters-in-law, embarking on your journey of giving birth and nurturing new life.

1 · WHAT WOMEN WANT

> I believe the best environment in which to deliver a baby would be within the ob wing, but in a more casual, home-like setting. I think a new mother should be allowed to have as much interaction with family members as she feels up to—including other children, parents, spouse.... The new baby should be allowed in the patient's room during these family gatherings if the parents so wish. I would also encourage as much mother-infant interaction as possible during the stay, interaction hopefully commencing immediately after delivery. I also feel "standing orders" for medication prior to and following delivery should be replaced with individualized recommendations.... Congratulations for caring enough to conduct this important survey.
>
> —Survey mother*

As health-care consumers, we have the right to have a big say in those services that affect our welfare so critically and that cost us so dearly. But instead of finding out what people want and need in their health care, doctors and other health-care providers too often tell us what we'll be getting. So far, that's worked because hospitals and doctors have had a monopoly in their business. In at least one area of health care—childbirth—the situation is changing rapidly.

Today more and more women know what they want to have happen in their childbirth experience. Really, they've known all along, but until recently no one ever asked them what they wanted.

In the late 1970s, three unique studies took care of this oversight. More than 2,000 women were asked to rate hospital maternity options in three different cities. They represented the Northwest (Wenatchee, Washington), the Mountain States (M.O.M. Survey, Boulder, Colorado), and the East Coast (COMA Survey, Baltimore, Maryland)—a cross-section of the nation.

Women of very diverse educational and economic backgrounds came up with virtually the same results: 2,067 women agreed that there are five major needs in maternity care.

*All quotes from women throughout the book are from the three maternity-preference surveys cited, unless otherwise noted.

- They want their husbands present for the labor, delivery, and recovery, and to have unrestricted visiting rights.
- They want cooperation and assistance from the hospital staff—doctors and nurses—in using prepared childbirth techniques.
- Women who breastfeed want effective help from nurses and doctors.
- They want a lot of contact with their babies, immediately after birth and throughout their entire hospital stay.
- They want their other children to visit them and to see and hold the new baby.

ISSUE NUMBER ONE: FATHERS' PRESENCE

The battle to have the husband present at labor and a vaginal birth has been won at most American hospitals. But there are still some doctors who refuse and some hospitals that won't change their policy. In the case of cesareans (at least one in six of all births), the fathers often are made to wait in a waiting room.

The women in the three surveys were in strong agreement on this issue: nearly all of them believe that the father's presence at all times, during labor and delivery and after the birth of the baby, is the most important issue to them. Here's what some of them said:

The only change I would make in my childbirth experience would be that my husband could be with me during labor, even if he doesn't attend a childbirth class ... just for comforting purposes. I was scared and lonely during labor.

The presence of the father throughout labor and delivery is of uppermost importance. After all, having a baby is a combined and most rewarding experience for both parents.

What Research Says About Fathers' Presence

Research supports women who want to have their husbands present during labor and delivery. Deborah Tanzer, Ph.D., was the first researcher to study husband participation in childbirth. She found that when the birth was unmedicated, and the husband was present, the marriage was strengthened. The husband appeared stronger and more helpful, more masculine, and more competent in his wife's eyes. One third of these women describe their births in such blissful terms that Dr. Tanzer concluded that they had what psychologists call a "peak experience," one of transcendent ecstasy. In contrast, none of the women who were alone in labor reported a peak experience. Apparently, the husband's presence was required for women to experience that kind of intense joy, and for women to view their husbands more positively after the birth than before.

One of the most likely times for severe strain in a marriage is in the first months after the birth of a baby, especially the first baby, studies show. Jane and James Pittenger, family counselors and childbirth educators, describe how the routine practices of doctors and hospitals contribute to an absent and disinterested father, an overwhelmed and dissatisfied mother, and confusion and ambivalence for them as a couple and as new parents. Often a woman looks to her doctor for the kind of support her husband could give. The pregnant woman's growing attachment to her doctor is at the expense of her feelings toward her husband. The foundation of the marriage, which combines both pleasure and commitment, is greatly weakened by a birth experience that makes them feel alienated from each other and from their baby.

However, the Pittengers also found that some couples were more satisfied with their marriages after the birth of their baby and found great pleasure in their new roles as parents. The differences between them and dissatisfied couples was that the satisfied parents took time to study together about birthing and parenting. They chose doctors who assisted and supported them, rather than took over. They were together in labor and delivery. Mothers in this group breastfed their babies for many months after birth.

ISSUE NUMBER TWO: INFORMATION AND HELP FROM DOCTORS AND NURSES DURING LABOR AND BIRTH

Nearly 98 percent of American babies are born in hospitals. Mothers go to hospitals to get what they believe is the best care for themselves and their babies. We were not surprised, then, to find that mothers believe strongly in getting informed, positive help from the hospital staff and doctors. A major concern of the mothers is having doctors and nurses trained in prepared childbirth techniques to help them in their labor and delivery.

Voluntary comments from mothers about staff help (or lack of it) during labor and birth were abundant.

The nurse needs to know when to help the husband help his wife or when to help directly—an art.

I will not have another birth in that hospital. Women want and need to be in charge of their whole childbirth experience. There is nothing more frightening for someone having a first baby than to be strapped down in bed, stuck with needles, examined by ten different people, experience terrifying pain and have no one explain it to you, and have absolutely no control over your body whatsoever. At this time a woman needs friendly advice, comfort, and warmth.

Many comments in this section had to do with the use of *anesthesia* (drugs that block sensation) and *analgesia* (drugs used to relieve pain).

I did not have a private ob. The ob that delivered my child was on staff at [X] hospital. I was very displeased with him. He kept trying to push drugs on me when I was in labor. The nurses were very helpful, very kind and understanding.

My last birth I almost had a natural childbirth, but I was too afraid not to have the spinal. I would like to see the hospital teach more about natural childbirth rather than push their own method of delivery. I figure natural childbirth has got to be better than that awful head and neck ache I had for a full week.

Women expect their childbirth education to reduce or eliminate the need for drugs in labor and delivery. But it doesn't work that way for many women, often to their dissatisfaction. The Baltimore survey found that fully 66 percent of the women who were given anesthesia felt that it was *not* necessary for them to deliver in comfort.

Several possibilities come to mind for why this is so. During the stress of labor women may ask for or accept analgesia or anesthesia and then later regret it. Some women tell us that they believe they could have avoided drugs if they'd had more human support and encouragement at crucial moments when relaxation and breathing techniques seemed to fail. Also, the lack of preparation for resisting the routine use of analgesia or anesthesia for almost all deliveries is another possible reason women get unnecessary drugs. Even a woman who may have decided to avoid drugs, if possible, could find herself in hard labor trying to explain to a doctor or nurse why she's different from other women in refusing "something for the pain."

What Medical Research Says About Drugs During Childbirth

Medical research strongly supports the preference of women for staff help in using prepared childbirth techniques to reduce or eliminate analgesics and anesthesia that are risky for mothers and risky for babies.

There is a delicate physical balance between mother and baby during labor and birth that can be disrupted by drugs, with the result that labor may be prolonged. Folklore from individual women and doctors holds that anesthesia has sometimes helped a woman finish dilating quickly after she seemed stuck at 8 or 9 centimeters for several hours. But no research shows that analgesia and anesthesia shorten labor. On the contrary, the slowing effect, particularly of anesthesia, has been documented in the medical literature. In fact, the drug Pitocin is often ordered to accompany anesthesia to offset the labor slowdown.

Analgesia and anesthesia may cause a drop in the mother's blood pressure, which may affect the amount of oxygen the unborn baby receives. Anesthesia often interferes with or eliminates the ability to bear down, requiring the use of forceps in delivery. There is often considerable transfer of the drugs from the mother to the baby, which can cause respiratory distress in the newborn, requiring resuscitation. The transfer of drugs causes short- and long-term effects on the baby. These effects are described in Chapter 7, "The Obstetrician's Black Bag of Interventions."

ISSUE NUMBER THREE: EFFECTIVE HELP FROM NURSES AND DOCTORS WITH BREASTFEEDING

Getting good breastfeeding help from the hospital staff was the third major preference of women. And from their comments it was clear that negative comments about breastfeeding were especially unwelcome.

The nurses were very helpful. They offered suggestions to make breastfeeding more comfortable for me and answered my many questions without making me feel dumb.

I feel all doctors and nurses and pediatricians should do further study on breastfeeding and not rely on ineffective theories about it.

In 1961 only 18 percent of newborns in the United States were breastfed. By 1982, nearly 60 percent of newborns started out being breastfed, reported La Leche League International. Many of these newborns, however, go home from the hospital already receiving bottles of formula or water or nursing through a breast shield placed over the mother's nipple. These kinds of nursing problems are the responsibility of poorly informed doctors and nurses. Most mothers want to breastfeed their newborns, but are not receiving support and information from the staff that will help them nurse successfully.

What Medical Research Says About Breastfeeding

As far back as 1967, Niles Newton, Ph.D., and Michael Newton, M.D., reported in the *New England Journal of Medicine* that failure in breastfeeding can often be traced to the doctor or the hospital experience. The surveys show this is still true. Drugs given to mothers during labor affect the ability of the infant to suck readily at the breast. Also, regulated, restricted, short breastfeedings advocated by many nurses in hospitals lead to reduced milk yield, poor weight gain, more nipple soreness, and greater likelihood of ending the breastfeeding altogether, according to the Newtons.

"The babies of our human ancestors were probably carried and nursed frequently for over 99 percent of our species' existence," says pediatrician John Kennell, M.D. In those cultures where successful breastfeeding continues for an average of two years, the mother and infant are inseparable from birth, and breastfeeding is so frequent that it appears to our eyes to be almost continuous. Dr. Kennell compares the fat and protein content of human milk to other animals', and concludes that human milk was designed for babies to be almost continuous feeders.

If breastfeeding results in more contact with the baby, it also means a larger time commitment on the part of the mother. In this modern world of fast-paced living and lots of demands on our time, why do it? Because hundreds of studies attest to the biochemical superiority of breast milk. New York researcher of pediatric infectious diseases, Jane Pitt, M.D., says, "There is hardly an antiinfective mechanism I can think of that we know of in the body that does not show up in breast milk."

"Formula-fed babies have 80 percent more infections than breastfed babies," says Mark Thoman, M.D., Iowa pediatrician and toxicologist. Only one quarter of breastfed babies "needed to be seen by a doctor even once in their first six months because of illness," reports La Leche League. But almost all (97 percent) of formula-fed babies needed doctor visits for illness in the first six months. And the sick formula-fed infants made more visits to the doctor than the sick breastfed infants. Dr. Thoman also points out that bottle-fed babies have an 80 percent greater chance of developing allergies. And for every nursing baby that succumbs to Sudden Infant Death Syndrome (SIDS), twenty formula-fed babies die of SIDS.

Formula itself is deficient in the more than 100 components of breast milk that have been identified, with more added to the list as research continues. Formula cannot duplicate these as-yet-undiscovered elements. But our breastfed babies are getting them, even though we can't yet give them a label. In addition, breast milk composition varies so enormously from woman to woman that some scientists speculate an individual woman's milk may be especially suited to her own baby's nutritional needs and age. It's not just a matter of your breastfed baby getting Formula A or Formula B, but of getting milk unique for him, and that changes appropriately as he grows older. According to Dr. Thoman, "Mama-lac is still the best."

However, simply breastfeeding because of a sense of duty to the baby isn't sufficient to keep most mothers breastfeeding very long. Dr. Niles Newton, La Leche League, and most successful nursing moms point out the physical and emotional pleasure to the mother that is a natural part of breastfeeding. This pleasure bond between mother and infant is what keeps the mother breastfeeding her baby in the face of difficulties.

The Pittengers describe the advantages of breastfeeding to the father, noting that fathers do not need to express their love for their baby by putting a bottle in its mouth. "In exchange, fathers gain an active, more responsive, sweeter smelling, and healthier baby, a wife who is more apt to be content in her role as mother, and exposure to the breastfeeding style of parenting with its frequent parent-child interactions, touching, and play," say the Pittengers. Almost all men whose wives have successfully nursed feel that the support and protection they give their wives is essential to the success of the nursing relationship.

Again, women are right on the button in their strong preference for breastfeeding help from doctors and nurses. For most mothers to be successful, positive information and support are essential. With an outside network such as La Leche League, many mothers are able to overcome breastfeeding difficulties that begin in the hospital. But the issue remains. Moms want doctors and nurses to give the very best information available on breastfeeding.

ISSUE NUMBER FOUR: CONTACT WITH BABY

A fourth vital concern of women is the contact they have with their babies. They want their babies with them from birth, so that the mother's body warms the baby, in preference to an incubator; so that the mother can start breastfeeding as soon after delivery as possible; and so that the mother can become acquainted with her new baby as soon as it is born.

I wish I had been more assertive about my wishes. I wanted my baby with me immediately after delivery and I was not allowed to see her until six hours later. I still don't know why. She was a normal, healthy, term baby.

When my second child was born, I was barely able to touch her tiny hand and quickly kiss her cheek before she was whisked away from me. I would have liked to have put her on my stomach. I had a hard labor and wanted to be close to her right away.

During their hospital stays, the mothers want a great deal more contact with their babies than is now possible in many American hospitals. Many mothers want their babies with them night and day, with the choice to use the nursery for short intervals. Hospitals call this "rooming-in." Significant numbers of mothers want no separation at all from their babies.

What Medical Research Says About Mother-Baby Contact

The strong desire of mothers to stay close to their newborn babies is nothing new. Ashley Montagu, Ph.D., was one of the first scientists to zero in on the critical importance of mother-baby contact immediately following birth. In his book *Touching,* he describes the benefits of uterine contractions during labor for the baby. "The stimulation the baby receives from the contractions of her uterus tone up his sustaining systems— respiratory, circulatory, digestive, eliminative, nervous and endocrine—for the functions they will be called upon to perform after birth." He believes "these uterine contractions of labor constitute the beginning of caressing of the baby in the right way—a caressing that should be continued in very special ways in the period immediately following birth and for a substantial period of time afterward." After the somewhat trying time of birth, both mother and baby "clearly require the reassurance of the other's presence," he says.

A usual hospital routine is for the newborn baby to be removed to a heated bed or incubator to warm him. Mothers who have wondered why their own bodies cannot warm their newborns will be reassured by nurse Celeste Phillips' research on heated cribs versus mothers' arms at Watsonville and Santa Cruz, California, hospitals. She found that newborn body temperature was as well maintained when babies were wrapped and held by their mothers as by the incubator. Because she noted cold delivery rooms during her research, Mrs. Phillips further suggests keeping the babies warmer by raising the delivery-room temperature regardless of whether babies are in their mothers' arms or an incubator.

After the baby was born we didn't get to spend much time with him. I would have liked to keep him with me longer and to nurse him. As it was, it was eight hours until I got to hold him and nurse him for the first time. They said his temperature had to stabilize and had him under a heat lamp. Wouldn't my body heat do the same thing?

Mothers say they prefer having their babies with them so they can immediately offer the breast when their newborn awakens. This avoids the painful breast engorgement common with mothers who feed their babies on a schedule. "Another very, very exciting and interesting thing we have found regards weight gain by the newborn," says Mayer Eisenstein, M.D., a home-birth physician in Chicago, writing in *Safe Alternatives in Childbirth*. "I was trained that it takes seven to ten days for a newborn to regain its birth weight, and I believed it. But we found our homebirth babies gaining very well, usually exceeding their birth weight by one-half to one pound by one week of age. We interpret this to be the result of no maternal separation."

Many mothers who have experienced this kind of complete contact with their baby during their hospital stay report they do not have the difficult adjustment from hospital to home described by other mothers whose babies spent long periods of time in the nursery. Research supports women in this also.

For years mothers accepted as inevitable the adjustment problems from hospital to home. Staying up all night with a crying baby the first night home seemed to start the awful, constant fatigue that wears down new mothers. "She's asleep when I'm awake, and I want to sleep when she's awake," became the common new mother's complaint. Every new mother and baby need time to adjust to each other. Sleep and nursing patterns that are mutually satisfying to mother and baby develop fastest when mother and baby are together from birth on, reports psychiatrist, Muriel Sugarman, M.D., from Brookline, Massachusetts. Multiple caretakers, different nurses on changing shifts who care for newborns left in nurseries, interrupt the progress of the mother and baby adjusting to each other. In fact, from her comprehensive review of the literature on maternal-infant attachment, Dr. Sugarman suggests that multiple caretakers of the newborn prolong the period of time needed by mother and newborn to adjust. New mothers and babies need lots of uninterrupted time to be with each other.

What is this age-old experience of maternal-infant bonding that mothers have always been aware of and scientists have just begun to study? This attachment is a unique, intense, learned relationship between two people, a long-term commitment between mother and child. It begins when their eyes meet at birth, and just may be the strongest kind of link we have with one another. Babies arrive with their bonding antennae well in tune. A newborn loves to look at a face. It seeks out the mother's eyes, and may mimic an act, such as sticking out the tongue. As its body is cradled by mother, the baby hears the heartbeat it has known for months. The child feels warmth and softness, detects mother's scent, and recognizes her voice. Brought to the breast often, the alert baby takes the warm sweetness of its mother's milk. The infant is secure and content. No more are babies looked upon as passive, unresponsive creatures who should be relegated to newborn nurseries.

Certainly the research on maternal-infant attachment most widely influencing doctors and hospital routines and supporting women's ideas is that of Marshall Klaus, M.D., and John Kennell, M.D. In one of their studies they compared two groups of women, all bottle-feeding mothers. One group had traditional contact with babies: glimpse after birth, brief contact between six and twelve hours, then thirty-minute visits for feeding every four hours. The other group had more contact. They enjoyed their new babies for one hour within the first three hours of life, and also had five extra hours of contact each afternoon on the first three days after birth, a total of sixteen extra hours of contact beyond the traditional amount given to the first group.

Observed at one month, one year, and two years, the mothers with extended contact fondled their babies more, were more soothing, gave fewer commands, and were more reluctant to leave the baby with someone else. "Incredibly," report Klaus and Kennell, "at five years of age these children had significantly higher I.Q.s and more advanced scores on language tests." Their early bonding studies were stimulated by knowledge of a high rate of child battering among children who spent their first weeks in premature nurseries separated from their mothers. Welcoming mothers into the nurseries and encouraging as much contact as possible between mother and child seemed to prove to be a successful abuse preventive for many premature babies.

Once again, mothers have been right all along. Doctors, nurses, and hospital administrators need to listen when women say it is vital to have their babies with them from birth, rooming-in, with the choice to use the nursery for short intervals.

I was made to feel that the baby was mine—not the hospital's property. I needed no permission, nor did my husband, to have access to our baby at any time.

I was not allowed to touch the baby, only look, although my delivery was uncomplicated, the baby was fine, and I had had no medication. I did ask the ob if the baby could be brought to me to hold after I was back in my room—he said, "Yes," but that he didn't believe in "all this bonding business," and he laughed at the idea that early mother-baby contact could be beneficial. I strongly believe the hospital could become the best place to deliver a baby if normal, uncomplicated deliveries were to take place in a homelike environment where the mother could be with her family. In this way, medical help and medical facilities would be close by, if needed, and yet birth could still be a normal, natural, family event.

ISSUE NUMBER FIVE: VISITS WITH OTHER CHILDREN

The desire of women for a strong family unit at the time of birth extends to their other children. Mothers want their other children to see the baby, and the mothers want to be able to see their other children, not waving through a window from a distance, but up close so they can talk to them, hug them, and reassure them.

I enjoyed having our two older children (ages three and five) visit me and the baby in the hospital. There were no traumatic spells of crying because they got to see the new baby and they were with both my husband and me as a family unit.

I think it's very important that your children are allowed to visit you. It was very hard to be able to see my children standing outside the maternity door when I couldn't go out there to hug them and they couldn't come in.

Those visits from their other children is the fifth crucial concern to women in their hospital experience. They strongly agree that they want their other children to visit them in the hospital, and they want their other children to see the new baby. Though the two other surveys asked women if they wanted to see their other children, the Baltimore survey was the first to ask moms whether they wanted their other children present soon after birth. An overwhelming 88 percent of the mothers want their other children there in the period following birth, during the recovery time.

I feel sisters and brothers should be able to hold the newborn as soon as possible after the birth, and that restrictions on family visitations be eliminated. After all, family means more to a baby than a nurse who works in a nursery.

What Medical Research Says About Visits From Other Children

Again, mothers are way ahead of professionals in perceiving that there is a crucial time for beginning sibling attachment to the baby; very few research reports compare the reactions of siblings who have been present at birth with those who have not.

Sandra Anderson, R.N., and Leta Brown, R.N., of the University of Arizona College of Nursing in Tucson, contributed a much-needed survey of the reactions of children present for a sibling's birth, compared with children who were not present. The positive reactions of the children seeing their sister or brother born continued in the months following the birth. The children who were present showed less regressive behavior (for example, fewer accidents in recently toilet-trained children) and less abusive behavior toward the new baby. In their book *Children at Birth*, Marjie and Jay Hathaway, through photos and prose, show the intense interest of brothers and sisters in their newborn sibling.

"What we're seeing," says David Stewart, Ph.D., of NAPSAC, "is that there is a biological prime time for attachment for all those who are present, regardless of age." Mothers whose other children are present at the birth or come in immediately after birth and see and hold their new sibling report that their older children have a deep concern for the baby's welfare.

In *Parent-Infant Bonding*, Klaus and Kennell refer to several studies showing that children who do not visit their mothers in the hospital are very distressed. These children showed "emotional distance" when their mothers tried to hug them after coming home: the children "either stiffened or turned away." Children who had visited their mothers were happy to see them at the end of the hospital stay. "Surprisingly, even one short visit seemed to allay some of the children's anxieties," said the authors.

WOMEN'S WANTS ARE ALL BACKED BY RESEARCH

It is abundantly clear that research strongly supports women's preferences. As health-care consumers demand change, they can have great confidence in their feelings about what is right for them and their families. Says Shannon Pope, who spearheaded the Wenatchee survey, "Never for a moment allow yourself to feel that, because you are a layperson, your viewpoint in childbirth is any less accurate or less valid than that of the person you are trying to influence. If you are a woman, you will be discounted on the basis of your 'obvious inability to separate the emotional aspects of childbirth from the factual.' But you have the advantage of recent scientific studies and *common sense* on your side! If you are a woman who has already experienced childbirth, you have the advantage of first-hand knowledge, and unless the person you are dealing with is also a person who has experienced childbirth, you are unique in possessing this area of knowledge."

ARE WOMEN SATISFIED WITH THEIR CHILDBIRTH EXPERIENCE?

Many women are satisfied, and their survey responses glow with their pleasure:

Beyond the joy of giving birth, I found another satisfying experience while in the hospital. The staff was consistently gracious, involved in my care and my excitement over childbirth. The best way to describe it is that I felt loved and "mothered" by the nursing staff.

I don't believe I would change anything. I had a very positive experience with the birth of my last child. All the hospital personnel were pleasant, efficient, and supportive of breastfeeding, prepared childbirth, rooming-in, sibling visits, fathers visiting anytime. All families should be lucky enough to have such a positive experience.

However, the above women are in a minority! Many women are not satisfied, concluded the three independently done surveys. Only 18 percent of the women would make no changes in their last birth experience, according to the Baltimore survey. (This was the only one to ask that specific question.)

I would not use the fetal monitor again—it really interfered with my relaxation positions and my breathing.

Labor experience went smoothly until the "rush" to the delivery room. During this time my husband was not allowed to be with me. I worried about him missing the delivery and I missed his coaching support. This interruption in our experience together was very disturbing to both of us.

Although the clinic had been highly recommended by family and friends, I found the doctors' attitudes toward me as an intelligent person very disgruntling—the problem was that they assumed I was not informed about my body or my birth and made no effort to change that assumption. There was no individualization of the care regime.

I would change a great deal. I would not have an obstetrician, but a nurse-midwife team. I would have no prep, no episiotomy (unless needed). I would like a Leboyer delivery in a homelike atmosphere. I would also room-in and would like my husband and the children to visit whenever they wished. I would never have another baby in the manner and atmosphere that I had my last child in.

Whether women would choose an alternative to the traditional hospital delivery, if available, is another measure of dissatisfaction. Twenty percent of the Boulder women said their first choice was a home delivery. Fifty percent of the Wenatchee women gave, as their first choice: home, birth centers, or birthing room. A whopping 76 percent of the Baltimore women said they would "choose to labor and deliver in the same bed, with a homelike environment, if it were available."

WHY HOSPITALS AND DOCTORS DON'T ALWAYS SUPPORT WOMEN'S WANTS

At this point many of you may be thinking, if research supports what women want, why in the world don't hospitals and doctors just give it to them? Why do I have to make an effort to get what I want? We've thought about that question a lot.

The only satisfactory answer seems both simple and complicated, and it took writing this book for us to answer it for ourselves. *Hospitals and doctors think that what they are doing is best, is right, is safe for the majority of women and babies.* Doctors' beliefs about what the best care is determine hospital policies.

Women's preferences in childbirth include a very broad view of birth; the *social*, the *psychological,* and *spiritual* aspects are as important to women as the *physical* act of giving birth. The doctor's viewpoint is different. He focuses on the *physical* act of giving birth. In other chapters we will examine the belief system of the doctor and how the way he views birth determines how it must be treated. A key issue in understanding doctors and in getting what you want is how the word "safe" is used. How is "safe" measured? How do you define "safe"? Doctors feel free to act as they do because they use maternal mortality and infant mortality figures to measure safety.

Because of what doctors believe about childbirth and how they view safety, they intervene in most births. To intervene means to get in there and get that baby out by applying technology. The doctor takes decisive action to speed or to end the labor and get the baby delivered. Intervention procedures are being carried out on a massive scale that most women do not believe is necessary. They are beginning to understand that one intervention leads to another, and the doctor may find himself on a treadmill he cannot stop without doing a cesarean delivery.

INTERVENTIONS AND SATISFACTION

Because of my last experience, I am convinced that the majority of gyn doctors are not the least bit interested in the mothers' preferences in childbirth. They seek the safest and quickest way to immobolize you and pull your baby out, regardless of your insistence that you are experiencing no discomfort and wish to have no drugs. I was not permitted to labor and deliver in the same bed, to have my hands free, or to nurse my child immediately following delivery. There was no medical reason for denying me these things, especially after we had talked about these very points before my delivery, and the doctors had all agreed. My doctor was able to harass me into having a spinal, which was being administered under my protests as my new son slipped into this world. I was in the hospital exactly forty-two minutes before my child was born, and it was filled with tears and loud arguing between my doctors and myself. Thank God it was not my first pregnancy, for if it were, I would surely not have another.

The Baltimore researchers measured the rates of medical-surgical intervention, and the mothers' opinions of them. The intervention level is so high that a typical woman having her baby at a Baltimore hospital will have a fetal monitor and IVs during her labor. She will have anesthesia for her delivery. Her chances are greater than one in two that she will have either a forceps vaginal delivery (33 percent did) or a cesarean delivery (19 percent did). There is also a strong possibility (one chance in three) that her labor will be started or speeded up by a drug. And while the rate of intervention was very high, many women did not believe it was necessary.

My last baby was born after my doctor induced labor. I would definitely not allow that again, unless there was a definite medical need. My baby was two weeks early and he didn't even look ready to be born. My first labor I was home except for the last half hour. I just made it into the delivery room. Because I had two very different labors, I believe that in most cases the following are totally unnecessary: prep, enema, induced labor, stirrups. I also believe doctors should be more supportive to the women who do not want pain relievers.

When my last child was born, an internal monitor was used and I don't feel that it is entirely safe since it pierces the baby's scalp. If I had known then what I know now, I would not have allowed them to use it.

Of the Baltimore women who had medical-surgical interventions such as fetal monitors, anesthesia, or induction, one half to three quarters of the women (depending on the intervention procedures they had) believed these interventions were unnecessary, less than best, or risky for themselves or their babies. The Baltimore authors said, "We can conclude that women are seeking less use of current routine obstetrical procedures and less anesthesia."

Something is very wrong here. Women are wondering why there is so much intervention. They are wondering, "Why me? I didn't want it. There could have been less intervention. I would have been more satisfied and the birth would still be safe." These women are right! In other chapters we will show again and again that research is on the side of the mother. The less intervention there is, the safer it is for mother *and* baby.

Women are right to take a broad view of the birth experience, to consider the social, psychological, and spiritual aspects as important as the physical act of giving birth. Meeting women's preferences makes the birth *more* safe. When a woman's preferences are met, she needs *less* intervention and has fewer complications for herself and for her baby. Chapter 3, "If You Don't Know Your Options, You Don't Have Any," demonstrates over and over that a good birth is a safe birth. The needs of the mother, father, and other siblings can all be met in a safe birth. Where you have your baby, who your birth attendant is, what options you have, and what interventions the doctor uses are all negotiable. You can have your baby the way you want to.

2 ▪ THE PLEASURE PRINCIPLE

Biologically, you are designed to receive great pleasure from your body not only during lovemaking and intercourse, but in birth and breastfeeding, too. This pleasure—*not duty*—is the best glue for happy families.

Are you stumbling on the word *pleasure*? Maybe you thought the birth process at its best was one of incredible exertion and stoic acceptance mixed with much pain—but a process that women have to put up with to get that longed-for baby. Yes, birth will be exertion, pain, and acceptance, but that pain and exertion will cause your brain to release endorphins (or "happiness hormones," as Seattle researcher J. C. Houck, M.D., labels them).

And Mother Nature built in another payoff. Birth offers sexual pleasure on a continuum from pleasant sensations (felt while your uterus rhythmically contracts in early labor if you're relaxed and feeling secure) to an intense birth climax (yes, just like an orgasm) as your baby slithers into the world of your waiting arms.

Does this sound like a fairy tale and not much like the Bible which says that women will bring forth children in pain and suffering? Our cultural view of birth provides some reasons for that. Even today, most women and their mates, plus doctors and nurses—in spite of the so-called sexual revolution—are not aware of the birthing woman's pleasure potential. But it's there. As world-renowned sex researcher, Virginia Johnson-Masters, D.Sc., said in a St. Louis interview, "The whole cultural message—subliminal if not direct—is that you shouldn't be sexual."

Niles Newton, Ph.D., is both a professor of behavioral sciences at Northwestern University Medical School and a researcher who frequently writes of the pleasure potential of all of women's sexual functions. In 1979 she said, "Duty is a recent invention in human relationships. Basic pleasure may be the foundation of family life. Pleasure in birth may be the starting point for optimal family relationships. Our knowledge of reproduction suggests there may be a biological reason for connecting pleasure in birth with the best outcome for the baby." Women who put great emphasis on the quality of their childbirth experience may well be intuitively seeking the kind of birth experience that enhances family stability.

If childbirth is supposed to produce sexual pleasure, why are so many women dissatisfied with their birth experiences? Standard hospital birth practices, from the shaving of your pubic hair to routine episiotomies (the "unkindest cut"), destroy much of this pleasure potential. Another reason women may not experience pleasure in birth is because we've not been taught that *all* of our reproductive functions are designed to give us pleasure—physically, emotionally, and spiritually.

Sexually, women are not carbon copies of men. Our sexuality involves far more than just making love with our mate, important as that is. Part of it can be the increased sexual energy a woman may feel during menstruation, the relaxing spurt of milk from her breasts when her milk lets down, and the sensitive tug of her baby's rhythmic sucking on her nipple.

But nearly all sex research has been done by men so it is not surprising that most sexual research concentrates on the study of intercourse. Women's other sexual functions have been less fully examined. But we can describe some of the similarities between sexual arousal and women's reproductive functions and the sexual bonus nature bestows on women who give birth.

Sexual Arousal and Pregnancy

Sexual arousal and pregnancy have strong bodily similarities. In both states, breasts enlarge and nipples become sensitive. There's also extra blood flow and lubrication in the vagina. Hormone production soars in both instances. And, according to Masters and Johnson and others, masturbation is common during pregnancy, even if never experienced before. However, not all pregnant women are hovering in a permanent state of sexual arousal. Many other influences—such as fatigue, nausea, worry, or just plain being busy—can affect a pregnant woman's sexual desires.

Your sexual interest during pregnancy probably resembles one of the following four descriptions:

■ Your sexual desire hasn't changed at all during your pregnancy.

■ You've felt tired and nauseated from day one. Now that you're past the first few months, you're not prostrate anymore, but you're not much better. Though you need your partner to hold and comfort you, sexual intercourse is not a priority. In fact, you'd prefer to do without it.

■ Even though you were sleepy and sometimes nauseated in the first trimester, now in the second trimester you marvel at your energy . . . and you feel wonderful. Surprisingly (because no one mentioned this as a pregnancy bonus), your desire to make love suddenly grows and is greater than ever before.

■ You are vibrating with good health and have felt that way since the beginning of the pregnancy. Your senses are more acute than ever. Food is appetizing, and you've never had a moment's queasiness. Your desire to make love with your mate continues to increase right up to the time of birth.

Whichever description most closely matches your own experience, you're in lots of good company. Other women have felt the same. An unchanged sexual response is the least likely, while increased desire in the middle trimester is the most common. But whether you're turned on or turned off, whether you want an orgasm or not, your feelings are normal, and may vary from pregnancy to pregnancy.

Oxytocin—the Caretaking Hormone

A seldom-studied hormone, oxytocin, flows in the woman's body during intercourse, during birth and again during breastfeeding. (Though oxytocin can be found in men, too, even less is known about how their bodies use it.) In intercourse, orgasm triggers this hormone's release; in labor, the onset of contractions finds oxytocin in the body; and in breastfeeding, it is liberated with each letdown of milk. This hormone acts on the uterus, as well as the breasts, causing the uterus to contract rhythmically during breastfeeding.

Unlike many other hormones, oxytocin is generated in sporadic bursts rather than in a steady stream. With orgasm or milk letdown, it usually produces a euphoric sensation, a relaxing sense of well-being. Its release is easily inhibited. Just as orgasm in lovemaking can be prevented by sudden noises, many a labor's progress has been stopped by an inhibiting hospital environment. Nursing mothers sometimes report their milk letdown slowing or stopping altogether when they're criticized, fatigued, or unhappy.

Oxytocin is very much involved in the bonding process. This hormone's presence in your body may actually make you want to take care of your baby. Breastfeeding often increases a mother's attachment for her baby; and the mother, in turn, has a physical need for her infant. Her breasts fill with milk and it's a pleasurable relief to have the breast emptied by the baby's sucking. And the baby's sucking gives rise to the gentle and prolonged stroking of one of the most sensitive parts of the female body—the nipple.

This caretaking hormone also bonds you with your mate through the pleasure of lovemaking and orgasm. Men and women care both physically and emotionally for each other in nearly all human societies when they live together. Caretaking, which is stimulated by the hormone oxytocin, is essential for human survival.

Parallels Between the Birth Process and Intercourse

You probably didn't learn in school that birth and breastfeeding are sexual events. They are. As sexual functions, they share many similarities with intercourse.

During intercourse, women do not want their concentration disturbed. In undrugged and uninhibited labor, they also do not want to be disturbed. In both intercourse and labor, Dr. Newton states, breathing is both deep and erratic, sometimes with grunts, gasping and sucking. Social inhibitions decrease as climax nears, and again as unmedicated labor progresses. In both instances, a tense (almost tortured) look appears on the face, and great effort is required, either to push out the baby or to sustain the intensity of orgasm. In both, the uterus rhythmically contracts.

Masters and Johnson data demonstrate that the uterine contractions in orgasm have the same recorded pattern as those of the first stage of labor—differing only in intensity. The cervical plug loosens and, for some women, the clitoris engorges. In fact, caressing the breasts can get a slowed labor going again by stimulating uterine contractions.

British natural-childbirth pioneer, Grantly Dick-Read, M.D., pointed out more than thirty years ago that anesthesia and analgesia inhibit the joy that often comes after the hard work of producing a baby. Medicated women remember the pain experienced before sedation but fail to have the compensation of elation that often follows the physical sensations of birth—feeling the arrival of a beloved baby.

Women experience intense emotion at birth when they are undrugged and have a supportive environment. Passionate emotions are released and sensory perceptions are heightened. Regardless of how much pain is endured, once into the second stage of labor, the pushing stage, many women report extraordinary pleasure. Some report a birth climax at the moment the head and shoulders slip through the vagina.

Some women describe giving birth, one month after the event, as being "like an orgasm," according to Deborah Tanzer, Ph.D. Most women who experience natural childbirth as Tanzer defines it (eliminating sedation in labor and delivery and consciously participating during the entire pregnancy and birth process) report feelings of triumph, enormous satisfaction, a natural high. They may or may not have experienced a lot of pain. That seems to be a separate issue. The euphoria following an unmedicated birth in a supportive environment can last for months. (And that memory helps many a weary mother cope with a fussy baby months later.)

The Role of Your PC (Pubococcygeus) Muscle

Your PC muscle surrounds and supports your sexual organs. The strength of this muscle not only enhances your sexual response during lovemaking, but it can enhance your physical sensations when you give birth.

In the 1940s gynecologist Arnold Kegel, M.D., emphasized the need for women to exercise their PC muscle to prevent unwanted urine leaking. (Hence, these exercises have ever since been known as "Kegels.")

Bradley childbirth instructor Rhondda Hartman, RN, MA, says:

> There's a misconception about the PC muscle. It isn't birth that weakens it. Rather, it's the weak PC muscle that creates complications in birth, such as tearing, and gynecological problems later in life.

There still aren't many doctors who suggest that pregnant women do their Kegels. For the last twenty years, childbirth educators have been the ones to spread the news. If your childbirth instructor hasn't already described these "tighten and relax" exercises, ask her to tell you. A strengthened PC muscle heightens your response before, during, and long after your baby is born.

The Natural Eroticism of Breastfeeding

Breastfeeding also resembles intercourse. In both, the uterus contracts, the nipples become erect, and the breasts receive extensive stimulation. The skin flushes. Soon after a baby is put to the breast, a letdown sensation brings the milk to the baby. As he or she sucks, the milk comes from the back of the breast, down into the nipple, and into the baby's mouth. While oxytocin, the pleasurable "caretaking hormone," is responsible for this milk ejection reflex, nursing mothers don't usually have orgasms when their milk lets down (though some occasionally report they do). However, nearly all nursing moms describe a feeling of well-being and a tuning in to their body. For a first-time mother, it may take a couple of months before she can recognize the letdown sensation, but it's there—and it feels good.

As a nursing mother, you will spend many more hours breastfeeding your infant than in either intercourse or childbirth. By the time your baby is three months old, she or he will have been put to the breast more than 700 times. This constant contact with the nipples often has unexpected advantages for you. For many, it reduces a sense of false modesty about not exposing or touching your breasts. Breastfeeding also enhances the response of your erogenous zones, especially if you occasionally nurse the baby skin to skin, unclothed. It is even common for breast milk to leak from a nursing mother during lovemaking. Some mothers then worry that there won't be enough milk for the baby's next feeding (but there will be). Some couples find milk-filled breasts an added sexual pleasure, and others don't. Of course, either reaction is normal. Breastfeeding's enhancement of your sexuality probably won't be noticeable until you have weaned the baby. While you're in the midst of nursing, you become accustomed to the constant breast stimulation.

Masters and Johnson report that many nursing mothers resume lovemaking with their husbands sooner than bottle-feeding mothers. For other mothers, the nearly constant body contact with their babies, and unavoidable fatigue, postpone their sexual desire whether these mothers are breastfeeding or bottle-feeding. It's probably part of nature's survival plan for you to be mostly interested in your baby during her or his early months. In fact, it is normal for estrogen levels to be lower than usual in new mothers, causing vaginal dryness for a few months. When you do desire to have intercourse after your baby's birth, consider using extra lubrication. Sexual desire will vary in any mother who has recently given birth, but all new mothers have an unusually strong need to be held and comforted. Just as in pregnancy, there's a wide range of sexual interest. Whatever you feel, whatever you want, is right for you.

Mother Nature's Sexual Bonus

Seemingly to make sure that women keep having babies, our capacity for sexual pleasure grows with each experience of birth and breastfeeding. M. J. Sherfey, M.D., reports that in all women (as long as obstetric damage doesn't intervene), pregnancy will bring an increase in the volume of blood flow in the pelvis, enhance the capacity for sexual tension, and improve your orgasmic intensity, frequency, and pleasure.

With increasing sexual experience and childbirth, your capacity for sexual pleasure unquestionably grows. Unmedicated birth that you feel *you* accomplished, with your own exertion, further enhances your erotic response.

Nature offers a double insurance policy of pleasure, to ensure a bonding of mother to baby. Even if you couldn't experience the pleasure of childbirth because your lower body sensations were numbed by anesthesia, you will still bond to your child through the pleasure of breastfeeding.

If you are still breastfeeding as your baby gets close to a year old, you'll see that the baby adores the breast (much as you've seen bottle-fed babies at this age "adore" the bottle). This adoration of the breast is normal, and is another source of pleasure to the mother. For more than 99 percent of our human existence, our ancestors' babies were probably carried and nursed frequently. Mutual bodily enjoyment, both mother's and infant's, is instinctive in humans. This pleasure conditions a mother to respond to her baby's needs. Sexual pleasure makes us want to take care of the partner—whether an adult partner in lovemaking, or the baby in birth and breastfeeding. Your sexuality, your pleasure in yourself as a woman are natural, biologically determined forces.

Vulnerability—A Necessary Ingredient for Caretaking

All three sexual functions—intercourse, birth, and breastfeeding—share the quality of vulnerability, which is essential to bring a pair-bonded couple closer together. Your vulnerability increases both physically and psychologically during pregnancy and birth, just as it does during intercourse. It's a mixture of risk, trust, and personal growth. During the process of birth, your body and emotions want to open up as surely as they do in lovemaking.

In pregnancy it's likely you'll experience the full gamut of feelings, from high spirits to low. Though your mate, your mother, or your boss may criticize you for being "too emotional," these feelings are a necessary preparation for your caretaking role. Experiencing increased emotions changes you. It makes you more receptive and opens you to respond to your baby. This period of special vulnerability helps you get in touch with what is deeply important to you.

As your pregnancy progresses, and you more closely approach the moment of birth, you look more and more for calm reassurance and support from those who care for you. Many career women, normally accustomed to assertively managing their lives, amaze themselves by this need for support. It's unexpected perhaps, but normal. You feel that you don't want anyone to bother you; while simultaneously you don't want to cause anyone any trouble. Perhaps more than at any other time of your life, you now feel that you want someone to take care of you.

As birth approaches, you withdraw and turn inward. You marshall forces to give birth and care for your baby.

The Importance of Touch During Labor

As we approach the time for labor and birth, we start to become aware that the reassurance and support that we want also comes from being touched. We sometimes forget how rewarding it can be to accept the comfort of touch when we're under stress. And labor surely is a stress. A tender, caring touch during labor can be sympathetic and restorative, as well as pleasurable. Research shows that laboring mothers do better when there is constant support that includes touch.

Our hesitation to touch each other is unknown in many other parts of the world. In other societies, mothers carry babies in their arms, or on their hips, or slung around their backs until they're two or three years old. This pleasure of intimate touching continues throughout childhood between the children and both parents. Raised this way, men, for example, feel comfortable touching other males.

Whether we can admit it or not, many of us are painfully inhibited about touching and being touched by other people— even those we love. Often we fail to realize how this separates us from those who share our lives. As a matter of fact, as you read this, you may recoil at the thought of others touching you in labor besides your mate.

Just as foreplay does in intercourse, touch enhances the physical sensations and the joy the birthing mother feels. A laboring mother in pain may recover her equilibrium through a sympathetic touch. A hand on her arm, a caress of her hair may blunt the stress of a contraction and imbue a sense of strength.

Negative emotions leave their effects, too—increased pain, a slowed labor, a tightened cervix. But positive emotions can work to aid the mother's body to open up to the birth process and experience pleasure, if a woman's confidence is enhanced, and not shattered with anxiety. The chief obstacle to pleasure in all of its forms is fear. The fear of pain, of ridicule, of embarrassment is common among women who have their babies in hospitals. Ensure that your vulnerability will be met by loving support—and touch. Have not only your husband with you in labor, but a doula (a supporting woman), too. (See Chapter 11.)

A New Way of Experiencing Birth

There's a new consciousness of birth, emanating from the home-birth movement. "Despite the fact that almost all of the people now alive in the world were born at home, the home-birth movement in the United States . . . is completely revolutionary," wrote lay midwife Rahima Baldwin in the *Informed Homebirth Newsletter* in 1978. She described three ways in which the new home birth is different. First, women who have home births today choose to feel, to know their bodies in the birth process. Second, these women "assume active responsibility for their bodies, their lives, and their birth experiences." Third, they recognize birth's spirituality. These parents demand "from the moment of birth, the recognition that their child is a whole and sensitive person, to be treated with care and respect."

Though only 2 to 3 percent of babies born in the U.S. are born at home, the needs and experiences of these parents have influenced hospital maternity care policies around the nation. They have also taught us there's much room for improvement in how birth is handled.

An optimal birth is more than the absence of such routine hospital procedures as enemas, shaves, IVs, and fetal monitors. It's understanding the need to be touched during labor and to feel comfortable and unafraid. It's experiencing the sensuality and joy in unmedicated childbirth—even when there's pain (if the woman is lovingly cared for and comforted). It's realizing that while anesthesia may be necessary, it makes you a spectator at your baby's birth. It's knowing that every birth is a family affair and an occasion when you need never be separated from loved ones.

In this new way of giving birth, women want active responsibility for their bodies. They choose to feel their body sensations. Feeling body sensations includes feeling the pain—not to be masochistic, but rather to experience a sense of endurance and triumph much like a long-distance runner's. Just as in a marathon race, labor, like a long race almost over, can cause excruciating pain. But would the runner want an epidural to finish, when she can see the finish line only yards away? Or would she want to use those reserves of physical, mental, and emotional energy with which she has primed herself to finish the race with her full senses. Biologically, our bodies want to finish labor and give birth triumphantly . . . with our senses intact.

Nature offers another reward for exertion—endorphins, the "happiness hormones." Hard exercise increases levels of this natural, narcotic-like painkiller in your blood. Lawrence Cherry, writing in *The New York Times Magazine,* stated endorphins are "substances that seem to be natural pain relievers several times more potent than morphine." Some researchers speculate that this chemical release explains the euphoria that joggers call "runner's high." The contracting pains of childbirth release endorphins and produce a sensation of enormous pleasure after the great physical exertion of labor and giving birth. Endorphins are found in the placenta and are released in both mother and baby through labor, nursing, and skin-to-skin contact. One researcher has found that the mother's endorphin level after a cesarean birth is lower than after the exertion of an unmedicated, vaginal birth.

No matter how much you know or don't know about the process of birth itself, you are right to want to experience the pleasure of birth. It's part of Mother Nature's plan. Make the most of this information. It's meant to broaden your knowledge about your sexual self and, we hope, expand your appreciation of your body, your birth, and your baby. When you are the center of your birth, instead of the hospital and its impersonal routines, you enhance and expand yourself, strengthening the quality of your own life as well as that of those you most love. And remember, your own perfectly normal reaction will vary from other women's along the continuum of pleasure.

3 • IF YOU DON'T KNOW YOUR OPTIONS, YOU DON'T HAVE ANY

> No one can tell a woman how to make the choice that is best for her. There is no one *right* choice. Today there are more choices and more support for trying than ever before in American history, which also leaves women with the burden of choice.
>
> —Gail Sheehy, *Passages*

For every one of you reading this chapter there is the strong possibility that within a fifty-mile radius of where you live you can find both a place for giving birth and a birth attendant that you will like. Change has come and is still coming, so fast it is difficult to keep up with the new possibilities. Find out what's available in your area.

The movement to humanize hospital maternity care started in the 1950s. The two main thrusts of this movement—called "family-centered maternity care"—were to keep mothers and babies together while in the hospital and to ensure the husband's presence before, during, and after birth. In the late 1960s, childbirth education had reached enough birthing women so that they began to "vote with their feet"—that is, they started going to those doctors and hospitals where their husbands were not only allowed, but encouraged to be present. This was the crack in the door to change in hospital maternity policies.

Today, while acceptance of the husband's presence at a vaginal delivery is *almost* universal in American hospitals, there is still an occasional hospital that denies a woman her mate's support during labor and delivery. Many, if not most, cesarean mothers are denied their husband's presence at delivery. And, while it is easier in many hospitals for mothers to get their babies on demand, interference in family togetherness is still widespread. So, more and more, demand for change has accelerated, and women continue to "vote with their feet" and go to those hospitals where they *can* get what they want.

Some women with their babies due *now* see changes in hospitals as turtle slow. They see their only choice as voting the hospital out altogether and opting for an out-of-hospital birth. Because childbirth is an annual $8 billion business in the U.S. today, there is a strong economic motivation for hospitals and doctors to keep you as a customer. While the actual percentage of out-of-hospital births is small, it is growing fast, and the threat of many women opting for out-of-hospital births is one of the most important reasons why hospitals have made changes demanded by consumers.

Getting accurate, out-of-hospital birth statistics is difficult. Enriqueta Bond, Ph.D., research scientist with the National Academy of Sciences, estimates 70,000 to 130,000 out-of-hospital births a year. She bases her estimate on national government figures for the low figure and home birth figures for the state of Oregon for the high figure. Oregon is one of the very few states to have accurate data on home birth. Because Oregon has several established home birth services and most states do not, using Oregon's data to estimate national figures may result in an overestimate of home births, according to Dr. Bond.

NAPSAC, the National Association of Parents and Professionals for Safe Alternatives in Childbirth, was founded in late 1975 by Lee and David Stewart, Ph.D., at a time when there were very few alternatives to the traditional hospital delivery. Interviewed in September 1982, the Stewarts said the national NAPSAC office receives 1,500 requests a month for literature and information. "The most frequent question we get—in the hundreds every month—is 'Where can I get a competent midwife or doctor for a home birth?' " said Dr. Stewart.

He estimates 2 to 3 percent of all births take place at home. "The difficulty in getting accurate figures probably comes from the lack of registration of home births," he said. "Parents just don't want to call attention to themselves by registering a home birth. They fear harassment of themselves or the lay midwives they tend to use."

Two to 3 percent is 70,000 to 105,000 home births a year. Although the numbers encourage home-birth advocates and frighten most obstetricians, home births barely twitch birth statistics. The numbers are tiny compared to three-and-a-half million or so babies born each year in hospitals in the United States.

Where To Have Your Baby

There are five different places where you may choose to give birth:

- In a traditional hospital with labor, delivery, and recovery rooms
- In a hospital birthing room

- In a hospital alternative birth center
- In a birthing center outside the hospital
- At home

One way of evaluating where to have your baby is to look at the likelihood of intervention for each place of birth. The fewer interventions there are the less risk there is to mother and baby. With fewer interventions there will be fewer problems as a result of intervention, fewer c-sections, and, we believe, a safer birth for the normal mother and baby.

Another way of evaluating where to have your baby is to look at how satisfied women have been with each option. That satisfaction can be measured in three ways—by how the family is kept together; by how much pleasure is involved; and by how much a woman's self-esteem is enhanced by the experience.

With less intervention, mother, baby, and father are more likely to have a strong attachment to each other, and this fragile new family will have the mutual loving start they need. The pleasure principle, the full expression of a woman's sensuality in birth, operates best with the least intervention. And finally, with less intervention, a woman feels more that she has "given birth" rather than that she has been "delivered." Her enhanced self-esteem from this achievement helps the woman in her new role as a mother. "The sense of achievement from a good birth experience is the strongest stimulus I know to greater self-esteem and effective functioning," said nurse-midwife Ruth T. Wilf, C.N.M., of Booth Maternity Center, Philadelphia.

In contrast to this, the greater the amount of intervention the more likely the mother will not have her preferences met, which can lead to regrets about the birth.

PLACE OF BIRTH: TRADITIONAL HOSPITAL

Birth in a traditional hospital will often resemble the birth described by Jenny in Chapter 7, "The Obstetrician's Black Bag of Interventions." This is because most births are attended by obstetricians, and it is unusual for an obstetrician to deliver anywhere but in the traditional area of a hospital. Birth there will be organized according to his belief that birth is a physical procedure with significant risks.

The laboring woman is first put to bed in the labor room, then moved to the delivery room. Delivery is often a surgical procedure (vaginal delivery with episiotomy and use of forceps, or a cesarean delivery) following an actively managed labor. She is then moved to a recovery room before being transferred to the postpartum room, where she will stay for the remainder of her time in the hospital. Her baby is removed from her at birth and placed in a central nursery.

The traditional hospital is where millions of American babies are born each year at a typical cost of $1,500 to $2,500, including the average three-day stay after birth. A cesarean delivery doubles those figures. The choices a mother may make in her labor and delivery vary greatly among hospitals. Some hospitals offer a great deal of flexibility; in other hospitals, almost all mothers experience the same routine. You *can* get what you want if you act ahead of time by choosing the hospital where policies are very flexible, and by negotiating with your doctor for agreement on those options most important to you. The second key to getting what you want in a traditional hospital is to have your husband as coach and a woman friend (your doula) to serve as your buffer and advocate with the staff.

The satisfaction of women delivering in a traditional hospital can be high when the staff is committed to a family-centered birth. As an example, only one out of every eight women was satisfied with her birth experience in the hospitals of the Baltimore metropolitan area surveyed by the COMA researchers. However, at Franklin Square Hospital, the satisfaction level of the patients was much greater than at any other hospital in the Baltimore area. One out of three women giving birth at Franklin Square was completely satisfied with the birth. One woman reported:

I would like to take this opportunity to praise the staff at Franklin Square and my obstetrician for making my childbirth experience the best of my life. The care I received was excellent. During the delivery I received so much praise and encouragement from the doctor and the attending nurses, it made things easy to do with no medication at all. We were even able to avoid an episiotomy. Also Franklin Square is a very flexible place that goes to great lengths to keep childbirth a family experience. My husband was with me the entire time. I also had rooming in on a twenty-four-hour basis, with the nursery taking the baby for about one-and-a-half hours a day for bathing and pediatrician's rounds. Any questions I had or assistance I needed was thoughtfully attended to by the staff. I wouldn't have my next baby anywhere else.

The rate of intervention at most traditional hospitals is very high. One of the reasons that mothers delivering at Franklin Square were much more satisfied than mothers delivering at other Baltimore hospitals may be that the rate of intervention at Franklin Square was lower.

The following chart shows the average rate of each intervention for all of the eighteen hospitals covered in the Baltimore COMA survey. The second column shows the highest rate of intervention recorded at any one hospital. The third column shows the rate of intervention for each procedure at Franklin Square Hospital.

Intervention	Average Rate for All Hospitals	Highest Recorded Use	Rate for Franklin Square
IV Fluids	81%	95%	66%
Prep	83%	96%	61%
Enema	57%	74%	48%
Fetal Monitor	67%	94%	77%
Anesthesia (General, Spinal, or Epidural)	65%	88%	53%
Lithotomy position for delivery	63%	74%	51%
Episiotomy	71%	80%	72%
Forceps used	33%	48%	23%
C-section	19%	32%	13%
Induction	22%	34%	21%

High rates of intervention in a traditional hospital setting carry a great risk of complications for mother and baby. Yet very little research has been done to document this risk. Lewis Mehl, M.D., Ph.D., Director, Institute for Childbirth and Family Research, Berkeley, completed one study of safety in home versus hospital birth. In his study, Dr. Mehl found the incidence of complications to mother and baby in a hospital birth was far greater than in a home birth. Because the rate of intervention is likely to be extremely low where the choice is for an unmedicated birth at home, and because the COMA survey data shows intervention to be very high in a traditional hospital setting, we agree with Dr. Mehl that it is the high rate of intervention that results in the greater risk of complications to mother and baby.

Dr. Mehl compared matched populations of 1,046 women planning home births to 1,046 women planning hospital births, with all the women defined as "low risk."* The home-birth mothers include those

---

*A "low risk" designation means that these mothers had no complicating factors of age, medical history or socioeconomic problems that might lead to difficulty with childbirth. For a more complete discussion of the somewhat controversial "low risk" and "high risk" designations, see Chapters 5 and 6.

who needed a hospital delivery though a home birth was planned. The hospital-birth women were more likely than the planned home-birth mothers to have had the following: five times more likely to have high blood pressure during labor, nine times more likely to have had a severe perineal tear, three times more likely to have had postpartum hemorrhage, and three times more likely to have had a cesarean.

The babies born to the hospital-birth women also had a higher complication rate than the babies born to home-birth women. In the hospital, the infants were six times more likely to have had fetal distress before birth, four times more likely to have needed assistance to start breathing, four times more likely to have developed an infection. There were no incidents of birth injuries at home, yet there were thirty infants in the hospital with birth injuries.

Hospital

To sum up:

- Insurance coverage.
- Birth takes place in several different rooms: labor room, delivery room, usually a recovery room, and a postpartum room (for the hospital stay after birth).
- Baby is taken to a central nursery.
- Immediate availability of emergency equipment.
- No one-to-one nursing care because nurses are responsible for several patients.
- High possibility of medical intervention.
- High risk of complications for mother and baby, regardless of a predetermination of "low risk."
- Most babies are born in a traditional hospital.

A Note on HMOs

Some readers of this book are members of an HMO, a health maintenance organization, in which payment for medical care differs from the more typical fee for each service. Members prepay a fixed amount to the HMO for all medical care and must use the physicians employed by the HMO. Among themselves doctors disagree heatedly on the merits and disadvantages of HMOs.

One 1981 study compared the quality of maternity care for members of a Boston-based HMO with care for women who choose fee for service (FFS) doctors. The cesarean rate for the first time mothers was high in both groups (18.3 percent for HMOs, 21.4 percent for FFS). On all other indicators, the quality of maternity care was better with HMOs than FFS.

Women in the HMO had more prenatal visits, less induced labor (21.1 percent for FFS compared to 12.3 percent for HMO), fewer cesareans among women who had previously given birth vaginally (7.3 percent for FFS compared to 2.3 percent for HMO), and an indication that the women in the HMO were more likely to be sent home if their labor was not well established (more than twice the HMO women had more than one admission for premature labor than the FFS women). The two groups had similar outcomes for babies. If you are a member of an HMO, you may expect somewhat less intervention than a typical FFS woman, but you will still have to negotiate for what *you* want for *your* birth.

PLACE OF BIRTH: BIRTH ROOM IN HOSPITAL

Three of the five places of birth are clear and distinct from each other in people's minds. Everyone—consumers, doctors, hospitals—seems to agree about what is meant by a traditional hospital birth, a birth center located outside of a hospital, and a home birth.

However, there is some confusion about how to describe hospital birth rooms and hospital alternative birth centers. Our description of these options is our best understanding of these two choices in the U.S. today. When you are investigating your own hospital options, go beyond the title you are given. Ask for a detailed description of that hospital's services, using our description and lists as a starting point.

For example, the definition of "rooming-in" varies from hospital to hospital. In some it means you can have your baby twenty-four hours a day. In others, it means you can have your baby once during the night or perhaps just all day. The variables for birth rooms and hospital birth centers are far greater. One description of hospital birth rooms lists labor, delivery, and recovery in the same room. However, we know there are some hospitals which do not permit laboring women into their birth rooms until they're at least 3 centimeters dilated (one good reason for staying at home as long as possible). Or hospitals may advertise a birth room, and women find the *only* difference is labor and delivery in the same room, with standard interventions such as IVs, electronic fetal monitors, and delivery on the back with legs in stirrups routine.

Birth rooms are one response to consumers' demands for improvements in hospital maternity care. More than 1,000 hospitals across the country have birth rooms where women may labor, give birth, and recover in the same bed. By providing birth rooms the whole belief system may change to one where birth is viewed as a normal event that can be a peak emotional experience for the woman and her mate.

A very great advantage of birth rooms is that almost all women can use them, unless a cesarean has already been decided upon or it is known that a difficult forceps procedure must be carried out in a delivery room. Most women, even those who may be at high risk for developing complications, can use a birth room. There need be no screening of potential users. However, many hospitals have strict screening for birth rooms that acts as a deterrent to women who want to and could use them. Usually this strict screening is instituted because the doctors are not committed to provide a real alternative to a traditional birth.

Emergency equipment is kept in the birth rooms. The bed is convertible and can be broken away to place the woman in a lithotomy position (on back, with legs in stirrups) if needed. The birth-room alternative is acceptable to some obstetricians and family practitioners, because doctors need not screen patients and because intervention can be carried out in a birth room if needed. Because birth rooms are homelike, however, the setting may discourage the use of routine procedures. Women get the feeling that they have much more control over what happens to them because their care can be individualized. Birth rooms have proven to be a satisfying alternative for those women who are distressed at the idea of a traditional hospital delivery and who want much less of the assembly-line feeling.

Manchester Memorial Hospital in Manchester, Connecticut, was the first hospital in the United States to open a birth room. Since 1969 over 4,000 births have taken place in the three birth rooms there. Currently, over half of all the births in the hospital take place in the birth rooms, with the rest in the traditional labor, delivery, and recovery areas. Obstetrician Philip Sumner, M.D., who was responsible for initiating the changes at Manchester Memorial Hospital, says, "The medical community resisted in every possible way." Local consumer groups assisted Dr. Sumner in his efforts. The medical staff gradually came around until today all of the ten other obstetricians on the staff use the birth room for some of their patients. Dr. Sumner and his two partners account for about half of the births in the birth rooms.

Dr. Sumner describes what happens when a woman gives birth in one of the birth rooms. " 'Celebration' is the theme of birth in the birthing room. When possible, rheostated dim lights are used as the baby emerges, with the mother herself reaching down and lifting her baby to her breast. In almost every instance the umbilical cord is long enough to permit her to determine her infant's sex for herself, and thus immediate bonding is encouraged. After the parents share the first 60 minutes, the family is transferred together to the newborn nursery where the baby is examined. If the mother or baby have no complications, they may then be transferred directly to a family unit. Breastfeeding, rooming-in, and sibling visitation are encouraged."

The satisfaction level of women giving birth in the birth rooms at Manchester Memorial Hospital is very high. They see the staff as giving support rather than trying to take control of the birth. This is one mother's story:

> One of the things that surprised me was that by my lifting her out, she was facing toward me and the doctor said, "Well, what do you have, a boy or a girl?" And I remember thinking, "Oh, my gosh, what a switch, the obstetrician asking the mother the sex of the baby. Usually it's the other way around." This time I got to tell him. It was a very nice tone of things. I wanted to reach down after the head was out and pull my baby out the rest of the way, which the doctor and monitrice helped me to do. I was a little unsure as to just when was the right time to reach down, but the monitrice guided my hands, and I reached under Tara's hands and I remember thinking, "What do I do now?" and just then the doctor said, "Now lift and push." Then it all made sense to me. So I pushed once and lifted her out and put her right up on my chest. That was a beautiful feeling.
>
> —Mother, quoted in *Birthing Rooms*

There is little available data to show whether using a birth room results in less intervention. The little data that is available suggests that it may. In Dr. Sumner's and his partner's practices only 10 percent of patients who used the birth room have analgesia. However, because these doctors believe anesthesia is useful in normal labors and deliveries, 51 percent of their patients have a paracervical anesthetic during labor and 33 percent have a pudendal anesthetic for delivery.

In 1976, in Decatur, Georgia, obstetrician Richard Stewart, M.D., and four certified nurse midwives in a group practice changed the whole maternity unit of Douglas General Hospital to the birth room concept. The obstetrical floor has three birth rooms and one delivery room with a traditional delivery table for cesareans or complicated vaginal deliveries (forceps and breech deliveries for example).

Women are admitted regardless of risk factors, and in the first 2,000 births, the rate of intervention has been very low. Women with diabetes, hypertension, twins, the need for induction, previous cesareans (many are delivered vaginally), or whatever complication receive the same low-intervention care. In 80 percent of all the births the midwife is the birth attendant (and is with the laboring woman from admission). If the birth turns out to be complicated and needs the obstetrician's presence and expertise, he comes in, but the midwife often completes the birth, as in twin and breech births. The only exception to admission is a woman in labor before her thirty-second week of pregnancy. In this situation of very early prematurity, if the labor cannot be stopped, the pregnant, laboring woman is transported to a regional neonatal intensive care hospital.

The expectant couple comes to the hospital when labor is well established. Women are encouraged to walk and assume any position giving the most comfort. Solid food in early labor and drinks as labor progresses are encouraged. Preps are not done. Enemas are given only if the laboring woman asks for one. Amniotomy (breaking the bag of waters around the baby) is not done. The cesarean rate is 9.4 percent (including repeat cesareans); forceps use is 5 percent. Of the vaginally delivered women, 3 percent had analgesia, 5 percent had anesthesia, and 27 percent had episiotomies. Maternal and infant outcomes are excellent.

These low rates of intervention are more than likely due to the birth attendants' beliefs rather than the place of birth. "Babies do not need to be delivered by obstetricians," Dr. Stewart told us. "Babies *need* to be delivered by midwives who give absolutely superior care." So sold on midwifery care are Dr. Stewart and his wife that when their daughter, Leslie Rebecca, was born, October 1, 1982, the Stewarts had the midwife on call as their birth attendant.

"The obstetrician has been the star of the show too long," said Dr. Stewart. "The star of the delivery is the mother. But most women are uncomfortable questioning their doctors. And too many women want anesthesia. Many women do want alternatives, though. The problem is that hospitals offer 'birth rooms' to get the women in, then don't let them use them or discourage women from using them. In one local hospital with 250 births a month, only 4 births are in the birth rooms. Women are going to have to work to get what they want."

Birth Room

To sum up:

- Insurance coverage.
- Labor, delivery, and recovery in the same bed.
- Immediate availability of emergency equipment.
- An alternative with high acceptance by some doctors.
- Almost all women can use birth rooms.
- Satisfaction of women is high; the family unit is kept together in one place.
- One-to-one nursing care is possible in some hospitals, especially if parents hire a private nurse.
- Intervention rate relatively high, but lower than in a traditional hospital.
- Almost no information available to compare complication rates in birth rooms with other alternatives.

PLACE OF BIRTH: ALTERNATIVE BIRTH CENTER IN HOSPITAL

In another giant step in providing maternity care alternatives, about seventy-five hospitals in this country have alternative birth centers (ABCs). These homelike, low-key birth settings are being built to lure into the hospital those women who might otherwise choose a home birth. In alternative birth centers, birth is considered a normal process. The atmosphere is relaxed. Routines are absent; flexibility is the watchword for everyone. And intervention is greatly reduced. The woman can participate as an equal partner with her doctor in decision making. Many mothers with their newborns leave for home within hours of birth.

The disadvantages of an ABC have to do with the screening required to ensure that only low-risk women are admitted, and with the resistance of most doctors and many nurses to using the alternative birth center.

Women who use these ABCs are highly satisfied because they feel in control in a homelike setting, yet they are in a hospital where they feel safer. A regular double bed, conventional furniture, hidden medical equipment, wallpaper, plants, and rocking chairs all contribute to the feeling that the woman is not in a hospital. However, it is the medical staff's attitudes of flexibility and support for whatever the woman wishes to do in her labor and delivery that contribute most to her feeling of control. The relaxed setting encourages her to walk, stand, or sit as she wishes during her labor, and to assume any delivery position she feels comfortable with. The father-to-be can lie on the bed with the mother to comfort her, as can any other support person present. The mother's other children can be present for the birth. In these ABCs, birth becomes a family affair, and often includes several close friends as well.

Because the alternative birth center is structurally separate from, though very close to, the ob floor, an ob nurse comes to the birth center when the mother arrives and follows her through her labor, delivery, and recovery, giving her one-to-one nursing care the whole stay. Some centers have that same nurse make a home visit at both twenty-four and seventy-two hours after birth to give medical follow-up to mother and newborn.

In the ABC, intervention and drug use is minimal or absent. Instead, the relaxed setting is an encouragement to all to wait out a difficult or prolonged labor and, instead of intervention, to offer the mother support by word and touch. About one mother in ten finds that pain remains the least-liked part of the alternative birth center experience, according to a 1980 report from Stanford University Hospital. Using an alternative birth center requires a commitment from the woman that no anesthesia, except for a local for episiotomy repair, will be used.

Only women considered at low risk for complications may use an alternative birth center. Strict screening for problems is done during pregnancy, to rule out women who have pre-existing medical problems such as heart disease, who have had previous severe delivery problems such as a stillbirth or a cesarean, or who have developed complications during pregnancy such as high blood pressure or premature labor. That still leaves most women eligible.

The flexibility and relaxed atmosphere of the alternative birth center, while it enhances the woman's control, reduces the control of the doctor. His role becomes one of lifeguard of the birth, not manager. Careful record-keeping from alternative birth centers shows that, because of this, obstetricians do not like to use this alternative, according to Madeleine Shearer, editor of *Birth*. British-trained midwife Linda Nelson, S.C.M., of Roosevelt Hospital in New York City, explained why obstetricians tend not to use the alternative birth center at her hospital. "Obstetricians view the use of the birthing room as more time-consuming, since they would have to be available for longer periods," said Nelson. "The births, although normal, do not entail the use of the various monitoring devices and other procedures with which obstetricians have trained and are comfortable."

When alternative-birth-center mothers and their babies are compared to low-risk women and their babies in traditional labor and delivery rooms the differences are nothing short of spectacular. The few studies of alternative birth centers give strikingly similar results. One 1980 report of 500 births in an alternative birth center comes from Robert C. Goodlin, M.D., of the University of California Davis Medical Center. The alternative birth center offered little obstetrical intervention. Mothers ate and drank as they desired (most took only fluids). No IVs were used. No anesthesia was given. No electronic fetal monitors were used. Only 6 percent of the mothers had minimal doses of analgesia during labor. In comparison, interventions were high among the 500 low-risk women who delivered in the traditional labor and delivery areas of the same hospital. All had IVs; 81 percent had the electronic fetal monitor; 70 percent had moderate-to-high doses of analgesia; and 30 percent had epidurals.

The following chart shows the difference in complications between the two groups.

Complications	Regular Birth (%)	ABC (%)
Mother		
Failure to progress in labor	18.3	5.2
Labor augmentation	21.2	3.1
Cesarean section	9.2	2.8
Infant		
Fetal distress	5.3	0.3
Meconium-stained fluid	11.9	2.3
Meconium aspiration	.2	1.2
Scalp infection	1.2	0
Jaundice	12.6	2.4
Neurological abnormalities	0.6	0.2

Mothers delivering in the traditional area were three times more likely than mothers delivering in the alternative birth center to have their labor diagnosed as "failure to progress," and seven times more likely to have their labors speeded with oxytocin. In the traditional area mothers were over three times more likely to have cesarean section. Before they were born, the babies delivered in the traditional area were fifteen times as likely to experience fetal distress and six times more likely to have meconium-stained fluid, another indication of possible distress. After birth, the infants born in the traditional area were three times more likely to have neurological abnormalities. They were six times more likely to have jaundice, a growing problem in pediatrics, possibly related to the much higher rate of Pitocin and other drug use in the traditional area. (See Chapter 14, "Your Baby Doctor.")

Just over one percent of the traditionally delivered babies got scalp infections from the use of electronic fetal monitors. Because the monitor was not used in the alternative birth center, there were no scalp infections. Follow-up for an average fifteen months after birth showed that 2.4 percent of the infants born in the traditional area were victims of child abuse, while none of the infants born in the alternative birth center were abused. The babies born in the ABC were more likely to breathe in meconium, a potential problem. Dr. Goodlin believes this reflects the absence of drugs in the ABC babies, who were more vigorous. Out of the six significant labor or birth complications for infants, the ABC babies did much better than the traditional-area babies in five complications.

Many professionals who use alternative birth centers believe that a better outcome for mother and baby is the result of two important factors. The first is the greatly reduced use of intervention. The second is the homelike setting itself, which results in a less anxious and more effective labor. Dr. Goodlin suggests that low-risk women benefit from a "service which seeks to reduce apprehension and insure tranquility."

Alternative Birth Centers

To sum up:

- Insurance coverage.
- Emergency delivery area readily accessible.
- Only low-risk pregnant women admitted.
- One in four women admitted is transferred to the regular delivery area.
- Most homelike setting in the hospital; relaxed, flexible setting and staff.
- One-to-one nursing care.
- Intervention rate very low.

- Risks of complications very low.
- Resistance to use by most obstetricians and some family practitioners; most midwives use readily.
- Satisfaction of women is very high; they feel control over the birth experience.
- Birth attendant may be midwife.

PLACE OF BIRTH: OUT-OF-HOSPITAL FREE-STANDING BIRTH CENTER

In 1975 there were 5 free-standing birth centers in the United States. By late 1981 there were 125 to 150 centers in twenty-seven states according to Anita Bennetts, C.N.M., Ph.D., and Ruth Watson Lubic, C.N.M., Ed.D., reporting in *Lancet*. Birth centers outside the hospital are similar in many ways to alternative birth centers within the hospital, and have the same homelike environment and relaxed, flexible atmosphere. There is very little intervention in the birth process, and the outcome for mothers and babies is excellent. The birth-center concept was developed by midwives who believe that it is the best alternative to both home and hospital deliveries.

As far as we know, the Denver Birth Center is the only privately run birth center in the country that rents space within the hospital. Because of this, when a patient requires transfer to a delivery room to handle a complication, it can be made very quickly. Most free-standing birth centers, however, are several minutes away from the hospital that serves as backup for complicated deliveries, so birth centers are strict in screening those women who wish to use their services.

About one out of five women who apply to an out-of-hospital birth center will be ineligible, either at the first prenatal visit or sometime during the pregnancy. "Horrendous emergencies can always be linked to high risk factors predictable before labor and delivery," said Linda Ross, C.N.M., nurse-midwife of the Denver Birth Center. This strict screening pays off for the birth center. During labor about one woman in seven requires transfer to a hospital—usually for failure to progress in her labor, for the development of hypertension, or for meconium staining. In contrast, in ABCs, as many as one in four is transferred to the regular hospital unit for deliveries. When this is needed, the midwife or doctor accompanies her to the hospital to deliver the baby, thus maintaining the continuity of care. Birth centers have emergency equipment available for the birth attendants to resuscitate a baby at birth or to stop a maternal hemorrhage, the two most frequent serious complications at birth.

The second factor distinguishing free-standing birth centers is that most deliveries are handled by nurse-midwives rather than doctors. Another significant difference is that all care, from early pregnancy through labor and delivery, postpartum and baby care, is given by the midwife in the same place where the woman will deliver. "Maternity care is viewed as a process of education to promote a healthy, safe and satisfying birth outcome in which there is a high value on the feelings and wishes of the family during childbirth," said Dr. Ruth Watson Lubic, nurse-midwife and director of the Childbearing Center, Maternity Center Association, New York City. "Maternity care, then, can be defined as preventive, health-oriented management of the childbearing experience, with high value being accorded to cultural, emotional, and spiritual, as well as physical needs of the family involved." The birth center emphasis on maternity care throughout the childbearing cycle is the most significant difference in free-standing birth centers from hospital ABCs.

A characteristic of all free-standing birth centers is described as "parent power" by Ruth Wilf, C.N.M., Ph.D., nurse-midwife, Booth Maternity Center, Philadelphia. Families are not only encouraged but expected to design their own birth experience. With home births as the standard, parents are encouraged to decide in every way how they will experience their labor and delivery. Maternity care is highly personalized for each family.

Because birth is viewed as a normal process and as an important beginning to a healthy family, the mother-to-be is encouraged to take responsibility for her health care during her pregnancy and delivery as the first step in taking care of her baby. Educating the parents to be responsible for their baby's birth is viewed as the best preparation for assuming the responsibility of raising their baby.

Unmedicated childbirth is advocated by free-standing birth centers. "You are designed to give birth without drugs," Loretta Ivory, C.N.M., nurse-midwife of the Denver Birth Center, tells her clients. Parents are encouraged to make all the decisions about who will be present at the birth, what the labor and delivery positions will be, and when they will be discharged. They are told to bring to the birth center anything they want to eat (many birth centers have kitchen facilities), and to do just about anything they want to do during the birth experience.

Women are encouraged to remain at home as long as they want to. "Women at term pregnancy, including women having their first babies, know when to come to the birth center if they have been encouraged by their birth attendant to listen to their own feelings," says Loretta Ivory. She describes how she handles the question of when a woman should come to the birth center. "When a woman calls me and says 'Should I come in?' I say, 'Do you want to?' and if she says, 'Well, I don't know, I thought you'd tell me,' then I say 'Stay home.' However, when she calls and says, 'I want to come in,' then it's time to come in. They know how long it takes them to get to the birth center."

The Childbearing Center of the Maternity Center Association, New York City, opened in the fall of 1975 and has been the model for other free-standing birth centers across the country. Over 1,300 babies have been born there. The popularity of the Childbearing Center is very high. The staff handles twenty to twenty-five births a month, which is their space capacity.

The Childbearing Center was designed as a demonstration project to test whether families who might otherwise have an unattended home delivery could have a safe, satisfying, and reasonably priced out-of-hospital alternative. In 1982 the staff of Maternity Center Association evaluated births in eleven centers in the United States.

Originally, the authors, Anita Bennetts, C.N.M., Ph.D., and Ruth Watson Lubic, C.N.M., Ed.D., had hoped to do a much-needed study that would match the women in the birth centers with a similar low-risk population in hospital births to compare complications and outcome. The authors could not get access to the needed data "primarily for political reasons," they say. "The American College of Obstetricians and Gynecologists (ACOG) . . . has squarely opposed out-of-hospital birth of any kind, and organized pediatrics has aligned itself with this opposition." As a result, they could not get the cooperation needed to study matched groups of women.

They settled for evaluating eleven birth centers. In all the centers, a certified nurse-midwife was the primary care giver and "the philosophy of the staff had to be one of minimal obstetric intervention," said the authors. Fifteen percent of the sample studied were transferred to the hospital after labor started, and all results include this transfer group. The only women who had anesthesia were the 5 percent who had cesareans. Five percent of the deliveries were assisted by forceps or vacuum extraction. Thirty percent of the women had local anesthesia for episiotomy repair.

The neonatal death rate for birth center infants *including transfers* is 4.6 per 1,000 live births. Because the authors were denied access to hospital data for a matched group of women, they did not have a hospital neonatal death rate to compare. However, the study neonatal death rate is almost identical to the rates for the safest birth attendants discussed later in this chapter.

Because of the excellent outcomes reported in this large study, the John A. Hartford Foundation gave a $250,000 grant to the Maternity Center Association to encourage out-of-hospital birth alternatives, especially free-standing birth centers. Maternity Center Association now provides consultation to assist individuals to start safe birth alternative programs in their communities. Part of the grant will be used to continue evaluating these alternatives.

About one half of the free-standing birth centers have doctors as the birth attendants. The NACHIS Birth Center in Culver City, California, was started in 1974 by obstetrician, Victor Berman, M.D., and his wife, nurse-midwife Salee Berman, C.N.M. Over 1,000 births have taken place at this center. Many of these babies had their sisters and brothers present at their birth. The NACHIS Birth Center was one of the chief sources of photos for the Hathaways' book, *Children at Birth*.

While intervention is very low in all free-standing birth centers, most have limited analgesia use. However, all women delivering at the NACHIS Birth Center have unmedicated births. (A numbing injection is given after birth for suturing an episiotomy, if needed.) If intervention is needed, the women are transported to a backup hospital. Twelve percent of the women required such a transfer for possible risk situations, lower than the typical free-standing birth center transfer rate. The intervention and complication rates are very low. Fewer than 3 percent of births were augmented with Pitocin. (Pitocin is only given in hospitals.) Fewer than 3 percent of the deliveries needed forceps or vacuum extraction. Under 50 percent of the women had episiotomies; fewer than 7 percent had third- or fourth-degree vaginal lacerations; and the primary cesarean section rate was under 7 percent.

Proponents of birth centers believe that they have the greatest potential for safety, satisfaction, and economy. Evaluation studies done on the deliveries of babies that have been born in free-standing birth centers show that birth centers are safe. Satisfaction is very high and is probably the most important factor in the explosive growth of birth centers. The cost of maternity care in free-standing birth centers is often far below that of general hospital maternity care. The total fee at the Childbearing Center is $1,000, about one third the cost of a normal delivery in a hospital in New York City.

Free-Standing Birth Centers

To sum up:

- Some insurance coverage, but some states refuse coverage, which limits new centers.
- Labor, birth, and recovery in a regular bed.
- No separation of mother, infant, and father.
- Equipment available for most common obstetrical emergencies; hospital backup provided.
- Very strict screening for admission.
- Complete pregnancy, birth, postpartum care, and pediatric care given at the birth center.
- Highly individualized and personal care, usually by nurse-midwives.
- Interventions nearly always absent; birth viewed as normal.
- 15 percent transfer during labor to regular hospital for delivery.
- Risk of complications very low.
- Parents educated and guided to take responsibility for their own health care.
- Satisfaction is very high.

PLACE OF BIRTH: HOME

> Should babies be born at home? What a question! Where else should they be born, if not in the home? The hospital? But I had thought that a hospital was a place where one went for relief from sickness or injury. I would not have thought, had I not known it to be a fact, that the most important event in the life of a family, the birth of a child, was celebrated away from home, away from the family, in a hospital.
>
> —Ashley Montagu, Ph.D.,
> quoted in *The Home Birth Book*

Almost all babies in the United States are born in hospitals. Home birth isn't seriously considered by most U.S. women today. However, there is a small but growing percentage of women who believe, as Ashley Montagu does, that the home is the best place to give birth, a place of celebration in the midst of one's family, with the hospital a place of medical refuge if needed.

The number of babies born at home, though small in relation to the millions born in hospitals, is growing dramatically. In many states, the percentage of babies born at home is about 1 percent. In a few states, the percentages are much higher. In Oregon, for example, 4.4 percent of all births take place at home. In some counties of California, estimates range as high as 15 percent.

The cost of home birth is minimal compared to a hospital birth. Almost all of the cost, in fact, is the birth attendant's fee, which varies from nothing or very little to six hundred dollars or more. Very few state insurance regulations cover the cost of home birth.

People who choose a home birth vary widely in their life styles and economic levels. Their reasons for having a home birth almost always have to do with a strong desire to have a self-directed rather than doctor-directed experience, to enhance family unity, and an inability to get what they want at a hospital. These parents see childbirth as a normal process. They believe that the addition of a new family member should take place in a way that is most conducive to acceptance of the new baby. The parents embrace full responsibility for decisions they make. The child is theirs forever, wherever it is born; the responsibility for the best outcome is theirs.

Most families who choose home birth do so in an atmosphere of widespread disapproval, so that they are often forced to carefully examine the reasons for their decision. In the area of safety, they see two key hazards of the hospital they are unwilling to accept: the risk of infection and high rates of intervention in normal births. They are willing to accept the risk of not having surgical delivery immediately available because they believe screening for risk can be effective. They believe that home birth is safer for a normal mother and baby than a hospital birth.

No one knows for certain whether it is safer today for a woman having a normal pregnancy to have her baby at home with a skilled birth attendant or to have her baby in a hospital.

In 1977 Neal Devitt, then a medical student at Rush Medical College, reviewed the medical and popular literature from 1930 to 1960 comparing the safety of home and hospital births. Because all the studies had scientific flaws of one kind or another, Mr. Devitt's conclusions suggest but do not prove that home birth was as safe as hospital birth during that period. Healthy women with normal pregnancies were better off at home because of a higher rate of birth injuries to infants and higher maternal mortality in hospitals.

There is an extraordinary lack of current research evaluating place of birth. In 1982 a joint Institute of Medicine-National Research Council committee described in detail the research needed to evaluate birth settings and safety for mother and baby. In order for research to be done, the cooperation of doctors and hospitals is required so that comparisons can be made between out-of-hospital and hospital births. So far, that cooperation is sadly lacking. Anita Bennetts, C.N.M., Ph.D., and Ruth Watson Lubic, C.N.M., Ed.D., experienced this lack of cooperation when they attempted to compare hospital and birth center births. They had to settle for evaluating outcomes of birth center births. Many obs are so convinced any kind of out-of-hospital birth is unsafe they will not sanction any research.

What research there is suggests that home birth is as safe or safer than hospital birth when the women have been screened to ensure they are low risk, and when they are attended by skilled birth attendants. Lewis Mehl, M.D., Ph.D., a family practitioner and statistician, carried out the first, and so far only, study comparing a group of women who gave birth at home to a similar group of women giving birth in a hospital. The 1976 study suggests a much better outcome for the home-birth group. One of the reasons for the much higher rates of intervention and subsequent complications in the hospital group studied by Dr. Mehl may be due to the difference in birth attendants. In the hospital group, three fourths of the women were delivered by obstetricians. In the home-birth group, two thirds were delivered by family practitioners and the remaining women by lay midwives.

A unique experiment in home birth continues to take place in rural Tennessee among a spiritual community of families called The Farm. The members of The Farm are a self-sufficient community who developed their own primary-health-care system. Over 1,000 babies were born at The Farm in the first ten years, 93 percent of them at home attended by lay midwives who learned their skills through practical experience and apprenticeship (called empirical midwifery).

Ina May Gaskin is The Farm's head midwife and author of *Spiritual Midwifery*, a text that is now being used in some medical schools. Statistics for The Farm deliveries contradict most hospital obstetrical statistics. Intervention is almost nonexistent. (The statistics include the women who delivered at a hospital after transfer.) Ninety-eight percent of the women gave birth with no analgesia or anesthesia; 28 percent had episiotomies, and less than 1 percent were given Pitocin to stimulate labor; less than one half of 1 percent of deliveries required forceps; and the cesarean rate was 1.8 percent. Their statistics for a ten-year period show none of the babies has had any neurological damage from the birth process. Not one of the babies had cerebral palsy, nerve damage, epilepsy, or mental retardation.

At The Farm, birth is viewed as a spiritual experience. One or two birth attendants support the mother early in her labor. Two or more midwives assist the mother in her delivery and early postpartum period. New or inexperienced mothers are housed with women who have already had several children so that the new mother can learn from the experienced mother. Ina May writes that all the parents speak of childbirth as a deeply moving religious experience, one where strong bonds are forged between the couple at the time of the birth of their child.

Home

To sum up:

- Insurance coverage unlikely, but costs low.
- Parent responsibility is high for finding a skilled birth attendant and for ensuring hospital backup is available.
- Screening essential to reduce risks.
- Approximately 20 percent transfer to the hospital during labor (mostly first-time mothers).
- Interventions absent.
- Complication rates extremely low.
- The risk of infection is low because the mother is not in an alien environment.
- The birth experience is directed by the parents.
- Mothers may feel more relaxed in their own territory.
- Siblings can easily participate in the birth at their own pace.
- The baby is part of the family from the beginning.
- Satisfaction very high.

The Choice of Your Birth Attendant

You have four choices for a birth attendant, and for the few parents who are unable to find a birth attendant they can agree with, a fifth choice is possible: themselves.

BIRTH ATTENDANT: OBSTETRICIAN

Whether a woman expects to have a healthy normal pregnancy, or whether she has been labeled "high risk," most American women choose obstetricians as their birth attendants. Obstetricians—surgeons trained to handle any gynecological or obstetrical problem—deliver four out of five American babies. Many women like the idea of having a specialist for their baby's birth, believing that, because the obstetrician can handle any complication that may develop, they have the best care available at all times.

In Chapter 4, "Understanding Doctors," we describe the obstetrician's training and practice. In a three-year residency the ob/gyn-to-be spends sixteen months on obstetrics. The rest of the time is spent mostly in gynecology, with some months in anesthesia, pathology, and endocrinology. He becomes a surgical specialist in diseases of the female reproductive system.

Most obstetricians believe birth to be a time of highest risk to the baby and that they are obliged to get the baby out as quickly as possible. They view a woman's birth canal as dangerous to the baby and believe that intervention is necessary in almost all births.

In a private practice review, reported in 1979 in *Ob.-Gyn. News,* a curious difference in the cesarean rates among obstetricians was revealed. "A surprisingly high rate of cesarean sections [were] performed by physicians who primarily practice gynecology," said Jack Pearson, M.D., registrar of ACOG, quoted in the article.

According to their data one could reason that gynecologists whose practice is primarily surgical are much more likely to give you a cesarean than obstetricians whose practice is mixed or primarily in obstetrics. If you go to an ob/gyn who specializes in gynecology for your obstetrical care, your chance of having a cesarean is one in two, or 50 percent. If you choose an obstetrician with a mixed practice, your chance of a cesarean is one in five. If you choose an obstetrician who primarily practices obstetrics, your chance of a cesarean is approximately one in four.

Obstetricians suggest that these differences are due to different patient populations; that is, they believe that gynecologists are probably getting women as patients who have already had prior cesarean sections or who are otherwise at high risk. However, no study supports this belief.

BIRTH ATTENDANT: FAMILY PRACTITIONER

Family practitioners, who deliver under 20 percent of American babies, are medical doctors who have taken an additional three years of residency after medical school.

A family practitioner chooses his specialty because he wants to treat the whole family. This is often the main reason some women prefer to go to a family practitioner for obstetrical care. They like the fact that he already knows the whole family, and they prefer the continuity of care that they receive by having the same person care for them and their newborn baby. Because the family practitioner's philosophy is to give primary care to the whole family, many family practitioners have a policy of delivering their obstetrical patients whether it is their night on call or not.

Family practitioners view birth as a normal process. Because they take care of newborns just as pediatricians do, they often see the complications from interventions. They view intervention in labor and delivery as risky and see themselves as skillfully using interventions only when necessary.

BIRTH ATTENDANT: CERTIFIED NURSE-MIDWIFE

Certified nurse-midwives deliver roughly one percent of American babies. They are registered nurses with an additional one to two years of midwifery training. During this time, the student midwife participates in over 100 normal deliveries. "The new nurse-midwife has more experience in normal childbirth than the average family practitioner," says Silvia Feldman, Ph.D., author of *Choices in Childbirth*. "She rapidly accumulates so much experience thereafter, working full time with normal births, that she soon knows more about managing normal pregnancies and childbirths than the average obstetrician."

The nurse-midwife's practice is limited to managing the maternity care of mothers whose progress through pregnancy, labor and delivery, and postpartum is normal. The training of a certified nurse-midwife is in normal childbirth, but she is taught to recognize an abnormal situation in pregnancy or birth, and to refer, or seek consultation with, a specialist. Education of the patient is a basic part of the philosophy of certified nurse-midwives. They view this education as helping the patient to participate in her own health care.

Certified nurse-midwives view intervention as risky, and prefer a more "hands on" approach, with the skillful avoidance of drugs. What some view as a disadvantage of midwives, that they are not trained to do surgery necessary in complicated deliveries, others view as the main advantage. Because she does not do gynecologic surgery, her time and efforts are not divided. Her only effort is to assist the childbearing family to have a normal delivery. "She is better equipped to give complete care to the normal [woman] than is her obstetrical physician colleague," said Ruth Lubic, nurse-midwife and director of the Maternity Center Association of New York City.

BIRTH ATTENDANT: LAY MIDWIFE

The lay midwives probably deliver 2 to 3 percent of babies in the United States each year, according to Dr. Stewart of NAPSAC. Lay midwives receive their training by apprenticing themselves to other midwives. They always deliver at home, though a few hospitals permit the lay midwife to accompany the woman to the hospital when a complication arises, and to remain with her through the delivery by someone else.

BIRTH ATTENDANT: YOURSELVES

Very few American women choose to deliver their own babies without a birth attendant. When they do, it's usually because they are unable to find a birth attendant who will give them the kind of birth they want either at home or in a hospital. Gregory White, M.D., a home-birth practitioner in Chicago, reports hearing from a registered nurse whom he had attended for her first three home deliveries. After she moved to Florida, she went to thirty different doctors, by actual count, to try to find a home-birth attendant. None would do it. Finally, she gave up and decided to have a do-it-yourself birth.

A number of do-it-yourself births are done by preference. Marilyn Moran of Leewood, Kansas, is the spokeswoman for this choice, believing that birth is a spiritual and sexual experience between husband and wife that should not be intruded upon if the pregnancy and labor are going normally. Believing it inappropriate for a woman to give birth into a stranger's hands, Moran suggests that a woman give birth into the waiting hands of the baby's father. For those who choose a do-it-yourself birth, Moran says it is crucial to have prenatal care to give the parents continuing information on the woman's risk status, and for the parents to study as much material about birth as they can, so they know the signs indicating a possible complication requiring hospital assistance.

Measuring the Safety of a Birth Attendant

One way to look at safety is to compare mother and baby death and complication rates for the different kinds of birth attendants. Obstetricians point to dropping maternal and perinatal mortality rates as proof of how well they are attending births. In Chapter 6, "Obstetricians'

Beliefs About a 'Safe Birth,' " we point out that overall death rates don't prove that what one is doing is safe; only evaluations of each intervention used could prove or disprove that. But death and complication rates can be useful in *comparing* birth attendants by specialty. If obstetricians who deliver most American babies have higher maternal mortality, perinatal mortality, and complication rates for their patients than family practitioners or midwives, that is a strong indication that, as a group, obstetricians may not be as safe as the other kinds of birth attendants.

Maternal mortality is based on the number of deaths of women per 100,000 live births. Maternal mortality rates in the United States are so good that it is difficult to distinguish any significant differences by specialty. The maternal mortality rate is about one maternal death for every 10,000 live births. Those are about the same odds of having triplets. For comparison, you have a fifteen times greater chance of becoming pregnant after your husband has had a vasectomy than you have of dying in childbirth.

However, there are a couple of reports suggesting more caution may be needed by obstetricians. Ob/gyns taking recertification exams in their specialty reported a tripling of maternal mortality among their patients, from 10 to 30 maternal deaths per 100,000 live births, from 1977 to 1978. That's "only" 20 more women who died for every 100,000 live births, but it was undoubtedly catastrophic for the families involved. According to ACOG's own report, the change may have been related to the increased cesarean-section rate for that year.

Another report, by Dr. Stewart of NAPSAC, concerned a medical and perinatal center in New Jersey, the College Hospital in Newark, whose staff has a high concentration of experienced, board-certified obstetricians. Giving testimony in the public hearing of the New Jersey Board of Medical Examiners, in 1980, Dr. Stewart reported that in the most recent nine-year span, College Hospital had 9 maternal deaths in 21,395 births. Dr. Stewart pointed out that was a maternal mortality rate of 42.1 per 100,000, more than double that of the state of New Jersey, and more than four times the national mortality rate. Of the 9 maternal deaths, 5 occurred over a ten-month period in 1978 and 1979, 4 of the deaths from anesthesia and one from toxemia. Dr. Stewart considers all of these maternal deaths preventable with the right kind of care.

There are differences in *infant* outcome by specialty that can be useful in comparing birth attendants. The best outcomes for mothers and babies in the industrialized countries of the world are, with the one exception of Japan, those countries where many or most of the babies are delivered by midwives. As an example, highly ranked Sweden has almost universal midwifery. Drug-free childbirth and 100 percent hospital births are also basic to Swedish maternity care.

One of the very few comparisons of neonatal mortality rates for babies delivered by either midwives or doctors was presented in the *American Journal of Obstetrics and Gynecology* in 1971. The neonatal mortality rate is the number of infant deaths per 1,000 live births during the first 28 days of life. For about three years, beginning in 1960, state funds were used for a nurse-midwifery demonstration project at Madera County Hospital in California. During the program, midwives managed "the vast majority of pregnancies and 78 percent of the hospital deliveries," according to the report. From mid-1963 on, doctors again handled all prenatal care and deliveries at the hospital. The program was terminated when, despite the good results, the California Medical Association opposed legalized nurse-midwifery.

This was a rare opportunity to compare birth attendants, all caring for the same kind of maternity population with the same mixture of low- and high-risk patients. The safest birth attendants were the midwives. During the period of time midwives practiced at Madera County Hospital, 1960 through 1963, neonatal mortalities were more than halved, dropping from 23.9 in 1959 to 10.3 neonatal deaths per 1,000 live births. The prematurity rate decreased by 40 percent, dropping from 11 percent to 6.6 percent. These neonatal mortality and prematurity rates were better than the average rates for the whole state of California.

The dramatic difference came, however, when the midwifery program was ended and doctors again became the birth attendants. During the next two-and-one-half years, the neonatal death rate more than tripled under doctors' care, averaging 32.1 neonatal deaths per 1,000 live births. The prematurity rate increased by almost 50 percent, rising to 9.8 percent, a lower rate than in 1959, but much higher than during the midwifery program. Midwives gave the best care at Madera County Hospital.

"Supervised Home Births Found Safest" trumpeted the newspaper headline describing a 1980 medical study by the Center for Disease Control, Atlanta, of neonatal mortality by place of birth and birth attendant. The six authors of the study were much more cautious in their conclusions, suggesting that, for low-risk women, delivery by a trained nurse-midwife in a birthing center was an acceptable alternative to a high-cost physician-hospital delivery. The study was carried out in North Carolina, where at the time of the study, lay midwives could legally attend home deliveries. Planned home deliveries, attended by lay midwives, had a neonatal mortality rate of 4 per 1,000 live births. The neonatal mortality rate for the hospitals, excluding low-birth-weight infants, was 7 per 1,000 (12 per 1,000 when low-birth-weight infants were included in the statistics). Lay midwives attended the planned home deliveries that had been medically screened for low risk. However, the women tended to be young, black, unmarried, and poorly educated, characteristics that caused them to be considered socioeconomically at risk.

The study included 100 planned home deliveries without a trained attendant. These women tended to be middle class, white, educated, and married, characteristics that initially would cause them to be considered socioeconomically at low risk. However, many had little or no prenatal care. Three of these infants died, giving a neonatal mortality rate of 30 per 1,000, seven to eight times higher than the home deliveries where the women were prenatally screened and had, as birth attendants, lay midwives.

The most comprehensive review of the literature on midwifery is given by Dr. David Stewart, editor of *The Five Standards for Safe Childbearing*. His historical review shows that midwife-attended deliveries have neonatal death rates well below national averages. In many, if not most, of the studies the midwives were attending the poor and high-risk client, where one could expect *higher* neonatal death rates.

He cited the outstanding example of North Central Bronx Hospital in New York City, reported in a public hearing of the National Institute of Health Task Force on Cesarean Birth in 1980. More than 30 percent of the mothers were labeled medically at high risk of complication. Another 30 percent were considered at risk because of socioeconomic considerations. Nevertheless, 83 percent of the births were completed by midwives. In spite of the risk status of many of the women delivered by the midwives, the neonatal mortality rate, which *included* many low-birth-weight babies, was an astonishingly low 4.2 deaths per 1,000 live births. No reports of doctor attended births of women with similar risks show as good outcomes as this low neonatal mortality rate achieved by midwives.

The midwives intervened in labor and delivery as little as possible. Amniotomy was not done, and only 3 percent of the women were given Pitocin to stimulate or start labor. Mothers were encouraged to walk during labor and permitted to eat and drink. Nearly 85 percent of the women gave birth in the labor beds in a semisitting position. Forceps were used only 2.3 percent of the time, and fewer than 30 percent of the births had either analgesic or anesthetic drugs used. The cesarean rate was 9 percent including repeat cesareans. More than half the women with previous cesareans were allowed a trial of labor. Seventy percent of these mothers gave birth vaginally.

Maternity systems based on midwifery have better mother and baby outcomes according to the literature. "The data base for these figures is in the millions, is global in scope, and spans almost a century, up to and including the present," said Dr. Stewart. He estimates that if all the women delivering between 1940 and 1980 had had a birth attendant with a midwife philosophy, mother and baby mortalities would have been halved and the rates of brain-damaged children and other birth defects would have been reduced by at least three fourths. According to his estimates, 30,000 mothers died in childbirth who should not have died; 1,500,000 children were severely brain damaged because of medical procedures; and 45 million children suffered minimal brain damage who would have been normal, had unnecessary intervention in normal deliveries been avoided.

Dr. Stewart agrees that it is the philosophy of care and not the title of the birth attendant that determines safety for mother and baby. This philosophy of care involves:

- Prenatal education and screening
- Continuous one-to-one labor support by a skilled labor attendant, who may also be the birth attendant
- The view that a woman's body is designed to give birth safely to her baby in her own unique way
- The belief that intervention should be used only when the need is greater than the risk

This philosophy is common among midwives, but can be found among some family practitioners and obstetricians, too.

Women at low risk for complicated deliveries have much greater rates of intervention and complication for themselves and their babies in traditional hospitals than in alternative settings, either within the hospital or outside of the hospital. Your chance of a normal birth is related to your choice of a birthplace and a birth attendant.

If you are willing to look, you have a great chance of finding a place of birth fairly near you that will satisfy your needs in childbirth. Many hospitals have eased their policies to allow flexibility in their routines. With your coach-husband, a woman friend, and an agreeable birth attendant, you can have a good and safe birth in many hospitals today.

4 ▪ UNDERSTANDING DOCTORS—WHY THEY DO WHAT THEY DO

> I'm proud of what I do. I'm proud that I've gone to school
> and become an educated person. I don't think I'm bet-
> ter than anyone else. We doctors are not pillars of society.
> We are part of society. Who's a pillar? The guy who
> sweeps out a gas station, pays taxes, doesn't commit any
> crimes, goes to church, loves his wife. Isn't he a pillar
> of society?
>
> —Obstetrician*

Most of you will have a doctor, probably an obstetrician, as your birth attendant. To get a good and safe birth, you need to understand your doctor. He's a unique person, with his own background, training that has shaped his thinking and beliefs, and his own pressures and successes.

TRAINING MAKES THE MAN

Most doctors-to-be know from their early years that they want to go into medicine. During high school and college, the doctor-to-be strives for academic excellence. If he doesn't have a high school report card with nearly all A's, he may not get into the college of his choice. Once he's in college, he's again working primarily for the best grade-point average, because competition for medical school is enormous. Each year many competent applicants are turned away.

The doctor-to-be learns early that he cannot allow himself to falter. For four years in medical school he studies harder than ever before. Finally, he graduates with that M.D. degree he has sacrificed so much for. Yet the demands on him intensify. He still has an internship and a residency ahead of him.

*This doctor's comments follow throughout this chapter.

Internship

Internship is a year in which new doctors sample all the medical specialties and choose one for themselves. Because the vast majority of doctors specialize, most will enter a residency program. Many hospitals have eliminated the year of internship, and students progress directly into a residency. This internship, or combined internship-residency, is a world in which single-minded dedication to medicine is mandatory, much like the seminarian's dedication to God.

In a 1982 issue of *Hospital Management Quarterly,* Julie C. Donnelly, Ed.D., reports on the stresses that face interns:

> The first year of postgraduate training is significant in that the individual is now an actual M.D., may legitimately be addressed as "Doctor," is now earning a salary for the first time, is now in a supervisory position over medical students, and has primary patient responsibility. At the same time, the intern is at the bottom of the medical training hierarchy and bears a workload of 70 to 100 hours per week. This typically includes an on-call schedule that demands being in the hospital every third night and weekend and often going without sleep for 36 hours.

Residency

In the usual residency the working hours and the elimination of a life outside the hospital hardly get any better. Michelle Harrison, M.D., author of *Woman in Residence,* describes her ob residency training: "Medical training works like brainwashing. Two major components are sleep deprivation and isolation from one's support system."

As if to verify this wearing down of the psyche, many doctors, looking back to their residencies, report daily reinforcement of their unworthiness. To survive, they had to learn to believe what they were told, to do what was demanded of them by their superiors. The hospital became their entire focus. Home was just a place to go to sleep occasionally. Although the above is true of all residencies, it is especially true, and accentuated, in surgical residencies such as ob/gyn.

I was in surgery seven hours from seven A.M. until two in the afternoon. Usually there were a half dozen or more operations, and I'd make rounds in between or after. The afternoons and evenings were for admitting new patients, performing physical exams, writing up charts, and prescribing tests or medications.

Typically, 75 percent of an ob/gyn's training is in surgery. Surgeons at their best are finely trained technicians. Learning to use technology is crucial for them, so that they can intervene automatically and quickly in lifesaving situations.

Obstetrics is the least scientific of all specialties. Traditionally in the past, the bottom half of the medical class went into obstetrics.

When I was in training, we still listened with a headscope. That was the state of the art. We were afraid to do a c-section and we knew nothing about the fetus. Now in ten years there has been an explosion of technology in obstetrics.

In the 1970s the glitter of high technology was added to the ob/gyn training program, making it a more challenging residency to new doctors. But it's more than the magic of science. "A lot of medicine is drudgery and trivia," one doctor told us, giving his opinion why doctors so readily accept new technology in their practice. "Medicine is often like an assembly line [a common complaint of the patient also]. New techniques and technology are exciting. They are like new toys, and you think you are doing things better. You become part of relentless progress."

Unless residents are trained to keep technology in perspective, I can see where they would get on a treadmill and rely upon machinery too much. Nurses are the same way. I was trained in the in-between era, where I saw both worlds. There is a place for technology, but people tend to rely on it too much. Doctors and nurses who are trained at high-tech centers have to make a conscious effort to not allow high-technology procedures to be their only tools. That's not easy. If that's the way you were trained, you'll be uncomfortable changing.

The most important skill for ob/gyns, from their point of view, is not delivering babies; it's surgery. This is an emphasis that is often not in women's best interests. Sociologist Diana Scully wrote of her three years' experience studying two hospital-training programs specializing in obstetrics and gynecology in her book, *Men Who Control Women's Health: The Miseducation of Obstetricians and Gynecologists.* According to her, "Most of a doctor's training in obstetrics and gynecology focuses on surgery and on gaining expertise in diagnosis and treatment of acute and pathological conditions. The majority of cases that a resident sees, however, do not require these skills." She concluded that in order to get enough surgical experience residents found patients whose problems might or might not indicate the need for surgery and then persuaded these patients to have surgery.

Residents are eager to do surgery. There is pressure on residents to find surgery because there is never enough to go around. I don't think I'm overtrained for surgery. I don't think you can ever be surgically overtrained. But you can very easily be undertrained. You can quickly get in the habit of doing surgeries that don't need to be done when there are alternatives, too.

Ob/gyn residents, like other specialists, practice almost exclusively on low-income women who frequent major medical centers. These women are the likeliest in our culture to be high risk, and the least likely to ask questions. This treatment, plus the normal vulnerability of pregnancy, labor, and birth, guarantees that many of these patients will not object to any procedure done to them. An ob/gyn resident is not encouraged to discuss with a patient what she wants; his daily training reinforces the belief that only he knows what's best.

I tell residents that they are going to find a different world when they go into private practice. Nobody ever told me that when I was a resident. If I said to a patient during my training, "You need a hysterectomy," she never said, "Why?" She said, "Yes, doctor, thank you, doctor." Well, that's not the real world. In my practice, there is a lot of consumer interest. And questions . . . and more questions.

Doctors who specialize in family practice treat the whole family—not just the pregnant woman. Like family practitioners, pediatricians in their three-year residencies often will see the same child and that child's family for many visits. A family-practice doctor contrasted his own residency training for us with the training he saw in ob/gyn: "I had fifteen patients of my own that I took care of from the very beginning of their pregnancy to their labor and delivery, and then I took care of their babies until I finished my three-year residency. That kind of follow-through in patient care is something you don't get at all in the standard ob/gyn training." Patients at major medical centers usually see a different ob/gyn resident for each visit and yet another stranger at the birth.

As a resident, I used to see forty to forty-five people in a three-hour clinic. I might have seven patients in labor at one time. All I could do was make a snap judgment, a quick decision. I couldn't really sit down and talk to people. There just wasn't enough time. I have a real easygoing practice now. I see about half the patients that the average obstetrician does.

I've made it a point not to treat my patients in my private practice the same way we treated women during my training. A doctor can change just like everybody else. It just depends on how human he is.

The resident obstetrician typically believes that he will learn all he needs to know about childbirth in his residency. That may leave him suspicious of any ideas that are different from what he learned.

I delivered 2,000 babies in my residency. If the patients didn't get medication, it was a rare exception. In fact, I was told that I failed in my duty if I did not provide the patient with medication. I trained in a big city ghetto hospital. There the women wanted and needed medication. There was no prenatal education, no Bradley or Lamaze classes. Most of the women were not married and didn't want to be pregnant. They didn't want pain. There was no reward for them to have that child and so in that situation, if I didn't provide them with anesthesia I wasn't doing my job. That's what I was there for.

Many an obstetrician feels that if an unmedicated birth was good for the baby and the mother, he would have been taught that in his training. If good communication skills were essential, they, too, would be taught in residency. If understanding women's need for the biological pleasure of birth was thought significant, that also would be part of residency training. However, these topics are seldom mentioned, if at all, in ob/gyn residencies.

I am way overtrained to deliver a perfectly healthy woman who is having her third child, who is going to go into spontaneous labor. She doesn't need a board-certified and surgically trained obstetrician for that delivery, nine out of ten times. One out of ten she might. My training makes it hard for me to sit on my hands and just wait and watch.

One obstetrician described the transition from training to private practice to us by saying, "Physicians are trained in a high-pace setting and have to unlearn rigidity, haste, and intensity." Asking an ob to "sit on his hands" and wait for nature to take its course goes against his beliefs, training, and experience.

"The exuberant years of medical research have set loose on an unsuspecting public a large number of physicians who are in command of highly complex, cost-intensive technologies of uncertain value, which they then proceed to implement," said Stanford University Economist Victor Fuchs in 1978. "They understandably want to practice medicine in the style to which they have become accustomed."

And that style definitely affects the care an obstetrician gives you.

SPECIAL INFLUENCES ON DOCTORS

Fear of Malpractice Suits

Malpractice is more than a specter for many obstetricians. It's a reality. Your physician knows colleagues who are being sued. That strongly influences what your doctor may or may not do during your pregnancy and birth. According to a 1979 report by Helen Marieskind, Dr. P.H., "The National Association of Insurance Commissioners estimates that an ob/gyn faces ten times the risk of being sued and being collected from than do most physicians. (And if he lives in California, Florida, or New York, his chances of being sued are even greater, according to a 1982 study reported in *Contemporary Ob/Gyn*.)

In a study of 591 physicians reported in 1982 in *Medical Media & Marketing*, "How Physicians See Themselves—And Their Image," Stephen W. Brown, Ph.D., concludes that many physicians are uncertain "as to what the public perceives about doctors and malpractice suits." But ob/gyns were the only specialty where a majority of the doctor-respondents said the public believes that physicians are at fault in most malpractice suits.

I talk to other doctors, and they are worried. This is especially true when I'm doing an ob consultation. I've read in the newspapers about doctors who deny that the fear of malpractice influences their decisions. Well, that's not true. Privately, we know a very large portion of an ob's decisions are based on the legal implications. It gets worse every day. The agencies that handle our malpractice policies come and give risk-management seminars for doctors.

The anxiety level about malpractice suits among most obstetricians is high. "The shadow of malpractice falls over our every act," states surgeon Ralph S. Emerson, M.D., in the *Bulletin of the American College of Surgeons*. And some lawyers encourage "defensive medicine." James J. Pagliuso, J.D., in his article, "Situations To Avoid If You Don't Want To Be Sued," in the March 1982 issue of *Contemporary Ob/Gyn*, stated: "I believe obstetricians and hospitals are taking substantial medicolegal risks if they don't undertake at least external monitoring from the outset of active labor."

I have people who come into my office and they say, "Why haven't you done the ultrasound yet?" and I say that I don't think it is indicated, and they say, "Well, my girlfriend had an ultrasound and I want an ultrasound; I want to see the baby." "You'll see your baby in six months," I say.

"Well, I don't want to wait," she tells me. She'll get her ultrasound. And strictly because if ever there was an anomaly or the slightest thing wrong, she is going to say to me, "Why didn't you do the ultrasound when I asked you to?" So I am pressured to do it. I don't do everything that a patient demands, but those kinds of pressures I cooperate with because I don't want to lose my practice. I have to earn a living, and I like what I do. I'm basically just like everybody else. If you work in a factory and the guy down the line does something wrong and gets fired for it, you are not going to repeat his mistake. It's the same with obstetricians.

Who's the least likely to get sued? The doctors who listen and talk to their patients, according to two Ohio State University marketing professors, Roger Blackwell and Wayne Talarzyk. Agreeing, Richard W. Boone, J.D., et al, said in a 1981 article, "What Every Perinatologist Should Know About Medicolegal Problems," "Developing a good relationship is the single most effective way to deter lawsuits."

The fear of a malpractice suit in your doctor's mind could cause you to receive unnecessary interventions, from extra office tests to a cesarean. Prevent "defensive medicine" from interfering with your pregnancy and birth by doing your part in developing a partnership with your doctor.

Insurance Companies Reinforce Your Doctor's Urge to Intervene

About 85 percent of Americans have health coverage. Nearly all hospital bills and two thirds or more of doctors' fees are paid by insurance. Health insurance allows most patients to buy services from both doctors and hospitals without concerning themselves about price. This arrangement is an effective incentive for doctors to use all the technology they have at their fingertips.

When a hospital buys ultrasound machines and electronic fetal monitors, the administration is counting on insurance companies to pay the tab—and that means using the machines. Insurance (ultimately the consumer) pays for all those other extras in the hospital, too—from IV bottles and Pitocin, to epidurals and anesthesiologists, nursery fees and baby bottles, sleeping pills and dry-up shots. Although your doctor doesn't get a cut of the insurance company's payment to the hospital, insurance companies reinforce the inclination of the ob/gyn to *do* something by virtue of what procedures they choose to pay for. Costs for cesareans, a surgical procedure, for instance, are usually reimbursed 100 percent. This is not always so with vaginal births.

Obstetricians have incentives to use technology during pregnancy, too. Insurance companies routinely pay for prenatal tests. Critics of the American medical industry point out that physicians with diagnostic equipment in their offices use that equipment more than physicians who use independent labs to do the work. You'll get more tests of all kinds if they can be done in your doctor's office. This is not to say that your doctor doesn't believe these procedures are necessary, but their use becomes habit, rather than thought out specifically with you in mind. Although pregnant women are very unlikely to get x-rayed, more and more obstetrical offices include ultrasound equipment. In these offices, every pregnant patient routinely has at least one ultrasound scan performed sometime before the birth.

In a foreword to the "Technology 82" issue of *Contemporary Ob/Gyn*, John T. Queenan, M.D., addresses his colleagues by saying:

> The field of medical technology is one of the fastest-growing areas in the fast-changing world of the physician. It is startling to realize the number of tests and equipment in common use now that were not available to us just two decades ago. Or even one decade ago. Stop and think what your practice would be like if these advances had not become part of your everyday life.
>
> New equipment has made an enormous contribution to our specialty in particular. Operating microscopes, colposcopes, laparoscopes, electronic fetal monitors, ultrasound scanners, office laboratory systems—these and other technical advances have made a huge difference in the way we practice.

Ob/gyns are trained to use high technology and they believe in its usefulness. Insurance companies pay for high-tech procedures. Knowing this incentive to use technology during both your pregnancy and birth, perhaps, when the question of tests, ultrasound scans, or hospital procedures comes up, you can discuss the pros and cons *for you,* with a clear explanation of the risks/benefits before agreeing with your doctor's suggestions.

What About Doctors' Drug Education?

Much of the drug education that physicians receive comes from drug companies themselves, rather than from a neutral, third-party source. Drug companies offer endless free samples to doctors, starting when they are medical students and continuing through their private practice years. Robert Seidenberg, M.D., Clinical Professor of Psychiatry at Upstate Medical Center, State University of New York at Syracuse, told a hearing of the House Select Committee on Narcotics Abuse and Control that "Physicians do not understand what conflict of interest means—that you don't get educated by your suppliers."

"Last year $215 million worth of advertisements were placed in the 150 leading medical journals, and that represents only the smallest part of the typical drug promotion campaign," reported *Time* magazine in 1982. "Hundreds of millions more go into snappy exhibits at medical meetings, glossy brochures presented to doctors by company 'detail men,' and educational videotapes for physicians."

Be responsible for your own drug use. Ask that both the benefits and risks of any drug that your doctor may recommend for you be explained. Read the package insert, available at pharmacies, on any drug you might take. Or look up a drug description in the *Physician's Desk Reference* at your local library.

Physician Income

Money talks in our culture. The highest paid physicians are surgeons (many earn more than $100,000 a year) and radiologists (who use expensive, high-tech machinery). Since ob/gyns are surgeons and the highest paid physicians working on hospital ob units, they have the most clout in establishing maternity-care policies or equipment purchase recommendations.

The typical obstetrician-gynecologist in 1980 netted (after expenses, before taxes) between $75,000 and $95,280, according to *Medical Economics*. Family practitioners netted between $50,460 and $70,810. (The higher-income figure was earned by physicians who are part of incorporated businesses.) Pediatricians averaged $61,070. In comparison, nurse-midwives took home $20,000 on the average; and the median family income for all occupations in the United States for the same year, 1980, was less than $16,000.

I know a lot of doctors who drive Chevrolets and Toyotas, have modest homes, and don't play golf every day. And they have a hard time paying their bills. I am under the same pressures as everyone else, so I want to make more money, too. Until I was into my thirties, my top yearly income was $18,000. That's not a lot of money. I was married early and had two children. I had $25,000 in loans to pay back, and it cost well over $50,000 to start my practice. Right there is a lot of incentive to make some money and make it fast. Many physicians think they deserve it. I don't know how to argue with that, because this is a money-oriented society and that's status and that's America.

The Coming Doctor Surplus—How It Will Change Your Maternity Health Care

Twenty years ago there was a public clamor for more doctors. But the number of doctors has grown proportionately faster than the population. Both insiders and outsiders of the medical profession now predict a doctor surplus—some call it a glut—at least by 1990. In 1980 a U.S. Government Advisory Committee projected an excess of nearly 70,000 doctors within the decade. Some of this crowding among doctors is already showing. In a *Medical Economics* "Continuing Survey," nearly half of the doctors surveyed said they were working at less than full capacity. Of those, 40 percent said it wasn't by choice.

In the government's report, one of the two specialties expected to have the greatest surplus is obstetrics/gynecology. (The other is pediatrics.) These physicians will not sit idly by and watch their number of patients, and therefore, their income, dwindle away. They'll find ways to overcome the financial drain of a doctor surplus. And some of the steps they're likely to take may not be good for you, the consumer:

■ *Increase the number of visits patients make, as well as the number of charges (including tests) per office visit.*

■ *Raise prices.* In cities where there's already an overabundance of doctors, prices do not go down, as they would in other industries. Prices tend to go up instead.

■ *Eliminate the competition.* With the U.S. birth rate not likely to increase very much, there already are not enough babies to go around for the people who are delivering infants now—ob/gyns, family-practice doctors, certified nurse-midwives, and lay midwives. If the projected number of ob/gyns for 1990 becomes a reality, each ob will have 25 percent fewer babies to deliver than he does now.

Each medical specialty wants other doctors to "stay on their own turf." Both the government and consumers are interested in nonphysician specialists. Nurse-midwives, pediatric nurse practitioners, and physician assistants, reduce medical costs and often provide more personalized care. All doctors—not just obs—are likely to fight the encroachment on what they believe is their exclusive territory.

I believe the demand for obstetricians in society will rapidly decrease. I think it should. We have too many specialists. There are women who do want an obstetrician, and they would no more go to a midwife or a family practitioner than they would live in an underground sod shack. I mean, they want an epidural; they want me; and they want to tell their friends that I'm a specialist and I'll deliver the baby. There will always be that demand. But that is going to be decreasing in the future and what are all those extra 20,000 obstetricians going to do? I've already lost some referring doctors because I have a nurse-practitioner in my office and I work with nurse-midwives.

Although obstetricians have made it hard for some family-practice doctors to get hospital privileges and virtually impossible for most certified nurse-midwives to get these same hospital privileges, the best example of the obs' efforts to eliminate competition is their battle against home births. Lay midwives have been harassed and accused of crimes. Some parents who've had their babies at home have been reported to state authorities and accused of child abuse. And doctors who participate in home births—or who give prenatal care to these women—are often hounded by their peers. These doctors are threatened with loss of hospital staff privileges; their malpractice insurance policies are usually dropped; and they are often treated like outcasts among other physicians.

Obstetricians are motivated strongly by their belief, learned in those training years, that all births should occur in a hospital, but there's no doubt that an economic incentive is at work. If birth can take place safely with a family practitioner or midwife in attendance, then fewer obstetricians are needed. With more obstetricians being trained, there is bound to be increasing conflict of interest.

Pressures of Medical Practice

Once a doctor hangs out his private-practice shingle, he puts in long hours, just like any other small business owner. According to 1981 American Medical Association survey figures, the typical obstetrician spends fifty hours in medical practice per week, though many individual doctors report sixty-, seventy-, and eighty-hour work weeks. Seeing patients takes up most of this time, including late-night deliveries and gynecological surgery time. Reading ob/gyn specialty journals adds more hours to an obstetrician's week.

If he's not already there delivering a baby, an ob can usually be found making rounds at one or more hospitals, checking patients first thing in the morning and often the last thing at night. If he's in a partnership, and nearly all obs are, he'll probably deliver several babies in any one twenty-four-hour period when he is on call.

Aside from long hours, it sounds like a good life. He's busy, he is doing what he wants, and he's well paid. He's obeyed without question at the hospital, and his patients are usually grateful to him. But that good life is a myth for many doctors.

> It wasn't that I was tired; it was emotional exhaustion. . . . The physical labor is minimal, the danger is infinitesimal. But what gets you—or rather what gets me—is the agitation of dealing with people. I don't think this is a unique reaction. Doctors, lawyers, psychiatrists, waiters, cab drivers, and shoe clerks suffer from the same syndrome. Anyone who deals with the public.
> People exert a pressure, deliberately or unconsciously. They force their wills. Their passions, wants, angers, lies, and fears come on like strong winds. Deal with people, and inevitably you feel you're being buffeted. No, that's no good. You feel like you're in a blender, being sliced, chopped, minced, ground, and pureed.
>
> —from *The Sixth Commandment*

Although this observation comes from a novel by Lawrence Sanders, physicians tell us it's a good description of the pressures they feel in their medical practice. Doctors are trained to believe that their job is to take over and cure. But the reality of medical practice is not that simple. Sometimes not much can be done for patients, yet many patients demand that the doctor do something.

I spend hours on the phone every week trying to talk women out of using Bendectin [a drug prescribed for nausea, which was removed from production in June, 1983]. "Do you understand there has been a lawsuit on Bendectin?" "Yes," she says. "Do you understand that we cannot guarantee the safety of any medication or substance you take during pregnancy?" "Yes," she says. "Do you understand that I don't prescribe the drug routinely?" "Yes," she says. "Do you understand that it has a package insert that says it's to be used only in unusual circumstances?" "Yes," she says. "So I prefer you take crackers and watch your diet and stay away from food," I tell her. "Doctor," she says, "I want Bendectin." These women are nauseated. I wouldn't want to be nauseated and not feel good. They say that I have to have something to give them. All I can give them is what they know already; that's all I have. So I get pressure from them.

Consumers complain that doctors aren't like they used to be, that they are always in a hurry and they don't want to listen anymore. In the Baltimore COMA Survey, the most important quality women looked for in their obstetrician was communication skills. In a 1981 magazine poll of readers, more than two thirds thought doctors should improve their explanations to patients. Yet most doctors are still trained to believe their job is to treat the physical problem, not listen. In *Medical Economics* one doctor expressed his frustration with "just" listening by stating, "But by and large, it's patients who do the most to fray a doctor's nerves. And pregnant patients are the worst. One of the most recurrent and annoying phone calls I get is from the patient in labor asking for instructions."

People expect more of doctors now. They don't expect mistakes. They are more aware of the shortcomings and faults that take place in medicine. And there's been another attitude change, too. If a woman delivers a baby that has a defect, people are much more surprised. In the past, people understood that there wasn't much we could do about it.

Patients have high expectations of physicians, and so do other physicians. Doctors expect all their peers to practice medicine much the same way.

There are fads—new, unproven techniques—in medicine, and they come and go. It's easier to go with these fads, no matter how unscientific they might be. You can buck the trend better if you are an established authority in a large medical center. It's a lot harder to do that when you are just an ordinary workaday obstetrician. You have no credentials and no research to support your viewpoints. Therefore, you are compelled to practice what is called the "standard of care," that is, what is reasonable in the community, what other obstetricians do. That's the threat, that's the problem. If you are outside the "standard of care," you are potentially leaving yourself open for liability, criticism, and loss of license.

The medical profession has always regulated itself. Now it's just beginning to be held accountable to different segments of society. Doctors believe they should be the only ones to regulate themselves. Self-regulation is always an invitation to abuse, especially when so much power and money is involved. But many doctors set that idea aside and believe it doesn't apply to them. Government regulation is perceived as an invasion of their privacy and an attack on their integrity.

We don't police ourselves nearly as well as we could. We've got a long way to go, but I think attitudes are changing. The older doctors resent any policing of hospital procedures, because they've been God so long. Nobody ever questioned them before. "Medicine is not fun anymore," they say. "Everyone is telling us what to do and what not to do." I think the younger physicians coming up are going to practice in an era of peer review. People are going to know what doctors are doing. Due to liability concerns and consumer demands, hospitals and doctors are going to have to protect themselves through self-regulation.

Although many other workers put in as many hours in a week as physicians do, there remains a big difference. Only physicians make life and death decisions on a regular basis. And this is perhaps the greatest pressure of all.

Even though they're trained in their residencies to believe only they can make those life and death decisions, that awesome responsibility still takes its toll on doctors personally. *Always* making the decisions places them in a position where they're not allowed to make mistakes—a tough order for someone merely human. To add to the stress of making these decisions, patients willingly give that power to doctors. Often we want the doctor to decide, thereby adding to his pressure to perform without error—like Superman. Surgeon Richard Selzer, M.D., commented on this issue in a magazine interview:

> Patients ordinarily don't want to know the alternatives. They say, "Do what you think is best." Even the most enlightened say that. When they're dreadfully ill, patients regress, they become childlike in a way. They want to be taken care of. It's an impulse that is in the tissues. A person wants to be held, comforted, and consoled. They want to be made well, to be touched. It's a laying on of hands. When I have tried to hold back that absolute blind faith and say, "Wait a minute, let's talk about this. It's your life, you should be the one to decide," this rocks the patient, it shakes them. They don't know what to do. Deep down, on the gut level, people want you to accept the responsibility. I would love to give over some of the burden of responsibility because I am full of guilt about it all the time.

Professional stresses spill over into a doctor's personal life. Many a doctor's wife can tell you about vacations canceled at the last minute because of hospital emergencies. Many a doctor's son or daughter knows that delivering a baby is more important than a high-school play. Not surprisingly, the divorce rate among doctors is higher than the rest of the population. Also, doctors are more prone to alcoholism, drug addiction, depression, and suicide than other people. (The drug addiction rate alone is 100 times greater than the rest of the population.)

Physicians do want the best medical care for you. However, your doctor is trained to believe that, of the two of you, he's the best judge of what that is. It probably won't be any easier for your doctor to change his ways than it is for the rest of us to change our unrealistic expectations.

He not only is trained to believe he's always right, he also has peer pressure from his colleagues to not rock that boat called "the status quo."

But there is a right birth attendant for you. Our next chapter describes how to find your "Dr. Right," a person who will be your health care partner—not your boss. The search is yours, because ultimately you, and only you, are responsible for your health and well-being.

5 ▪ FINDING DR. RIGHT

> Women must realize first that they do have a right to say
> how they want their babies delivered, with whom and
> where.... Like everything else—one must care to have
> things a certain way. If there is no strong desire, then
> the doctor, as most people do, will follow whatever prac-
> tices that are convenient for him. We need to educate
> women who will then demand proper services from doc-
> tors and hospitals.

Knowing what birth options you want is no guarantee that you'll get them or that you'll experience all birth's potential pleasure. But it's a step. Understanding your doctor's point of view based on his training and background is also a necessary step. Next in getting the birth you want is not only choosing the right birth attendant, but establishing a relationship, based on thorough communication, that works in the best interests of you, your baby, *and* your doctor.

This chapter tells you one step at a time how to find Dr. Right, what to do once you're in his office, what to say/do/ask when you're face-to-face with him, what questions you need answered, what's in it for him to work with an informed consumer (for a change), your legal rights, and, of course, what his responsibility is to you and what your own responsibility is in your health care. To know where you're starting from, compare your attitude to the following list:

1. You want your doctor to take over and be totally in charge.

2. You want the doctor to keep you informed, but you want him to make all the decisions.

3. You want to be informed, and when it comes to making medical decisions, you do it in partnership with your doctor.

4. You consider a doctor your consultant only and will make all decisions regarding your health care, except in a life and death emergency.

If your choice is #1 or #2, you are in the mainstream of American medical consumers. Doctors are most accustomed to and comfortable with working with people like you. If your choice is #3 or #4, you are a pioneer in developing the partnership between pregnant women and their doctors. Like a pioneer anywhere, you're preparing the way for others, while risking criticism for yourself.

"The majority of doctors feel threatened by exploratory interviews," stated Charles Flowers, M.D., in a 1981 magazine article. You may find that some doctors will be most unreceptive to your questions, particularly if your attitude is #3 or #4. However, these attitudes are your best chance of getting the birth you want, and when you do find Dr. Right, the search will have been worth it.

HOW TO FIND DR. RIGHT

Let's take it from the beginning. You think you're pregnant and you start to look around for the right doctor for you. You look at your current doctor. Your friends also make suggestions. The Baltimore COMA researchers asked women to list all the reasons for choosing their ob. Nine out of ten women put at the top of their list these two reasons: he already was her gynecologist, or he was referred by a friend or relative. (The other most important reasons were his ability to communicate and his hospital affiliation.) Maybe after you've done a search, you'll still wind up with your gynecologist.

Because nearly all of you will choose a physician, we call your birth attendant Dr. Right. For most of you, he is an obstetrician. For others, a family practitioner, or for a few, an osteopath. If your search is for a midwife, you can still follow the same process.

Making a List

I am again shopping for a doctor, a doctor who delivers at a hospital with practices I agree with. I would like to have a doctor who has a midwife working with him or her. I definitely know what I want and don't want next time and I will try not to get myself into an undesirable situation again. I plan to find out what I can about the doctor even before I see him or her, and then, during the first visit, make sure our ideas are in accord.

Start with the recommendations of others and make a list. When getting names, ask why the doctor is being recommended. You'll soon discover that many of the reasons aren't sufficient for a well-informed consumer like yourself. The key is to know what you want and find the doctor who will give it to you. Though interesting, would you choose your partner in your health care for these reasons?

- He goes to my church and lives in the neighborhood. (He may even vote the same ticket, but that doesn't mean he's familiar with a Leboyer gentle birth or that he will help you avoid drugs in labor.)

- Your Aunt Sally says he has a wonderful bedside manner. (Your doctor probably won't get to the side of your bed until you're ready to deliver the baby.)
- She's the only woman doctor in town. (If your number one priority is a woman, and your town doesn't have midwives, then this is obviously a valuable piece of information to add to your list. But if one of your reasons for having a woman doctor is that she's likelier to give you what you want because she's a woman, don't count on it. Women doctors experience the same medical training that men do. Chances are though, like other women, a woman physician will pay more attention to your personal relationship with her than her male colleagues might. Since 25 percent of medical students are now women, your chances of finding a woman practitioner increase all the time.)

Some people also look in the Yellow Pages or their town's medical directory (available at the public library). That can help you get a geographical fix on the doctors in town. But mere names and locations don't tell you enough.

Physicians often suggest to consumers that a hallmark to look for when doctor-shopping is board certification. This term means that a doctor has completed the required years of medical training and, in addition, has passed a series of professional competency exams in his specialty. Board certification, in the case of obstetricians, however, may work against your having your baby your way. Those who put in that extra effort may be even more likely to want to use the interventive skills they've learned in their training. Board certification is no guarantee that your doctor will listen to your preferences, or that he has experience or interest in assisting you with your birth, free of unnecessary interference.

Checking It Twice

There are three valuable groups of people who can help you double-check your list: nurses who work on hospital ob floors; childbirth educators; and La Leche League leaders.

Before you call any of these, though, make up a list of key issues for your birthing experience, in order of priority. (If having your other children visit you after the birth is crucial, ask that question first—not last.) If you've never had a baby before, talk to your friends who might qualify as "informed consumers" and read a few books to help you think about what you want. Just because you've never had a baby before doesn't necessarily mean you won't have strong preferences when the time for your labor and birth arrives.

Hospital nurses are proud of their ob units and are generally happy to help pregnant women who call for information. The nurse can tell you which doctors are likeliest to help mothers with unmedicated births; what the hospital's cesarean rate is and which doctors do the fewest sections; who doesn't routinely have laboring women hooked up to IVs and fetal monitors; who's the most enthusiastic about fathers in the delivery room; and more. These hospital ob nurses can also give you the phone numbers of local childbirth educators and La Leche League leaders.

Most women giving birth in the U.S. today attend childbirth-education classes in the last trimester of pregnancy. Increasing numbers also go to early pregnancy classes. If you are in one of these classes now, talk to your teacher. If you aren't currently in a class, you can still call a childbirth teacher. She'll be glad to help you. Also, consider contacting La Leche League.

Both of these groups of women, La Leche League leaders and child-birth educators, are very knowledgeable about birth and caring for babies. They offer monthly meetings that attract large groups of women— pregnant or, in the case of La Leche League, new mothers, too. Though they may not give you direct physician referrals, they'll certainly answer your questions about the reputations of the doctors on your list, and about the care that individual hospitals in your area give to new mothers. Be specific with them about your preferences. If you want your baby with you immediately after birth, with your body warming your baby's and not an incubator, say that. Don't ask which doctors believe in "bonding." That's too vague. You'll quickly zero in on those doctors most willing to give you your preferences.

Don't Forget the Hospital

Next time I will shop for a hospital as well as a doctor. Next time I definitely want rooming-in; I definitely want my first child to be able to visit me in the hospital, and to see her new brother or sister; I would really like to have a Leboyer delivery; I would really like to have the baby with my husband and me in recovery; I want to be able to feed my baby after its birth and have a period of closeness with it. To me the issue of bonding is much more important than whether I have an enema, prep, or an episiotomy.

You need to find "Hospital Right" as surely as you need to find Dr. Right. One mother who lived in a town without its own hospital found the right hospital for her by sending a questionnaire to ten hospitals within a fifty-mile radius of her home. All but one administrator responded, and her decision was easy based on the replies.

Some of the questions you will ask about hospitals may be the same ones you'll ask of prospective doctors. Following is a sampling:

1. *Do you have a birth room?* If so, who can use it? (Regulations vary from hospital to hospital.) Is the birth room always staffed? (Some hospitals do not have nurses in birth rooms all the time. It is possible to have your doctor plan to use this facility, but when you get there in labor, no one may be available for nursing duty.)

2. *How many nurses are available at a time for how many women in labor?* If the hospital has a shortage of nurses throughout the ob unit, but in every other respect is the right hospital for you, you might want to consider hiring a private duty nurse (a monitrice) for your labor. (More on that later.)

3. *If a cesarean becomes necessary, can the father stay?* If they say yes, ask which doctors (including anesthesiologists) allow fathers in the cesarean operating room.

4. *When is the baby separated from the parents?* Pursue specific details. If you're told babies can be with parents all the time, ask, "You mean for twenty-four hours a day? There's no routine taking the baby back to the nursery for a newborn check or pediatrician visits?"

5. *What's the average cost?* Costs vary from hospital to hospital, with teaching hospitals generally the most expensive. Even if you have insurance, many policies do not pay 100 percent of hospital maternity costs.

6. *Can fathers visit twenty-four hours a day?* In some hospitals dad can not only be there all the time, but the hospital will provide a bed for him in your room. In other hospitals, he's confined to visiting hours. Hospitals vary just as much in their policies about siblings visiting mom and the new baby.

It's essential that you know every hospital maternity floor has two sets of rules—one written and one unwritten. It's possible that any rule you might want to break has already been broken at least once (if only by a doctor's wife).

The written rule is the policy determined by the ob committee of the hospital—and includes rules about being able to labor and deliver in the same bed or not having your other children with you during labor and birth. Policies are hard to break, but not impossible.

On the other hand, the unwritten rule is the doctor's protocol—his routine recommendations for his patients. All hospital ob nurses know each doctor's routine. (That's why the ob nurses you called could answer your questions, not only about what the hospital rules are, but about what options individual doctors offer.) Examples are: routinely ordering a prep (shave of the perineum) or an IV on admission, an epidural at 8 centimeters, or water for your baby in the nursery.

Issues like these are almost always doctors' routines, not the hospital's. Protocols vary tremendously from doctor to doctor in the same hospital, even for doctors who are partners in a practice together.

You will have difficulty getting information on rates of intervention in your local obstetrical unit unless a consumer group or childbirth educators have surveyed for this information. It's easier to find out about individual doctors than hospitals. One way to get information on intervention in general at any one hospital is to contact the head nurse or director of nursing and ask what percentage of mothers avoid episiotomies or do not have analgesia or anesthesia or do not use a fetal monitor. Turn the figures around to estimate intervention rates.

Asking the Initial Questions

After you've talked with friends and relatives, scoured the Yellow Pages, consulted with hospital nurses (not only about doctors, but hospital options, too), childbirth educators, and LLL leaders, you'll be able to narrow down the list to the two or three doctors who you believe will meet your preferences. The next step is to find out all you can on the phone *before* you have that first appointment for a consultation. Call the doctor's office and ask for the following information. In some offices, nurse/receptionists freely offer these answers on the phone; in others, you'll have to get some of them directly from the doctor himself.

1. *How much does maternity care cost?* In most places, the obs charge the same fee. Family practitioners often charge somewhat less. Birth centers have a package fee for both the birth attendant and the place of birth.

2. *What is the scheduled length of his appointments?* The closer his appointments are (ten to fifteen minutes apart, rather than twenty to thirty, for instance), the more likely it is you'll do a lot of waiting, as well

as be rushed through your appointment when you do see him. Ask how long patients wait to see him. (If it turns out that, for other reasons, he's Dr. Right, find out when you should schedule an appointment to reduce waiting—perhaps first thing in the morning, or just after lunch.)

3. *Does he deliver babies at more than one hospital? If so, which ones?* Doctors in metropolitan areas usually deliver babies at more than one hospital. As mentioned earlier, each hospital has its own set of maternity options. Some permit twenty-four-hour rooming-in, for example; most don't. Some have labor and delivery beds or birthing chairs; most don't. You'll already have some idea of what each hospital offers from the calls you made to hospital ob nurses. (In your search for the best birth attendant and best hospital, you may have to resolve the dilemma of Dr. Right not being on staff at what could be "Hospital Right.")

4. *How many babies does he deliver in a month?* If it's fewer than ten, he's more likely to give you more of his time and interest. If his number is closer to thirty, beware. Remember, babies aren't delivered an average of one a day. He may deliver as many as five or six babies on a single day. If your baby is one of the five or six, you might rightfully be concerned whether you'll get adequate attention from him.

5. *What percentage of his patients does he deliver himself?* If you hire an ob, you naturally assume he'll deliver your baby. But many a woman has a rude awakening when someone else is there to deliver her baby. Now he may say (and many have), "Of course, I'll deliver your baby, except if I'm not on call or if I'm out of town." At first hearing, it sounds as though he'll be there. Check further. Ask, "Well, about what percentage of your patients do you personally deliver—75 percent, 50 percent, 30 percent?" He'll have some idea. We know from our Boulder M.O.M. Survey how important it is for the majority of women to have their own doctor there—especially if you've gone to a lot of trouble to choose him. In a look at obs in our survey, the chance of any one of them being there was only about 60 percent. Most of the obs we've discussed this with were surprised that women found this issue so important.

After all, how many of them have ever had a baby? Even many of the women doctors delivering babies today have not given birth. They do not know from personal experience how crucial it is to have familiar, nurturing birth attendants present. There are enough strangers (the nurses) to cope with as it is. Also, if the doctor you're talking to is an obstetrician, it was part of his training to be at births on a potluck basis, that is, only if he was on duty. He probably never saw any woman twice at his residency hospital during any part of the prenatal, birth, or postpartum period. From his point of view, it's just not a big deal.

If your doctor delivers fewer than ten babies a month, our research shows that the chances are good he'll be there for your birth. If he's part of a joint practice with other doctors (and most obs are), then the chance of his being there decreases as the number of partners goes up. Health maintenance organizations (HMO) are proliferating rapidly. If you are a member, you may have no control over who will be there for your baby's birth. Incidentally, many family practitioners and most nurse-midwives (as well as lay midwives) deliver their own patients even when they are not on call—it's part of their philosophy of continuity of care.

Even knowing your ob may not be there, you may still decide that a particular doctor is Dr. Right. If so, tell him that you would like to meet all the doctors who might cover for him when your baby is born. There may be more than just his partners. (There literally can be a dozen or more doctors who might be on call for you when you are in labor. In some HMOs the number of doctors has been as high as sixteen!)

When you do meet these other doctors, review with them the agreements that you and Dr. Right have made about maternity options.

My other complaint is obstetricians who have partners with ideas incompatible with their own. If it's your chosen obstetrician's night off, nine months of planning can go down the drain because the partner pushes anesthesia or just goes along with the routine.

If you specifically do not want a particular associate of Dr. Right to deliver your baby, find out if you can request someone else, even if the doctor you don't want is the one on call. Sometimes you can, sometimes you can't. If you can't, make extra sure he and the nurses know what you want.

A special problem occurs for women in small towns with only one or two doctors to choose from. What do you do if Doctor #1 always delivers babies with spinals, and Doctor #2 usually induces labor—both options you don't want? Try to negotiate the best you can with what you've got. Or look farther afield. Draw a fifty-mile radius around your hometown and check into what hospitals and birth centers are in that range. The inconvenience of extra traveling may be far outweighed by the pleasure of having the birth the way you want it—unless you have really quick, quick labors and aren't likely to make it that far.

Face-to-Face Negotiations

When you've made your list of possibilities and gathered what information you can by phone, then make an appointment. Traditionally, initial visits for pregnancy include an internal exam to confirm pregnancy. Just because it's office routine, however, doesn't mean you have to do it that way. You do not need to have a particular doctor examine your body to find out if he is the right one for you.

STEP ONE: SCHEDULE A "CLOTHES-ON, SIT-UP" CONSULTATION

One mother confided, "The worst part in finding a new doctor when I was pregnant was going through an exam with yet another stranger. I didn't realize until my fourth pregnancy that I didn't have to do it that way. I could just schedule a consultation."

This is very important: schedule a "clothes-on, sit-up" consultation. Tell the receptionist that you want a consultation first with Dr. X so that you can become acquainted and discuss the maternity options you want. Usually doctors charge for this, some occasionally do not.

The receptionist may say, "Fine." But perhaps she'll say, "We don't do that here; all initial visits include an exam."

Try saying, "I know this is not what you usually do, but it's very important to me." Repeat yourself, calmly, until she budges. (It usually doesn't take more than three times.) If you can't get a "clothes-on, sit-up" appointment, we suggest you scratch that doctor off your list.

Here's why. If you go ahead with the exam first, one of two outcomes is likely: You will find changing doctors extremely difficult even if the one who examined you is *not* Dr. Right; or, after he's examined you, the doctor is more likely to become angry at your questions, your taking your time to make up your mind, or your decision to change doctors. Remember, you are negotiating first whether this doctor is Dr. Right.

Some doctors (or more likely, office nurses) may argue that your pregnancy must be confirmed first by an exam before you do any talking. Let's say you have your consultation first, and then you decide he *is* Dr. Right. Now you have your physical exam, only to find out you're not pregnant, for heaven's sake. You may be embarrassed, but it's an honest mistake. It does happen. Know that you are that much farther along in your search for the right medical care when you do get pregnant.

Persistence in pursuing the consultation first generally gets you past even the best gatekeepers. Those are the folks who help the doctor run the office. Their goal is office efficiency through tried-and-true methods called the "routine." That is their job, and it is appropriate for them to want to fit you into their way of doing things. It is also appropriate for you, the paying customer, to have some say in how you and the doctor will work together.

STEP TWO: CONDUCTING YOUR INTERVIEW

The time arrives for your "clothes-on, sit-up" appointment. Take your husband with you if you can. An increasing number of dads go to some of their wives' prenatal visits. He may often have more questions than you do. While he is a primary part of this new venture, his presence also helps you get the doctor's full attention. Male doctors respond more respectfully to other males. We're not saying this is the way it ought to be; but this is the way it is. Use what works.

If your husband is unavailable, take another adult with you. More attention is paid to patients (whether in the doctor's office or in a hospital) if they are accompanied by another adult. The other person is effective whether he or she says one word. It's especially helpful if the person appears to be taking notes—even if he or she is only writing a grocery list. Doctors, like other people, are more careful when others are writing down their words.

So, you and your companion arrive at the doctor's office. Now it may all go according to plan, and the two of you may be ushered into the doctor's office for your consultation.

Or what might happen is that the receptionist may invite you into an examining room and ask you to disrobe. Remind her that you're there for a consultation, and repeat your phone conversation until things go your way.

Perhaps at this point, you'll think to yourself, it's not worth making a big deal about this. Sooner or later, I'll need to be examined anyway, you say. Go over in your mind why it's important to consult first, examine last.

- It's difficult to change doctors after that initial exam.
- You give the impression to the doctor that you will be his patient when what you need is information and time to decide.
- Many women find it difficult to meet a new doctor while flat on their backs, their legs in stirrups, counting the dots on the ceiling tile to pass the examination time.

These are some possible reasons. You may have others. So stick by your goal. This is a consultation appointment.

Now you're in the doctor's office. You've introduced your husband or the other adult by saying, "So-and-so is here because this is a very important appointment for me and he [or she] will make sure I don't forget any major questions I have." Most doctors don't mind this; they want patients to understand their explanations, and they know that two sets of ears are better than one.

Now, it's your move. Your body language, and your carefully asked questions, will determine how this interview will proceed. Before we list questions (and possible replies) we'd like to suggest some behavior that will make this a conversation among equals.

Body Language

You're nervous and want to appear calm. How should you express this through body language?

When we have done workshops with women on "Getting What You Want From Your Doctor," questions that come up repeatedly are: "How can I make my doctor listen to what I'm saying?" and "How can I establish equal footing with him?" Here are some body-language tips that could help.

Don't: Cross your legs tightly, hold your back straight, and keep your hands crossed on top of your knees (while sitting). If you do, guess what! Your head automatically drops, and now you're looking at the doctor with your eyes lifted—just like a little girl at a birthday party. You can't negotiate for what you want in that position.

Do: Think about how powerful men sit—with their legs loose and relaxed, never crossed. Try it; your body automatically feels more at ease. Wear a loose skirt or slacks and keep your legs uncrossed so you can relax your back, hold your head up, and look him right in the eyes. The ultimate body-language position of power, of course, is sitting back, with arms draped easily over the back of the chair. But most doctors' offices have chairs where this position is nearly impossible.

You're conscious of trying to establish a relationship of equals with this new potential partner. You want to have a meeting ground where you will have equal say. How do you do it?

If he stands, you stand. Keep your body at least on the same level with his. If he's sitting behind his desk (which is likely) and leans toward you, across the desk, you mirror his gesture and lean forward yourself. (Notice how that keeps you feeling equal.)

Another thing to keep in mind: People in subordinate positions smile often at the person in power. We're not saying that you should never smile, but if you find your smile muscles are hurting, you may be smiling too much.

These body-language strategies are built-in equalizers. You may not feel comfortable doing all of them, but they all get easier with practice. They're certainly shortcuts to getting what you want, because they make people pay attention to you.

The Problem of Names

Our intent is to help you train your ob to listen to you differently. It's well established that similarity in how we address each other encourages equality. The words you choose, in this instance, are not a matter of etiquette—they are an indication of power. So, now for that special problem—what do you call each other? If you call him "Doctor" and he calls you by your first name, you have several choices:

a) *Call him by his first name.*

A mother at one of our workshops confided, "It was easier for me to call him by his first name than to get him to call me by my last name. He was startled when I first called him "Bob," but after that we were both comfortable. It helped our rapport."

If this first-name basis shocks you and makes you feel disrespectful, remember this: it's common in employer-employee relationships that the boss addresses his employees by their first names, but he remains "Mr." It helps maintain a respectful distance. Your doctor is not your boss. You're paying him.

b) *Tell him you'd prefer to be called Mrs. (or Ms.) Smith.*

If the idea of calling your doctor by his first name appalls you, why not suggest he address you by your last name?

All of us have anxious moments when we try new things. That's only normal. But it doesn't have to stop us from doing things we never have done before. The anxiety will pass. It really does get easier with practice.

c) *Make no changes.*

It's not a big deal, you say to yourself. Names are not the only sign of equality.

It's Time for the Questions: Will He or Won't He?

Following is a sampling of questions to ask prospective doctors:
Can my husband be with me during the labor and birth?

For some women, if the doctor, or hospital, doesn't allow fathers to be present during labor and birth, that's the end of the interview. But let's say you're willing to discuss the issue further.

If he can't be present all the time, when would he have to leave?

Some doctors encourage husbands to be there all the time, even for cesareans. Others want husbands to leave for all procedures, including progress checks (to see how far along labor is) or insertion of an IV needle. Chances are good you'll want your husband there all the time. If he's asked to leave, you or he can just insist he stay, but that's a hassle you don't need. You should negotiate *in advance* whether he ever has to leave, so that if you run afoul of hospital routine, you can say, "Dr. X said my husband never has to leave. If you have any questions, ask Dr. X."

How many other people can be with me during labor and delivery?

In some hospitals (and in birth centers and home births) many mothers invite others to be present for the labor and birth, for both moral support and companionship, as well as specific help in breathing techniques and relaxation. Some want their children, too. However, your doctor may say that the hospital has a policy that only allows the husband to be present. Well, maybe yes, maybe no. This rule is almost always doctor-decided. It may be easier for him to "blame" the hospital, but he and his peers have made the decision. How does this information help you? Well, perhaps you can negotiate a special arrangement for yourself. Try saying:

Dr. X, it's really important to me that my best friend be there with me during labor.

His answer could be that the room is too small for additional people, or that it's distracting to the nursing staff. Or he may laugh and say, "Do you want me to put up bleachers and sell tickets?"

What do you do? You keep repeating the same phrase:

Dr. X, it's really important to me that my best friend be there with me during labor.

Repeat it in the same calm way until you're satisfied, one way or the other.

Example:

DOCTOR: "Your friend can stay, but if she gets upset or interferes with nursing routine, I may ask her to leave." Or, "That's absolutely out of the question."

You may accept the first reply as a reasonable compromise. The second reply may lead you, however, to find another doctor. It depends on how important it is to you. If part of your fact-finding early on was talking to hospital ob nurses, then you'll have a good idea which doctors do permit other people in the labor room, as well as which hospitals encourage or discourage it.

YOU: *I want you to hand me my baby as soon as it is born and I don't want it to leave my arms for at least two hours.*

DOCTOR: You want that messy baby? We'll clean him up before we give him to you.

YOU: *I want you to hand me my baby as soon as it is born, and I don't want it to leave my arms for at least two hours.*

DOCTOR: Sure, but we must check the baby for vital signs, weigh him, and clean him up first.

YOU: *I'm perfectly agreeable to your checking him while I hold him. I have no objection to your cleaning and weighing him. I'm just asking you to do it later, at least two hours later.*

DOCTOR: It will take only five minutes to check your baby to see if all is normal. We can do it in the delivery room. Except for that five minutes, your baby will be in your arms.

You decide if that's reasonable. If not, keep talking or look for someone else.

YOU: *I want to see my other children immediately after the baby is born, either in my own room or in the recovery room. I want them to see and hold the baby, too.*

DOCTOR: Our hospital policy prevents children from coming into the recovery room.

YOU: *It is very important for me to see my children immediately. They could be brought up to my private room where I could go with my baby straight from the delivery room.*

DOCTOR: The nursing staff doesn't like children on the floor.

YOU: *I'll see to it that the adult caretaker with my children makes sure they move quietly through the halls and only enter my room. I agree with you that children should be respectful of others, but it's still very important to me that I see my children immediately after the birth.*

DOCTOR: If your birth is normal, I can arrange for you to go immediately to your postpartum room instead of the recovery room. Your children can visit you there if, indeed, there is an adult caretaker with them.

You decide if that's reasonable. If not, keep talking or look for someone else.

Do you ever recommend an ultrasound scan? If so, for what reasons?

An ultrasound scan works by bouncing sound waves off the abdomen to determine the shape and position of the fetus. This allows doctors to "see" the fetus, for detection of pregnancies outside the uterus, for the presence of two or more babies, or for the diagnosis of some fetal anomalies. Just like the electronic fetal monitor, ultrasound scans originally were used only on a minority of women, and then to confirm or diagnose suspected problems. Now half of all women have at least one (but usually more) ultrasound scans performed while they are pregnant.

Although there is obvious widespread use of ultrasound scans, there's much concern about the possible side effects. According to a 1982 report from the American Medical Association, "Until physicians can say with assurance that ultrasound does not produce subtle or delayed harmful effects, it should be used only when medically indicated." In 1980 Marion Finke, M.D., director of the FDA's New Drug Evaluation Division stated: "There's increasing concern regarding the fetal safety of widely used diagnostic ultrasound in obstetrics. Animal studies have been reported to reveal delayed neuromuscular development, altered emotional behavior, changed brainwaves, abnormalities and decreased survival. Genetic alterations have also been demonstrated."

Ultrasound scans are often used to determine the gestational age of the fetus, but ob/gyn John L. Duhring, M.D., stated in "High-Risk Pregnancy—Part I," in *The Female Patient* that when using ultrasound in the last trimester "the predicted date of confinement can be off by four weeks."

There are many unanswered questions about the risks of ultrasound. Beware the doctor who has an ultrasound machine in his office. If your doctor suggests an ultrasound scan, make sure he explains to you the reason.

What is your definition of "high-risk" pregnancy?

According to authors Roger K. Freeman, M.D., and Susan C. Pescar of *Safe Delivery: Protecting Your Baby During High-Risk Pregnancy,* the following conditions are high risk: diabetes, hypertension, heart disease, Rh incompatibility, kidney disease, some thyroid disorders, severe asthma, incompetent cervix and uterine malformation, a sexually transmitted disease, cancer, or some other disease that could affect the pregnancy's outcome.

A lesser list includes a history of any of the following: miscarriage, premature birth, stillbirth, bleeding problems, a previous abnormal child. Or you've been exposed to rubella and you are not immune, certain toxins, extensive radiation, certain chemicals, specific drugs. Other factors: a family history of hereditary disease or genetic disorder, smoking cigarettes, chronic alcohol consumption, taking unnecessary or potentially damaging drugs and being seriously overweight or underweight. Add women who have had three previous births or who are past age thirty-five to the high-risk group, as most doctors do, and it's no wonder that Dr. Freeman estimates that "20 percent to 25 percent of pregnant women are probably in the high-risk group."

So how does that affect you? "The term 'high-risk pregnancy' means something different to everyone," state Freeman and Pescar. Just as with the terms bonding and rooming-in, there's no uniform accepted definition. But if you are labeled "high risk" whether you truly are or not, you automatically will be exposed to many pregnancy and birth interventions, starting with ultrasound scans and perhaps ending with a cesarean.

What can you do? Get a second opinion. And don't assume that if you, for instance, have a history of miscarriage, that means you automatically need amniocentesis, or that you'll need to be monitored electronically during labor, or have your labor induced. Always pursue specific answers to your questions about you. Ask what your options are, what the risks/benefits are.

Your line of questioning is seldom going to be answered with a simple yes or no, as we've shown you here. A doctor's replies are based on his own standard of care—his belief about what good medical care is, and his belief system is different from yours. His own personal experience affects every answer he gives you. Do not expect a doctor to be enthusiastic about something he has never tried before (allowing several people to be with you during labor and the birth, for instance, or letting you give birth in a supported squatting position).

That doesn't mean he won't try something new, but you should anticipate some of his concerns. Defuse his concern with a statement like, "I know this is new to you and you are probably uncomfortable changing your routine." He can deny that, in which case you have brought him along the path to working in partnership with you. Or he can agree with you. Then you can further reassure him by saying, "I appreciate your cooperation."

Getting It All in Writing

Perhaps after your first interview you'll be satisfied that this, indeed, is Dr. Right. So you can tell him right then. Or you can let the doctor know later.

Whether you're sure he's Dr. Right or not, thank him for his time and tell him that you'll call the office with your decision. Don't pressure yourself to make a decision while you're sitting there. He doesn't need to know instantly. If you're not sure he's Dr. Right, interview the next doctor on your list.

I have a very progressive doctor and he asked me for a list when I was pregnant of what I wanted in my childbirth experience, in terms of anesthesia, enemas, preps, stirrups, the whole bit. I wrote it all out— including the labor, the delivery, the postpartum experience. He took my list, we went over each item. He said okay to everything that was on my list. It became part of my chart and I never had any problems with anybody.

Now your doctor may not ask you for a list, but that's no reason why you can't give him one.

Somewhere about the sixth or seventh month of pregnancy, after you and your doctor have had several chances to talk over your desired options, it's time to get it in writing. It may seem that asking your doctor for his signature shows a lack of trust on your part, but your doctor will not be with you all the time you're in the hospital. This signed paper takes your doctor's place.

Summarize your options on paper. Get your doctor's signature on it, in case he's not there at the labor and birth or, more likely, doesn't get there until some hours after you do. Give a copy to each of the possible substitute doctors when you meet with them. Have Dr. Right's partners sign the agreement, and leave a copy with each possible substitute. Other copies go to the nurses at the hospital, to your own ob, and in your hospital overnight bag. You'll be amazed at how this reduces hospital hassle. When there's a question about this or that being different from the routine, just wave your paper and say, "My doctor has agreed to this. If you have any questions, ask him." Incidentally, if he refuses to sign the paper, write down his verbal agreement and use the paper anyway.

Penny Simkin and Carla Reinke have a birth plan in the form of a chart that is available for fifty cents from the pennypress, inc. (See Appendix D.)

Does that mean that your labor and birth will follow your birth plan to the letter? Not necessarily. It does mean that any changes in your plan will be thoroughly discussed with your doctor.

However, your job is not done after you've passed out the list. You have to continually reinforce it. Repeat every visit: "Remember, I'm the one who wants. . . ."

Changing Doctors Mid-pregnancy

> During my first visits, my ob was thorough, very nice, and talked about her kids. She had been my gynecologist for years. When I was 7 months pregnant, my husband and I took in our birth plan. The interview was a complete disaster. We wanted no routine Pitocin; she threatened us with possible infant brain damage if we didn't use it. When I said I didn't want medication; she said, "You can hurt as much as you please and you will." It went from bad to worse. When I said I didn't want a routine IV; she said she'd be "sloshing in my blood which would be all over the floor." Brain damage, agony, and death? Hardly the image of joyous childbirth I had imagined. I knew I had to change doctors and discovered it wasn't as difficult as I thought it would be. I was welcomed by the birth center I transferred to and thrilled with my birth there.
>
> —Colorado Mother

What if you get this far—or even farther—in your pregnancy, and you discover this is not Dr. Right. You realize you can't compromise as much as he wants you to. Should you change doctors? The natural vulnerability and dependency of pregnancy work to keep women from switching, but some women do change doctors. From our experience interviewing many women, those who have changed are very satisfied. The new Dr. Right will welcome you as a paying patient. You will find cooperation much easier to get because you have gone to the trouble of changing doctors in mid or late pregnancy. Although it doesn't happen often, some doctors—when faced with your requests—will dismiss you as a patient. They'll send you your records and tell you to go elsewhere. Count your blessings. He or she obviously wasn't Dr. Right.

Sometimes when pregnant women decide they must change doctors, they will agonize unnecessarily over how and what to tell the first doctor. You don't owe him a lengthy explanation, certainly not an apology. Your new doctor will handle the request for a transfer of your records, or he will ask you to call your former doctor's office and request that your records be transferred. You can let your former doctor know why you're transferring, but a brief letter is adequate. Most of the time, this will be the end of it. Don't expect him to agree with your decision or even to be civil about it. That's okay. It's your decision, not his.

What's in it For Your Doctor to Negotiate With You

When a doctor answers a woman's questions, explains pertinent facts, and offers choices, he puts himself in a win-win partnership with the woman. The woman gets her preferences. The doctor gets an informed patient, less likely to call anxiously at all hours with fearful questions. That means fewer time and energy demands on him.

And, as pointed out previously, doctors who have trusting relationships with their patients have far fewer malpractice suits. Besides, consumers have a right to good communication, some doctors say. They believe it's the birth attendant's role to educate patients about their bodies so they can be informed partners in health care. It's like getting a warranty. Education goes with the product.

Also, doctors who are partners, not bosses, have less pressure on them to be godlike. Doctors know in their hearts that medicine is an inexact science. All of us can, and do, make mistakes—including physicians. Inviting a doctor to be your partner ultimately allows him to function at his best, as an equal who shares responsibility with you, the patient.

But let's also be frank. The doctor makes his living from delivering babies. The more patients he has, the more money he makes. The doctor wins economically if you buy his services. And the word will get around very quickly (probably from you) that this doctor is one who supports women's preferences.

Responsibility—His and Yours

You have a right to an explanation of, and the reasons for, any procedure that might be done to you by your doctor or the hospital. You also have the right to refuse any procedure. You have the right to be informed of the probable consequences to you and your baby and of any alternative to that procedure. The patient must have a chance to weigh the benefits against the risks.

The New York state legislature established a law that "requires that a physician or nurse-midwife must provide expectant mothers with information regarding the possible risks of obstetric drugs to the mother and her baby." While this specific, informed-consent law is on the books in New York, all doctors are certainly expected to inform their patients adequately enough to enable them to make decisions—or else they risk malpractice liability.

You have to do your part, too. It's your responsibility, not the doctor's, to ask for plain English when you don't understand medical terminology. It's also your responsibility to keep notes during your pregnancy of your conversations with your doctor, regarding explanations of procedures and descriptions of drug side effects. Don't rely on memory alone, no matter how good a memory you have.

Communicate your preferences clearly, frequently, and repeatedly. If you don't, no one will read your mind. Doctors are as poor at mindreading as the rest of us. Doctors have repeatedly told us that their patients don't tell them what they like and don't like. How can you blame him for not giving you what you want if you haven't asked?

Your Legal Rights

Stuart and Susan McElhinney, J.D., reported that the issue of the rights of birthing parents "is really an unclear area of the law.

"Generally, however, any patient has the right to refuse any treatment. Because the law in most states has refused to recognize the fetus as a person, separate from the mother, the mother may be entitled to refuse treatments—including sonograms [ultrasound], fetal heart monitors and cesarean sections—which directly affect her fetus. However, we all must be aware that this rule is changing and that in many instances the fetus is held to have separate rights which the court may act to 'protect.' Of course, we note that this 'protection' usually takes the form of orthodox medical actions."

In the same article the authors describe a case at a Denver hospital in 1980. A woman was in labor and her electronic fetal monitor registered what appeared to be severe fetal distress. Hospital staff urged her to have a cesarean. She refused. The staff called in a judge who declared that the fetus was endangered and the woman had to submit to having a cesarean. And she did. Although the staff had expected an infant in severe fetal distress because of the EFM readout and the time that had elapsed (nine hours after the recommendation of a cesarean), the actual outcome of the baby was good. Nevertheless, the staff and attorneys felt they had taken proper action.

You can avoid confrontations like this at your hospital by discussing with Dr. Right all issues important to you (including when and why he does cesareans) ahead of time, while you're still pregnant.

All of the steps we suggest may not apply to your situation or you may be reluctant to try every one. However, even doing one thing differently in your contact with your doctor is a sure sign of success. One step leads to another, and each time you try something new it gets easier the next time. A woman in labor is in no condition to fight with her doctor or the hospital staff. She must negotiate her options ahead of time. We also believe that a true partnership with your medical caretaker— accomplished carefully visit by visit, question by question—is a guarantee of your own personal satisfaction with the whole birth process.

6 ▪ OBSTETRICIANS' BELIEFS ABOUT A "SAFE BIRTH"

> No doubt about it, if ten women went into the jungle to have a baby, nine would walk out with healthy babies.
> —An obstetrician in practice for twenty years

> I think I should practice the best medicine. All of my patients are hooked up to fetal monitors and IVs during labor.
> —The same obstetrician

Why is it so difficult to get what you want? Why do you have to negotiate with your physician for what surely is a perfectly normal experience? In these modern times, why can't you just go to the hospital and have your baby your way? You've read articles in magazines that paint a beautiful picture of giving birth: the mother labors with her husband's assistance, nurses' help, and the doctor's encouragement. She delivers with great joy and immediately gets to hold her baby. Then mother, father, and infant spend the first few minutes after birth getting acquainted. Isn't that the way it always is? No, it isn't.

Of your four friends who just had babies, one had a cesarean, two had drugs to start or speed their labors, and also regional anesthesia they had hoped to avoid. Only one had her baby the way magazine articles describe as typical.

You may have wondered as you read the two quotes by the same obstetrician at the beginning of this chapter: How he could say two things that seem so contradictory. Easy! Most obstetricians say they believe anywhere from 80 percent to 95 percent of births are "normal." Turning that around, they also believe that from 5 percent to 20 percent of births will have problems. One obstetrician told us, "Five percent of the time there are problems that arise, and these are the problems that we are here for." Yet most physicians believe those kinds of labels can only be put on a birth *after* the birth is over. As an eminent pediatrician wrote to the *Denver Post,* "There is no such thing as normal childbirth except after the fact." A prominent obstetrician said, "Normal pregnancy is really a retrospective diagnosis." Obstetricians believe that at the time they are handling your birth they are handling a very dangerous situation.

Confirming our statement that most obstetricians believe that birth is a dangerous, high-risk procedure was a *McCall's* magazine report on a national survey of 243 obstetricians. *McCall's* stated, "The majority of obstetricians continue to picture childbirth as an event fraught with danger best left to the hands of an expert." Individual survey responses expressed that view: "The consumer ideas aren't going to decrease mortality and that's what it's all about." And another: "Some patients are trying to tell doctors how and when to deliver. That's ridiculous." And another: "The majority of pregnancies are high risk."

What Is High Risk?

Women who are high risk are simply more likely to have problems in their pregnancy or with their childbirth or baby than those who are low risk. The words "high risk" applied to a pregnant woman mean that she should be watched carefully for complications which may affect her or her baby. The factors that make a pregnant woman high risk are medical and social. The social factors known to make her high risk include being unmarried or poor, for example. Medical factors include high blood pressure, toxemia, or other serious diseases in the mother.

A high-risk labor includes women who have been labeled medically at high risk during pregnancy and all premature and induced labors. (Some doctors see augmented labors as high risk also.) These labors can result in a normal birth, but they are more likely to require the birth attendant's intervention for the best outcome for mother or baby. High-risk deliveries include cesarean and breech births.

A high-risk designation does *not* mean a woman or her baby will have problems. One of the drawbacks with labeling is that the doctor or the pregnant woman may forget that. Once a woman is labeled high risk the doctor and woman may act as if she or her baby *will* have problems. Unnecessary interventions to end the pregnancy may then take place. For example, a doctor may tell a woman he wants to deliver her breech baby by cesarean section a week before her due date. That presumes that the woman or her baby will have problems if she is allowed to go into spontaneous labor and deliver vaginally. The doctor and woman have forgotten that the high-risk label is a decision made in the minds of those who use the words, and it may or may not really exist for that particular woman.

Over half of dead, injured, or defective babies are delivered by the 20 percent or so of pregnant women who are labeled high risk. "The bulk of unsatisfactory outcomes of pregnancy derive from a relatively small proportion of the obstetric population," said Richard Aubry, M.D., writing "ACOG's Standards for Safe Childbearing." By intensifying care for these women, by applying high-quality, prenatal care and high-technology childbirth care to them *when needed,* many doctors believe the greatest gains can be made in reducing the number of dead or damaged babies.

Many Doctors Believe All Birth is High Risk

The words "high risk" are so widely applied today that most obs look at most of their patients this way. "We'll take [high-risk or difficult birth] patients the community hospitals can't, and we should," said William Clewell, M.D., of University Hospital of Denver, interviewed in 1982. "But the term 'high risk' gets kind of muddy. What some are calling high risk is not what we're calling high risk."

Most obs believe they are handling a dangerous situation with all births, including the low-risk woman. She's the healthy, married woman who has carried her baby to term, who has no serious medical problems, and who has started labor spontaneously. "You never know which woman will have complications or which baby will need intensive care; therefore we need to treat all women as high risk," is the belief. Doctors point out that 30 percent of the admissions to neonatal intensive care units come from babies born to low-risk pregnant women. And more than half of the complications of childbirth occur in low-risk women.

"This seems to be a *damning defense* of the present system of obstetric care," said author Doris Haire, D.M.S., president of the American Foundation of Maternal and Child Health. "It compels one to ask what proportion of these complications, which had their onset *during* labor and birth, are the direct result of aggressive obstetric procedures." She quotes Professor G. T. Kloosterman, M.D., chairman of the department of obstetrics at the University of Amsterdam, Netherlands, "The spontaneous labor in a healthy woman is an event marked by a number of processes which are so complex and so perfectly attuned to each other that any interference will *only* detract from their optimal character. The doctor, always on the lookout for pathology and eager to interfere, will too often change true physiologic aspects of human reproduction into pathology."

Where Doctors' Beliefs Come From

Doctors certainly do not believe that what they are doing causes complications in births and problems in the babies. "It is threatening to be told that what you are doing is not good, that you may have been hurting people," Vic Berman, M.D., director of the NACHIS Birth Center in Culver City, California, told us. "Doctors simply can't say what they have been doing for twenty years is wrong. If it were wrong, *they* were hurting babies. That's a totally unacceptable idea."

The obstetrician's training and his peers tell him that what he is doing is right. And his everyday experience with complications in birth shows him he needs to get in there and do more, not less. Besides, interventions and technology make an obstetrician's practice more interesting. "Every doctor enjoys his intervention," John Franklin, M.D., chief of staff at Booth Maternity Hospital, told writer Alice Lake. "That's what his skill and training are for. Some think that nature is in constant need of improvement and others that nature can't be trusted, but one kind of intervention leads to another and then the doctor is kept busy seeking remedies for his own actions." The doctor's definition of "safe" is decided by his training, his peers, and his personal experiences—all of which tell him that all childbirth is high risk.

A Safe Birth

If all childbirth is seen to be dangerous, the overriding concern of the obstetrician, naturally, becomes "a safe birth." Those are "buzz" words we find obstetricians using frequently: "I can't do that because it's not *safe.*" "I find an epidural is a *safe* way to deliver a baby." "The delivery room is the only *safe* place for your baby to be born."

Women are very vulnerable when the doctor uses the word "safe" or "unsafe." *Of course* you are going to do what you are told will ensure your baby's safety. But you will come far in the art of negotiating to have your baby your way if you understand what "a safe birth" means to many obstetricians. There are six key elements. A "safe birth":

- Is actively managed
- Is predictable
- Is controlled by the obstetrician
- Takes place in the hospital
- Is attended by an obstetrician
- Is solely measured by a live baby and a live mother

A "safe birth" is actively managed. Among themselves, obstetricians call this "the aggressive management of parturition," writes Sandra Anderson, R.N., M.S., an instructor in community health at the University of Arizona College of Nursing. "In an effort to decrease maternal and infant mortality, modern obstetrics has developed its intervention to the point of 'active management' of not only the high-risk group but almost all labors and birth." But why active management of all labors and births? In *Patient Care* magazine, George Ryan, M.D., Professor of Obstetrics and Gynecology, University of Tennessee, Center for Health Sciences, is quoted: "A short obstetric hospital stay is a retrospective accomplishment. All patients require the same facilities and services during labor and delivery." But why all? An obstetrician explained to us, "You have to understand that we look at things virtually 180 degrees differently from you [consumers]. You are all saying this would be very pleasant and nice. Unfortunately, in medicine we have to do things for the minority situation, which is 5 percent of the time when things go wrong. We'll never have a meeting of minds on this issue because you look at things from the opposite standpoint. We are doing things and setting up rules and regulations for the small number of cases that are going to be bad, not for the large number that are going to be good."

Obstetricians honestly believe that all women, and babies about to be born, deserve the very best in technology. A West Coast family practitioner described to us what it was like to work with obstetricians: "The impression I got was that if you didn't do all these fancy things for the mother and the baby, somehow you were not providing optimal care. Optimal obstetrical care was that which used all the new technology." Technology is essential to the active management of labor and delivery.

A "safe birth" is predictable. When a birth is actively managed, it is quite predictable. The obstetrician knows the risks of his procedures, and he has faith that he can handle them with another procedure, if necessary. For instance, if the epidural he's given to a mother slows her labor, he can speed it up with Pitocin. If that same epidural prevents her from pushing, he can use forceps.

His basis for measuring whether your labor is going "normally" comes from a generally accepted medical standard called the "parameters of normal labor." For instance, if a woman's bag of waters breaks, it is expected that she will soon start to labor, and will deliver within twenty-four hours. Whenever labor begins, the woman is expected to deliver within twelve hours. When a woman is in what is called "active labor," after three or four centimeters dilatation, obstetricians expect her cervix to dilate at least a centimeter an hour. In the second stage of labor, the delivery, the belief is that a woman shouldn't have to push for more than one or perhaps two hours, less if she has already given birth. For the third stage, or the delivery of the placenta, it's generally agreed to give the woman about a half hour before the birth attendant begins to extract the placenta. However, as one doctor told us, "Nobody waits that long. Everybody starts pulling on the cord sooner."

If your labor and delivery do not follow the above timetable, the obstetrician's belief in the active management of labor requires that he do something to bring your labor within the "normal" range. Using his tools of intervention carries some risk to the mother and the baby, but the obstetrician believes he can handle any complications that result from his own procedures. For example, two of the most common complications of "intensive obstetrical care" reported by Madeleine Shearer, R.P.T., editor of *Birth,* are newborn scalp infections (from fetal monitors) and maternal intrauterine infections. Both of these complications the obstetrician believes can be handled easily with antibiotics.

A "safe birth" is controlled by the obstetrician. Your doctor believes that he is giving you a safe birth and protecting your baby's interests when he denies you a part in the medical decision-making process. At the Northwest Regional International Childbirth Education Association convention in 1981, author and lecturer Suzanne Arms spoke to this issue when she said, 'Society now has experts who believe we must leave important life decisions to them, that they know best." Doctors still hold to the view that they really do know what is best for you. As one doctor told us, "You do have to give us some credit for knowing technically what is best for the situation." Believing that he really does know what is best for you, he also supposes that you then have total trust in him.

This control by the obstetrician is the toughest issue to face in negotiations. He believes he knows what is best. You need to know what "best" means to him. You need to find out how your doctor handles childbirth.

In her book *The Hidden Malpractice*, Gena Corea writes that physicians consider it a misguided effort to inform women because it only leads to anxiety and loss of confidence in the physician. The prevailing attitude is Don't confuse women by asking them to make decisions that are beyond their comprehension. Because obstetricians do not believe that women should make important decisions about their own deliveries, doctors sometimes become angry with inquiring pregnant women. The *McCall's* survey mentioned earlier analyzed responses from obstetricians across the country. The results "suggested a widespread disinterest in basic change and considerable irritation that accepted routines are being questioned at all."

You may have already experienced your obstetrician's irritation. Certainly a lot of women have. No one is necessarily immune. Suzanne Poppema, M.D., a family practitioner herself, was pregnant with her first baby when she had this experience. She was seeing an obstetrician substituting for her regular doctor. He spoke of using the fetal monitor on all of his patients. When she questioned him, suggesting that she didn't want to be attached to a machine, he became irritated with her. She later said, "I got the distinct impression that somehow I cared less about my baby than a woman who would have agreed that monitoring was the best way to go. When I shared with him the information that a very good study showed no evidence of benefit to monitoring low-risk labors, he said he didn't believe in the study. The impression I came away with was that, somehow, I wasn't quite as concerned about my baby as I should have been."

Where do the mother's preferences for her delivery fit in with a "safe birth"? Family Centered Maternity Care is a label that has been applied to maternity care that takes into account the social and psychological aspects of birth as well as the physical ones. The obstetrician's belief system does not give much value to the psychological and social dimensions of birth. Richard Schmidt, M.D., while president of the American College of Obstetricians and Gynecologists (ACOG), held a press conference to clarify ACOG's position on family-centered maternity care. Reported in a *NAPSAC News* editorial, Dr. Schmidt said that ACOG was not in a position to dictate policy in obstetrics to U.S. hospitals and that ACOG would be reluctant to "box hospitals in with rigid recommendations based more on human feeling than on scientific data." During the course of our negotiations with our local hospital, we came up against this belief system many times. In one session, a local obstetrician told us, "You need to understand our point of view. We are interested in medical safety, not TLC [tender loving care]."

The experience of childbirth for the woman is too often unimportant to the doctor. As one pediatrician told us, "It's okay for the doctor to follow the wishes of the patient when it doesn't make any difference one way or the other. But we need to communicate to the patient those things she wants to do that are dangerous." When we discussed the result of our M.O.M. survey with a surgeon, he unknowingly summarized the belief system of obstetricians in terms of control when he said, "You may know what women want, but it may not be what they need."

If the experience of childbirth for the woman is too often unimportant, the doctor's comfort is. Since he controls the situation, he becomes the key person in the whole experience. The kind of bed or delivery table used, the labor and delivery position of the woman, the temperature of the delivery room, are all designed to contribute to his convenience and comfort, not that of the mother-to-be or the newborn infant. A nurse, who has worked in newborn intensive care units, was discussing with a obstetrician whether the cool delivery room could be contributing to breathing distress in the newborn. She asked him who he felt was the most important in terms of comfort in the delivery room, the infant or him. He replied, "I am."

Obstetricians believe very strongly that their control of the decision making for the birth process is an important key to a safe birth. The titles of two articles in *Patient Care* magazine clearly distinguish the dichotomy that doctors believe there is between what women want for their birth and what doctors believe is best. The first article is entitled "Mother's Wishes Vs. Doctor's Duties." The second is entitled "U.S. Experts: Safety Vs. Sentiment." An underlying assumption in both articles is that doctors care more about safety than mothers do.

Some doctors go much farther and call all women's preferences "gimmicks" and "risky." Marsh Steward, Jr., M.D., wrote an editorial in 1981 for the California Association of Obstetricians and Gynecologists in which he said:

> It is even more frightening if, in addition, we also consider the fact that obstetrics has become almost totally consumer dominated. This "consumerism" has resulted to a large degree from the extensive media exposure given to an extremely vocal but misguided minority. It has panicked some hospitals into providing some poorly thought-out gimmicks in an effort to be seen as responding to these demands, i.e., the practice of "bonding," of putting the baby to breast on the delivery table, the "ABC Room," the birthing chair and other cult rituals. If we are to avoid being done in by the malpractice problem we must reassert our control over the patient and insist that we exclusively make the decisions relative to patient care, putting an end to nonpatient interference in this process.

A "safe birth" takes place in the hospital. If you believe that the active management of labor is best for all mothers and babies, then the associated risks of intervention are much too great to take place anywhere other than in a hospital. In this and other countries, midwives and doctors who deliver women at home or in birth centers are doing sophisticated screening of patients to identify those who are likely to develop complications requiring regular hospital care. However, because of their own personal experience with sudden emergencies in the hospital, obstetricians do not believe that successful screening is possible. Therefore they reject any kind of out-of-hospital delivery, whether in a free-standing birth center or at home. One of the "Standards for Safe Childbearing" of ACOG is that all births occur in hospitals. Warren Pearse, M.D., Executive Director of ACOG, is the author of the extreme opinion shared by obstetricians that "home delivery is maternal trauma—home delivery is child abuse!"

A "safe birth" is attended by an obstetrician. Accepting the assumption that birth is a dangerous procedure that must be actively managed with risky interventions, you can understand why obstetricians feel they are the only ones qualified to attend the birth, not midwives or family practitioners.

While a small number of hospitals have certified nurse-midwives on their staffs, and growing numbers of health-care consumers are lobbying hospitals to give certified nurse-midwives delivery privileges, most obstetricians are unaware of the high quality of care given by midwives. When we called the Washington, D.C., ACOG office to request some information on certified nurse-midwives, we were told that the information was not readily available since "we put midwives together with home birth; we don't separate nurse-midwives into their own file." In a speech in 1980 to family physicians at their annual meeting, Dr. Pearse referred to the growing trend toward midwivery as a "serious problem" and as "worrisome."

Obstetricians feel uneasy about family practitioners, too. In the United States today, 80 percent of births are attended by obstetricians, less than 20 percent by family practitioners. In fact, the percentage of babies delivered by family practitioners has been steadily decreasing—down from 1968, when 31 percent of the babies born in the United States were delivered by family practitioners. Believing that the care that they give is superior to that of other birth attendants, obstetricians are passing around a catchy phrase that best describes their feelings toward family practitioners and midwives: "Why settle for a Ford when you can have a Cadillac?"

*　　*　　*

A "safe birth" is measured solely in terms of whether or not there is a
live mother and a live baby. We all certainly agree with doctors that a
live mother and baby are foremost in our minds, too. When everything
reasonable has been done and death still occurs, there is some solace
in knowing that every safety precaution was followed. That's the reason
we are going to the doctor in the first place. Obstetricians, however,
justify their interventive measures on the basis of improved maternal
and perinatal mortality rates. "It has been the sophisticated medical
technology afforded by the fetal monitor and the cesarean section that
has vaulted this country's [perinatal] mortality rate to the best in the
world," said William A. Cook, M.D., to an interviewer. Proclaimed
Clayton T. Beecham, M.D., in 1981 at a Philadelphia meeting of the ACOG:

> By tolerating or encouraging "natural childbirth" methods and the
> escalating use of midwives, American gynecologists and obstetri-
> cians could jeopardize the impressive decline in maternal mortality
> rates achieved in the past fifty years, which is directly linked to
> the spread of modern medical techniques in childbearing.

The obstetricians' keys to a "safe birth" (i.e., the birth is managed,
predictable, and controlled by them; takes place in a hospital; and is
attended by an obstetrician) are all justified because obstetricians believe their technology and interventions are the reasons for improved
maternal and perinatal mortality rates. Improved maternal and perinatal
mortality is their overriding concern, their measure of success and the
justification for their belief in their activity as scientific. We will look
closely at that claim.

Maternal and Perinatal Mortality—Causes for the Decrease

The maternal mortality rate is measured by the number of deaths of
women per 100,000 live births. The maternal mortality rate has gone
down steadily since the beginning of this century, when more than 700
women died out of every 100,000 live births.

Year	Maternal Deaths per 100,000
1940	376
1950	83.1
1960	37.1
1970	21.4
1980	9.2

Perinatal mortality includes the deaths of fetuses from seven months of pregnancy through birth and to seven days of age of the baby. In other words, perinatal mortality measures deaths of babies around the time of birth. Perinatal mortality is so much higher than maternal mortality that it is measured per 1,000 births.

Year	Perinatal Deaths per 1,000
1950	33
1960	28.9
1970	23.2
1980	12.8

Obstetricians tend to claim most of the credit for the steadily decreasing maternal and perinatal mortality rates. Because the decreasing death rates are so impressive, obstetricians' feeling that "what I'm doing must be the reason" might be easy to accept. But it's just not that simple.

The falling rates are due to complex interrelated factors having little to do with what obs believe are the keys to a safe birth. For example, dramatic falls in the maternal mortality rates in the 1940s were aided by the development of antibiotics, which controlled infection, and by the development of blood banks, which allowed needed transfusions for the mother to survive a severe postpartum hemorrhage. It wasn't until 1950, according to Herbert Ratner, M.D., former director of public health in Chicago, that birthing women were free from pelvic bone abnormalities caused by rickets, which had been a major problem complicating births. With better nutrition—especially the addition of vitamin D to milk, which started in the 1930s—this was the first generation of women who could give birth without the complications of rickets and other diseases of malnutrition.

In those years, too, obstetricians were in the forefront of changing maternity care. Then, as now, most births were normal, i.e., uncomplicated, vaginal deliveries. Then, as now, complicated births (both vaginal and cesarean deliveries) resulted in the highest rates of maternal and perinatal mortality. Obs made a major contribution to reducing mortality rates by starting to use—and by setting high standards for training in the use of—analgesia, anesthesia, forceps, and IVs in the care of those complicated births. Dr. Ratner paints a dramatic picture of the ob's role in reducing maternal mortality: "The actual fact is, and it must not be forgotten, that if it weren't for the contribution of obstetrical specialists, some of your mothers, and some of your grandmothers, would have died in childbirth and some of you in this audience would not be here today. . . . These specialists played an important role in the continuing reduction of preventable maternal deaths by reforming correctable professional and hospital practices." Obstetricians took the lead, and still do, in changing the care of complicated deliveries to make them safer for women.

Another factor contributing hugely to maternal mortality rates in all deliveries, complicated or not, was puerperal fever (called "childbed fever" long ago, "postpartum infection" now). Antibiotics saved women who developed infections. Instituting strict sterile techniques at birth and during vaginal exams before and after birth cut infection and death rates dramatically through prevention.

Right up to the present many factors having nothing to do with labor and delivery affect maternal mortality rates, such as falling birth rates and the availability of family planning. (Maternal mortality is higher for women who have already had several children.)

"Some may argue that the improved statistics are due more to improved availability of family planning and abortion services," said Richard Aubry, M.D., co-director, Perinatal Center, State University of New York, Syracuse. "They are certainly significant factors and the ACOG is proud to have been in the forefront of making those services available and ensuring that the proper physician training allowed for their implementation with maximum safety. However, it should be noted that a major part of the reduction in maternal mortality occurred before effective family planning was widely available [the sixties] and clearly well before the availability of abortion services [the seventies]." That's right. As shown in the maternal deaths chart, the giant drop occurred in the forties—long before the spread of technological interventions (the "active management of all births") came to the ob floor.

The drop in perinatal mortality is also complex. Factors that affect maternal mortality also affect perinatal mortality. For example, babies who come near the end of a large family are at greater risk of dying around the time of birth, so falling birth rates can improve perinatal mortality.

The greatest cause of perinatal mortality in the United States today is the same as it has always been: respiratory distress syndrome, most often found in premature or low-birth-weight babies. Specialized pediatricians, called perinatologists, have reduced perinatal mortality by saving more babies born with complications, and by saving smaller and smaller babies. "That newborn intensive care can lower mortality in low-birth-weight infants is widely accepted," reported Nigel Paneth, M.D., M.P.H., et al., in a special article for the *New England Journal of Medicine* in 1982.

Low birth weight remains the most significant factor, far outweighing all others affecting perinatal mortality. What an American Medical Association news release in 1982 termed "the heavy burden of low-birth-weight babies" affects our standing internationally in infant deaths. The major reasons for perinatal mortality in the United States were traced by researchers J. David Erickson, Ph.D., and Tor Bjerkedal, M.D., who compared perinatal mortality in Norway and the United States and reported their findings in 1982. A high number of low-birth-weight babies born into economically deprived families is the major reason for the United States' perinatal mortality rate, "poor" in relation to Norway's, say the authors. They concluded that any major improvement in the United States' rate will await a reduction in the births of low-weight babies.

Finding ways to reduce prematurity, for example, would be one of the ways to reduce the number of low-birth-weight babies. High-quality prenatal care reduces prematurity. Lack of prenatal care is one of the best predictors of low birth weight and resulting perinatal mortality, reported researchers from Massachusetts Department of Health comparing Massachusetts with Sweden in 1982. Getting high-quality care to all women is a problem. The AMA reported that, in 1981, one fourth of new mothers in the United States gave birth with little or no prenatal care.

International Comparisons

Many factors affect mortality rates, so the rates by themselves can't be used to justify the way a baby is delivered. The mortality rates are useful in looking at obstetrical care, however. Remembering that we have to look at many interrelated causes in the mortality rates, let's look at infant mortality between countries.

The infant mortality rate is a different measure from perinatal mortality. Infant mortality measures the death of a live-born baby within the first year of life. For international comparisons it is the measure commonly used. The relative standing of the United States, where the U.S. is, high or low, in comparison to other countries, tells us how well we are doing. Though the infant-death rate for 1982 in the United States was the lowest in history—11.2 deaths per 1,000 live births—population experts call the rate high for an industrialized nation. The countries with the lowest infant mortality—fewer than 10 infant deaths per 1,000 live births—are Sweden, Japan, Finland, Switzerland, the Netherlands, Denmark, Norway, and France.

In these eight countries there is a national commitment to providing quality prenatal and birth care for all women. Also, birth rates are low, partly because contraception and abortion (which reduce birth rates) are readily available; for seven of the eight safest countries, many or most births are attended by midwives. Are midwives the safest birth attendants? Records show that midwives, or doctors with the midwife philosophy of care, *are* the safest for mothers and babies.

Randomized Controlled Trials—The Only Measure of What Obs Do

What we know from looking at mortality rates is that obstetricians can't measure what they do in labor and delivery by using mortality rates (called "crude mortality rates"). They cannot say the dropping maternity and perinatal mortality rates are due to interventions such as using fetal monitors, Pitocin, cesareans, or other procedures. The active management of all births is an invention of the seventies, long after the greatest decreases began and continued in maternal mortality. Perinatal mortality was decreasing before the seventies too, and the decrease has many different reasons behind it. Current research clearly shows, however, that any major decreases in perinatal mortality will now come from prevention—reducing the large numbers of low-birth-weight babies in the United States.

Obstetricians call their tools beneficial, but can they prove it? They need to show the benefits, risks, and safety of each intervention by testing it separately. For the most part, research to evaluate the interventions of obstetricians on the basis of whether or not the interventions are better for the mother and baby than not using them has simply not been done.

Iain Chalmers and Martin Richards, British medical researchers, examined the tendency of obstetricians to claim their activities cause the falling maternal and perinatal mortality rates. Chalmers and Richards say:

> One is left wondering how a profession which has always thought
> of itself as scientific could have remained complacent in the face
> of such haphazard changes in practice. Certainly the relative re-
> search design has been available for many years: Johnston and
> Sidall in 1922 allocated alternate women to experimental and con-

trol groups in a prospective study which failed to demonstrate any beneficial effect of perineal shaving prior to labor. The fact that these findings, although confirmed by subsequent research in 1965, do not seem to have a major impact on actual practice, raises the question of whether well-conducted research influences practice to a greater extent than opinion and anecdote.

The evaluation that the authors refer to is called "randomized controlled trial" (RCT), which shows whether or not a new way is better than the old way, and whether doing nothing is better than either the old or new way.

In the example given, women were assigned on a chance, or random, basis to either of two groups. In the first, "the experimental group," the perineal area was shaved. In the second, "the control group," the women were not shaved. The reason usually given for the perineal shaving is that it reduces infection. There was a slightly higher infection rate for the experimental group (with perineum shaved). From several RCTs involving thousands of women, we know perineal shaving does not reduce infection so there is no reason for shaving the perineal area of a woman in labor.

The use of randomized controlled trials of the various interventions of the obstetrician would tell us whether any one intervention was of any benefit and what the risks were. A doctor can only claim to be scientific if he uses the scientific method in his practice; if he either carries out research using RCTs, or in his practice uses only those interventions that have been evaluated and proven beneficial. "What constitutes science is the use of scientific method and not the status or the hopes of its practitioners," says author M. D. Riley in *The Benefits and Hazards of the New Obstetrics.*

Senators at a health subcommittee hearing on obstetrics were appalled to discover that there has been no systematic evaluation of the interventions used by the obstetrician. Former Senator Jacob Javits said that many routine activities and interventions of obstetricians had "never been conclusively tested for the relative risk and benefit." Senator Edward M. Kennedy added "the development of obstetrical technology far outstrips our capacity to assess its appropriate value. As a result common practice is established before appropriate practices can be defined."

Some doctors are troubled that routine practices have not been evaluated scientifically. The oxytocin challenge test (OCT) is one such intervention, used primarily when a woman's pregnancy is more than two weeks past her due date. The woman is given just enough oxytocin to stimulate several hard contractions while the fetal heart rate is monitored in response to the contractions. The theory is that, if the fetal heart rate is abnormal, labor must be induced immediately. G. Eric Knox, M.D., of the University of Alabama Medical Center, said in a discussion evaluating the use of the OCT in prolonged pregnancies:

> I also concur with Dr. Kirschbaum that the OCT itself has never been validated in the way that he suggests appropriate (prospective, randomized trial with non-intervention control group). Be that as it may, what has happened is that enthusiasm for this test [OCT] like many other previously touted forms of fetal assessment [HPL, estriols, etc.], becomes so widespread that when investigators go to a Human Use Committee and ask if they may compare an OCT versus non-intervention or expectant management, they are told, "No, by denying this patient this test you would be performing an unethical study." I would suggest, and I assume Dr. Kirschbaum would agree, that through this type of reasoning we are perhaps doing an unethical thing by introducing therapies into our practice prior to having them well validated by appropriate, controlled studies.

We don't want to just *tell* you that what obstetricians do is unscientific. We will show you.

7 • THE OBSTETRICIAN'S BLACK BAG OF INTERVENTIONS

Jenny and Dick talked eagerly about their first baby due in a week. "It seems like we've waited so long for this," Jenny said. "We were married two years when we decided to have a baby, then it seemed to take forever to get pregnant!" she added, blushing now. "We've finished our Lamaze course," Dick broke in with a sparkle in his eyes, "I know we can use everything we learned." Jenny seemed to be reminding Dick when she said quietly, "Our teacher emphasized that this is not natural childbirth, and I shouldn't be a martyr. She said just enjoy it, and do whatever is best for the safe delivery of the baby."

As the days went by, and the due date came and went, Jenny became discouraged; it seemed so difficult to move around now. One week after her due date, she awakened slowly, aware that what woke her was a heaviness, a tensing in her lower abdomen that had come and gone several times before she was fully awake. Was this it? She glanced at the clock and saw that it was almost time to get up anyway, so she sat up and started timing her contractions. Disappointed, she noticed there wasn't much of a pattern—first ten minutes, then eight minutes, then twelve minutes. By now Dick was waking up and he asked what she was doing. When he found out she was timing contractions, he jumped up and scurried around nervously getting ready. Jenny told him she didn't think it was labor. But within an hour the contractions had settled into a fairly regular pattern of every eight minutes, and she decided to call her doctor. He told her to come in since he was already at the hospital (it was seven A.M.). It sounded to him like she was probably in labor. Now they both really got excited. This was the big day! By the time they got to the hospital, it was eight o'clock. Jenny missed Dick, who had gone to sign her in, but she was busy undressing to get into bed. She was disappointed to find out from the nurse's examination that she was only two centimeters dilated. The contractions were already hard to handle, especially without Dick there.

Before the years of high-technology births, mothers-to-be were often sent back home if they came to the hospital in very early labor like Jenny. But sending a mother home, once she comes to the hospital— even in very early labor—is now almost unheard of.

Mother Put to Bed to Labor

In most countries women in labor are encouraged to walk around rather than go to bed, but there is a belief system in the United States that it is safer for the woman to be in bed. Several times in one year, Denver General Hospital did not have enough beds for all women in labor, so women in early labor *had* to stay upright, either sitting or walking the hospital halls. A misinformed nurse observing these women told a *Denver Post* reporter, "That's dangerous!" In fact, it is *not* dangerous; it is beneficial to the laboring woman and the fetus.

There is no research showing any benefit in putting the laboring woman to bed. On the contrary, there is research that shows a danger to the fetus when a mother labors on her back, and benefits to a side-lying, upright, or walking position in labor. A world authority on the supine (or flat-on-the-back) labor and delivery position is Roberto Caldeyro-Barcia, M.D., director of the Latin American Center for Perinatology and Human Development of the World Health Organization (WHO) in Montevideo, Uruguay. He and later researchers in the late seventies, using randomized controlled trials, discovered that the supine position is the *worst* one for labor and delivery. It has the disadvantage of "adversely affecting pain and comfort, uterine activity and maintenance of normal blood pressure," says Frederic Ettner, M.D., in *21st Century Obstetrics Now!* A drop in the mother's blood pressure affects the circulation of blood within the uterus, resulting in poor oxygen supply for the unborn baby. Dr. Caldeyro-Barcia states, "Except for being hanged by the feet, the supine position is the worst conceivable position for labor and delivery."

Raising the woman to a semisitting position in bed, sometimes called "the Lamaze position," for labor and delivery has the same problems as the supine position, says certified nurse-midwife, Katherine Camacho Carr, in her 1980 review of the medical and cross-cultural literature on a woman's position in labor and birth.

Standing, strolling, sitting, kneeling, or on hands and knees are the ways for a woman to labor upright. When the upright position is used, labor is much shorter than in the on-the-back position. The upright position, with the assistance of gravity, increases the strength of contractions and dilates the cervix faster. Women report less pain in the upright position. There is also less need to use drugs to speed up labor, or relieve pain, and babies are in better condition at birth. Finally, women *like* being upright. According to Caldeyro-Barcia, 95 percent of women given a choice choose to be upright. It's also important to point out that there is no research showing that the on-your-back or the semisitting position for labor gives as good results as the upright positions.

Carr, who presented her review of labor and birth positions to a 1980 conference on "Benefits and Hazards of Hospital Newborn Care," referred to J. Roberts' research at the University of Illinois in 1980, showing the side-lying position was one of more uterine efficiency than was the sitting position. In terms of efficiency of contractions and shortening of labor, Carr's review concludes there is an order from best to worst for labor position:

1. Walking or standing
2. Side-lying
3. Sitting
4. Lying down or lying on the back in a propped position (Lamaze position)

By now Dick was back with Jenny, trying to get her back in control, helping her with her slow breathing, encouraging her to relax. At this point the nurse came in with some equipment and asked Dick to leave. Jenny felt miserable and embarrassed as she submitted to the prep and enema and the procedure to put an IV opening in the back of her left hand "just in case," the nurse said. Jenny realized that her contractions were not regular at all now, sometimes very mild, sometimes a little uncomfortable. Jenny was still at 2 centimeters dilation.

IV

In most other industrialized countries, a normal laboring woman is allowed to eat and drink lightly. In the United States, as a substitute for this light eating, an IV or intravenous pathway is inserted into the woman's arm. Fluids may be given through the IV to sustain the woman as she fasts throughout a long labor. And the IV allows a quick means of giving general anesthesia, analgesia, and fluids for emergency surgical intervention. The woman is required to fast "just in case" of an emergency. If a woman receives general anesthesia, she is unconscious. If she is not watched carefully, she may vomit, and inhale the fluids—and may die. The responsibility for observation rests with the anesthetist, who can quickly turn a woman's head if she vomits and avoid any peril. The most common use of the IV, however, is to give Pitocin, either for induction of labor or to speed up labor.

There is no research that shows that an IV needs to be used before there is an emergency, or that having an IV in place in a normal laboring woman has made a difference in an emergency. Hospital ob nurses and birth attendants know how to start an IV quickly when needed.

There are risks to an IV. The woman may develop an infection at the site of the IV. Also, the "nothing by mouth" rule for a laboring woman according to a medical textbook can lead to abnormal blood chemistry ("metabolic acidosis"). This condition in the mother results in less oxygen for her unborn baby.

Prep

The prep is the shaving of the perineal or pubic area. Over half of American women giving birth routinely have their perineal or pubic area shaved as part of being admitted to the hospital. The medical reason given us is that it reduces infection. Research in the 1960s, using randomized controlled trials involving 7,600 women giving birth, showed that the infection rate was lower among those who were *not* shaved.

Enemas

Enemas are still a routine part of hospital admissions for over half of laboring women. There is no research proving any medical benefits of an enema. Many mothers experience a natural bowel cleansing in labor. They may have several bowel movements over a period of minutes or hours as the baby moves down in the pelvis. Some birth attendants believe this cleansing gives the baby more room in the mother's pelvis. If a mother does not have this natural diarrhea, she may feel more comfortable having an enema. Also a fear of passing feces with pushing contractions may inhibit some women who have not had an enema. These possible benefits suggest the choice of an enema should be left up to the laboring woman.

Jenny had now been at the hospital two hours, and her contractions were becoming weak and irregular. The doctor examined her for the first time and found she was still at 2 centimeters dilation. He said he was going to break the amniotic sac "to get things moving." Jenny didn't feel anything, just a little wetness between her legs. However, within minutes, her contractions became strong again, and she needed

Dick to help her with her breathing. Dick, feeling anxious now that he was doing the real thing and not just practicing, worked with Jenny, reminding her to take her cleansing breath at the beginning and end of the contractions.

Amniotomy

Amniotomy is the deliberate breaking of the bag of waters surrounding the baby. The nurse or doctor uses a blunt, sterile instrument to puncture the amniotic sac. Amniotomy is so common in laboring women in hospitals that few nurses and doctors have ever seen a laboring woman with a bag of waters intact during late labor or delivery. Trying to change the practice of routine amniotomy can be difficult.

In a 1979 discussion of fetal monitoring in the *American Journal of Obstetrics and Gynecology,* Robert Munsick, M.D., professor of ob/gyn at Indiana University School of Medicine, notes that early amniotomy becomes a "routine reflex; how else can the scalp electrode be placed?" He told how difficult it was to get his ob/gyn residents in his hospital in Indianapolis to stop amniotomy. "Attempts by me through entreaty, counseling, and even cajolery failed to influence this practice." What finally worked was to post a "Wanted" notice in the residents' lounge: "Wanted—Delivered Alive—$50.00 Reward!—A fetus delivered in a caul." Within ten days of posting the notice, four infants were delivered in a caul (with amniotic sac intact).

Amniotomy is done to speed up labor, to induce labor (usually accompanied by Pitocin), and to get the bag of waters out of the way to apply the electrode to the fetal scalp, necessary when using an internal fetal monitor.

There is a speedup of labor when the bag of waters is ruptured early in labor. Researchers, M. Martell, M.D., et al. found in 1976 that early amniotomy reduced labor by about an hour. In 1974 Dr. Caldyro-Barcia found that early rupture of membranes speeded labor by "a little more than half an hour." The question is, is it worth it? Is the amount of time saved worth the loss of protection normally given by the amniotic fluid? Before rupture, the bag of waters provides a cushion of even pressure from contractions, and protection from excessive molding of the head as the baby moves through the mother's pelvis. After rupture, the pressures on the baby's head during contraction are direct and uneven. Also, the umbilical cord can be compressed, sometimes denying the baby necessary oxygen. "I didn't know, when I was an intern, about the literature showing that the amniotic fluid protects the head," a family practitioner told us. "To me it was just something that was in the way, and the sooner you ruptured the membranes the better off you were."

When the bag of waters is not ruptured artificially, 95 percent of women who start labor spontaneously at full term, and have uncomplicated, unmedicated labors, will have the bag of waters intact until very late in labor or even during delivery. This provides a significant measure of protection to the baby and to the baby's lifeline, the umbilical cord. Most women who have their bag of waters rupture naturally—even in early labor—can have normal labor and deliveries. However, whenever possible, it seems reasonable to allow the extra margin of safety the intact bag of waters provides. There is a direct benefit to the mother, too, since the longer her bag of waters is intact, the lower her risk of infection is. "Avoiding amniotomy would probably reduce many of the abnormal factors seen so often in labors, including severe drops in fetal pH, cord compression, infections, and increased numbers of cesarean sections," says certified nurse-midwife Katherine Camacho Carr, reviewing obstetric practices that protect the unborn baby during labor and birth in the journal *Birth*.

Within a few minutes of the amniotomy, two nurses came in pushing a large machine, the electronic fetal monitor. They had Jenny spread her legs again so they could screw the electrode to the baby's scalp. Dick was fascinated by the machine, by the colors and sounds—the winking and blinking of the lights. He felt they certainly were receiving the best in care. The only problem Jenny noticed was that whenever the nurse came in the room, she went straight to the fetal monitor as if Jenny were no longer there. The nurse didn't ask anymore how Jenny felt.

Electronic Fetal Monitoring

Fetal monitoring is keeping track of the baby's heartbeat as a means of measuring fetal distress and possible need for intervention. Traditionally, this has been done by the nurse listening to the baby's heartbeat with a stethoscope (auscultation). In the seventies a substitute for auscultation was found. Electronic fetal monitoring (EFM) has become almost universal in the United States. A task force of the National Institute of Health estimated that by the mid 1970s, 60 to 70 percent of all labors in the U.S. used EFM. In Baltimore, 47 percent to 94 percent of mothers were electronically monitored in the eleven hospitals covered by the COMA researchers in 1979.

There are two kinds of electronic fetal monitoring, external and internal. *External* electronic monitoring is indirect monitoring that picks up the fetal heart rate by the use of ultrasound waves. The external monitor is considered much less accurate than the internal monitor, having unreliable readings from 43 percent to 65 percent of the time, reports Madeleine Shearer, editor of *Birth*.

The *internal* fetal monitor measures the fetal heart rate directly by an electrode inserted in the baby's scalp, and measures the mother's uterine contractions by an electrode placed just inside the uterus. Electronic fetal monitoring is high technology with beeps and readouts that seduce you into believing you're getting useful information. For some onlookers, the machine is mesmerizing. "It is almost like watching television to stand in a labor room and watch this monitor," says Shearer. "The paper comes out and lies in folds in the drawer of the cabinet upon which the machine is set. A lighted green window up on the left of the monitor has an oscilloscope display of the fetal heart pattern. Then right next to that is a digital display in red, the numbers constantly flickering with each beat of the heart. I stand and watch and think to myself, 'How could I possibly question this advanced technological breakthrough in obstetrics?' Just the added information alone must be worth the effort."

Many, if not most, obstetricians wholeheartedly believe in electronic fetal monitors. They do not believe there are enough nurses in hospitals to give the one-to-one care necessary for the nurse to regularly monitor the baby's heartbeat with a stethoscope. That a machine can substitute for a nurse is a widespread misunderstanding; *someone* must monitor the machine. Editor L. J. Stonstegard, R.N., commented in 1981 in the *Perinatal Press*, "None of the studies perceived that the monitor allowed the professional care provider to perform other functions due to decreased time requirements for patient care. Rather they noted that *more* attention might be necessitated." The cost of electronically monitoring half of all laboring women is $400,000,000 annually, estimate Drs. Banta and Thacker in a report done for the U.S. Department of Health, Education and Welfare. That kind of money could hire a lot of nurses to give one-to-one care.

In 1982 researcher Judith Lumley, Ph.D., of Queen Victoria Medical Centre, Melbourne, Australia, described as "sobering" that the United States, "the richest country in the world [is] unable to provide women giving birth with the necessary one-to-one patient care."

Doctors see the electronic fetal monitor as useful, proven, and, therefore, essential for assessing fetal well-being. They cite studies done with thousands of births that show that where fetal monitors are used, the perinatal death rate goes down. They conclude that the decrease in the perinatal death rate is due to the use of the fetal monitor. However, these studies only compare years of use of the fetal monitor with years when the fetal monitor was not used. When comparisons are made involving different time periods, the limitation is that you can't pick out any one factor, such as the fetal monitor, to explain the decrease in the death rate. That conclusion could only be made scientifically if randomized controlled trials (RCTs) are done.

The five randomized controlled trials that have been done comparing electronic fetal monitoring and nurse fetal monitoring show *no benefits* for machine over nurse. All five studies show that electronic fetal monitoring increases the risk of cesarean birth two to three times over the group of women whose labors were monitored by nurses, *while there was no better outcome for the baby.*

There have been two large-scale reviews of the medical literature to evaluate studies on electronic fetal monitoring. The first was done by the staff of the U.S. General Accounting Office, and a second was done by Drs. Banta and Thacker of the Department of Health, Education and Welfare. Both reviews came to the same conclusion. Research that simply measures the use of electronic fetal monitoring over a period of time, and arbitrarily relates it to falling perinatal death rates, cannot determine the safety and value of the monitoring. Only randomized controlled trials can do that, and the five that have been done to date show little or no benefit of electronic fetal monitoring over auscultation.

Banta and Thacker and other researchers point out the lack of precision of the electronic fetal monitor in distinguishing normal fetus stress in labor from abnormal fetal stress. In about three fourths of cesareans done because of fetal distress, supposedly confirmed by the electronic fetal monitor, the condition of the babies at birth contradicted the diagnosis of fetal distress. In addition, a significant number of infants are distressed at birth when the EFM readout does not indicate distress. In other words, the electronic fetal monitor overdiagnoses fetal distress and results in unnecessary cesareans, and yet sometimes does not diagnose fetal distress that might need intervention.

Because of these recognized problems of unreliability with EFM, fetal scalp sampling is now encouraged by obstetricians to verify a monitor's readout of fetal distress. This involves taking a sample of blood from the unborn baby's scalp. While Albert Havercamp, M.D., et al., of the Health Sciences Center in Denver and Denver General Hospital found that fetal scalp sampling was somewhat helpful in reducing unnecessary cesareans, other researchers have shown little correlation between the baby's well-being or condition at birth with the blood-chemistry measurements made from the fetal blood taken during labor. In other words, the fetal-scalp-sampling technique has the same problems that the EFM does, of sometimes indicating a distressed fetus when the baby is normal, and at other times showing the baby to be normal when it is distressed.

In 1979 a National Institute of Health Consensus Development Conference on electronic fetal monitoring concluded that because there is a *possible* (but unproven) benefit, the use of electronic fetal monitoring should be strongly considered in high-risk labors. The Conference found no evidence that EFM was of any benefit in other labors (i.e., low-risk or normal labor) and should *not* be used because of possible detriment to the mother and baby.

The risks of EFM to a normal laboring woman and her baby are greater than the unproven and uncertain benefits. The widespread use of EFM in the United States is the best example of the unscientific nature of American obstetrics. Auscultation will be discouraged because doctors and hospitals have decided to use and promote EFM and they have the power, according to Dr. Lumley. In her 1982 article, "The Irresistible Rise of Electronic Fetal Monitoring," she quotes another writer describing the stages of medical innovation, ". . . The success of an innovation has little to do with its intrinsic worth (whether it is measurably effective as determined by controlled experimentation) but is dependent upon the power of the interests that sponsor and maintain it, despite the absence or inadequacy of empirical support."

The risks of *external* electronic monitoring are far less than internal monitoring, but the readouts are much less reliable. In addition, external electronic monitoring carries the risks associated with putting the mother to bed on her back because she must lie quietly in that position for the monitor to work.

The risks to the mother of the *internal* fetal monitor are greater and include the necessity of putting her to bed and performing amniotomy, because the bag of waters must be broken for the scalp electrode to be attached to the baby. With internal fetal monitoring the mother has greater infection rates, possibly from increased internal examinations, the problems associated with starting her on the road to active medical management in labor and delivery, and an increased likelihood of having a cesarean that she may not need.

"Failure to progress" in labor and "fetal distress" are the two most likely causes for cesareans in women who use an internal fetal monitor according to Havercamp et al. in 1979, and Minkoff and Schwarz in 1980. These two diagnoses are very important in the increasing rate of cesareans (see next chapter). Both researchers found "failure to progress" the most common reason for cesarean when EFM is used. "Monitors may play a key role in *causing* the increased cesarean rate for failure to progress," say Howard Minkoff, M.D., and Richard H. Schwarz, M.D., of the Downstate Medical Center, Brooklyn, New York. The researchers suggest that "the stress that monitoring might create for patients" is responsible for failure to progress in labor.

Thirty to 40 percent of women react negatively to the use of the EFM. Dr. Munsick presented a possible explanation of how the mother's psychological reactions may result in cesarean section for failure to progress.

> We begin by restraining a woman early in her labor. We allow her to see the FM's chattering stylus and its winks; often we even torture her unnecessarily with hours of its staccato sounds at 150 beeps per minute and we watch the monitor and not her. She dare not interrupt our silent vigil. Anxiety gives way to fright and anger . . . [leading to] abnormal contractions and these in turn cause arrest of labor. . . . And we then apply the modern-day obstetric panacea—cesarean section.

Negative reactions or not, failure to progress or not, more women have cesareans when internal fetal monitors are used, two to three times more often. According to Havercamp et al.'s study in 1979, 6 percent of women monitored by stethoscope had cesareans. Twelve percent of women who had EFM plus fetal scalp sampling had cesareans. Eighteen percent of the women who had EFM alone had cesareans. There is a risk of dying from the cesarean operation, and enthusiasm to use EFM on *all* women fails to justify the increased risk of cesareans to the women. If the risk of having a cesarean increases two to three times for a woman having EFM, so does her risk of dying increase over the nurse-monitored woman.

The risks to the baby include the loss of the protection of the bag of waters because of amniotomy, as well as injuries from misplacing the scalp electrode, infections, and (rarely) death due directly to infection from the scalp electrode.

The NIH Consensus Development Conference concluded that for most labors, the nurse should monitor the fetal heart rate every fifteen minutes in the first stage of labor and every five minutes in the second stage. This demands a high degree of one-to-one nurse-patient contact for laboring women in hospitals and many hospitals do not have adequate staff to do that. If your hospital is understaffed, consider hiring a private duty nurse (a monitrice) to give you the nursing care you need.

At noon, when the nurse came in to check the fetal monitor, she also gave Jenny another exam and remarked, "You certainly are not cranked up yet; you're just three centimeters." Those had to be about the most discouraging words Jenny had ever heard. When the doctor suggested that a "little" Pitocin would make Jenny's labor more normal, Jenny readily agreed. The nurse pulled in a stand with a bottle on a six-foot pole and quickly got the "Pit" going since the IV was already in place. Jenny felt an immediate change in the contractions. They seemed much closer and more intense. Dick redoubled his efforts to help her stay in control, massaging her arms and legs, and lightly stroking her tummy. Soon the contractions were three minutes apart and sixty seconds long, and getting harder to cope with. Jenny switched to accelerated breathing. The nurse came in about every fifteen minutes now, and several times made an adjustment in the IV that increased the Pitocin drops flowing into Jenny's hand.

Induction and Augmentation of Labor

Induction of labor means to start it artificially. Augmentation of labor means to speed up a labor that has started naturally. "I have seen hundreds of deliveries screwed up because of unnecessary intervention," said one nurse interviewed by writer Judith Glassman. "In many hospitals 60 percent of labors are chemically induced or stimulated even though Pitocin often causes overly strong contractions, as well as blood pressure problems in both mother and child. It's just easier for the doctor to administer Pitocin than to supply emotional support."

In the medical management of labor and delivery, the usual way to artificially begin labor is to break the bag of waters and start the intravenous administration of Pitocin. The staff of the U.S. General Accounting Office estimates that 12 percent of all labors in the United States are artificially begun. Rates varied by region, however, with a high of 16.4 percent in the Northeast. However, some doctors believe that rates of induction would be much lower if it were done only when the risk of continuing the pregnancy was greater than the risk of inducing labor and delivery. The conditions where continuing the pregnancy presents a threat to life or well-being of mother and baby include severe blood incompatibility between mother and fetus, some diabetics, severe pre-eclampsia, severe high blood pressure, kidney disease, and an overdue pregnancy (postmaturity) where there has been *proven* a danger to the fetus. If induction of labor were carried out only when these conditions were present, Dr. Caldeyro-Barcia estimates that, at most, 3 percent of births would be induced. If that is so, it means that three fourths of the inductions in the U.S. today are putting the mother and baby at risk for a less than sound medical reason. Authors Iain Chalmers and Martin Richards, writing in *The Benefits and Hazards of the New Obstetrics,* concluded:

> It has not been possible to demonstrate any striking advantage or disadvantage of a widened use of the induction of labor. The truth of the matter is that we are ignorant about the circumstances in which the benefits of induction outweigh the disadvantages and are likely to remain so using the research techniques employed so far.

Intervening to speed up a labor begun naturally is much more common than induction. Estimates of augmentation range from 20 to 30 percent of all labors that start spontaneously. "We used to have women laboring twenty-four, forty-eight, and even seventy-two hours!" an obstetrician told us. "We won't allow that anymore. I don't think augmentation is overused." Speeding up the labor goes along with the belief that the stages of normal labor must fit within a carefully defined standard of time. "Shortening the phases of normal labor when there is no sign of fetal distress has not been shown to improve infant outcome," says Doris Haire, D.M.S., maternal advocate and president, American Foundation of Maternal and Child Health.

Pitocin is a synthetic version of the hormone oxytocin, which is produced in the body of the laboring woman and is one factor in the progress of her labor. Pitocin is usually (but not always) highly effective in beginning or speeding up labor, as many of you reading this book can testify. If Pitocin must be used, administration through an IV is preferred, because it offers the best means to control the dosage over a period of time.

However, even the most careful administration of Pitocin simply does not duplicate naturally occurring labor. This is because the progress of labor is under the dual control of the baby and the mother. The complex chemical and hormonal interrelationship of the mother and baby in starting and continuing labor is still not clearly understood. But we do know that it is impossible to reproduce normal labor. Mothers given Pitocin often describe the contractions as being longer and stronger, and with a shorter period between contractions, than those they experienced in unaugmented labor.

During both normal and induced or augmented labor the blood supply to the uterus (and therefore the oxygen supply to the baby) is temporarily reduced. With normal contractions, however, there is time between contractions to allow the baby's blood to be well oxygenated, to enable him to "hold his breath," so to speak, during the next contraction. In induced or stimulated labor, there are two ways the baby's oxygen supply can be shortchanged. The time between contractions is shorter; there is less time to oxygenate his blood between contractions. The contractions are longer; the fetus goes for a longer period of time before he receives a full supply of oxygen. For the unborn baby, it can be like being pushed into a swimming pool before he had a chance to catch his breath, and then having someone push him down deeper, just when he had bobbed to the surface for much-needed air. This possibility of an inadequate oxygen supply for the baby is one reason that all induced or augmented labors are considered at risk for developing complications.

Research shows the most significant risks of either induction or augmentation of labor to be:

- Higher rate of complicated labors and deliveries
- More use of analgesia or anesthesia because of the intensity of the contractions
- Fetal distress
- Higher rate of jaundice in the newborn
- Greater chance of delivering a premature baby (induction only; why all induced labors are "high risk")
- Postpartum hemorrhage (induction only; there has been no research to determine if hemorrhage is associated with augmentation of labor)
- Higher rate of ruptured uterus and placental separation, which may lead to the death of the mother or baby

While there is consensus that the risks of Pitocin are worthwhile when continuing the pregnancy would be life-threatening, there is no evidence of benefits outweighing risks in the vast majority of inductions and augmentations being done. "The timing of spontaneous delivery is controlled by complex mechanisms which are still incompletely understood . . . and which have as their end point the delivery [of the baby when] survival of the newborn is most likely," said an editor of *Lancet*.

"The data on induction, oxytocin, and cesarean section all point to the same conclusion: Intervention is resulting in iatrogenic [physician-caused] pathology in women and their babies who might well have had spontaneous vaginal deliveries if they had been left alone," said Richard W. Beard, a British medical doctor, criticizing the widened use of induction in his country.

The first randomized control trial of Pitocin versus the upright position was finally done in 1980 at the Los Angeles County/ University of Southern California Medical Center. This RCT studied the effectiveness of Pitocin versus the upright position in getting stalled labors going again. Women whose labors had slowed were randomly assigned to one of two groups. In the first, women were given the usual routine of Pitocin. In the second group, women were not given Pitocin; instead, they stayed out of bed, either walking, standing, or sitting. The study showed stimulation of labor was more effective by using the upright position than by using Pitocin.

Jenny, scared, began to complain about the contractions. They were more overwhelming than painful. The tremendous sensations she felt in her lower body were unlike anything she had ever felt before. It seemed to take too much effort to stay in control, to work with her body; otherwise there was pain. "I wish there was more time in between. It seems like only a few seconds from the time one is over until another one starts. They hurt." At this point the nurse returned to check Jenny and said that things seemed to be on track now, she had dilated a centimeter in the last hour and was now 4 centimeters dilated. Jenny's contractions were now every two minutes and she thought "I think I need the anesthesia now, I can't take this if it's going to get worse than this." She told Dick she needed something and he rang for the nurse. The nurse said, "I'll let the doctor know." A half hour later the doctor arrived to give Jenny an epidural injection remarking, "If I were having a baby, I'd want an epidural as soon as I could." He added, however, that 4 centimeters was about the earliest he felt he could give an epidural. Within fifteen minutes, Jenny became talkative and could hardly feel the pain. She felt good about being able to talk coherently to her husband now without grimacing with discomfort.

Analgesia and Anesthesia

Analgesia are drugs used in labor to relieve pain. Anesthesia are drugs administered in labor and delivery to block or obliterate sensation. Most mothers given analgesia or anesthesia believe them safe and that they are given to relieve pain and discomfort. According to *Williams Obstetrics*, a textbook used by obstetrical residents in their training, "Vast experience has shown that obstetric analgesia and anesthesia, when judiciously employed, are in general beneficial rather than detrimental to both baby and mother." The obstetrician's belief system requires the use of analgesia and anesthesia because it is thought to result in "more careful, gentler, and frequently easier deliveries" and in "healthier mothers and more living babies," according to the textbook. Recognizing the risks of drug use, the writer of the text goes on: "The search continues for drugs that singly or in combination produce effective analgesia, amnesia, and sedation during labor but at the same time are completely safe for the mother and the fetus." The purpose of any drug, whether analgesia or anesthesia, then, is not just for pain relief but also to produce memory loss of labor, to quiet the mother, to make deliveries easier, and to ensure healthier mothers and more living babies.

Analgesia and anesthesia use in the United States is very widespread. National data of use are incomplete, but comprehensive reports from many hospitals indicate that almost all (90 to 100 percent of birthing women, depending on the hospital) receive analgesia, anesthesia, or both. The analgesia (drugs given for pain relief) rate seems to range from about 40 to 70 percent. The anesthesia (drugs given to block sensation) rate is estimated at around 80 percent. It's unusual to find a hospital with better rates than these.

Almost all birth attendants agree that in complicated deliveries, whether vaginal or cesarean, analgesia and anesthesia are beneficial because they sedate or anesthetize a woman so that essential intervention can be carried out. The disagreement comes in deciding what is a complicated delivery and whether the birth attendant may, by intervening, be *causing* complications. In traditional settings the complication rate, intervention rate and drug use rate are much higher than in alternative settings. The excellent outcomes for mother and baby in alternative settings show us that complications—and the need for intervention—can be avoided in most births. There is no research that proves that for these uncomplicated deliveries, analgesia and anesthesia use "permit more careful, gentler and frequently easier deliveries resulting in healthier mothers and more living babies" as the medical textbook indicates. There is evidence that, especially for those normal mothers and their babies, the risks may outweigh the only proven benefit, which is pain relief for the mother.

Analgesia and anesthesia:

1. May slow labor by changing the strength and frequency of contractions so they are less effective, requiring the use of Pitocin.

2. Almost always cause some drop in the mother's blood pressure, and may cause a serious drop, with life-threatening consequences to her or her baby.
3. Dull the experience for the mother, reduce or eliminate the physical pleasure of birth, and, immediately after birth, may make her less responsive to her baby.
4. Anesthesia may slow the second stage of labor by relaxing the vaginal walls, and often interferes with the mother's ability to bear down, requiring a forceps delivery.
5. Anesthesia prevents the mother from feeling how hard she is pushing the baby against her perineum and, because she does not have the "protective reflex" of feeling the birth, the birth may be too fast to gradually stretch the perineum and may cause perineal tears and damage.
6. With anesthesia the mother risks headaches from misplaced injections or other neurological damage which may be temporary or, rarely, permanent.
7. Cause short-term neurological and behavioral abnormalities in the baby, such as breathing and sucking difficulties, and may cause a dulling of the baby's ability to respond to the mother in the attachment process.
8. May cause long-term neurological and behavioral disorders in the baby.

The results of extensive research on the effects of analgesia and anesthesia on the newborn are frightening. Yvonne Brackbill, Ph.D., and her associates have done the most comprehensive research on the short- and long-term effects on infants whose mothers were given drugs during labor and delivery. Esther Conway and Dr. Brackbill, working through the University of Denver, published their results in 1970, showing that anesthesia and analgesia impaired the muscular, visual, and neural development of the baby two to five days postpartum. At that time, Conway and Brackbill suggested that it was possible that anesthetics and analgesics caused permanent damage to the infant.

Nine years later, Dr. Brackbill, research professor of psychology and obstetrics and gynecology at the University of Florida, reported on the lasting behavior effects of obstetric medication on children to two different government bodies, a Senate subcommittee in 1978 and a committee of the Food and Drug Administration in 1979. For her reports, Dr. Brackbill reviewed forty-one studies on obstetric medication and infant/child behavior. All but two of the studies found significant drug effect. Dr. Brackbill reported four key findings from the studies. First, obstetric drugs affect the child's behavior negatively (they interfere with normal function). Second, the behavioral effects are dose-related; that is, the stronger the drug and the larger the dose, the greater the behavioral effect. Third, Dr. Brackbill reports, "At all ages, the effects are more clearly visible when the tasks are difficult, that is, when they require the child to exert itself to make an effort to cope with problems." And fourth, the behavioral effects of obstetrical medications persist for years.

For her 1979 report to the FDA, Dr. Brackbill presented additional evidence of obstetric drug damage. Working with Sarah Broman, Ph.D., a psychologist at the National Institute of Health, Dr. Brackbill had analyzed data from a study of 53,000 women who gave birth at twelve different teaching hospitals from 1959 through 1966. Broman and Brackbill studied the data on the 3,500 women in the project who were the *healthiest* and who had the *most uncomplicated* pregnancies, labors, and deliveries, trying to rule out the possibility that any results showing damage to the babies would be due to complicated pregnancies or deliveries. In this select, healthy group, Drs. Brackbill and Broman found that obstetrical medications affect the children's behavior at least through seven years of age.

Among the older children whose mothers had received drugs during labor and delivery, there were lower reading and spelling scores, and lower scores on a visual-motor test. Dramatizing the results of their analysis, Dr. Brackbill concludes, "On the whole, I estimate that 95 percent of births in the United States hospitals nowadays are medicated. This means 3,500,000 medicated births out of 3,700,000 total births per year. If the average I.Q. loss per medicated birth is four points, this means 14,060,000 I.Q. points lost to new U.S. citizens every year. Cumulatively, that figure should put the problem of obstetric medication at the head of the class of national health priorities."

Doctors are concerned, however, that if women have full information on the risks of brain damage to their unborn babies when drugs and anesthesia are used, they will be frightened away from using them when needed. This issue came up in Dr. Brackbill's presentation to the Committee of the FDA. Another doctor questioned that a mother might refuse a needed cesarean section because of the risks of anesthesia. Dr. Brackbill's reply was, "I see evidence everywhere I turn that women are capable of making risk-benefit decisions." The American Academy of Pediatrics Committee on Drugs agrees, and has recommended that doctors "use the smallest possible amount of medications when it is needed, and to discuss the benefits and side effects with the mother, preferably in advance of the birth."

A related issue in the use of analgesia and anesthesia is the lack of research on the safety of the drugs used. Toxicologist-pediatrician Mark Thoman, M.D., says, "Every drug is a controlled poison." Many of us believe that the Food and Drug Administration would not allow drugs to be used in obstetrics that are unsafe. In a study of this issue, Doris Haire, D.M.S., reports that the dictionary definition of safe ("free from harm or injury") is not the definition used by the FDA; in fact, they have no definition of what "safe" is. In a letter to her, the director of the FDA advised her that the FDA does not guarantee the safety of any drug, even those drugs that the FDA approves as "safe." Furthermore, the FDA does not require the drug given to a woman during labor or delivery to be proven safe for the unborn baby. Says Dr. Haire, "There is no doubt in my mind, and in the minds of many other individuals working with brain-injured children, that a large proportion of brain-injured and learning disabled children are the result of obstetric drugs administered to women to relieve discomfort or pain, or to induce or stimulate their labor. Most women are unaware that obstetric drugs diminish the supply of oxygen to the unborn baby's brain and can result in brain damage."

The American Academy of Pediatrics discourages the use of drugs for the laboring woman and states that no drug has been found safe for the baby *in utero.*

In the next hour and a half, Jenny and Dick chatted. They even became a little bored. Jenny felt hungry, but knew she couldn't eat. Her sense of smell seemed very sharp; everything reminded her of food. She hadn't eaten since last night's dinner, and it was almost twenty-four hours since then. Jenny felt nothing from the top of her tummy down, but she could, strangely, feel the baby moving around. At 3:30 she became aware that the epidural was wearing off. About that time the nurse came in for a check and told her she was 6 centimeters dilated and doing fine, but she helped her turn on her side because her blood pressure was "a little low."

Jenny wasn't so sure that she was doing fine. She was afraid of feeling the overwhelming contractions again. She asked Dick what she should do. He suggested they start timing the contractions again, and get back with the breathing. By 4:30 she was 8 centimeters dilated and feeling unable to handle the contractions again. She rang for the nurse to come back. "Please, I need something now!" She felt she didn't do very well the next half hour waiting for the doctor, losing her breathing rhythm, even though Dick was now breathing along with her with each contraction. Nothing seemed to be working. At 5:00 the doctor arrived, found she was at 9 centimeters dilation, and gave her a second injection of epidural anesthesia. As the sensations of labor began to disappear (much to her relief) she overheard her doctor talking to the nurse outside her door, "If I could have talked her into waiting another half hour or so for the first one, I probably wouldn't have had to repeat it." By 5:30 Jenny was feeling nothing, and became very excited when the nurse coming in to check her told her she was nearly fully dilated and almost ready to push.

A few minutes later the doctor returned to check her and confirmed she could now push. Dick and the nurse helped Jenny round her back and grab her knees. "Push as long as you can!" the nurse encouraged. After about twenty to thirty minutes the stretcher was wheeled in for the move to the delivery room.

Mother's Delivery Position

The usual position for an American woman giving birth in a delivery room is on her back, with her legs in stirrups. This is known as the lithotomy position. More than three fourths of obstetricians consider the lithotomy position best for delivery, according to a *McCall's* survey. "Maybe the position is undignified for the mother," one doctor wrote, "but it's convenient for me." And that's the only good thing about it. The position is for the convenience of the delivering doctor. There are no benefits and several serious drawbacks for the mother and baby.

In *The Cultural Warping of Childbirth*, Doris Haire, D.M.S., summarized the literature indicating the problems in the lithotomy or on-the-back position for delivery.

1. It adversely affects the mother's blood pressure and the blood supply to her heart and lungs.
2. It decreases the normal intensity of contractions.
3. It makes it difficult for the mother to push the baby out and, therefore, increases the need for forceps. (You feel as though and you are, in fact, pushing the baby *uphill.*)
4. It makes it difficult for her to expel the placenta, which increases the need for procedures such as pulling on the cord, which put her at risk of hemorrhage.

5. Because the mother's legs are pulled wider apart than is normal for an easy delivery, and the baby's head presses against the back of the perineum, there is an increased need for an episiotomy to prevent tearing.

Many mothers find delivery not only safer but far easier curled on their side, or in a semisitting position with the soles of their feet on the bed, with a comfortable relaxed spread of their legs. However, there are five upright positions that use gravity to assist the woman in delivery. They are: sitting, squatting, on hands and knees, kneeling, and fully supported standing.

Jenny liked the idea of moving to the delivery room. Now she knew her baby was almost here. As the nurse and Dick helped her slide onto the delivery table, she felt another contraction coming, a tightening of her tummy with no other sensation. "I need to push!" she exclaimed. But she had to wait while her legs were positioned in the stirrups, and the sterile draping carefully arranged around her legs and stomach. Dick placed himself at her head. The nurse put a pillow under Jenny's shoulders. For another twenty minutes, Dick and the nurse encouraged her to push fully with each contraction. Finally the doctor told her he was going to help her with forceps and "a little cut." She'd probably feel some pressure in her back, he mentioned. As he worked positioning the forceps, he said, "This one is staying in one spot, so push hard. It's pretty tight ... okay, now we're moving, just lie back and let me do the rest." An eight-pound girl slid into the world at 6:18 P.M. The nurse took the baby from the doctor who cut the cord immediately. The nurse brought the baby around to Jenny and Dick for a brief look. Jenny and Dick were thrilled to see their new daughter. Both had seen the delivery in the overhead mirror with feelings of awe from watching the miracle of birth. The nurse took the baby over to check and clean up. Within a few minutes the nurse brought the baby to Dick and asked if he'd like to take his new daughter to the nursery "while the doctor finished up here." The doctor explained that Jenny had torn, even with the episiotomy, since the baby was in there "awfully tight," and he'd had to go a little higher with the forceps than usual.

Episiotomy

Episiotomy is the cutting of the perineum to enlarge the birth opening. This practice is so widespread that there is hardly an American woman today who has given birth vaginally who has not had an episiotomy. The current estimate is that 85 percent of women giving birth receive an episiotomy. This compares to an 8 percent episiotomy rate in the Netherlands and a 3 percent rate in Sweden—information that leads one to believe that it is not women's perineums that are different from country to country, but medical fad.

Doctors give three reasons for doing an episiotomy. In *Williams Obstetrics* the reasons are stated as fact. First, an episiotomy substitutes a straight incision for a tear, and that is better for healing than a laceration would be. Second, an episiotomy "spares the baby's head the necessity of serving as a battering ram against perineal obstruction. If prolonged, the pounding of the infant's head against the perineum could cause brain injury." And third, an episiotomy reduces the likelihood of deep tears, called third-degree or fourth-degree (through the rectum) lacerations. An underlying belief of many physicians, touched on in the textbook, is that an episiotomy prevents excessive stretching, which would lead to a relaxed perineum and reduced sexual pleasure for the woman's male partner.

There is no research to support any of these beliefs. Dr. Lewis Mehl's research comparing two large groups of women who delivered either at home or in hospital gives interesting information that suggests that an episiotomy doesn't prevent severe laceration. In the home-birth group, only 10 percent had episiotomies, and yet fewer than 2 percent had either third-degree, fourth-degree, or cervical tears. In the hospital group, 87 percent of the women had episiotomies. Nevertheless, just over 14 percent of the women had third-degree, fourth-degree, or cervical lacerations. The in-hospital women had seven times more severe lacerations, though they had nine times as many episiotomies as the home-birth women. The high rate of episiotomies and the many severe lacerations in hospital deliveries occur because 1) obstetricians simply are not trained to ease out the baby's head any other way than to enlarge the opening with an episiotomy, 2) the lithotomy position is nearly universal for hospital delivery, and 3) large numbers of deliveries have forceps used.

If your birth attendant is not familiar with, or unwilling to try, a delivery without an episiotomy, you can increase your chance of avoiding an episiotomy and tears by:

1. Choosing an upright or side-lying position for delivery
2. Avoiding anesthesia
3. Pushing only when you feel the need, for five to six seconds at a time

4. Stopping pushing if you feel a burning sensation (perineal tissue is stretched to tearing point)
5. Preparing your perineum with the Kegel exercise
6. Asking your birth attendant to avoid forceps if at all possible

Forceps

Forceps, in use since the 1500s, are a metal device placed around the baby's head to lead it through the birth canal. Forceps shorten the delivery and prevent possible brain damage to the baby from pressure on the baby's head against the mother's perineum, according to the beliefs of obstetricians. These reasons are given in the textbook, *Williams Obstetrics*. The book describes "elective low forceps" as forceps used when "the obstetrician elects to interfere knowing that it is not absolutely necessary for spontaneous delivery may normally be expected within approximately fifteen minutes. The vast majority of forceps operations performed in this country today are elective low forceps. One reason is that all methods of analgesia interfere to a certain extent with the mother's voluntary expulsive efforts."

The elective use of low forceps is sometimes called preventive use of forceps (meaning "to make delivery easier") and is widely used in the United States. Forceps are used in one fourth to one third of all deliveries, according to estimates, going as high as 65 percent in some American hospitals. This contrasts with obstetrical care in Europe where, until recently, many centers had instrument delivery rates of lower than 5 percent. "The incidence of forceps delivery remains low in the Netherlands where childbirth is still considered a physiological process and is much more a matter of social and emotional support than of surgery and pharmacology," according to W.M.O. Moore writing in *Benefits and Hazards of the New Obstetrics*.

There is no research to support the elective use of forceps. Forceps are being used without a scientific basis, in normal deliveries, when there is no need to hurry the delivery. The risks to the infant are of hemorrhage within the head, and damage to nerves serving the face and arms. For the mother, episiotomies almost always accompany the use of forceps. In spite of this, severe lacerations of the mother's perineum are more frequent when forceps and episiotomies are used.

Summary: Interventions of the Obstetrician

Obstetricians are not scientific in their practice. None of the ob's interventions has been evaluated and proven helpful, beneficial, or better than avoiding the interventions for the 80 to 95 percent of women who could have normal labors and deliveries—and most of the interventions have substantial risks. What they do "depends on training and how they make a living, not on the result of randomized control trials," said Thomas Chalmers, president of Mt. Sinai Medical Center of the City University of New York, speaking about all doctors when quoted in *USA Today*.

The only scientific means of evaluating the interventions used by the obstetrician is by randomized controlled trials. A few studies have been done for three of the ob's interventions. For two of these, shaving of the perineum and the use of the fetal monitor, randomized controlled trials have shown no benefits in normal labors, and in fact, show some risks to the mother and, in the case of the fetal monitor, risks to the baby, too. The third intervention tested was Pitocin to stimulate labor. The upright position—walking, standing, or sitting—was *more effective* in the randomized controlled trial than was the Pitocin in stimulating labor.

Most obs' interventions, then, are experimental—that is, we don't know if using them is more beneficial than not using them—because randomized controlled trials to prove their benefits have not been done. Obstetricians *think* they are beneficial because of their experience in using them. There are, however, known risks, and when the doctor says the interventions are "safe" he means he *feels* safe using them. You, however, may not agree that an unproven intervention is "safe." It's your decision.

There is some research that does indicate which of the ob's interventions are the most dangerous to your baby. Amniotomy, induction or speeding up labor by drugs, the use of the on-the-back position for delivery, and anesthesia and analgesia were identified by several speakers as among the most common causes of infant brain damage and mental retardation at a conference in New York City in 1975 sponsored by the American Foundation for Maternal and Child Health. Writer Gary Stimeling, reporting the conference, suggested in the *Journal of Legal Medicine* that these common delivery techniques may soon be considered "malpractice."

At the 1977 American Public Health Association annual meeting, Lewis Mehl, M.D., reported his computer-assisted research on what determines the condition of the baby at birth. The four obstetric interventions identified most closely with poor outcome for the baby were Pitocin for induction or stimulation of labor, analgesia, forceps, and amniotomy. Testifying before a 1978 Senate Health Subcommittee Hearing on obstetric interventions, Dr. Haire said she believed "that at least a large percentage of learning disabled and handicapped children result from obstetric practices which interfere with normal biochemical checks and balances provided by nature to assure the normal progression of labor and a good maternal and infant outcome."

It has been as scary for us to write about the unproven interventions of the obstetrician as it is for you to read it. We are afraid for the risks being taken with the lives and health of women and their babies, when those risks are unjustified in normal births; and we can hear women who are reading this book say, "Why are you telling me this? It's only making me frightened of what might happen."

The active management of normal labors and deliveries is new in the history of childbirth. As recently as the early to mid 1970s several of the obstetrician's interventions were only used in complicated cases of labor and delivery, where the health and welfare of the woman or her baby clearly justified them. Now the technology is being used on most women in labor whether the labor is normal or not. *It will probably be used on you if you don't negotiate to prevent its use.*

Usually when complications happen in childbirth, the birth will still result in a live mother and a live baby. Advances in obstetrical technique are saving more babies from complicated births. Perinatology (the care of the unborn and the newborn) has resulted in the greatest saving of babies in trouble. If your baby is two pounds or more, it is more likely than ever that your baby will live, regardless of what kind of childbirth you have. If the obstetrician's interventions were reserved for the 5 to 20 percent of births where they can be justified, we could be pleased about the advances made to ensure a healthy baby in a complicated birth. However, the technology is also being used in the other, normal deliveries; yet the risks to the health and welfare of the mother and baby seem very great for the unproven benefits.

These interventions may not only be unsafe, they are also changing the experience of childbirth for women and babies, with far-ranging results. What have we lost? The mother becomes a nonparticipant in the birth of the baby and is denied both the joy and pleasure that is possible. And because of problems resulting from the interventions—problems either in mother or infant requiring intensive treatment after birth—the infant is separated from the mother. What we are losing here is the experience of childbirth at its best: An exuberant experience of enormous courage, effort and incredible pleasure. We are losing the kind of childbirth experience that makes us feel better about ourselves as women, that helps us grow and develop as mothers, that is important in the attachment process with our babies. More than that, the active management of labor and delivery is leading to an epidemic of cesarean births at costs that we are just beginning to tally.

8 ▪ THE CESAREAN EPIDEMIC

> The most common cause of cesareans today is not fetal distress or maternal distress, but obstetrician distress.
>
> —Dr. Gerald Stober,
> New York City obstetrician

Typically, a laboring woman sees her doctor very little in the hours before birth. Then he strides in, takes charge, and accomplishes an efficient, quick delivery. But, often, he *is* there in the hospital, waiting and anxious, in the doctors' lounge or the nurses' station. In his mind, the danger is mostly to the baby. He believes a safe birth produces a live mother and a live baby. He almost never "loses" a mother, but no matter how hard he tries, he does lose babies, 13 times out of every 1000 births. The constant anxiety in his mind is "Am I going to lose this one?" The uncertainties of labor's progress result in more anxiety than almost any obstetrician can handle. He usually gets in there and does something.

Belief, Training, and Money Are Behind the Cesarean Epidemic

When physicians are asked why cesareans have increased, the most frequent reason they give is the threat of a malpractice suit, according to Helen Marieskind, Ph.D., a Seattle public health specialist. She reviewed the literature, interviewed more than one hundred physicians, and evaluated the increase of cesareans in the United States for the Department of Health, Education and Welfare. In the interviews, physicians called cesareans "defensive medicine" and said that, even if a baby was "less than perfect," if a cesarean had been performed, they were covered, reported Dr. Marieskind.

Because he fears being sued, the doctor feels the need to try everything, including a cesarean, if he is at all concerned about the progress of the labor. However, the facts do not substantiate his belief that a cesarean protects him from a malpractice suit. Obstetrician-gynecologists are successfully sued more than most physicians, according to the National Association of Insurance Commissioners. Most of the successful suits are unrelated to birth—they are malpractice suits against the doctor when he's wearing his gynecologist hat. Performing a cesarean for fear of a lawsuit, practicing "defensive medicine," is being done without good foundation for the doctors' fears.

"Cesarean sections mean better babies" is another important belief causing the dramatic rise in cesareans.

- "You get pregnant to have a healthy baby, not a vaginal delivery."
- "We are looking for a neurologically and psychologically sound human being."
- "Now, in an advanced country, we expect a baby to survive."

The above comments were by medical experts interviewed by Silvia Feldman, Ph.D. Until the 1960s, the obstetrician's emphasis was on saving the mother, since maternal death rates had been so high. When maternal mortality rates dropped dramatically, the emphasis shifted to the baby.

Mothers generally no longer need to worry that they will die in childbirth, so their concern has switched to having a healthy baby and a good birth experience. Yet they now find themselves faced with the ultimate intervention—a cesarean—because the doctor's emphasis has switched from the mother to the baby. He believes that cesareans result in fewer damaged or dead babies. The need to "guarantee the product" (so to speak) puts so much stress on obstetricians that they have coined the term "premium baby" for any baby especially desired by the mother— particularly the older, first-time mother. Women thirty to thirty-four years old have cesarean rates 20 percent higher than women in their twenties. Women thirty-four to thirty-nine years old have cesarean rates one third higher than women in their twenties, according to the U.S. Public Health Service. "Anyone over 35 years old is by definition considered to be high risk and far more likely to be delivered by cesarean," says Jennifer Niebyl, M.D., an obstetrician who cares for high-risk women at Johns Hopkins Hospital, Baltimore.

A National Institute of Health task force studying cesarean sections looked at the increasing rates and the evidence that cesareans improve the outcome in complicated deliveries. Using data covering nine years, the task force studied a massive amount of material from more than 200 hospitals. They concluded that there is no good evidence that babies born by cesarean have better outcomes than if they had been delivered vaginally. Yet, despite the lack of evidence, the widespread belief that a cesarean is better for the baby persists among obstetricians and the public. It is often given to a mother in labor as a persuasive reason to undergo a cesarean. And certainly, told that something might happen to her baby if she goes ahead with a vaginal delivery, a woman is unwilling to take that risk.

An obstetrician's training contributes to his anxiety about the dangers of childbirth and to his urge to resort to a cesarean delivery. "I believe the present high-risk childbirth model is creating more anxiety than obstetric personnel can handle, and the increasing cesarean rate is in part a manifestation of this anxiety," says Philip Sumner, M.D., co-author of *Birthing Rooms*. Many doctors recognize the problem that obstetrical training emphasizes high-risk care. Doctors get little or no training in normal obstetrics, and are, therefore, poorly prepared to handle normal labors, according to Dr. Marieskind in her cesarean evaluation study. Residents receive little or no training in normal birth, in monitoring the fetal heart rate by stethoscope, in vaginal breech deliveries, or in vaginal births after a cesarean, for example. By contrast, they receive extensive training in the use of technology in labor and delivery: in the use of electronic fetal monitoring, ultrasound, scalp sampling, anesthesia, forceps, and surgical deliveries. Obstetricians are more likely to perform cesareans when they are trained in the high-risk model of obstetrics.

In addition to the obstetrician's belief and training, there is a financial incentive behind the increasing cesarean rates. "A combination of economic factors can exert influence toward the more profitable, in this case surgical approach, while at the same time providing no incentive to persist with a vaginal delivery," says Dr. Marieskind. Some of those economic factors are:

- Obstetricians are paid more when they perform cesareans than when they deliver babies vaginally.
- The number of obstetricians has increased.
- The number of babies born each year has decreased.
- Each obstetrician handles fewer births.
- Obstetricians can better plan their time by doing a cesarean.
- Insurance coverage is sometimes better for cesareans than for vaginal deliveries.

In spite of fewer births per doctor, the income of ob/gyns has more than kept pace with inflation, making them one of the highest paid medical specialties. "It seems to me, that in order for those obstetricians to maintain that sort of livelihood, they are forced to resort to more expensive and elaborate technologies, of which, I think, cesarean section is one," says Arden Miller, M.D., a public health physician, interviewed by writer Gena Corea for *Mother Jones* magazine.

Waiting around in the hospital during a mother's labor is one of the biggest annoyances of the obstetrician, doctors tell us. "It's a waste of time, it fouls up your schedule, and you're not making any money," said one. Some get tired of waiting. Evidence of unnecessary cesareans for convenience comes from three different reports, the first from Susan Doering, Ph.D., a research scientist at Johns Hopkins University. Reasoning that if cesareans are true emergencies, they should be spaced randomly over a twenty-four-hour period and as many emergency cesareans will be done from seven P.M. to seven A.M. (at night) as are done from seven A.M. to seven P.M. (during the day). However, in her review of a small sample of emergency cesareans, Dr. Doering found that 80 percent were performed during the day, and 20 percent at night. She also reported on L. K. Gibbons', Ph.D., unpublished research which showed a significant time difference when cesareans were done on a number of first-time mothers, supposedly emergency situations. He found 58 percent of the women had cesareans between seven A.M. and seven P.M., but only 42 percent had cesareans at night. Similar results were found in a third study, a survey of five New York City hospitals by personnel with New York State's Division of Maternal and Child Health. In women having their first babies, 62 percent of cesarean deliveries took place during the working day (from seven A.M. to six P.M.). Only 38 percent of the emergency cesareans in first-time mothers were done between six P.M. and seven A.M.

While the above financial incentives to perform a cesarean are impressive, the NIH Task Force found that the evidence was not good enough to say that economic incentives are a *major* reason behind the increase in cesarean sections.

Cesarean Rates Differ According to the Doctor or Hospital

Cesarean rates vary according to hospital size and geographic location, but rates vary much more between hospitals. The size of a hospital is measured according to the total number of beds for patients. Hospitals with 500 or more beds have higher cesarean rates than hospitals with 100 or fewer beds. The northeastern part of the United States has higher cesarean rates than the Southwest or Central United States. The most dramatic differences, however, occur between hospitals in any one city or state. Rates of 12 percent to 32 percent were reported by the Baltimore

COMA Survey among the ten hospitals with the most deliveries covered in their report. Cesarean rates ranging from 2 percent in one hospital to a high of 22 percent were found around the state of New York in a state Department of Health study. That means whether you have a cesarean depends much more on the hospital you choose—and the doctors who practice there—than you.

Your choice of birth attendant also affects your risk of cesarean, regardless of how your labor goes. One reason for an increased cesarean rate is that more and more women choose obstetricians (who more readily use cesarean delivery for their patients) than family practitioners. Cesarean rates vary greatly among obstetricians themselves, however. Our M.O.M. Survey data showed that, among the eleven physicians in the survey (who delivered most of the babies), the cesarean rate ranged from 5 percent to 23 percent. A practice review carried out by the ACOG showed that the cesarean rate ranged from 19 percent to 54 percent according to the specialty of the obstetrician, with the ob/gyn whose specialty is gynecology having the highest rate of cesarean births. "If you go to a doctor who likes to do cesarean sections, you're going to get sectioned," said Andrew Fleck, M.D., director of the Maternal and Child Health Division of the New York State Health Department, interviewed by writer Gena Corea.

One way to avoid unnecessary cesareans is to find a hospital and birth attendant whose cesarean rates are low, 10 percent or less. This will not be easy, however, because a c-section rate of 15 percent or more is fast becoming the accepted standard for a hospital or doctor. "A cesarean section rate of 15 percent seems proper for now and for the immediate future," said Leon A. Carrow, M.D., writing for the American College of Surgeons in January 1982.

Hospital administrators and doctors become defensive when questioned about their cesarean rates, and some doctors do not keep track of them. High cesarean rates are always explained on the basis of a hospital or doctor having more women who are high-risk patients. Because we know that cesarean rates vary so much between doctors or hospitals who treat the same kinds of patients, we don't buy it. Some doctors simply don't keep track of their c-section rate. "If I thought I were doing any unnecessary ones, I might figure it out [my c-section rate]; but they've all been necessary," said one physician to us in acknowledging that he didn't know his c-section rate.

THE EPIDEMIC

An epidemic is an outbreak of anything that spreads or increases rapidly. Given that definition, there is certainly an epidemic of cesareans. In the decade before 1970, about 3 percent of all births were by cesarean. Doctors looked at a cesarean birth as a last resort, a life-saving measure for the woman or her baby. By 1970, the cesarean birth rate had climbed to 5.5 percent, very low when compared to today's rates. The rate increased just over 1 percent a year until by 1981, the U.S. Public Health Service reported that 17.9 percent of all births that year were cesarean deliveries.

Nearly one fifth of all births today are by cesarean delivery. There is little indication that cesarean birth will be less frequent in the future than it is now. Major medical centers in New York City now have cesarean rates nearing one in three births. The United States has the highest cesarean rate in the world, but there is also an international trend toward a much greater use of cesarean delivery.

A cesarean rate of 17.9 percent of all births is so high, health care providers now separate cesareans into two groups; those that are primary or first-time cesareans, and those that are repeat operations— operations for another birth after a previous cesarean. Almost one fourth of all cesareans are repeats, and three fourths are primary, or first-time cesareans. That means about 5 percent of all births today are repeat cesareans, and 14 percent of all births are first-time cesareans. Before 1970, when doctors were extremely cautious in doing a primary cesarean, repeat cesareans made up half or more of the total 3 percent cesarean rate for all births. That meant the primary cesarean rate then was a small 1.5 percent or less of all births. If you are having your first baby, or you have never had a cesarean and are having another baby, your chances of having a cesarean delivery today are more than nine times greater than before 1970. That's a startling change in the way babies are delivered. Authorities agree that this means there has been a fundamental and widespread change in medical practice.

The cesarean epidemic has not gone unnoticed by the popular press, by government watchdogs, or by doctors themselves. The media has been highly critical of the increased cesarean birth rates, documenting huge increases in cesareans with few benefits shown. Over a period of a year, under the direction of the National Institute of Health, a nineteen-member task force, two thirds of whom were physicians (one third were obstetricians), studied cesarean delivery. A complete printout of world literature relating to cesarean births was available to the task force. This literature, which altogether weighed more than ten pounds, as well as some unpublished studies were the major sources of information relied upon for a final, comprehensive, 537-page report titled *Cesarean Childbirth* published in late 1981. In their report, the authors said that cesarean delivery, once considered a failure in vaginal birth technique, has become another approach to try to improve fetal outcome. The increased safety for the mother makes that approach easier for the doctor to take. Because of their complete review, the task force authors believe there are no simple ways to improve fetal outcome, to reduce infant damage and death rates. They decided that it is extremely difficult, if not impossible, to know if the increased cesarean birth rate has resulted in better fetal outcome. There is no information now available that shows that cesareans result in "better babies."

Epidemic Worse for Women With First Births

We need to make a distinction between women laboring for the first time (called primiparas) and women who have already had babies (called multiparas).

William Cook, M.D., obstetrician and author, describes his view of the difference:

> The fact that a first childbirth is usually so different from subsequent births as to be almost unrelated is of such prime importance that it should be emphasized by every childbirth instructor and author (but isn't) . . . the effect of much childbirth education is to blur the distinction between the often long labor and difficult delivery of the first child and the shorter and easier labor and delivery of subsequent births.

Primiparas have more interventions and cesareans than multiparas. Some intervention differences reported in *Birthing Rooms* are:

Intervention	Primiparas	Multiparas
Moved from birthing room to delivery room	12%	3%
Forceps	30%	4%
Anesthesia or analgesia during labor	78%	43%

The cesarean delivery rate is much higher in primiparas than in multiparas who have never had a cesarean, according to a Massachusetts Department of Public Health study in 1981. The purpose of the study was to compare quality of care between HMO (Health Maintenance Organization) and fee-for-service doctors. The cesarean delivery rate for primiparas was 18.3 percent in the HMO and 21.4 percent for women having fee-for-service doctors. The primary cesarean rate for multiparas (repeat cesareans were excluded) was far lower, 7.3 percent for women with fee-for-service doctors, and a small 2.3 percent cesarean rate for multiparous women using an HMO. The risk of a primiparous woman having a cesarean is eight times (HMO) to three times (fee for service) greater than a multiparous woman.

Doctors have long recognized primiparas have a higher risk of cesarean delivery. With smaller families the rule now, primiparas make up a larger part of the childbearing population, from 34 percent to 42 percent in 1977 according to Dr. Marieskind. Doctors have pointed to the increase in the proportion of the childbearing population that are first-time mothers as an important reason for the cesarean epidemic. Marieskind's analysis of changes in the number of primiparous women in relation to multiparas leads her to say, "The changes, however, would not seem to be of such size as to justify, by themselves, the increase in cesarean sections." The risk of cesarean delivery has increased for everyone, but the risk is much greater than it used to be for a first-time mother.

Why the Epidemic?

A doctor is legally required to give a specific medical reason for performing a cesarean. "The fear of a malpractice suit," "a better baby," "first birth," or "I don't know how to do a vaginal breech birth," are not reasons obstetricians write on medical records. Not so long ago, when our teenagers were born, the most likely medical indications for cesarean delivery were different:

- Baby's head too large to pass through pelvis (severe cephalopelvic disproportion—CPD)
- Life-threatening maternal bleeding (hemorrhage), usually caused by the placenta detaching from the uterine wall before birth
- Placenta blocking the birth canal (placenta previa)
- Severe toxemia
- Severe Rh factor incompatibility, making a premature delivery necessary
- Repeat cesarean

These factors were the more likely reasons for cesareans performed before 1970. Then, the primary cesarean was viewed as an emergency life-saving event for mother or baby. However, most cesareans are done today for very different medical reasons. "The dilemma for the obstetrician is that she or he now feels pressed to operate when there is any *possible* indication of fetal distress that might remotely injure the infant—or at least uses that as a rationale," says Cynthia Cooke, M.D., Assistant Clinical Professor of Obstetrics and Gynecology at the University of Pennsylvania. Ninety percent of the increase in cesarean section rates in the 1970s was ascribed to the following four medical reasons:

- Abnormal labor
- Repeat cesarean birth (for a mother who had a previous cesarean birth)
- Cesarean section for breech position of the baby
- Fetal distress

Abnormal Labor

The most important reason for the increase in cesarean birth rates is due to the much more frequent diagnosis of "abnormal labor," a diagnosis that accounts for one third of the increase. *Dystocia* (pronounced dis-toe-sha) is the medical term for abnormal labor. Dystocia means that there is difficulty in the progress of the labor ("failure to progress"), for any of three reasons: weak contractions ("uterine inertia"); a poor position of the fetus; or an abnormal size pelvis that prevents the baby descending or passing through the mother's birth canal (cephalopelvic disproportion—CPD).

Drs. Banta and Thacker, in their report on fetal monitoring for the United States Department of Health, Education and Welfare, found that many hospital reports show a huge increase in the use of CPD as the reason for cesareans. Because researchers have found that true CPD occurs rarely (in approximately 2 percent of *first-time labors*) most of the time the label CPD is a catch-all term for any kind of abnormal labor. Richard Hausknecht, M.D., went even further in the NIH task force report, noting the "indiscriminate overuse of the wastebasket term, 'dystocia.' "

The task force reported that doctors are most likely to diagnose dystocia in labors where the infant, when born, weighs over five-and-one-half pounds—meaning the diagnosis is most likely in full-term deliveries where the infant is of normal birth weight. The task force found that when the diagnosis of dystocia or failure to progress is made, there is no survival advantage to the infant to have a cesarean delivery compared with a vaginal birth. In addition, the task force found no information available proving cesareans prevented brain damage when dystocia was diagnosed.

> There is no magic number of hours beyond which labor should not continue.
>
> —Emanual A. Friedman, M.D.,
> Developer of "Friedman curves"

Doctors use the "Friedman curves" to decide whether a labor is abnormal. E. A. Friedman, M.D., analyzed the progress of normal labor, averaged the time for many normal labors, and drew graphs to show normal and abnormal labor. He describes two stages of labor, latent and active. The latent phase is early labor, the period of time when the cervix becomes effaced (thinned out) but dilates slowly, up to about 3 to 4 centimeters. A normal latent phase, according to Friedman, can last up to twenty hours in a first-time mother, and up to fourteen hours in a woman who has already had a baby, but averages about nine hours. The active phase of labor (sometimes called "true labor"), when the cervix dilates faster and steadily, is from 4 centimeters to 10 centimeters of dilatation. The *average* time for the active phase is about four to six hours.

Birth attendants misuse the Friedman normal labor curves, according to Susan Doering, Ph.D. They equate slow progress with abnormal progress, because they assume any labor not matching the average on the graphs is abnormal. Birth attendants tend to forget that the graphs are based on averaging many labors of widely varying lengths. Most obstetricians view a normal labor (to full dilatation of the cervix) as lasting no more than a total of twelve to fourteen hours for early and active labor. Yet twelve to fourteen hours is the length of the *average* first labor, according to the Friedman curves. Many perfectly normal labors will last longer than that, some much longer.

Obstetricians have good reason for their concern about prolonged labor. Very prolonged labor is associated with increased perinatal mortality. That is, according to the research, in very long labors there is an increased risk that the infant will not survive. However, according to authors, Drs. Hellman and Pritchard, of *Williams Obstetrics*, the text-book used to train obstetricians, we don't know if the increased perinatal mortality is the result of the longer labor itself, or if it is because of complications from the interventions that the doctors use to speed up or end the labor.

Interventions can cause the very problems they were used to prevent. Friedman found that the use of analgesics or regional anesthesia (such as epidural, caudal, or spinal anesthesia) given before the mother has gone into active labor often results in a prolonged latent (early) phase of labor. Hellman and Pritchard warn that "one of the most common mistakes in obstetrics is to try to stimulate labor in patients who have not been in labor at all." They direct doctors to consider Pitocin only when the woman is in active labor, dilated to 3 or 4 centimeters or more.

Anesthesia can slow active labor also. Dr. Doering summarized the special problems of epidurals in causing abnormal labors. In her review of the literature she found "epidurals slow and weaken contractions considerably for at least a half hour after each dose. Since fresh doses are commonly given every 60 minutes, the result is often a drug-caused dysfunctional labor. This result is so widely recognized that many physicians routinely combine epidurals with oxytocin stimulation, hoping to counteract the effects of one drug with the other. Also epidurals often interfere with the flexion and descent of the baby's head during labor." The result of these complications can be a diagnosis of abnormal labor and the need for a cesarean.

The second stage of labor is the pushing stage, the time from full dilatation until the woman pushes her baby out. Most obstetricians allow one or at most two hours for the pushing stage, believing that longer than that is dangerous for the baby. The results of a 1976 study of the pushing stage of 4,403 first-time mothers by Wayne Cohn, M.D., of Harvard Medical School show there is "no adverse influence of a long second stage on perinatal or neonatal mortality in nulliparas [first-time mothers]." The author concluded, "It would thus appear that the elective termination of labor simply because an arbitrary period of time has elapsed in the second stage is clearly not warranted."

What to Do for "Abnormal Labor"

Especially if this is your first baby, you should consider staying home from the hospital as long as possible. Stay home until *you are sure* you are in active labor and you feel you don't want to stay home any longer.

"What is wrong with a woman waiting until it is time for her to deliver, coming into the hospital, staying two to eight hours and taking her baby home?" said Paul Wexler, M.D., chairman of the department of obstetrics and gynecology of Rose Medical Center, Denver.

Hospital staff tend to measure the length of your labor from the time you arrive at the hospital. Because first labors tend to be longer and often harder for the mother to handle (she's never experienced this before and her cervix is opening for the first time), staff distress goes up. You are likely to avoid many problems, such as diagnosis of abnormal labor, if you go to the hospital when you feel certain your labor is very well established.

The NIH task force noted that "failure to progress is frequently classified as dysfunctional labor and placed in the category of dystocia, when it may, in fact, be false labor or prodromal labor or otherwise not abnormal." False labor is the "practice" contractions of the last few weeks (for many first-time mothers) or the last few months (for many subsequent pregnancies). Prodromal labor is very early labor or, some would say, the contractions that signal labor may come soon (hours or a few days away).

- If you are not in true labor (4 centimeters or more), you just may need to go home and wait for the real thing.
- Your long labor may be perfectly normal for you.
- Basing normal labors on a graph means the slow labors will be defined as abnormal.

If you are in active labor, 4 centimeters or more, and have been diagnosed as failing to progress, the NIH task force recommends (in the absence of fetal distress) the following alternatives to cesarean section:

- Walking in labor
- Letting the patient rest—sleep if she needs it
- Emotional support
- Sedation
- Oxytocin stimulation
- Hydration—fluids by IV or mouth

The sedation and oxytocin stimulation are drug possibilities you may wish to try last. Diony Young of the International Childbirth Education Association recommends trying the following nonmedical alternatives:

- *Ask for more time.*
- Try position changes. If you're lying in a semisitting position, try lying on your side for a while, then try sitting upright with your legs crossed—maybe what you need is *variety.*

- Walking.
- A warm shower or bath.
- Loving encouragement (tell your helpers you need their encouragement in words and touch).
- Change in environment (ask if you can leave the hospital for a walk in the park—or at least try the early labor lounge or lobby).
- Privacy with one's partner (shoo everyone else out, leave a guard at the door, and you and your mate can cuddle, kiss, massage, or whatever you need—maybe talk!).
- Breast and nipple stimulation. Remember, breast and nipple stimulation can make the uterus contract and can work for those women who have enjoyed it as part of lovemaking and either are uninhibited in a hospital setting or can arrange for the privacy they need.
- Removal of persons who cause stress (be honest).

To avoid failure to progress in the second stage of labor, use one of the efficient delivery positions discussed in Chapter 7. If you have no choice but to use the delivery table, you can help your second stage in several ways, most of which need to be agreed on ahead of time.

- Have the delivery table tilted down at a slight angle; you won't feel you are pushing uphill as much.
- Avoid stirrups. They can quickly be swung into place if needed. Your legs should be relaxed and spread apart so you are comfortable. (This position allows you to relax your perineum, so your pushes are more effective. It also protects your perineum from tears and episiotomy, because there is no tension holding back the birth.)
- If you must use stirrups, have the nurse adjust them for you in an upright, supported sitting position, so you are not forced to lie back because the stirrups are fixed for that position.
- With each pushing contraction, have your helpers lift you to an upright position, round your back, hold onto your knees, but don't pull on them (causes perineum tension), relax your perineum, and push, using your abdominal muscles.
- Have a stack of pillows behind your head and shoulders so you can relax between contractions without lying flat.

Repeat Cesarean Births

"Once a cesarean, always a cesarean," has been a strong belief in American obstetrical care since the early 1900s. The practice of requiring repeat cesareans was started to avoid the risk of uterine rupture at the scar site, a life-threatening situation.

Even today, any uterine scar may rupture (a more serious, sudden bursting of the scar) or separate before or during labor. However, a change in the kind of incision done in cesareans has resulted in a greatly reduced possibility of separation or rupture, and a greatly reduced threat to the lives of the mother and baby. The "classical" cesarean operation was performed through a long vertical incision from the navel to the pubic hair, and then a similar vertical incision in the uterus. However, today's preferred method for cesarean delivery is a low horizontal incision in the uterus, after first cutting a similar low skin incision. Over 90 percent of cesarean deliveries are now done this way. The skin incision is called a "bikini cut," implying that it won't be visible when you wear next summer's bikini. This widely accepted, newer technique has greatly reduced the risk of separation or rupture of the uterus in subsequent pregnancies or labors—to less than one percent.

More than 90 percent of the problems consist of a partial separation of the old scar with no dangerous results to mother or baby. A rupture of a low horizontal cesarean scar is exceedingly rare and less serious than a rupture of a classical uterine scar. In their extensive review, the NIH task force found not one maternal death connected to a rupture of a low horizontal cesarean scar. The danger to the fetus is almost nonexistent. Discussing the safety of a vaginal birth after a previous cesarean, Harold Schulman, M.D., of Albert Einstein College of Medicine reports, "At least in the past thirty years, you will find no maternal and only one fetal death from a rupture during labor of a previous transverse incision."

Most countries do not have a policy of repeat cesareans. Trials of labor and successful vaginal deliveries following cesarean are common. However, 98 percent of American women who have a cesarean and become pregnant again have repeat cesareans. Yet, largely due to doctors willing to challenge the status quo and women willing to question their doctors, vaginal deliveries after cesarean are being tried in some places in the United States today. Twenty-five studies conducted between 1950 and 1980 in different medical centers showed that many repeat cesareans are unnecessary. These studies documented 28,000 successful vaginal deliveries after previous cesareans.

One such study, reported in 1980 by C. E. Gibbs, M.D., covers a period of nine years at the University of Texas Health Science Center and included 1,200 women allowed to labor after a previous cesarean delivery. The women given a trial of labor had one previous cesarean with a low horizontal uterine incision and no indications for a cesarean in the present pregnancy. Two thirds of these women successfully delivered vaginally. There were six scar separations or ruptures during labor, all of which were repaired at the time of a cesarean or by abdominal surgery following a vaginal delivery. No infants were lost in those labors where there was a separation or rupture. Maternal death in the nearly 1,200 trial of labor patients was zero.

Because of the increasing numbers of reports of successful vaginal delivery following a previous cesarean, many more obstetricians now believe that a vaginal delivery after a previous cesarean is as safe for newborns as is a repeat cesarean, and that it is even safer for the mothers. Cesareans have a higher risk of maternal death, and a much higher risk of complications in the mother than vaginal deliveries. The NIH task force referred to studies reporting that the risk of maternal death is at least two times greater in a repeat cesarean than in vaginal deliveries of all kinds. The NIH task force recommended that "in hospitals with appropriate facilities, services, and staff for prompt emergency cesarean birth, a proper selection of cases should permit a safe trial of labor and vaginal delivery for women who have had a previous low segment transverse cesarean birth." In 1982, the ACOG, the professional organization of obstetricians, reversed its seventy-five-year policy on repeat cesareans and announced encouragement for a vaginal delivery after a cesarean.

Breech Presentation

About 10 to 15 percent of the increase in cesarean delivery rates is due to the decision to deliver many breech presentations by cesarean. Most babies are born head first. In a breech birth the baby's bottom comes first, called a frank breech presentation, or rarely, the baby's feet come first, called a footling breech presentation. Breech presentation happens in 3 to 4 percent of deliveries. The labor lasts no longer than the average head-first presentation. Breech position is nine times more common earlier in pregnancy than at term, which means that most breech babies naturally rotate to a head-down position before the end of pregnancy.

Perinatal mortality and complication rates are higher in breech presentations than in head-first presentations. There are often other problems, such as prematurity and placenta previa along with the breech presentation. However, even when problems such as these are not present at breech deliveries, the outcome for the baby in a breech presentation may not always be as good as for head-first presentation. Because of this, there has been a shift to cesarean delivery of most breech births. Some obstetricians will not deliver any breech presentations vaginally (and some of them have not had any training in vaginal breech deliveries either).

The trend toward cesarean delivery of breech presentation is a major area of controversy among obstetricians, however. The reason for the controversy is that cesarean birth increased from 12 percent of all breech presentations in 1970 to 60 percent in 1978. In spite of the greatly increased use of cesarean delivery, there is no evidence of a better outcome for the baby: there was no overall decrease in mortality for breech presentations during that period, and no evidence of a neurological difference ("better babies").

More and more studies report successful vaginal deliveries with breech presentations. Several older, experienced obs told us, "So, what's new? I've always delivered most breech babies vaginally." The consensus of the NIH task force was a recommendation for vaginal delivery of a frank breech presentation of a term pregnancy by a physician experienced in vaginal breech delivery. Ultimately, the best solution may be to get the breech baby in a head-first position. "External version" is a term used to describe gentle manipulation by the doctor of the mother's abdomen late in pregnancy to turn the baby from a breech to a head-first position.

In 1981 a randomized prospective study of external version was done at Women's Hospital in Los Angeles. "Where no version was attempted the cesarean rate for breech presentation was 74 percent; where version was attempted, the vaginal delivery rate was 72 percent," said Martin Gimovsky, M.D., reporting in *Contemporary Ob/Gyn*. About 20 percent of the control group spontaneously converted from breech to vertex (head down) position during the study. Increasingly successful efforts in external version mean "we may be able to reduce the incidence of breech delivery to approximately 1 percent to 1.5 percent," according to Edward Quilligan, M.D., a Los Angeles obstetrician with the University of Southern California School of Medicine.

A simple and successful exercise to turn the baby to a head-first position is called the tilt position, originated by Juliet De Sa Souza, M.D., retired professor of obstetrics and gynecology at Grant Medical

College, Bombay, India. If, by the beginning of the eighth month of pregnancy, the baby is still in a breech position, the mother lies in the tilt position for ten minutes, twice a day. With an empty stomach, lying on her back on the floor, with her knees bent, so her feet are flat on the floor, the mother puts three good-sized pillows under her bottom. Dr. De Sa Souza reported in 1977 that 89 percent of 744 babies in breech presentations turned to a head-first position with this exercise, most within two to three weeks. Once the baby has turned from a breech to a head-down position, discontinue the tilt exercise.

The pelvic rock exercise has also been effective for turning a breech for some mothers. Use it daily, as well as the tilt position. (The pelvic rock is a good exercise for *all* pregnant women—it's great for strengthening your back and relieving the common backache of late pregnancy.) To do the pelvic rock: On your hands and knees, keeping other muscles relaxed, tighten your buttocks muscles; your lower spine will tilt forward. Release. Do as many pelvic rocks as you can. Work up to eighty a day.

Fetal Distress

The diagnosis of fetal distress accounts for 10 to 15 percent of the increase in the c-section rate. Fetal distress is most often defined by variations in the fetal heart rate which are considered abnormal. An abnormal fetal heart rate may mean the baby is getting too little oxygen, which can lead to brain damage. Birth is a normal stress on the fetus that naturally causes its heart to beat faster. The difficulty is in telling whether the fetus is simply normally stressed or is in distress. The NIH task force found no evidence that there is more fetal distress than there used to be, yet the diagnosis of fetal distress is made more often. It is probably being overdiagnosed. The reasons for the overdiagnosis of fetal distress lie in the general high-technology approach to childbirth and an increased concern for fetal outcome, both of which raise the distress level of *the birth attendant*.

One intervention of the high-technology approach that has been definitely associated with an increase in the diagnosis of fetal distress is the electronic fetal monitor (EFM). This may be because the abnormal readings of the fetal monitor are difficult to evaluate. An abnormal reading when the baby is not in distress is called a "false positive." The fetal monitor, then, can show distress when there isn't any.

Albert Haverkamp, M.D., an obstetrician and researcher at the University of Colorado Health Sciences Center, started studying the results of electronic fetal monitoring with the belief that the use of electronic fetal monitors contributed to better fetal outcome. In several randomized control trials, he did not find this to be so. He studied high-risk mothers, the very group for whom electronic fetal monitoring was believed to give the best evaluation. There was no difference in outcome for the baby between mothers who were electronically monitored and mothers who had a nurse listen to the baby's heart rate with a stethoscope. The difference was in the rate of cesareans. The electronically monitored women had almost three times as many cesareans as the women who had nurses monitoring the baby's heart rate. A full 17.6 percent of the EFM group had cesareans versus 5.6 percent of the nurse-monitored group. "I feel that fetal monitoring gives the doctor and nurse information. More information doesn't necessarily give a better outcome," said Dr. Haverkamp, testifying before a 1978 U.S. Senate Health Subcommittee. "It seems that in the ob patient, the more information you receive the more anxious you become about its significance and the more aggressive. . . . Every piece of information that looks irregular . . . is like a red flag to a conscientious physician to get in there and do something. C-sections are done by conscientious people who are nervous, not knife-happy."

In their comprehensive review of the literature, the NIH task force summarized the most common suggestions for reversing fetal distress without resorting to surgery:

- Give the mother oxygen.
- Change the mother's position.
- Give intravenous fluids (hydration).
- Turn oxytocin off if it is being used.

A simple means of preventing the overdiagnosis of fetal distress is to use a nurse to regularly monitor the baby's heart rate. In addition, the widespread use of oxytocin needs careful evaluation. Pitocin can intensify natural contractions, reducing the oxygen supply to the baby and triggering fetal distress. Because this is so well known, women receiving Pitocin are usually placed in the high-risk category. So another way to prevent a diagnosis of fetal distress would be to avoid the use of Pitocin in the first place. Try other means of stimulating labor, such as having the mother walk.

Other Reasons for the Increase

The remaining 10 percent of the increase is due to a wide variety of reasons: increased "elective" (by choice or option, not emergency) cesareans for mothers at high risk (for example, for some mothers with serious kidney disease), or increased elective cesareans for babies at high risk (for example, multiple births—twins, triplets—or cesareans when *active* genital herpes in the mother is identified). Many of these reasons are widely accepted as necessary, but others have no evidence of better outcome. For example, twins may be delivered by cesarean, or the first is delivered vaginally and the second by cesarean, with no evidence of better outcome for the babies. Cesarean for premature rupture of membranes is another reason for a small percentage of the increased cesarean rate.

Premature Rupture of Membranes

PROM, as it's called, does not refer to the old high school dance. The letters stand for premature rupture of membranes, meaning that the mother's bag of waters has broken before labor begins. The rupture is considered prolonged if it happens several hours or more before labor starts. It is one of the most common complications in pregnancy and can result in a c-section, often unnecessarily. A vaginal delivery after PROM is possible, but that depends on *your* doctor's point of view.

There is strong controversy among obstetricians over what to do about premature rupture of the membranes. Some argue for immediate delivery to reduce the risk of infection in the mother and the baby. Others say that because premature rupture of membranes is often associated with a pregnancy not yet at term, that is with prematurity, nothing should be done. These two approaches are termed "aggressive" and "conservative." The aggressive approach means delivery within twenty-four to forty-eight hours of ruptured membranes by induction or cesarean if necessary. The conservative approach means waiting with close attention for either spontaneous labor or signs of infection. Several studies now show that the conservative approach results in less respiratory distress syndrome in newborns. The longer a baby is allowed to mature inside the uterus the less likely he is to have distressed breathing at birth. His lungs are more ready to breathe.

More and more, obstetricians are coming around to believe that it is better for the baby to take the conservative approach with PROM, if delivery is going to mean a premature baby. Most, however, still believe that if premature rupture of membranes happens in a *term* pregnancy, and spontaneous labor does not begin within a few hours, they must induce labor or do a cesarean to make sure the baby is born within twenty-four hours.

Strong support for using the conservative approach whenever premature rupture of the membranes happens, whether at term or not, comes from a 1979 study by Kenneth A. Kappy, M.D., et al. of Tufts University School of Medicine and St. Margaret's Hospital for Women, Boston. Over a two-year period, a conservative approach was used for 188 patients with premature rupture of the membranes; 78 of the women were at the end of their pregnancy.

Most of the women who were not yet at term with PROM went *more* than twenty-four hours before labor started. Nearly 20 percent continued their pregnancies more than seven days before labor began, and the longest period of time between premature rupture of membranes and labor was 58 days.

Most of the women whose pregnancy was at term with PROM went into labor *before* twenty-four hours. However, several women had their pregnancies continue up to a week or more before labor began; in one case, for fourteen days. Infection rates (the fear of doctors when they diagnose PROM) were very low in comparison to other studies. A critical difference in this study was that *no* internal exams were done, that is, no birth attendants put gloved fingers in the women's vaginas to examine the cervix. One of the reasons for higher rates of infection associated with PROM is probably that infection is introduced at the time of an internal examination after the membranes have ruptured. The key reason doctors give for the aggressive approach—infection—is often the iatrogenic (doctor-caused) result of internal examinations.

Another highly significant finding of the Kappy et al. study was that waiting for spontaneous labor in mothers with PROM at term meant fewer cesareans. Among the mothers with PROM at term, some were immediately induced. Half of these had cesareans for failure to progress. Among the mothers with PROM at term who were allowed to go into spontaneous labor, some days later, a far lower number of women had cesareans for lack of progress of labor, one in seven compared to one in two of the women who were induced.

The uterus continues to manufacture amniotic fluid and sometimes the tear in the membranes seals over. The study by Kappy et al. shows that it is safe to allow a pregnancy to go on for days or weeks after premature rupture of membranes, whether the woman is at the end of her pregnancy or not. If it happens to you, talk to your doctor about this study. Most of the following common sense measures suggest how to avoid getting an infection:

- Allow *no* internal examinations.
- Avoid intercourse.
- Avoid sitting in water, take showers instead.
- Stay home until labor starts, rather than go to the hospital.
- Avoid contacts outside the family (alien germs).
- Watch for signs of infection, such as an elevated temperature and pain or tenderness in the abdomen.
- Keep in touch with your doctor.
- Wait for spontaneous labor to begin.
- If you have active genital herpes and PROM, you will need a cesarean within six hours to avoid the possibility of infecting your baby.

Cesarean Delivery for Active Genital Herpes in the Mother

Genital herpes is a viral, venereal disease that doctors are not required to report to health departments. Numbers are only estimates. The Center for Disease Control in Atlanta estimates that 20 million men and women have genital herpes, with as many as 500,000 new cases expected each year. Genital herpes is an incurable disease that becomes latent (without symptoms) but can reappear in the infected man or woman. Usually, the first infection, called primary genital herpes, is the most uncomfortable and lasts about three weeks. Recurrences are usually milder and last nine or ten days.

Genital herpes is a serious disease for the baby of a woman who may have a primary infection or recurrence of it at the time of delivery. When the woman is known to have herpes at delivery, the chance of her infant contracting it in a vaginal delivery is nearly 40 percent. The risk of death or chance of the infant becoming abnormal as a result of contracting the disease is very high.

An automatic cesarean for every woman with herpes is *not* necessary. "Thousands of babies are born every day to women with genital herpes," said Lawrence Corey, M.D., of the University of Washington School of Medicine, Seattle. "Vaginal deliveries are usually possible, and the babies are perfectly normal." Reviewing the research, Dr. Corey says that "Only women who are shedding virus at term transmit virus to their infants. Just because a woman has genital herpes does not mean that she has to have a cesarean section. . . . However, even abdominal delivery is not foolproof. Neonatal herpes infections have occurred after abdominal delivery."

According to Dr. Corey, most authorities agree on the following program for women with a history of genital herpes in them or their mates:

- Vaginal and cervical cultures should be started between thirty to thirty-six weeks of pregnancy.
- When labor begins, the doctor should do a careful examination for active genital herpes.
- During early labor a Pap smear (a scrape of tissue examined under a microscope) can be done. The test is only about 50 percent accurate (even if the smear shows no herpes virus cells, they may still be present), but it can be done quickly.

"For women with no lesions, no evidence of viral shedding [from the cultures], and a negative Papanicolaou smear, we usually deliver the infants vaginally," said Dr. Corey.

Another report, in 1981, of the successful use of cultures to determine whether a woman with a history of genital herpes should have a vaginal or cesarean delivery comes from Frank Boehm, M.D., et al. of Vanderbilt University Medical Center. Over a five-year period, 120 pregnant women in the Nashville area who had a possible history of genital herpes were cultured. Three fourths had negative cultures throughout their pregnancy. Of the forty women with positive cultures, twenty-four had time to repeat cultures before delivery and eighteen of the twenty-four women then had cultures that were negative. Women with negative cultures were delivered vaginally unless there was evidence of a possible genital herpes lesion when the women came to the hospital in labor. Women with positive cultures were delivered by cesarean. The authors concluded that by using cultures for women with a history of genital herpes, the rate of cesarean section and infection of the baby with herpes can be kept to a minimum. Most women with a history of genital herpes will have negative cultures throughout pregnancy, and active genital herpes will be uncommon toward the end of pregnancy.

A special risk to the infant of a woman with a history of herpes in her or her mate is the use of the internal fetal monitor. Edward M. Kaye, M.D., and Elizabeth C. Dooling, M.D., of Boston City Hospital reported in 1981 on neonatal herpes associated with fetal scalp electrodes. In the cases reported, the mothers had no signs of active herpes, but their babies contracted herpes at the site of the insertion of the electrode.

Because of this reported risk, a woman with a history of or suspicion of past genital herpes in her or her mate should strongly consider refusing the use of an internal electronic fetal monitor. "We have shown that neonatal herpes simplex virus must be considered an added risk of fetal monitoring," say the authors, who question the use of internal fetal monitoring in low-risk pregnancies because of this added danger.

CESAREAN SURGERY

"A cesarean section has become less a matter of last resort and truly simply another method of delivery," said Basil Maloney, M.D., discussing breech delivery at a West Coast ob/gyn meeting in 1979. What most physicians don't know, and might even be shocked to discover, is that most women don't take cesareans quite as casually as they do. The aftereffects and recovery from a cesarean birth, for some women, are about as close to hell as they choose to get. For others, it can be less dramatic, but still traumatic.

The surgery itself, however, *is* an easy, quick, and usually safe procedure. Because cutting into the abdominal wall is involved, all cesareans are major surgery. In preparation for surgery, a catheter is put into a woman's bladder, the abdomen and perineum are shaved, and an IV is inserted in the back of her hand. The IV and catheter remain in place for about twenty-four hours after the surgery. Regional anesthesia (a spinal or epidural), which allows the mother to be awake but without feeling below her waist, is administered. In an emergency situation, a general anesthesia (gas) can be used. The advantage to gas is that it takes effect immediately, in preference to the fifteen to twenty minutes taken by regional anesthesia. A drape is placed at about chest level, to keep the woman from observing the surgery. Then the abdomen is sterilized with a cold anesthetic solution.

The first incision is made in the abdomen, usually a four- to six-inch "bikini cut" just above the pubic hair line. The bladder is separated from the uterus and pushed down out of the way before another horizontal incision is made in the lowest part of the uterus. The baby is lifted out of the uterus within ten minutes from the beginning of surgery. The afterbirth is removed, the uterus is sutured, the bladder is stitched back into place and the abdominal incision is closed. The total surgery takes about an hour, with most of the time spent in sewing up the incisions.

How Safe Is "Safe"?

Well, why not have a cesarean? With the cesarean section rate so high, your chances of having one are pretty good, one in five in fact. Why fight the system? It's an easy, simple, safe operation for the doctor to perform, and if he says, "I think you need a cesarean," isn't it easier to just go along? Yes, it is. And if you do have a cesarean, the chances are overwhelming that you will survive, and so will your baby.

Cesarean Risks to Baby

Although cesareans are safe today, they are certainly not as safe as vaginal deliveries, much of the time, either for the mother or the baby. A baby is always considered at high risk for complications when born by cesarean section. Madeleine Shearer, editor of *Birth*, reviewed the literature and summarized the four most frequent complications of cesarean to the infant, in order of their frequency:

- Jaundice
- Fewer quiet alert periods after birth
- Iatrogenic (doctor-caused) respiratory distress
- Drug effects

Jaundice

Jaundice is an overdiagnosed, overtreated problem in more than half of all newborns and is a recognized risk of cesarean delivery. Why is not known. Newborn jaundice sometimes requires treatment of the infant under bilirubin lights. Having a blindfold placed over his or her eyes for nearly twenty-four hours a day for several days can be uncomfortable, frustrating, and perhaps even terrifying for the infant. Certainly, the treatment interferes with early contact between mother and her baby.

Fewer Quiet Alert Periods

Infants born by cesarean section have fewer quiet alert periods after birth, the time when the infant is most likely to respond to its mother. Mothers and babies need all the help they can get in the early time they are getting acquainted with each other. A cesarean-born baby has fewer of these ideal times, when he is neither sleeping nor crying, but awake and taking in his surroundings—most importantly, his mother. All cesareans require anesthesia in the mother, which may be the reason for this complication in the baby.

Respiratory Distress

Breathing difficulty or respiratory distress is the most feared of the frequent complications of a cesarean baby. "Babies delivered by cesarean section are at a considerable disadvantage during the first few days of life," concluded British medical researcher John E. H. Brice and Colin H. M. Walker, studying respiratory distress in a special-care baby unit at Ninewells Hospital, Dundee. Dr. Haverkamp explains why: "A baby delivered vaginally is squeezed by the uterus in labor and by the vagina during birth and has fluids in its lungs pushed out. But in a cesarean section some of these fluids may remain in the lungs and the baby may not be able to breathe well for a few hours, or even a few days."

Breathing distress may be temporary or may be the much more serious respiratory distress syndrome. This disease varies from mild to severe, often requires mechanical assistance for the baby to breathe, and is due to the lungs being too immature to work properly.

"The respiratory distress syndrome (RDS) associated with premature delivery remains the greatest single cause of perinatal morbidity and death in the United States today," said R. L. Goldenberg, M.D., et al., in 1975, studying how doctors can cause RDS. The authors observed that a major factor in RDS was a misjudgment of gestational age of the fetus and a too-early termination of the pregnancy by induction or cesarean. "The ill-advised timing [by doctors] of cesarean sections is threatening to become the leading cause of respiratory distress syndrome, or hyaline membrane disease in infants," said Lewis Gluck, M.D., of the University of California Medical Center in San Diego. In other words, doctors are misjudging or ignoring how far along the pregnancy is. However, M. Douglas Jones, Jr., M.D., et al. found in a 1975 study of the records of 16,485 births at University Hospital, Denver, that cesarean delivery itself carries a risk of RDS. At all gestational ages more babies had RDS when delivered by cesarean than vaginally.

Drug Effects

Drug effects on the cesarean infant can be noticeable and are the fourth most common complication. The infant may appear to be drugged, or slowed down, because of drugs or anesthesia given the mother during labor and delivery. The baby may also have an elevated blood pressure from drugs given to the mother to correct her *low* blood pressure as a complication of the anesthesia.

Additional Complications

In addition to these four common complications the medical literature shows babies born from *planned repeat* cesareans (cesareans done before labor begins) are at risk from two additional complications. They are more likely than babies born vaginally to have abnormal neurological responses, and more likely to have these abnormal neurological responses still present when the babies are a year old. Planned repeat cesareans may mean a low-birth-weight baby. A low-birth-weight baby most often results from the doctor misjudging the fetus's maturity and operating before the baby is ready to be born. The same misjudgment of maturity would seem to be a factor in abnormal neurological responses in some planned repeat cesarean babies; this is a rare complication in repeat cesareans performed after labor starts.

Long-Term Effects

Long-term effects on the baby are more difficult to judge. Because a woman has to have anesthesia and at heavier doses than in a vaginal delivery, a cesarean baby may be more likely to have long-term effects on its motor development and intellectual ability. If the cesarean is scheduled before labor begins the baby will experience no labor. "There is good evidence that even a little labor is good for the baby," says Murray Enkin, M.D., Associate Professor of Obstetrics and Gynecology at McMaster University Medical School. Two writers go even further to suggest that labor and a vaginal delivery are best for the long-term development of the baby. Babies born by cesarean miss the vital skin stimulation of labor and a vaginal delivery that is the human substitute for other animals licking their newborns, said anthropologist Ashley Montagu, Ph.D. (*Touching*) and psychologist Arthur Janov, Ph.D. (*The Feeling Child*). Dr. Montagu suggests that labor conditions are essential for the baby's gastrointestinal, genitourinary and respiratory systems to work best. Dr. Janov suggests that the lack of physical stimulation results in cesarean babies being more fearful and restless. Yet, despite these two reports, many doctors say they observe no differences between cesarean and vaginally born babies. Perhaps cesarean mothers have made up for the lack by naturally cuddling, stroking and touching their babies in the course of normal mother-infant contact. We hope so.

Cesarean Risks for Mother

There is no medical question that a vaginal delivery is safer for the mother almost all the time. Regional anesthesia, availability of blood transfusions, a horizontal uterine incision, and antibiotics have made cesareans safer for mothers than ever before. Yet, the maternal death rate after a cesarean is *still* higher than it is for a vaginal delivery. There is some controversy about how great the difference is. Maternal mortality for vaginal deliveries is generally placed at about one death for every 10,000 live births. During the seventies, when cesarean births became common, obstetricians knew the maternal mortality rate for cesareans was higher than for vaginal births, but they were told in their journals that it was only about four times higher, or about 4 maternal deaths for every 10,000 live cesarean births.

Later studies show that the maternal death rate after cesareans is much higher than originally believed. Women who deliver babies by cesarean section face a risk of death twenty-six times greater than those who deliver vaginally, according to John R. Evrand, M.D., and Edwin M. Gold, M.D., Brown University researchers reporting in 1977. Their study, covering an eleven-year period in Rhode Island, reported a much lower maternal death rate following vaginal deliveries than is commonly accepted, (.27 per 10,000 rather than one per 10,000 deliveries) and a higher cesarean death rate than reported before (7 per 10,000).

Other information showing more maternal deaths from cesarean delivery than formerly believed comes from a 1981 study done by George Rubin, M.D., et al. of the Center for Disease Control, Atlanta. They found maternal mortalities actually higher than reported. If a cesarean mother dies after she leaves the hospital (from a pulmonary embolism, for example) her death is not likely to be recorded as a "maternal mortality." Comparing death certificates of women with birth certificates of babies born up to sixty days before a woman's death, the authors found a maternal death rate of 9.7 per 100,000 live births (or the typical 1 per 10,000) for vaginal deliveries, but a rate of 105 maternal deaths per 100,000 live cesarean deliveries (or slightly more than 10 per 10,000). The cesarean mothers were more than ten times likely to die than the mothers who gave birth vaginally. The authors consider these mortality figures low because they limited their search to sixty days before the women's deaths and they excluded maternal deaths associated with stillbirth.

In both these studies, half of the maternal deaths after a cesarean were directly caused by the operation, from pulmonary embolism (a blood clot migrating from the surgical incision to the lungs) or from complications of the anesthesia. About the same time other researchers were also finding that half of the maternal deaths associated with cesarean section are directly caused by the operation itself. Death from pulmonary embolism and complications of anesthesia are "an inevitable risk of any pelvic operative procedure," say authors Iain Chalmers and Martin Richards, writing in *Benefits and Hazards of the New Obstetrics.* In a study of cesarean section deaths in England and Wales, these authors found that half the maternal deaths following a cesarean section were caused by these two complications. "Earlier studies have underestimated the risks of cesarean sections," concludes Rubin. "Physicians should carefully assess the risks whenever they are considering performing cesarean sections."

The true cesarean maternal death rate, or the odds of a mother dying after a cesarean delivery, are about one per thousand. Certainly this relatively high rate, compared to vaginal delivery, should be a strong reason for caution when the question of cesarean comes up.

Other reasons for caution are the complications, the physical problems, that cesarean mothers have: severe pain from the operation itself, pain from the intestinal gas resulting from shock to the intestines, and possible future cesareans. Hospital stays are longer, costs are much higher, and the physical recovery from the surgery and birth takes much longer than the recovery from a vaginal birth. The woman who has a cesarean may also find she no longer has maternity insurance coverage for her next birth. Industry-wide, the usual policy is to terminate maternity coverage after a cesarean delivery for a woman with an individualized insurance policy or a group policy that has a small number of employees (ten or less).

Almost half of cesarean mothers have serious complications from the surgery, some complications more easily treated than others. The three most frequent of the serious complications are infection, hemorrhage, and internal problems from scarring or injury to other organs, according to editor Madeleine Shearer's review of the literature. Women who are internally monitored during labor, and then have a cesarean, have uterine infection rates ranging from 35 percent to 65 percent. When the mothers are not internally monitored, the uterine infection rates are still a high 20 percent to 40 percent in cesarean mothers. That compares to a low 1.4 percent rate of uterine infections following vaginal deliveries. The cesarean mother is at greater risk than the vaginal mother of developing other infections too, for example, in her bladder and in her abdomen.

Need for Caution

If you are advised to have a cesarean you must be ready to ask, "Is this really necessary?" It's probable that this crucial question must be asked by your husband or your doula to protect you, because you are likely to have been laboring for hours, to be tiring, to be vulnerable and open to any suggestions around you.

Most doctors will not like your questioning their decision. Because there is no evidence that cesareans improve infant outcome when the diagnosis of abnormal labor is made, you and your doctor will have to re-learn toleration of a long labor. You may have to remind your doctor to try other measures to reverse fetal distress, such as those recommended by the NIH task force. Knowing that a vaginal birth is possible in place of a repeat cesarean or for a breech presentation, you have to doctor-shop during your pregnancy to get what you want. Finding Dr. Right is still your best bet for a vaginal birth.

The Emotional Pain of a Cesarean

Almost all cesarean mothers survive the surgery, and their wounds eventually heal. However, the emotional pain can be much harder to heal, and this is an area physicians pay little, if any, attention to. Whatever the reason for the cesarean, it tends to promote a poor self-image for the newly delivered mother: "My body screwed up," is the common complaint. If a woman has had a vaginal birth before this cesarean delivery, the feelings about herself may not be as poor. But most women need to try to understand what happened, why *they* couldn't give birth vaginally. Yet many women complain that their doctors leave them with little or no lasting understanding of all the medical concerns leading up to the cesarean.

Another emotional problem can occur with maternal-infant attachment, which may be difficult because of the inevitable separation during the first hours or day following delivery, when the mother is in so much pain. Some mothers who have been given a regional anesthesia for the surgery and no drugs to knock them out have found they can take advantage of the first hour in the recovery room before the anesthesia wears off. They are not yet feeling the pain of the incision and can respond to their babies. But maternal-infant attachment can be affected by the surgery. "We are finding that mothers are upset with their babies because they had to have surgery," said nurse Debbie Pile, interviewed for a television documentary on cesareans in 1981. Nurse Pile says the mothers feel toward the baby that "it's your fault I had to have the cesarean. I was relaxing and breathing and it was you who developed fetal distress."

All new mothers are vulnerable and need loving care from those around them so that they can learn to love their babies. Cesarean mothers need more loving nurturing and for a longer period of time after birth. Many decide they just won't go through it again and make sure of that by having themselves sterilized. Postpartum sterilization is far more common for cesarean mothers at all ages, according to the U.S. Public Health Service.

The physical pain and emotional trauma of the cesarean experience has been much overlooked by doctors. Our next chapter gives one mother's story.

9 · HAVING A CESAREAN IS HAVING A BABY

Sandy's Story of Two Cesarean Births

With my first baby, I was in labor for nineteen hours before my doctor decided a cesarean was indicated. I was very, very upset, and my husband was very frightened. All the rules of the game had been changed on me. I had totally lost control. I had never had surgery, and I was angry and frightened at the thought of it. The abruptness of it all shocked me, and then, of course, there is always the underlying threat that maybe things will not come out well. It was very traumatic.

The anesthesiologist on call preferred to give gas, and my doctor recommended I go along with his specialty. They put me out and then it was over. When I finally woke up—after five hours of fading in and out—everything ached. I was intensely sore where they had cut. I wasn't inclined to move, to hold my baby, or to breastfeed her—which broke my heart and disappointed my husband greatly! My body just hurt too much.

The physical pain was one thing, but the emotional and psychological pain was, I think, worse. Sometime before I finally woke up, they had shaken me awake, and told me three times that I had a girl. I felt very empty, very empty, very detached from the whole experience. They said, "Hey, take a look at this," and I thought "big deal." I did feel my husband's presence in the room when I would wake up for a minute before falling back to sleep. I would see him sitting in the chair holding the baby and there was a great deal of comfort in that. When I finally unfogged enough to talk to my husband and my sister, who is an obstetrical nurse, I felt good that they were there and that they were taking care of the baby; at least the baby was in the hands of the people that I loved.

One of the things that upset me most in my first cesarean was that neither physician, neither my family practice doctor nor my ob asked me anything about how I felt about the cesarean. There was no emotional support or concern from either of them. There I was feeling, okay, now here you are, you have this pain in your belly. You have this baby you feel detached from. You have what was supposed to have been a wonderful experience all turned upside down.

You do need someone to talk to after a cesarean, regardless of whether it's a traumatic one or not. My sister was there for me, and we talked continuously for hours. She also got after me to start walking really soon. It was very painful to get up and walk around. It almost didn't hurt too much if you lay still and didn't move, but moving—changing your position in bed, or trying to get up—was enormously painful. I didn't want to do that. But she told me that the sooner you start walking, the sooner you start passing gas, which means that the intestines have begun working again and you are beginning to recover. That was the magic word!

I had wanted to nurse my baby as soon after birth as possible. Well, that was a joke. I knew that nursing helps the uterus to contract, but I was so fearful of any additional pain, I wasn't going to let that baby anywhere near me. My sister knew my fears and told me that, because this was my first baby, I probably would not feel the uterus contracting, especially because there was so much pain down there anyway. She very gently kept urging me to nurse, and with her help I did it. She helped me get the baby on the breast, and I discovered that there was no additional pain . . . just a wonderful joy.

After that, I felt emotionally very good for the rest of my three-day hospital stay, because I had my sister, my husband and my baby all rooming-in with me. My sister acted as my advocate after the surgery, and it was wonderful for both me and my husband to have her around. Together, she and my husband made me feel good about everything— about the baby and the experience—and I felt optimistic about the future. So, all in all, I would describe my first cesarean as a positive experience, because I felt so cared for during my hospital stay (by my family), and later, when I went home. I felt emotionally high for months afterward.

After my second cesarean I was extremely depressed. As high as I was with my first, I was that depressed with my second. We had a trial of labor, sort of as an experiment, because a vaginal birth after a cesarean had only been done three or four times at my hospital. I was 4 centimeters dilated when they decided to do a cesarean. I thought they were pretty quick to jump in as soon as they saw that the labor wasn't going fast.

I realize now that I was very apprehensive about another cesarean, and I would have been willing to labor forever to avoid surgery. I should have talked out my fears long before the labor. My worst fear was the overwhelming remembrance of the pain. That, and remembering the recovery, remembering just how complicated the whole thing is, emotionally and physically.

I had decided beforehand to have an epidural if a cesarean were needed, so that I could stay conscious and have my husband with me. He had to wait outside while I was given the epidural, and I felt alone and frightened. I had to curl up into the fetal position, which was difficult for me because of my big belly. The better fetal position you get into, the better chance the anesthesiologist has of hitting the epidural space. My back was numbed, but he had to poke around several times. I was afraid, thinking, "What are they doing behind me?"

Later, as I lay on the table holding my husband's hand, I barely knew he was there. I kept thinking, "They are going to cut me up again, dammit." I felt that the anesthesiologist was moving too fast. Everything was moving too fast, and no one cared how I felt. People were bustling about in the delivery room, and I was feeling very helpless. My second chance at a vaginal delivery was shot. Once again I had lost all control over the situation. Why the hell was this happening to me again?

Once the surgery started, it happened within minutes. They were taking the baby out, but I didn't know it. I was still thinking, "When are you going to start?" I was holding my husband's hand, just looking at him, trying to block everything else out, frightened to death. My sister, who was with me again, all of a sudden said to me, "It's a girl," and I didn't know that they were cutting me open yet.

They showed the baby to me just briefly. I started crying and shaking a little bit, and they said later, "Oh, Sandy was so touched, it was such a euphoric experience because she was crying." I was crying because I thought, "God, it's another girl and I have to go through this one more time to have a boy, and I can't do it. I can't do it again." My sister went down with the baby to the nursery. They called back over the intercom to say that she weighed ten pounds. That's the one positive, happy feeling that I will have from the whole experience—the utter astonishment I felt at having such a large baby.

I was so cold in the delivery room and shaking with chills. I shook more and more until I was out of control—apparently because I had hemorrhaged so badly, and my body was compensating for the loss of fluids. That really frustrated me. The anesthesiologist gave me something, and I went out. It was all over. Once again, I didn't have a chance to be with my baby after the delivery.

The pain after my second cesarean was more intense, because my emotions were so negative, I believe. It was also made worse by my getting a spinal headache. The anesthesiologist was not able to get into the epidural space well enough; and the epidural had turned into a spinal. It was complicated by a tightening of all the muscles in my back which was more painful to me than the headache. Two days later they ended the headache and muscle spasms when they did a "blood patch" —injecting some blood from my arm into the epidural space. Because of the headache, though, I hadn't been able to get up and move around to help my recovery. Also I didn't have the same kind of support in the hospital as I did the first time. At the last minute the person I had lined up to care for my two-year-old couldn't come, and my sister went home to take care of her.

Emotionally I was a mess. My baby was in the nursery more than she was with me—no rooming-in this time. I was feeling very negative that I had had another painful experience, and I didn't have anyone in the hospital to help me. When I got home, my sister did not have the physical energy she had the first time to sit and talk with me, to empathize. She was too busy keeping up with the two-year-old, the cooking, and the rest. My husband was involved with his work, so he wasn't available very much. So I felt alone, and it was very stressful for me. After three months my belly was still hurting every day, all the time, because every time I lifted my two-year-old, I pulled on my incision.

I finally figured out that the physical part would have been barely noticeable *if* I had felt good emotionally. But I was mad at everything. I was mostly mad at my husband. Yet there was no way he could have been what I wanted him to be. I wanted him to make it all go away, and he couldn't. I was mad that I had no energy, and every little stress became impossible to cope with. I was mad at my physicians, and it wasn't until weeks later, at the urging of a friend, that I actually even acknowledged that. I was mad as hell at the anesthesiologist for knocking me out after the delivery, and for screwing up my recovery with a spinal headache. I was even mad about having hemorrhoids.

I am still angry about the whole experience, and I still haven't talked to anybody about it. My poor husband is afraid to bring it up; he's just trying to keep his head above water to keep me from biting it off all the time. He can't begin to understand my anger, and I'm just now beginning to accept that he never will, and it's not his fault. I've alternated from thinking I am going to get a stress-related disease, because I'm not coping well, to my marriage is going to break up because I've turned into such an unhappy shrew. What alternatives!

After my first cesarean I felt I was physically recovered after three weeks, although it was three months before I felt that all the fog was out of my head. But I was feeling very high, and very well loved, and very excited about the first baby. This second time I didn't have the gas, which I am grateful for, but I have an awful lot of anger bottled up. There were even times when I have felt suicidal in the last four months. After three months I began feeling better because I went home for Christmas and let other people take care of the baby, and I just slept and relaxed, so I broke the fatigue and self-pity cycle. Once or twice since then, I have regressed and have felt like I was going back to the old depressed mode. It's now four months postpartum. I announced to my husband a week ago that my incision didn't hurt anymore. But, then, after spending a whole day painting my daughter's bedroom, it began hurting again, and it's been hurting ever since. Nothing to run to the doctor about, but just enough pain to annoy me.

Finally, after four months, I am feeling more in control of my life again—but I'm working at it damned hard. The phrase that I often use when I think about the difference in the cesareans is that the first time I was surrounded by "a love bath," that is, love, concern, and security coming from my mother and my mother-in-law (who were both there to help when I came home from the hospital); my sister, who took care of my emotional needs and taught me how to care for my new baby; and my husband, who was just thrilled with the new baby. I felt good about myself and about my baby. After the second cesarean, there was no love bath. It just didn't happen. For some reason I just felt all alone and negative—about myself, the experience, and especially about my future.

Some people would say, "Just give me a cesarean and forget the pain of labor." Well, I don't think there is a comparison between the pain of a cesarean and the pain of labor. Labor is a transitory pain. It's over when it's over. Labor pain is a physical thing. With a cesarean, however, there are so many other factors involved besides the physical: the emotional pain of apprehension and fear, the resentment and the anger, and the feeling of having lost all control—first over your body in pregnancy and in surgery, but also over your life. That's why—unless there is enormous support to make it a positive experience—the pain of a cesarean is really so much worse. When labor is over, the pain is over. When the cesarean is over, I don't think the pain is ever over—unless it was nipped in the bud by some very energetic, loving people.

Sandy is every cesarean mother. She is also a real person, though her name has been changed to protect her privacy. The fear, the disappointment, the anger, and the grief are almost universal feelings of cesarean mothers—albeit to different degrees. Support groups have sprung up across the country just for women who have had cesareans, so every cesarean mother can have the chance to express her intense feelings about her baby's birth, and to feel the support and understanding of other women who have had the same experience.

Where do these incredibly deep and intense feelings come from? Almost all women know how babies grow and how they are born. Nearly every woman grows up believing that some day she will become pregnant and give birth. A woman's monthly menstrual cycle is a regular reminder of her fertility and how her body is made to bear children. A woman's very image of herself, carried with her for years, is shattered when she must have a cesarean delivery. "I felt like a terrible failure," said one mother, Jane Richardson. "It was like training for the Olympics, then falling down the stairs. I had practiced so hard. I did nine months for this delivery. I know other women who feel guilty too, and they say 'if only I had breathed better and tried harder.' I felt disappointed, cheated, deprived, ugly, and angry."

The feeling of failing is intensified in women who prepare for childbirth. They are prepared to be in control, to participate in the delivery of their child, to experience the joy of giving birth vaginally. Suddenly all that is taken away. They lose the support of their husband when they need him the most, and they lose the moment of becoming acquainted with their newborn baby after birth, a time they have looked forward to as the culmination of their pregnancy. Cesarean mothers have suffered a loss, a loss of the birth experience they had prepared for, a loss of intimate contact of the mother, father, and newborn, and a loss of the very image of themselves as able to give birth vaginally. Grief is the normal human response to loss. Knowing that a cesarean was done for the sake of their baby is a great comfort to cesarean mothers, but it does not make up for the sense of loss and need to understand "why me?" Cesarean mothers need a long time to heal emotionally.

In spite of what they have been through—the major surgery, the physical pain, the grieving—cesarean mothers cope. They learn to mother their babies. They heal and often go on to have another baby, even though it often means another cesarean. Cesarean mothers nurture, touch, and breastfeed their babies just the same as mothers who give birth vaginally. However, cesarean mothers need more comfort, more understanding, more help after their babies are born. They also could use a lot more respect for their incredible courage in immediately putting their baby's needs first, and readily giving up the kind of birth experience for which they have waited so long.

Every birth is a perfect experience in its own way. It takes profound courage for a laboring woman to confront complications and to willingly open her already open self even further to include unfamiliar people and procedures into her experience. Monks spend lifetimes in soggy caves trying to achieve this state of humility that women are able to experience through giving birth, being then vessels through which the ultimate creative impulse is served and manifest. There is truth to be gotten and beauty to be seen in all births. Who is to say if one set of circumstances is more perfect than another, and who is to say that the mother whose child is taken from her at birth did not "bond" with the child?

—Kate Botlos,
Assistant Editor, *Mothering*

"Grapefruit are sectioned but women give birth," is a phrase cesarean mothers have come up with to remind doctors that cesarean mothers, too, need family-centered births. By using the information we've assembled, you the reader can greatly reduce your chances of having a cesarean. But mothers sometimes really do need cesareans. You may have done all you can to reduce your risk of cesarean, and then find yourself in labor with the necessity to have an abdominal delivery.

Because the possibility is there for all women, you need to know what you can do to make your baby's cesarean delivery as good an experience for you, your husband, and your baby as it can be.

What Cesarean Mothers Want for Their Deliveries

Women who have had cesareans are very sure about what is important to them. Cesarean mothers across the country strongly agree that they want to be awake. They want their husbands with them, and they want as much visual and physical contact with their baby as possible. In other words, like all women, cesarean women want a family-centered birth—plus lots of the extra help that they need, because of their surgery, in holding and caring for their newborn. In surveys cesarean mothers' opinions were stronger and more unanimous than those women who had vaginal deliveries. Because of what they have been through, they are much more sure about the importance of the father's presence and about having contact with their babies. Cesarean mothers want hospitals and doctors who will give them the following options:

- To be awake, if possible
- To have the father with them during and after surgery
- To see the baby immediately after it is born

- To hold the baby when surgery is completed
- To be encouraged to hold and care for the baby if it must be in a special nursery
- To care for the "well" baby in their room whenever they want

Every mother needs to have her care individualized. Because almost all cesarean mothers want these options, doctors need to support their patients in getting them. Hospitals also need to change their policies so that family-centered maternity care is as strongly supported for cesarean mothers as for mothers who deliver vaginally. The care a cesarean mother receives needs even more sensitivity to her preferences, however. For example, while almost all cesarean mothers have a lot of pain following surgery, they will vary greatly in what they are willing to try to do—walk the first day, nurse their babies, have rooming-in, or have visitors.

Most cesarean mothers want to be awake. Currently 60 percent of cesarean deliveries are done with regional anesthesia (so the mother is awake), and 40 percent are done with general anesthesia (where the mother is not conscious). Although any kind of anesthesia has its risks, the National Institute of Health's task force recommended that women have the option of receiving regional anesthesia when they have a cesarean.

Women want to have their husbands with them during and after surgery. A woman's fear and anxiety when a cesarean is recommended is high enough without having her key support person denied her. Husbands also are reassured by staying with their wives. Many hospitals are easing their policies to allow men to be with their wives for a scheduled or repeat cesarean. It's unusual, however, to find a hospital that will allow fathers to stay with their wives in an emergency—one that is decided on during labor. It's unlikely though, in most emergency cesareans, that the need for the cesarean is so urgent that a staff member cannot take the time to include the father in the preparations, allowing him to change his clothes into a scrub suit and stand by his wife. Emergency cesareans allow plenty of time for careful preparation, explanation, and some choices on the part of the parents if the baby is not in acute fetal distress. Having their husbands with them is so important to cesarean mothers, it should be the exception, not the rule, when husbands are asked to wait outside during an emergency cesarean.

If your husband is with you, he will not be able to see the surgery, just as you will not. The cesarean mother lies on her back on the delivery table. A drape is raised above her midsection, so she cannot see beyond that point. She does not see her baby born through the abdominal incision, and neither does her husband seated next to her head. If the doctor keeps up a running commentary on what he's doing, however, the parents can participate in the excitement of the few minutes before the baby is born. Then the baby should be carried around the drape for them to see. If the baby is not in breathing distress, there is no reason why the father cannot carry his newborn to the nursery for an examination while the doctor closes the incisions on the mother. If the father does accompany his infant to the nursery, the new mother may prefer to have a familiar person stay with her. The doula, perhaps.

Cesarean mothers want to see the baby immediately after birth and to hold their baby when surgery is completed. Women who have had cesareans are keenly aware of what a difference it can make in their feelings toward the baby if they are given the chance to view the baby immediately after it is born, and, then, when surgery is completed, to hold and get acquainted with their baby in the recovery area before the anesthesia has worn off. For many women it may be the only chance they have to get acquainted with their babies for another twenty-four to forty-eight hours because of the pain following surgery.

Women want both parents to be encouraged to hold and care for the baby if it must be in a special-care nursery. Klaus and Kennell's research strongly supports this preference, because many women who are separated from their babies have much more difficulty developing a normal mother-baby relationship.

Women want to care for their "well" baby in their room whenever they wish. The pace of each mother's recovery will vary, but after the first day or so she will have the strength and inclination to begin to care for her baby. If the husband and doula take over the care of the baby for the first day, the mother can, as Sandy did, gain great comfort from knowing her baby is being watched over and cared for by those she loves. Having the husband and doula stay with the mother for much of her hospital stay gives her the extra care and assistance she needs.

Questions for Your Doctor: Will He or Won't He?

To get what you want for a cesarean birth you must negotiate in advance, during your pregnancy. If you know you must have a repeat cesarean, or if you are going to have a trial of labor and *may* be having another cesarean, you are more likely to have strong preferences to negotiate for during your pregnancy. If you have not had a cesarean, your chance of having one today is high enough that if you want it to be as family centered as possible, you must negotiate for this ahead of time. Although most of you are not anticipating a cesarean delivery, we are suggesting that you negotiate for what you want in a cesarean birth, just in case. Decide what you *may* want (you can change your mind later) and get that insurance policy in writing, just as you did for the other options you want for your vaginal delivery.

Many hospitals have eased their policies to make cesarean birth more family centered. Allowing fathers to attend cesarean deliveries that have not been anticipated, however, is unusual. Looking back, surveyed mothers felt most strongly about having their husbands there. If the hospital and doctor you have chosen already allow fathers to be present for cesareans that are planned, the next step is to persuade them to permit your husband to be with you should you need an emergency cesarean. To do this you need to find out the position each hospital anesthesiologist takes on letting your husband into the surgery, since he can veto your doctor—and often does. Negotiation is your tool for getting what you want. (Review Chapter 5.)

Cover your own list of preferences with your doctor. Our examples, based on what surveyed mothers said is important to them, are for those mothers who do not expect to have a cesarean delivery. The mother who knows she must have a repeat cesarean, or the mother who is attempting a vaginal birth after a previous cesarean, will negotiate in advance much the same way.

You have chosen Dr. Right, and you have seen him for prenatal care once or twice. It's time to get agreement on your preferences for a cesarean delivery, if needed. You might want to make a special appointment with your doctor right in the middle of your pregnancy to talk about the possibility of a cesarean, bringing your husband along to impress on the doctor how important your preferences are. Don't allow him to dismiss the subject by saying you won't be having a cesarean—he just doesn't know at this point anymore than you do.

You are working in partnership with your doctor so that he knows what is important to you for your birth, and if it is medically possible to do so, he will make sure that you get what you want. Negotiate during a regular prenatal visit.

YOU: *By the way, you know I really want a vaginal birth, but just in case I might need an emergency cesarean, I still want my husband there with me.*

DOCTOR: We only allow husbands with scheduled cesareans.

YOU: *Of course, since we are discussing this issue ahead of time, and you know how important it is for my husband and me to remain together, even if we have an emergency cesarean, there must be a way for you to make this special arrangement for us.*

DOCTOR: I don't know. If you are sure it's something you want, I might be able to arrange it with the anesthesiologist. It's not easy though. We just got the change through the anesthesiologists to allow fathers to be present for scheduled cesareans. This might mean they wouldn't allow any fathers at all anymore.

YOU: *I understand that I'm asking you to do something very unusual. I want you to know how very important it is to me not to be separated from my husband. I also understand there could be an emergency cesarean. But if there is any possible way to have him with me I want to arrange it. Can you tell me now which anesthesiologist might allow my husband in, and which might not? I'd like to meet with them beforehand to see if one would be willing to come in especially for my surgery, if needed, even if he's not on call.*

DOCTOR: I'll see what I can do, but I won't promise anything.

End the negotiation here for the time being, and at your next appointment check with him on the progress he has made in making the special arrangements for you. *Keep checking until you are satisfied.*

Next, you may want to get your doula there too.

YOU: *I'll have my good friend with me during my labor, and I'm sure things will go well, and I'll have the vaginal delivery I want. If they don't though, I'll need her to help me stay calm. You know how anxious women get with emergency cesareans. It's very important to me that I have these two people, my husband and my friend, stay with me even if I must have an emergency cesarean; then when my husband goes with our baby to the nursery for examination, my friend can stay with me.*

DOCTOR: A cesarean is a surgical procedure. We can't have all kinds of lay people in there.

YOU: *I know this is unusual, but they can both sit with me at my head and stay out of your way. I'm going to need all the help I can get if I must have major surgery.*

DOCTOR: I don't think the anesthesiologist will allow more than one person with you in surgery.

YOU: *I really need to have my husband with me. Perhaps you can help influence the anesthesiologist on our behalf? As an option, perhaps he will agree that at least, when my husband leaves with the baby to go to the nursery, my friend can come in with me to take his place.*

DOCTOR: Just one at a time.

YOU: *Fine; also if the baby's okay, I would like the baby, my husband, and I to stay together in the recovery area before the anesthesia wears off. I want regional anesthesia so I can be awake.*

DOCTOR: I think I can arrange for your husband and baby to stay with you in recovery if you are awake, but as a matter of fact, only one of the anesthesiologists gives regionals (spinals or epidurals). He might not be on call when you come in.

YOU: *Well, my husband and I would like to meet with that anesthesiologist. I don't want anything before the anesthesia to sedate me either, because I want to be fully awake. So I don't want anything besides the anesthesia until after the birth. I think we might need to talk with him. What's his name and how can I reach him?*

The anesthesiologist is *the boss* in the operating room. He decides whether your husband and doula can be there; he decides on the anesthesia for surgery; and he decides the drugs routinely given "pre- and post-op" (before and after surgery). Your doctor knows which anesthesiologist may be flexible and go along with your preferences. He can often handle the negotiations for you. But if your doctor can't "put it in writing," you may want to negotiate in person by scheduling an appointment for you and your husband with the anesthesiologist. A personal interview may be the only way to convince the anesthesiologist that you want *him* to be on call for you, so you can avoid pre-and post-op sedation (until the anesthesia wears off), and so you can have the regional anesthesia.

Depending on how important cesarean delivery options are to you, if you cannot negotiate for what you want, remember you can change doctors during your pregnancy. You'll feel discouraged if you have to start your search over again for the hospital and Dr. Right. And you'll have to overcome the natural feelings of dependency in pregnancy. But having your baby *your* way is the reason you are going to all this trouble, remember?

If your cesarean-born baby must be in a special-care nursery after birth, you will need to negotiate with the pediatrician so you and your husband can have as much contact with the baby as possible.

YOU: *I'd like my husband to spend a lot of time with the baby in the nursery from birth, and I would like to come to see and hold the baby whenever I am able to.*

PEDIATRICIAN: Why don't you just let us take care of the baby and you take care of yourself.

Maybe you've got the wrong pediatrician. Experts agree that parents with a baby in a special-care nursery need to be involved in the care of their baby from the very beginning.

YOU: *It's very important for us that, if our baby needs special care, we are encouraged to see and touch him as much as possible from birth. We really need your backing on this.*

DOCTOR: Well, I don't think it's necessary, but if you insist, you can see the baby whenever you want.

YOU: *Good, that is what we want.*

VAGINAL BIRTH AFTER CESAREAN (VBAC)

"The best way to reduce the number of cesareans is to be sure the *first* one is necessary," says Gerald Stober, M.D., New York City obstetrician. But for the 600,000 or more women who are given cesareans every year in the United States, that advice comes too late. Many of these women are looking to the future, not the past, and want to have a vaginal delivery for their next baby. If you are one of these women, scientific evidence strongly supports your having a vaginal birth after a cesarean. Experts now agree that if a woman has had one previous cesarean with a low horizontal uterine incision, a vaginal delivery is as safe for her newborn as a cesarean—and even safer for her. Experts may soon agree on VBACs for women with two or *more* previous cesareans because of growing numbers of such births.

Although ACOG has come out with an endorsement of VBAC (pronounced Vee-back), the guidelines laid down to allow a trial of labor are restrictive:

- The woman should be delivered in a hospital that can perform an emergency cesarean within fifteen minutes.
- The reason for the previous cesarean should not have recurred.
- The fetus should be a single one in the head-down position and weigh less than 8.8 pounds.

- The woman should be told in advance of the risks and benefits of vaginal delivery and of the possibility of having to undergo cesarean section anyway.

Most obstetricians interpret these guidelines to mean that VBAC must take place in a hospital with 24 hour staffing (an obstetrician and anesthesiologist there at all times), an open blood bank, and an operating room ready to move into in 15 minutes, reported *The New York Times* writer Joan Rattner Heilman. Except in teaching hospitals or the unusual community hospital, a chance for a VBAC is eliminated if this interpretation is followed.

Happily, more and more obstetricians are willing to try a VBAC, but you have to look for them (a family practitioner backed by an obstetrician can also give you a vaginal birth after a cesarean). However, if your doctor believes you must come to the hospital in early labor, and he must be there as soon as you come in, he will have to spend hours with you, something he is not accustomed to doing.

The amount of time involved to monitor your labor is a big drawback for the doctor. At a conference reported in the *Ob. Gyn. News* doctors objected that the management of a vaginal birth after cesarean was too time-consuming for obstetricians in private practice. "Total patient care should come before consideration of the physician's time and money," replied Thampu Kamarasamy, M.D., speaking at the conference. That kind of altruism may be hard to find.

You can reduce the time your doctor must spend in the hospital by staying at home until labor is reasonably established. In medical centers where VBAC has become more standard procedure than the exception, mothers are told to stay home until they are sure they are in labor, with contractions five to ten minutes apart or less.

"Women wanting a VBAC should go to the hospital when a normally laboring woman would," Richard Porreco, M.D., Director of Perinatal Services, St. Luke's Hospital, Denver, told us. He considers the attending doctor's attitude a key factor in whether a woman will have a VBAC: "Success is related to the doctor's enthusiasm for VBAC. You can't treat her like a time bomb." In a two-year study of several hundred VBACs at Kaiser-Permanente Hospital in San Diego, he and Paul R. Meier, M.D., concluded that unless a new reason for a cesarean is present, a trial of labor is "the best and safest form of obstetric management." To insure a high success rate, "Pitocin and regional anesthesia ought to be used for the same indications as for any other laboring woman."

How to Increase Your Chances of a Vaginal Birth After Cesarean

Your choice of birth attendant can make a difference in whether or not you have that vaginal delivery. Just as cesarean section rates vary between doctors and hospitals, so, too, do the rates of vaginal delivery following cesarean. Success rates of 25 percent to 85 percent vaginal delivery after previous cesarean are reported in the medical literature. So ask what your doctor's success rate is.

You can be misled by a doctor who says he is in favor of VBAC. One doctor we know has been allowing labor trials for almost all of his patients who had previous cesareans, but only 30 percent of them deliver vaginally. His low rate of success seems to come from his belief (as told to another physician) that he can tell during the first hour of labor whether a woman can deliver vaginally after a previous cesarean.

The two most common reasons for a repeat cesarean after a trial of labor are "failure to progress" and "fetal distress." (Review these in Chapter 8.) Failure to progress is such a poorly defined term that your long labor may be perfectly normal for you. Staying on your feet and walking slowly during your whole labor may be particularly important to prevent the diagnosis of failing to progress. If your baby is not in distress, ask for more time to labor. To avoid a misdiagnosis of fetal distress, have a nurse regularly monitor your baby's heart rate rather than use an internal fetal monitor. And finally, there is some evidence that your belief in your own ability to give birth naturally is important to your success.

Nancy Wainer Cohen cofounded C-SEC, Inc., in 1973, the first cesarean parents support group. Following a cesarean delivery with her first child she had two vaginal births (the last one at home). In 1981 she founded CPM, Cesarean Prevention Movement. She has counseled hundreds of women in VBAC. More than 90 percent of those who have delivered have had vaginal births. Except for the cesarean itself for the remaining 10 percent, no mothers or babies, whether delivered vaginally or by cesarean, have had any complications. Among the women who delivered vaginally were twenty-five or more who had more than one previous cesarean, women who had breech presentations, some women who delivered babies weighing over ten pounds when they had had cesareans for CPD with five-pound babies, and three sets of twins. "I believe most cesareans can be prevented, and certainly most repeats aren't necessary. We work on attitude, pain confrontation, emotions, creating a positive environment—all with the aim of allowing a woman to relax. We stress nutrition, exercise, vitamins, and relaxation techniques. I believe there is an inseparable relationship between mind and body and that birth is just as spiritual as it is physical," said Mrs. Cohen, interviewed by Joan Rattner Heilman for *The New York Times Magazine* in 1980.

Cohen does not like the use of the term "trial of labor" because "it undermines women's confidence." Mrs. Cohen's clients not only want a vaginal delivery very badly, but they believe that they can do it. Mrs. Cohen, who coined the term VBAC, explained to us why she thought the women she counseled were so successful:

> They are free to have the same labor as anyone else. They have no IVs, no electronic fetal monitor. They walk in labor. They eat or drink as they desire. They have confidence in their body, and they have loving support during labor. They have no time limit on their labors.

Cohen added that some of the women had very long labors of up to forty hours, some at home before going to the hospital for the birth, and some in the hospital.

Elizabeth Conner Shearer, M.Ed., M.P.H., was a member of the NIH Task Force on Cesarean Birth. She is a childbirth educator who gives classes in vaginal birth after cesarean. In a 1982 article, "Education for Vaginal Birth After Cesarean," she wrote about the similarity of educating VBAC women and women who have not had a cesarean. "The uterus works the same whether it has a scar on it or not," said Shearer. "Effective preparation for childbirth helps women accept the pain of birth, to appreciate it as a sign of how strong and well their bodies work, quite different from pain that signals injury or illness."

The special difference for VBAC parents, Shearer said, is "to know, trust, and rely on their bodies to give birth . . . when their bodies did *not* 'work right' the first time." Shearer makes special note of "how unscientific 'CPD' and 'failure to progress' are as diagnoses. All 'CPD' means today is that *the baby did not get out in the time the doctor thought s/he should*" [Shearer's italics]. Shearer also says that parents need to understand the reason for the cesarean to be realistic about their chances for a vaginal birth after cesarean.

Marianne Brorup-Watson with the Childbirth Education Association in Terrace, British Columbia, had a vaginal birth after two previous cesareans. Pregnant with her third, it was her doctor who suggested she try another doctor in Vancouver for a vaginal birth. From her experience she suggests the following:

1. Make use of all available resources: childbirth groups, labor coaches, other women. Pass the word; there's always someone who knows someone who has done what you want to do.
2. Read everything you can lay your hands on. Libraries, public health units, childbirth groups all have literature you can borrow.
3. Get a second opinion if you are refused a VBAC. Never take one doctor's word for it.
4. Enlist the help of a supportive doctor.
5. Put together a birth plan and make sure you give all your attendants a copy.
6. Take exercise and good nutrition seriously. Train for your birth like a runner trains for a race! Labor is the hardest work you'll ever do.
7. Attend the best prenatal classes available.
8. Find yourself a good midwife. This is well worth the money and effort. Midwives deal in birth as a natural function. A midwife can make it safer to stay at home as long as possible during labor.
9. Concentrate on the upcoming birth. Remove any negative influences from your environment. A positive frame of mind is essential to your success.
10. Make sure you and your mate have someone with you throughout labor, who knows exactly what you want. It is impossible to make an informed decision when you are in hard labor. And your mate will get tired and need a break. Check to make sure your hospital allows more than one person in the labor/delivery area; if not, change hospitals.

Having a VBAC is unusual in most places in the United States. Just as it took time for husbands to become widely accepted in the delivery room, it will take time for most obstetricians to feel comfortable with VBAC. Having a VBAC is a pioneer effort. You'll need persistence and determination to find a willing birth attendant. Just as important for you, you'll need to have people around you who are loving, caring, and supportive of your labor. But what if you still end up needing another cesarean? Counselors, such as Nancy Cohen and Elizabeth Shearer, who help women prepare for a VBAC, say that every woman is glad she made the effort, for she had the labor, she knew it was the best time for her baby to be born, and she would never look back and wonder what might have been. She had done her best.

10 ▪ UNDERSTANDING YOUR FEELINGS: IT'S NOT ALL HORMONES

> As a first-time mother I still find myself, more than half a year later, remembering my (our) birth experience. I think I am finally coming to an understanding of the many feelings I had then and accepting the miserable ones as well as the elation.
>
> —A mother quoted by Leah Yarrow,
> "When My Baby Was Born,"
> *Parents* magazine, August 1982

Few of us are prepared for childbirth's impact on our feelings. We open ourselves up—physically and emotionally—to a degree not thought possible. And if it's our first baby, ready or not, we're thrust into the new role of motherhood. We now see the world with different eyes, while coping with up and down emotions. These feelings are normal.

You've looked forward to caring for your baby, but now that the baby's here, you worry. Maybe you really weren't prepared enough, you say to yourself. Bone-weary collapse seems just around the corner. As most of the 64,000 readers who responded to a 1982 *Parents* magazine survey said, the biggest surprise about parenthood is the fatigue. Fatigue alone can produce a kaleidoscope of feelings, mostly negative.

Women's intense feelings after childbirth are certainly not new. "As long ago as the 4th century B.C., the medical writer Hippocrates was theorizing about the biological basis of this strange sorrow and/or madness that could invade the mind of the new mother," reported Maggie Scarf in her book on women's depression, *Unfinished Business*.

Some of the new mother's emotions bother both herself and those closest to her. She's just not herself, and no one knows why. She experiences mood swings, more than the usual amount of tears, irritability, and constant energy lows. These symptoms are usually labeled "postpartum depression." On the other hand, when the new mother thrills at feeding and holding her baby, and when her tears are tears of joy, these actions are labeled "maternal." But the truth is that, to some degree, *all* of these feelings are normal, not just the so-called positive ones. No one, including a new mother, is ecstatically happy all the time.

If some combination of all of these feelings is normal, why are the majority of women who give birth in hospitals much more troubled with negative emotions than they are pleased with good feelings? "Most [American] women show some postpartum depression," said Dennis A. Frate, Ph.D., at the 1979 annual meeting of the American Public Health Association. Luis E. Sanz, M.D., and James A. Patterson, M.D., said two years later in *Contemporary Ob/Gyn*:

> In postpartum blues, there may be mild depression, weeping anxiety, and minimal intellectual clouding. These symptoms usually begin by the third or fourth day after delivery and can last from a few hours to days. This is a very common phenomenon in obstetric wards, with an incidence of 56% to 87% in various institutions.

And British sociologist Ann Oakley, author of *Women Confined: Towards a Sociology of Childbirth,* found that 60 percent of the normal English mothers she studied were victims of postpartum depression.

Are hormones the culprits? If they are part of the reason, they're certainly not all of the answer. "Scientists are very far indeed from a full understanding of the hormonal changes associated with pregnancy, childbirth, and the onset of lactation," states Scarf. To exonerate female hormones even more, in many other cultures and in home births in this country, women reportedly seldom experience postpartum depression.

At The Farm, an agricultural community in Tennessee, midwives find that of the thousands of births that have taken place there, only .03 percent of their mothers experience depression in the months after their babies are born, reports principal Farm midwife Ina May Gaskin. Nancy Mills, a California lay midwife who's attended hundreds of home births, said in 1975 that home-birth mothers "rarely experienced postpartum depression."

MISSING PIECES

A combination of birth experiences we call the "missing pieces" can cause your emotional see-saw to continue on the downside longer than is comfortable. You don't have to undergo all these experiences to feel the impact of postpartum depression. Many women feel the effect with only a few. The missing pieces are unfulfilled expectations, unrealistic expectations about pain and self-control, invasion of your privacy, distractions, memory loss, unwanted interventions, and separation from your baby.

Unfulfilled Expectations

There are reasons unique to our times why today's new mother may be especially perplexed and sometimes profoundly confused by her feelings. Women, especially younger women, have come to expect the best.

You're harder to please. Simply having a live baby is not enough anymore. You want the best experience, too. If you can control conception with the Pill, you expect to be in control of your birth and enjoy its pleasure, too. Maggie Scarf points out, "You're told now you can do it all, have it all; and when you end up not having it all or not doing it all well, you feel guilty—and depressed." And perhaps shortchanged.

Because there's more information available on birth now, the process is not so mysterious anymore. Nearly all of you go to childbirth-education classes. You know to eat well and avoid drugs. As far as you know, you're doing everything you can to have a good and safe birth. Why, then, doesn't childbirth always result in what you wanted? Because birth isn't that predictable and neat a package.

Parents magazine writer Leah Yarrow said that the letters they received after their poll of 64,000 readers "suggest that women spend considerable time struggling to come to terms with the disparity between the expectations they had of their labors and births and their actual experiences."

The truth is that the act of giving birth plunges you into the hands of a force much bigger than your ability to control it or fully anticipate it.

Pain

Many new mothers are stunned, not only by their roller-coaster reactions after birth, but by the pain they felt. No one said it would hurt so much, or if someone did, you didn't think it would happen to you. Pain in childbirth is not new to women, of course. When your mother or your aunts, perhaps, told you a horror story about birth, you knew those were pre-Lamaze times your relatives were talking about. After all, you had much more information available to you now than they had.

Many of us have been told that if we did it right—breathed and relaxed correctly—we'd feel a contraction, not pain. For some laboring women, that's true. For many others, it's not. In the 1982 *Parents* magazine survey, most of the mothers found childbirth to be painful and one third said childbirth was "the most painful experience" they had ever had. Only one third of the mothers reported that "medication took all the pain away." Not only does pain persist, some women become passive spectators because of the drugs and the lack of exertion. Psychologist Niles Newton, Ph.D., says this may lead a new mother to feel that the medical profession—not she—produced the child.

Ann Oakley says, "The deliberate misrepresentation of the pain of childbirth adds to the risk of postpartum depression, since it makes realistic anticipation impossible." She continues, "A woman who has been misled about 'painless childbirth' has been found to be more likely to panic and request drugs when those sensations turn out to hurt. . . . Furthermore, a man who withstood hours of severe pain, refusing anesthetic to benefit another, would be a hero, but a woman who experiences pain is made to feel inadequate." Her pain becomes a "mark of failure."

Yes, the latter part of the first stage of labor is painful. But contrary to what many doctors believe, the second stage—the pushing part—often is not. For the baby's safety, most women don't receive anesthesia until they are quite near the pushing stage. Consequently, they never know that the most painful part is nearly behind them with the exhilaration of pushing just ahead.

Labor can be painful, exhausting, and still euphoric. We know. It's happened to both of us and to many other women. In 1983 British researchers confirmed that women who give birth without anesthesia suffer more pain than anesthetized women do, but they also experience greater pleasure. The laboring woman is aware of the pain, but the physical high from endorphins comes too. Pain can also be moderated with the appropriate people support.

Loss of Control

Prepared childbirth classes lead you to believe that you will be making your own decisions about how delivery will be handled. My own experience was quite the opposite. The staff treated me as a "body," not a person. They administered anesthesia for delivery without asking me if I wanted it, but simply because that was the usual routine.

Maintaining control means many things to a laboring woman—the control of pain, the control of her actions, and the control of emotion. Researcher R. Rubin found "loss of control in any form may result in loss of self-esteem and bring on a feeling of shame and humiliation."

Then there's the staff view. Doctors believe pain relief is of first importance, when in reality, women's worst birth memories are of the interventions used. As for who guides the course of your stay in the hospital, routine usually prevails. And emotion—nurses and doctors often become anxious if a laboring woman expresses deep feeling. According to Barbara Katz Rothman in her book, *In Labor: Women & Power In The Birthplace*, childbirth educators go along with the idea that a woman needs to control her emotions:

> According to the rules of the game, if the laboring woman chooses to deal with her pain by crying or calling out, she has entirely forfeited her right to make decisions. Much is made in childbirth-preparation circles of the woman's being in control during labor, but all that is meant by that is control over her expressions of pain. A woman who maintains a fixed, if somewhat glazed, cheerful expression and continues a regular pattern of breathing is said to be "in control," as she is carted from one room to another and literally strapped flat on her back with her legs in the air.

Lack of Privacy

Psychologist Newton believes that people, being territorial animals, are more relaxed in the home. However, birth in our society usually takes place in a hospital. What is it that women don't get in hospitals that is part of their biological need? Privacy, for one thing. It's difficult to provide true privacy for any hospital patient. You are handled by strangers (the nurses on duty, a doctor on call for your own, perhaps medical students, interns, residents, nursing students).

Thousands of hospitals are taking a step in the right direction by offering a more homelike appearance with wallpapered and curtained birth rooms. But having your baby in one of these birth rooms is no guarantee that you'll feel at home. "It is not the way the room looks that matters," sociologist Rothman states. "What matters are the attitudes of the attendants—the beliefs, values, and ideas they hold about women, babies, and birth."

Distractions

A woman in labor craves peaceful surroundings, yet many laboring women have described how disturbing overheard conversations and laughter from the hall can be (or being asked questions by the staff when you're in the middle of a contraction). Because of the physical and emotional intensity of giving birth, laboring women's senses soar. According to Elizabeth Loftus, a psychologist at the University of Washington at Seattle, in her book *Memory*, hearing memory is apparently stronger in humans than touch, sight, or smell memory. Twenty and thirty years after the event, many a woman still remembers the conversations staff members had (as if she, the woman in labor, was merely an object) while she was in the labor room or on the delivery table.

Memory Loss During Labor and Delivery

It's normal to talk about your births. You'll want to replay the experience again and again. In fact, you need to. So much so, that if you can't remember everything, you're often troubled and anxious.

Dyanne D. Affonso, Professor of Nursing at the University of Arizona, coined the term "missing pieces" to describe postpartum feelings after interviewing 150 women in Hawaii and Arizona. She found "that more than three fourths of the women interviewed indicated that they could not remember, or were distressed by vague ideas of, some period or periods during their labors or deliveries." Women described finding themselves thinking often about what they could not remember.

One of the reasons for the memory loss the author gives is the use of "high-risk equipment like the [fetal] monitor." Use of this equipment "may result in a laboring woman not hearing what is said to her, or if she heard it, she may forget it later." Her anxiety about the use of this equipment creates a crisis in her mind. Upset and distressed, she literally can't hear what's said to her.

Women who receive little feedback from doctors or nurses about their progress—where they are in labor, how fast they're dilating, and the condition of the baby—also have a sense of not understanding or remembering what happened, whether their labors were long or short, states Affonso. During their hospital stay women who couldn't remember found themselves asking the same question over and over to one person, or even asking "the same question to different persons such as the nurse, doctor, husband, or even the cleaning lady. . . ."

Drugs used for a vaginal birth have their effect on memory loss, too. And about cesareans, Affonso said, "especially women who encounter an unexpected cesarean section are vulnerable to forgetting certain important areas of their childbirth experience." According to the *Parents* survey, women who have cesareans (half of whom were not awake at their child's birth) experience the most shock of any new mother when they compare their experience to their expectations.

Unwanted Interventions

Sociologist Ann Oakley found that "having the blues during postpartum hospital stay was associated with epidural block, dissatisfaction with the second stage of labor and instrumental [forceps] delivery." She also found that "becoming depressed at some point in the five months following birth was also preceded by obstetric intervention and feelings of dissatisfaction about the birth per se." She associates this dissatisfaction with the mothers' sense of loss of control in labor and the management of the birth itself.

Routine hospital procedures often trigger a sense of low self-esteem. In her book *Birthing Normally: A Personal Approach to Childbirth,* Gayle Peterson points to draping, shaving of the pubic hair, enemas and routine episiotomies as unrecognized attempts to hide the fact that birth is sexual. They also serve to make women feel demeaned.

Separation From Your Baby

> When the mother is really the first human being to have contact with the baby and that contact is continuing within several hours, she is the expert for her baby, and feels it, and develops a tremendous amount of confidence, even skills; fathers too, and others. They all feel very close to the baby, very responsible for the baby. There is no third party interfering with this. . . ."
>
> —Midwife, quoted in
> *In Labor: Women & Power*
> *in the Birthplace*

Most of you want to be with your baby after the birth. That's clear. But according to the *Parents* survey, less than half of women have their babies with them as long as twenty minutes after birth. Author Yarrow states: "In our cross-tabulations we discovered that the amount of time mothers were allowed to bond with their babies after birth may have a significant impact on their assessment of the birth experience. Mothers who stayed with their babies for less than ten minutes were much more likely to say their birth experience was negative or a mixture than were those who bonded for a longer time."

Rooming-in mothers developed maternal feelings significantly sooner and felt more confident and competent in caring for their newborns than did mothers having limited contact with their babies, according to 1977 research reported by Niles Newton. Further it was shown that mothers who felt confident about themselves consequently gave more affection and evaluated their own children in more positive terms, thereby increasing the self-esteem of their children.

In spite of all the pluses rooming in offers, American hospitals don't provide as much rooming in as you might suppose. In the *Parents* survey, "a little more than half (56%) did have some form of rooming-in, but only a small percent (6%) of all mothers had their babies with them all the time."

The Need for a Support System

The missing pieces of your birth can be prevented or diminished by family and friends. You probably will have your husband with you during your labor and the birth, so you will have the presence of someone who cares for you. What more could you need or want? Another woman, that's who. As wonderful as it is to have your mate with you, we believe you need even more support than that.

From the beginning of time, the traditional companions for a laboring woman and the new mother have been, and continue to be, women. In a study of 186 cultures reported in 1982 in "Birth, Interaction, and Attachment," pediatrician-anthropologist Betsy Lozoff, M.D., was able to "find only two cultures in which a man actually did something to help deliver the baby."

Traditionally, women have helped other women give birth. Isolated families where new mothers have only their mate for support are not the best environment for women. It's too easy for the new mother's needs and emotions—and the new father's—to be overlooked. We encourage you to set up a support system to help both you and your husband before birth and after, to reduce or eliminate a chance of postpartum depression. We consider this support essential.

Peacemaking, Apologies, and Misplaced Compassion— How They Might Get in Your Way

Your behavioral style may get in the way of your pleasure in your birth and your baby. If it's important for you to please other people and always play the *peacemaker*, if you want to avoid criticism at all costs, speaking out about your childbirth preferences may not be the thing for you to do. The price you pay for silence, however, is anger and/or depression—now or later.

You may speak out daily on your job or in your home, but react differently in your dealings with the authority of doctors and hospitals.

"Oh, what will they think of me?" you wonder. This attitude stops you from getting what you want. We often feel responsible for everyone's comfort and well-being, including that of the hospital staff. As women, we should learn to count to ten before taking the blame or backing off from a request we've made. And if that doesn't work, count to twenty!

How do you know when you're in your *apologizing* (or "I won't make trouble") mode? You'll know, if you've said some of the following statements to yourself:

- It's very important to me that I don't have an electronic fetal monitor; I'm probably not right, though. After all, the doctor must know more than I do about this.
- My doctor doesn't agree with me that I should stay out of bed and walk around during labor; I must be wrong, so I'll do what he wants me to do.
- I couldn't convince the nurses to bring me my baby—they probably know better than I do. And I hate to be obnoxious by insisting.

And then there's *compassion*. Many women try to "out good" everyone else by always being fair and understanding (especially of men). There's nothing wrong with compassion and fairness; they are noble attributes. But they can stand in the way of getting what you know is best for you and your baby. For example, one mother told us that she didn't use the hospital's alternative birth room, even though she wanted to, because the doctor said delivering a baby on that double bed might hurt his back. Another mother spent a miserable night anxiously listening to the cries from the nursery, fearing her baby was crying for her. She was in tears and her breasts were full, yet she feared disturbing the nursing staff by asking for her baby.

Many people adopt a passive, nonassertive attitude for coping with difficult situations. Even though that's not always the best response in our daily life, in pregnancy it is a *perfectly normal* response. For you, as a laboring woman, the most important reason for avoiding hassles in the hospital, for avoiding disagreements of any kind, is your physical and emotional vulnerability. That's true no matter how assertive a person you are ordinarily. Enlist the help of your husband or doula (see next chapter) to fend for you.

Sometimes, it's true, you may feel that yielding is simply the most rational way to cope with some situations. And it certainly can be. We only encourage you to first understand your choice of options, and their individual importance to you, then choose your own actions.

Coping With Your Anger From a Past Birth

I would have liked to have been allowed to find my own best position for comfort in labor and delivery. I found it excruciating to lie flat on my back—yet it was insisted that I do so (because of fetal monitor). I tolerated labor very well in a standing, bent over position, but I was forced to lie in bed—which I hated. Also, to be moved from a bed to the delivery room was further agony—I really didn't want to be disturbed at such a crucial point. It was only through the help of my husband that I managed. Then they kept me from my baby. I still get angry when I think about it.

So what do you do if you've already had a birth (or a gynecological) experience that's left you feeling angry? You find ways to cope with that anger and, hopefully, use that energy in a positive direction.

Give yourself permission to be angry. Having a baby is one of a woman's most important life experiences. If your baby's birth wasn't what you wanted, you have a right to be angry. You can't go back and do that birth over, but you can understand what you're angry about.

Write down all the things about your birth experience that made you unhappy. This will help you answer, "At whom am I angry?" Maybe you're angry at everyone. The nurse, for ordering you to lie down when you felt more comfortable sitting up. Your husband, because he didn't speak up enough to protect you or left when you needed him. The hospital, because you weren't allowed to use the birth room—someone else got there first. Your friends, because they didn't tell you what to expect. Your doctor . . . ah, your doctor. Most of us just *can't* allow ourselves to be angry at our doctor. Whatever happened, someone besides him was responsible: the nurse, the hospital, your mother, or your husband. After all, the doctor "gave you" a healthy baby. But, the fact is, most of what happens to a woman in a hospital is the responsibility of the doctor.

What about being angry at yourself? Are you beating yourself over the head with: "If I had only . . . arranged ahead of time . . . demanded my baby . . . stood my ground . . . held out a little longer before accepting drugs . . . ?"

Make a list, and identify what you're angry about, and at whom. This is an important step. Now look at the list again. Is it enough for you to place blame? If it satisfies you, okay. However, most of us find it doesn't relieve us of our anger. Besides, placing blame just isn't so simple. If you blame your doctor for your treatment, remember he's only doing what he was trained to do. You could blame the nurse—except you know she's only doing what the hospital expects of her. So who are you going to blame? Your husband? You have to live with him. Besides, he probably did his best. Like you, the experience was far different from his expectations. He may be angry as well. Yourself? You have to live with yourself, too. Now that you know you're disappointed, perhaps feel betrayed, angry, or enraged, what are you going to *do* about it?

Make a decision about what you'll do next. What are your choices?

■ *Do nothing.* One option that we all choose sometime or another is to do nothing. You can leave that anger buried deep within you. We've been asked why we would recommend doing nothing. Is it as productive as other suggestions? Maybe not. But we believe every woman has her own timetable for working through her feelings. And some of you will need to put that anger on a shelf in the back of your head for awhile before taking it down, dusting it off, and deciding what to do next.

■ *Take action.* Anger creates energy that you can funnel into not only helping change doctors' and hospitals' attitudes, but changing your actions in the future for your health care.

■ *Talk about it.* Whether your birth expectations were met or not, whether you reacted with anger or not, whether you have "missing pieces" from the birth or not, you have a need, common to all women, to talk about your baby's birth. In doing the M.O.M. Survey, we were struck by the depth of feeling—often rage—of many women who answered our questions. And *Parents'* Leah Yarrow stated: "The need to examine and explain the birth experience was dramatically evidenced in the torrential response to our recent birth experience poll."

Get a friend who will listen to you, someone who will comfort you when you cry. For if you are grieving, you are grieving over a real loss. Boulder Hospice nurse, Marcia Lattanzi, says, "You don't recover from grief, you manage it." And the more important the loss, the more profound the experience will be.

Women who had children long ago produce vivid accounts of their own birth experiences for us, as if they are still working on understanding them. And maybe they are. One mother, who gave birth to twin daughters thirty years ago, still wonders what the twin looked like who was born dead and then immediately taken away. Another wonders what her labor was really like with her oldest son, now in his twenties. She was drugged as soon as she arrived at the hospital and was left alone to labor. There was no one to ask about what happened. But you're not likely to be left alone in labor today. In fact, we encourage you to have at least two people with you.

One cesarean mother who had been asleep at her daughter's birth told us that when her baby was one day old, she asked the nurse who had been with her during her labor and who also accompanied her to the operating room, to tell her, in detail, just what happened. That mother taped the conversation she had with the nurse and treasures it because it fills in some of the missing pieces of her memory.

Talking it out is cathartic, but it's more than that. Women have a need to preoccupy themselves with all the details of pregnancy, labor, delivery, the hospital stay, and those first few weeks at home. They talk of the pain and the pleasure, all the while putting the pieces of the experience together. Having a baby, especially the first time, changes your life dramatically. You're suddenly an equal with your own mother, and a sister to every other woman who has borne children. You're affected profoundly and you yearn to understand.

■ *Write letters.* Even if it's been several years since your child's birth, you can still write a letter to your doctor or the hospital, telling them what you liked about their care, and what you didn't like. Hospitals pay attention to these letters, and will pay special heed if you also send a carbon copy to the chairman of the hospital's board of trustees. This board is responsible for getting patient/consumer input. You'd be helping the board to do its job by giving them your opinions.

If your complaint is about your doctor, write a letter, being as clear and specific as you can, to the local medical society. Do this especially if you had anything done to you against your wishes. Ask for a copy of the letter they send to the doctor. Your public librarian can tell you what medical society covers the geographic area of your doctor's office (it may not be the same as where you live). If you don't receive satisfaction locally, you can appeal to the state level, the state attorney general's office, the state medical licensing agency, or the grievance committee of your state's medical society.

■ *Tell doctors and hospitals directly.* When the M.O.M. Survey brought out angry comments from women about their past maternity care, every obstetrician we talked to told us (and we believe them) that they didn't think women were unsatisfied with their care because their patients hardly ever expressed these complaints to them. Doctors are not likely to change if they believe women are satisfied with their medical care. We know it's probably a lot easier for all of us to tell other women what we think, and we know that confrontation makes many people ill at ease. It's certainly not always easy to say, "By the way, Doctor, when I was in labor and called for you, I can't tell you how disappointed and angry I was that you weren't on call. A doctor I didn't even know delivered my baby. I expected you to be there." However, it's still most effective to tell your complaints to your doctor.

To complain, follow the same steps as in negotiating. Plan ahead what you want to say, practice in advance, remain logical and self-controlled. Take a friend to help you stay calm.

■ *Become hospital changemakers yourselves.* That's what we did. Why and how we worked with our community hospital to make maternity care changes that women wanted is described in the Appendix, "How to Be a Changemaker."

■ *Do things differently in the future.* If you're angry about your previous birth experiences the most important step for you to take is to resolve to do things differently in the future. What happened then, happened, and it's over now. Do what you can and move on.

But you don't have to be angry to want to do things differently the next time. Take what you learned from your experience and, step by step, develop a new relationship with health professionals.

11 · YOUR SUPPORTERS—YOUR HUSBAND, DOULA, CHILDBIRTH EDUCATOR, AND MONITRICE

> I relied heavily on the constancy of my husband, allowing his strength to sustain me through despair, tears, exhaustion, and hints of epidurals and analgesia.
>
> —Nona L. McNatt, R.N., C.N.M.,
> quoted in *Obstetrics & Gynecology*

Your lineup of supporters is your best guarantee for avoiding unnecessary interventions in the hospital, for getting the options you want, and for receiving the pleasure you deserve.

Although American childbirth practices have changed dramatically in the last ten years, far too many women still give birth emotionally and physically alone. They have no husband, no family, no friends in the delivery room, just doctors and nurses who are usually too busy to have much time to give to a laboring woman. Yet through the ages women have intuitively known that a laboring woman needs a lot of emotional and physical support.

In this chapter we'll discuss the role of four different supporters for you. The first two are familiar to you—your husband and a childbirth educator. The other two are innovative in hospital births in our culture today—the doula and the monitrice. *Doula* is a Spanish word (popularized by anthropologist Dana Raphael, Ph.D., in her book *The Tender Gift*) describing a woman who nurtures and cares for a mother in labor and birth, as well as her and her baby later—a woman who "mothers" the mother. *Monitrice* is the 1960s Lamaze word for a labor coach, but in our use, the monitrice is a nurse hired to give one-to-one care to you in the hospital.

THE HUSBAND

> Pam and Gerry stared at each other during her labor continuously—
> each strengthening the other. He kissed her face often and she
> thanked him with both looks and words for understanding her need.
> When she finally got to the pushing stage she was most comfort-
> able standing up. Gerry held her up for hours, letting Pam's body
> be as limp as possible. Immediately after both of their babies were
> born, the voices in the delivery room hushed as we watched Gerry
> and Pam. Each was lovingly cradling one of their twin daughters
> and gazing into the eyes of that infant.
>
> —Doula

When the Lamaze method of prepared childbirth was developed in France, a woman trained to be a labor coach stayed with the mother. When this childbirth education method crossed the Atlantic to the United States, the husband took over the role of that woman. We believe the husband's presence is crucial and not to be duplicated by any other person. He is most important to the mother as her lover and the father of her baby.

During the last twenty years, more and more fathers-to-be entered labor and delivery rooms. For most women, their husband is the most important support person for them. The husband's presence and partici- pation is necessary for the woman to have a "peak" experience in childbirth, according to psychologist Deborah Tanzer, Ph.D. Tanzer's research found evidence that joy and ecstasy in childbirth are directly related to the husband's presence. This peak experience is also possible for cesarean mothers whose husbands stay with them through the birth.

In our M.O.M. Survey, 99 percent of the women reported they wanted to have their husbands with them in both labor and delivery. Robert Bradley, M.D., who made popular the husband-coached childbirth concept, said, "I include the father because there is simply no substitute for him. People watching husband-coached childbirth often say that they feel like intruders in a room where a man and woman are making love." This emotion shared with the husband replaces those heartfelt, sincere displays of affection that many a woman used to give to her obstetrician when he caught the baby . . . and the father was nowhere in sight.

Fathers are not only there now, but many hold their newborns in a Leboyer warm-water bath within minutes of the birth; and occasionally a father delivers his own baby in a hospital setting. A group of doctors in southern New Jersey make a practice of it. Since 1974 hundreds of fathers have thrilled at the touch of their own newborn emerging from their wife's body. Is the how-to-do-it complicated? Author Leah Yarrow states, "As for learning how to deliver the baby, it's strictly on-the-job training. When the couples first hear that all the training they get is a set of brief instructions as the wife is pushing the baby down, they are aghast. It seems that delivering a baby should require at the very least a week of coursework and demonstrations on models. But the hands-on method is actually the very same one used to teach medical students."

These three New Jersey doctors—Robert Block, M.D., Myron Levine, M.D., and Robert Dilks, M.D., distributed a questionnaire to parents in their practices. "So far," Yarrow says, "the results show that fathers who deliver their babies are more active in the baby's care and feeding, that the couple resumes sexual relations earlier, and that their marital relationship is better even than those of couples in which the father was present at the delivery as a coach."

It's clear that the more that's done to keep birth in the hands of the new mother and father, the better they each feel about themselves and each other. This intimacy, says Lucy R. Waletzky, M.D., a Washington, D.C., psychiatrist, can reduce the stress many new fathers feel. In her article, "Husbands' Problems With Breastfeeding," she states that the most common negative reaction of a new father is jealousy. Among Waletzky's suggestions to men for more enjoyment of their fathering, she includes: Attend prenatal birth classes; stay with your wife when she's in the hospital for the labor and birth; and then stay with your baby and your wife as much as you can after the birth.

Historically, the husband has not been the person who gives the major support to the laboring woman. And not every father wants to be present for his child's birth or throughout labor. That's his choice. Having your mate there is not the only way to have a baby. You know your own husband. Some husbands feel guilty because they don't want to be there. If he's not interested, plan to have at least one doula with you. What's important is that you receive the physical and emotional support that you need.

When the husband is there, his role in childbirth has become more than that of a lover, or rarely, the baby catcher. Most times husbands are also labor coaches and doulas. They help their wives to cope successfully with labor contractions. They comfort their wives with word and touch. They attempt to keep track of the hospital options the couple wants.

But if the husband's presence were enough, 82 percent of the women in the Baltimore COMA Survey wouldn't have been dissatisfied with their birth experiences. The huge increase in medical intervention in childbirth leads us to question whether the father alone can adequately meet all the needs of a laboring woman in hospitals today.

THE DOULA

As a Lamaze teacher, I'm often asked to go to the hospital and stay with a woman and her husband during labor. It's exhausting work, but so worthwhile. I love to go when I can. I do more than coach the woman in labor. I also explain to the couple the things the staff has told them, but which are still unclear to the couple. I try to ask questions that the mother wants to ask but is obviously too preoccupied to mention. I comfort the father, who often wonders if he's doing the right thing. Usually I find that the nurses are glad to have me there, especially if they're understaffed.

No childbirth class can totally prepare a couple for what happens in the hospital. I don't just mean the labor. It's more than that. It's being in a strange place. It's expecting that you'll get what you want just because you talked to your doctor about it before. It's just not that simple. I'm the go-between for the couple and the staff. I try to clarify any confusion, especially when the staff suggests interventions the couple said they didn't want. But most of all I do what I can to create the best environment for the woman and her husband. I know it's one of the most important days in their lives.

—Doula

In all but one of 150 nonindustrialized cultures studied by anthropologists, a family member or friend, usually a woman, is present during the labor and birth. Studies by researchers John Kennell, M.D., Marshall Klaus, M.D., Steven Robertson, Ph.D., and Juan Urrutia, M.D., give evidence that having a caring, attentive woman present during childbirth is healthier, not only for you, but for your baby as well. This research, conducted in a Guatemalan hospital, showed that one group of laboring women who had doulas with them had fewer complications and healthier babies. These mothers were also more affectionate with their newborns than another group of women who were alone. The women with the healthiest outcome were continuously attended to by these untrained women, who simply held their hands, rubbed their backs, and talked to them throughout labor. With doulas present, the average labor time was cut in half. The researchers say these results suggest anxiety may slow or stop labor and may cause fetal distress—prime reasons for medical interventions.

The laboring mothers in this study did not have their husbands present, so the question is raised: Couldn't the father take the place of the doula? Yes—and no. In fact, even greater benefits may be expected when the father *and* a woman friend remain with the mother throughout the labor and birth. We think the father plays a unique role, and that no woman can substitute for what he does. But we also believe there is a special role for a doula, which the father can't fully duplicate.

The Guatemalan research shows clearly that having a doula can prevent problems in the laboring woman. Women without doulas had three times as many complications, such as cesarean birth, stillbirth, forceps, and slowed labor requiring the use of Pitocin. We believe that in a hospital birth today, having a good and safe birth requires a doula not only as comforter, but as both buffer and advocate with doctors and nurses for the laboring woman and her husband.

Ideally, a doula is someone who is related to the mother or already knows and cares for her. She doesn't have to be a childbirth education teacher, though thousands of these compassionate women have been doulas for their students. Hopefully, she's a mother herself, wants to help other women, and will be accepting of the laboring mother's wishes. Don't overlook prospective grandmothers. These women are generally very supportive to both the laboring mother and the father, and their support helps to strengthen the bond of the newly extended family. And, of course, grandparents are often invaluable once the baby's born.

Some women may want more than one doula. In fact, it is common to find several women in attendance in alternative birth centers or at home births. When you have your baby, you, too, may want to invite several women; but check with your hospital in advance (going to the hospital administrator if you need to), since many hospitals have a limit on how many people can be with you in the labor room. You may have to negotiate to have more.

You may be wondering if laboring women ever have brothers or prospective grandfathers present. Some certainly do. In fact, according to anthropologist Raphael, the doula occasionally is a man. One mother who gave birth in a birth center told us euphorically how her brother held her while her husband caught the baby as it was being born. Yet we still believe that a female doula is needed.

■ *She calms the father.* Though the father's unique role makes him the key to the mother's joy and rapture, he can also benefit from the doula's presence. Fathers, especially first-time dads, can be unsure of what's expected from them during the birth process. As labor becomes progressively more intense, the woman becomes consumed by her body's contractions, and all attempts at casual conversation are gone. Some fathers may worry that all is not well. It is at this point, especially, that the doula can encourage and reassure the father—telling him that what he's doing (talking softly to the mother, kissing her face, wiping her brow, whatever) are all comforting and crucial. Also, though the father is not physically giving birth, he's still investing enormous energy. The doula's helpful presence and her kind and encouraging words can help to reduce the father's anxiety.

■ *She nurtures the mother.* The doula rubs the mother's back, holds her hand, and, as much as possible, keeps in soothing body touch with her. Since the father is doing this, too, isn't that enough? Some of the time it is, sometimes it isn't.

The doula also offers the "female" connection, a same-sex empathy much like the identification men have with other men in a time of crisis—like soldiers on a battlefield. The doula probably has had a baby herself, so she has the link of experience. She understands the physical, emotional, and spiritual processes of childbirth. Some mothers who have given birth with doulas present tell of receiving an energy from these women, often described as a healing strength. Giving birth draws women together, while not precluding the simultaneously special relationship the laboring woman has with her husband. Often doulas describe reliving their own birth experiences—a feminine link through the ages.

It seems right to be with other women. Another woman present at the birth often can help the mother discard inhibiting social concerns, such as worrying about making too much noise, or complaining too much, or not pleasing others. A doula can help the mother know that she—and she alone—is the center of this birth. Her needs and the needs of her baby, are the only ones that matter just now.

■ *She serves as a buffer.* Some nurses understand the laboring mother's need for encouraging glances and comments, but they can also be severely limited in how much time they have for each patient. Others, though well intentioned, deflate mothers and may delay the progress of the labor by comments like, "Gosh, your contractions aren't as strong as they should be," or "Get hold of yourself—quiet down," or "If you don't hurry up, they'll probably give you a c-section." The mother doesn't need any negative statements during labor. In contrast to this, the doula continually reminds mom of how well she's doing.

The doula can also calm the staff. During the course of one labor a doula reported that the nurse would look visibly upset when she'd come into the room and find out that the electronic fetal monitor was malfunctioning because of the position of the belt on the mother's abdomen. Knowing that the mother now thought she had done something wrong or that her baby was in trouble, this doula intervened and cleared up an accelerating misunderstanding. "The machine's malfunctioning again, isn't it?" said the doula to the nurse. "The baby's just fine. It's the machine that has the problem." When the nurse readily agreed, the mother visibly relaxed.

Just having another person present during the labor, in addition to the father, reduces the chance of negative comments from the staff, since we're all generally on our best behavior when there's an audience.

One mother reported that she wanted to get up and move around during labor, even though she had an IV hookup and fetal-monitor attachments. The doula's reminder to the nursing staff, along with her readiness to help the staff work out the problems of the patient moving while attached to machine cables, led to a satisfactory solution that allowed the mother to walk around. If someone hadn't taken the role of the diplomat, the go-between, it's unlikely that mother would have moved from her bed.

The doula's there to see that hospital routine does not overshadow the parents' needs. The presence of the father and the doula can form a protective bubble around the laboring woman.

■ *She serves as advocate.* Active labor is not the time for a pregnant woman to be assertive. She has more important things to do than to have to remind nurses and doctors of what birth options had been agreed to. The mother needs to focus her mind solely on her body sensations. She can hardly do otherwise. So it might fall onto the dad's shoulders to renegotiate options. But this is a dissipation of his energies as well. Having a doula there to handle these matters allows the father to concentrate solely on his wife and her needs during labor.

As labor progresses, you may feel yourself getting "bogged down" in middle labor (4 to 7 centimeters), or when approaching the pushing stage. Quite normally you'll wish you were somewhere else. Or you'd give anything if the birth could happen "right now." You may even reach the point where you don't care whether you have anesthesia or not, a cesarean birth or not. That's normal.

If labor seems to slow, a lot of people (especially nurses and doctors) get nervous unnecessarily. That's when the doula can step in and gently remind everyone that the baby is fine. She can also monitor to see that the mother's preferences—from no routine IVs to a sitting-up position for birth (which may require a special prop behind her in the bed or on the delivery room table)—are honored. When the doula calmly reminds those present of what the mother wants, she helps everyone—parents and staff alike.

This part of the doula's role may make the parents uneasy before they even get to the hospital. What if the doctors and nurses become angry with the mother because this person is interfering? And what if parents in the future won't get what they want because they and the doula are too demanding now? One mother expressed the fear that if she were too exacting about her baby's cesarean birth, the hospital would change its policy of allowing fathers to be present at cesarean births.

It's not the doula's intent to tell the staff how to perform their jobs; it's her purpose to remind everyone of what the mother wants. Nurses and doctors, of course, want to do their jobs well. They, too, want a healthy, satisfied patient. Although parents may have an initial fear of reprisal, women who have played the part of the interface between staff and parents have not usually been criticized. It does occasionally happen in a tense moment. Nurses and doctors are human, remember? But we have never heard of hospitals eliminating options they once offered because of the presence of a doula.

You may be convinced that you want a doula with you and your husband when you're in labor, but are reluctant to ask a friend to come with you. It seems like a lot to ask of someone. But women we've talked to who have played the role of the doula consider it a privilege, a rare opportunity.

Once you've selected a doula (or two), before you go into labor, review with her what's important to you for your birth. Describe what agreements you have with your doctor or the hospital. Be as specific as you can about what you want her to do. You may not be comfortable with a doula providing all the functions we describe in this chapter. Fine. Tell her what *you* want her to do for you.

■ *She helps after the baby's born.* While you've been pregnant, you've probably gotten a lot of attention, especially if this is your first baby. After birth, who is there to turn to? Your baby's needs take from you. That's your infant's right. A mother needs mothering herself to love and care for her infant. A doula is priceless after the birth. We know from the surveys that such friends are important breastfeeding supporters, and they are essential for mothering after you go home, too. She may, or may not, be the same person who was your doula during your labor and birth. Find someone whose attitude mirrors that of the lay midwife who told us that her most important role with a woman is to help her through her transition to motherhood—to give her encouragement and confidence as she learns to be a mother. On The Farm in Tennessee new or inexperienced mothers are housed with women who have already had several children so that the new mother can learn from the experienced mother.

Psychiatrist Lucy Waletzky encourages fathers, too, to find a support system for themselves after the baby's born. She says, "Perhaps it would help to have someone mother the father." Mothers have friends and family to call, plus volunteer organizations like La Leche League. Men can talk to their own fathers, their friends, or men they work with who have children.

Since many hospitals are accustomed to having only the father stay with the mother during the labor and birth, as well as be a constant visitor once the baby's born, you will probably have to make special arrangements in advance for the doula. Check with the hospital and your doctor. If you have one doctor for the birth and another for your baby, check with both. If possible, arrange to have your doula come at any time while you're in the hospital. The hospital visiting hours may not suit your needs or your doula's schedule.

No one cares for you as much as your family and friends. Inviting them to help you is a plus for them, too. It's an invitation to share in some precious moments in your life and the life of your baby and can be a form of insurance for you that they will always care for your child. Klaus and Kennell report in *Parent-Infant Bonding* that Raven Lang, lay midwife, "noted that the observers of the labor and birth became more attached to the infant than other friends of the family who did not witness the birth."

What can you do if you live 1,000 miles from your nearest relative and none of your friends have babies? Make new friends. Find someone else who has a new baby—she'll talk your language. What about your neighbors, a co-worker, someone from your childbirth education class or La Leche League? Create your own circle of supporters.

THE CHILDBIRTH EDUCATOR

Childbirth education in the United States began in the forties, largely influenced by British obstetrician Grantly Dick-Read and his book, *Childbirth Without Fear: The Principles and Practice of Natural Childbirth*. During the fifties and sixties Dick-Read was followed by Robert Bradley,

M.D., and his husband-coached childbirth; ASPO (American Society of Psychoprophylaxsis in Obstetrics), a teacher-certification group responsible for the widespread use of the Lamaze method, and ICEA (International Childbirth Education Association), an umbrella organization of childbirth educators and consumers.

Childbirth educators offer instructions on relaxation and breathing during labor, physical exercises, and a description of the course of labor. A tour of a local hospital ob unit is included, and most instructors have added information on analgesia and anesthesia, breastfeeding, and changes in sexuality. Most of the classes are taught at the end of pregnancy (six to eight sessions), but more and more instructors also have one or two prenatal classes in the first trimester.

Childbirth educators have done an excellent job of informing couples about pregnancy and the process of birth. Along with La Leche League, childbirth educators have been at the heart of the consumer movement in maternity care in the United States. They've helped women take more responsibility for their own health care. Millions of couples are closer today because of the powerful effect of sharing the woman's labor and birth, and because of the knowledge they gained from these educators. Some of these educators, in addition, act as doulas for their students.

But childbirth educators are often criticized for not delivering more. Repeatedly, women say, "My experience at the hospital didn't match what my childbirth instructor said would happen." Or, "She led me to believe that I would get what I wanted." Or, "Why didn't she tell me the contractions would hurt so much?" You could say that some of these new mothers blocked out the words of the instructors that as pregnant women they didn't want to hear or weren't ready to understand. But it's more than that. You may be expecting more than a childbirth instructor can give you.

Lamaze is far and away the most widespread of the childbirth methods. In fact, many people think the word *Lamaze* is a generic term synonymous with all childbirth-education methods. Superb national organization plus cooperation (some critics claim co-option) with physicians has made it so. The Lamaze method has strong physician support and there's good reason for that. Lamaze is taught almost exclusively by nurses, trained and certified by ASPO, who are likelier to tell couples what they'll get in the hospital, than what options are available. Many hospitals and doctors hire their own childbirth instructors for their patients, further ensuring that couples will conform to established routine. Lamaze instructors often see themselves as an arm of the medical profession. Bradley instructors, on the other hand, tend to see themselves more as parent advocates—not antidoctor, but proconsumer.

Many childbirth educators say they walk a fine line between giving consumers information and getting along with doctors. For instance, one childbirth educator said she encouraged couples to use the birth room in a local hospital because they were likelier to get the options they wanted there. The doctor this educator worked for, however, wouldn't use that room because he was more comfortable in the delivery room. The childbirth educator finally quit telling couples about the birth room.

Independent childbirth educators, those who are not in the direct employ of hospitals or doctors, rely on referrals for new customers. Some couples choose a class because of a suggestion from a friend, but most couples choose a childbirth educator because of a referral from their doctor. So even some self-employed childbirth educators try not to go out of their way to anger local doctors by volunteering negative information about the use of fetal monitors, for example, when educators know that the local hospitals use these monitors routinely.

In years past, Lamaze instructors taught women distraction and conditioned responses (like special breathing techniques) to use during labor. Bradley instructors, on the other hand, encouraged women to breathe normally and tune in to their bodies. Childbirth educator and author Penny Simkin, R.P.T., told us that many Lamaze instructors have changed their classes because of the influence of British childbirth educator Sheila Kitzinger. Many Lamaze instructors now encourage women to have a greater awareness of their bodies during labor. And like many Bradley instructors, they take an eclectic approach—they teach their students techniques from many sources, including yoga breathing and visualization.

Shop for a childbirth educator as you would for a physician or hospital. Childbirth educators vary enormously in what they offer, in their beliefs, and in their experience. Take the issue of pain. If you want to cope with pain drug-free, you need to know *how* to do that, not just that it is safer for the baby if you do. Some instructors spend time describing nondrug methods of coping with pain. Others spend a whole class and more describing analgesia and anesthesia—with the admonition, "Don't be a martyr."

Interview childbirth educators on the phone. Ask your friends. If possible, look at each teacher's class kit (the handouts couples get). How consumer oriented is the material?

Childbirth educators cannot guarantee that you'll have your version of a "good experience." The person to ensure that is you, by virtue of information you gather, your choice of both birth attendant and location, and whether you have enough support during your labor and birth.

THE MONITRICE (YOUR PERSONAL OB NURSE)

Although the hospital you plan to use may be fully staffed with nurses, most of you will be having your baby at a hospital that's not. Eight out of ten American hospitals do not have enough nurses for routine care. And the shortage may be on the ob floor.

I do not consider myself a complainer—but believe me, when you need something, have a question, or are in pain, and ring for a nurse, you don't expect to wait for two hours before they answer your call. Many a time I had to call two or three times.

We know a hospital that advertises an alternative birth center, but laboring mothers are routinely turned away because there isn't a nurse available to work in that section. Although the mothers are promised the use of the birth center by both physician and hospital, the mothers are sent instead to the traditional ob unit. If this happens to you, you may find that one nurse will be responsible for as many as six to eight women in labor.

> There is often the problem of too much to do with too few nurses to do it. But closer observation of these situations may find staff practicing avoidance behavior, such as refilling supply cupboards, sorting chart forms, and making gauze sponges. Even closer observation may find staff simply avoiding the laboring women except for routine assessments. Supporting women and their families in labor day after day is exhausting and depleting work. In the traditional routinized and compartmentalized maternity system, there are few rewards for nurses.
>
> —Philip E. Sumner
> and Celeste R. Phillips,
> *Birthing Rooms: Concept and Reality*

What can you do to avoid paying the consequences of a nursing shortage when you're in labor? We're serious when we tell you to consider this: hire a private-duty nurse, a monitrice, to be with you. Hiring a nurse to provide primary, or one-to-one, nursing care for you is uncommon for hospital births but not new.

To overcome resistance to their efforts to institute the birth room program at Manchester Community Hospital in Manchester, Connecticut, in 1969, Philip Sumner, M.D., and his colleagues had to supply their own nurses for the first birth room used. "What at first seemed to be a hardship turned out to be the greatest single asset of our program," says Dr. Sumner, "since it enabled us to introduce the concept of the monitrice. One-to-one, uninterrupted support by the highly motivated and sympathetic monitrice has helped ensure the success of our program."

Fourteen maternity nurses trained in the Lamaze method of prepared childbirth were on call on a rotating basis for patients of Dr. Sumner and his partners. They were hired privately by the patients, came to the hospital when the woman arrived in labor and stayed with her through labor, delivery, and recovery. The monitrice monitored the fetal heart rate with a stethoscope, continuously if necessary, so that electronic fetal monitoring was used for normal births only when the monitrice felt she would like the additional data it might provide.

In Baltimore, three nurses started a monitrice service, Monitrices of Maryland (MOM). (No connection to our M.O.M. Survey.) They "provide individualized and continuous nursing care on a one-to-one basis during labor, delivery, and the immediate postpartum period for the family." All of the monitrices are registered nurses who are trained in relaxation and breathing techniques.

"We have an extensive orientation for our nurses in each hospital where we work," said Patricia Curran, R.N., codirector of MOM. No doubt this has contributed to their trouble-free efforts at getting hospital privileges and having general acceptance from nursing staff. MOM's monitrices can provide all nursing care from admission procedures to auscultating the fetal heart tones. "The patient does not have to come into contact with the hospital nurses except for a few procedures," said Curran, "like inserting IVs."

An average fee for the Baltimore monitrices in early 1983 was $120 to $150 a birth, depending on the number of hours the monitrice stayed with the laboring woman. In late 1982 the monitrices in Manchester, Connecticut, disbanded their service when the Manchester Hospital administration opted to provide one-to-one nursing care for laboring women by hiring additional staff nurses. When the Manchester Monitrices provided their services, the charge averaged $110 per birth.

What about insurance? William L. Kuehn, Ph.D., then Director of Communications for the American Nurses Association, pointed out in an interview, "I would suggest pregnant women check this out, since insurance reimbursement depends on physician approval. Nurses have no direct reimbursement methods." MOM's Curran said: "Blue Cross would not give us blanket coverage, but a physician can write the order that he wants a patient to have a private-duty nurse. Some patients have been reimbursed, but the patient has to keep after the insurance company." In Manchester, Connecticut, the monitrice fee was part of the hospital's bill and was paid for by insurance companies.

Do you definitely need a private-duty nurse in addition to your husband and your doula? Will your care suffer if you don't? Yes and no. What if you're in a hospital that routinely uses electronic fetal monitors on all patients, and you want to be an exception to the rule? When you discuss this preference with your physician, your argument will be much more persuasive if you tell him that you're willing to hire a private-duty nurse who will monitor your baby's heart tones by stethoscope. Having a nurse of your own do that—whether your hospital is short of staff or not—makes this option more manageable for your physician. Your willingness to hire a nurse also shows how important this preference is to you. (Do check with the nurse you're hiring to find out if she's been trained to use a stethoscope for fetal heart tones.)

To find a monitrice, call hospital ob units and ask if they have on-call ob nurses. If they do, contact one of them. She will already have gone through the hospital orientation and have hospital privileges. If an ob nurse tells you they don't use on-call nurses (and/or they have enough nurses on staff already), unless they provide one-to-one care, go further. Call the director of nursing or the hospital administrator. Undoubtedly, there's a procedure for hiring private-duty nurses at your hospital, because most likely your hospital already has private-duty nurses available for the medical-surgical patients.

Ask your childbirth educator. Since most childbirth educators are also nurses, some of them will have hospital privileges and, in addition, may be working at your hospital part-time. Ask your doctor if he knows of nurses who work part-time on the ob floor.

Nurses don't agree on what the ideal number of obstetrical patients per nurse is. But research shows that the ideal ratio for you, the consumer, is one-to-one nursing care. Unquestionably, both you and your baby will be healthier. Primary or one-to-one nursing care is standard in alternative birth centers, and lay midwives stay with mothers during all of the labor and birth at home. If you plan to have your baby in a traditional hospital unit, you can't expect the hospital to provide one-to-one care. You'll have to provide that yourself by hiring a monitrice.

All women benefit by having their husband, doula and monitrice present. But if you are expecting your first baby, these supporters are especially helpful to you. First-time mothers are likelier to have interventions of all kinds than women who have already had a baby. Labor and birth will be an entirely new and untried experience to you, and you will need all the help and reassurance you can get.

12 • HOW TO HAVE A NORMAL VAGINAL BIRTH (and Avoid an Unnecessary Cesarean)

In her seventh month of pregnancy Kathy finalized her birth plan with Dr. Right. By then she had discovered there were a lot of things that seemed very important to her, such as checking into the hospital as late as possible, hiring her own nurse to be with her at all times (a monitrice), and having other women there with her (as well as her husband).

When Kathy told her doctor she wanted to stay home as long as possible in labor, and to call him when she felt like coming to the hospital, he agreed. But his sudden laughter showed that he felt she wouldn't last very long at home. Hiring the nurse was okay with him, too, since there was a shortage of ob nurses at the hospital. To avoid having a fetal monitor, he said, the private-duty nurse, or monitrice, would have to check the fetal heart tones. Getting him to agree to these things was easier than she had expected. However, getting him to agree to the presence in labor of her mother-in-law, Maria, and her friend, Julie, was more difficult. He suggested the monitrice and her husband were enough. He couldn't understand why she wanted other women to be there, but finally he agreed to that point as well.

When Kathy was negotiating with Dr. Right, she noticed that he paid more attention to what she said when she talked about what was safe for her baby. When she told him what she wanted, he listened, but not as carefully as when she said she wanted to avoid interventions unless absolutely necessary because they might not be safe for her baby.

Kathy listened and agreed when her doctor said that her birth-plan preferences might have to be overridden in an emergency situation. Kathy typed up two copies of her birth plan. Both she and Dr. Right initialed them. Then he took one copy for her hospital chart, and she kept the other with her.

Kathy had been a light smoker when she became pregnant. Cigarettes had not tasted good to her during the nausea of early pregnancy, so she quit smoking. She had been an occasional drinker but she found, as her pregnancy proceeded, that alcoholic drinks didn't seem to taste good anymore, either, so she cut back on this too.

The unborn baby is the loser when a woman smokes or drinks during her pregnancy. Studies done in the 1970s in various medical centers have linked smoking with an increase in the risk of miscarriage, premature birth, premature separation of the placenta from the uterine wall (placental abruptions), placenta abnormally low in uterus (placenta previa), premature rupture of membranes (PROM), fetal distress during labor, and low birth weight. Heavy smokers tend to gain less weight during pregnancy than nonsmokers, and this may be one reason for their baby's lower birth weight. However, studies indicate that smoking directly affects the unborn baby, reducing the amount of oxygen that reaches the baby and causing growth retardation.

Pregnancy and alcohol don't mix either. Doctors have long known that a heavy daily use of alcohol is connected with a set of birth defects in the baby known as fetal alcohol syndrome. As researchers began to take a closer look at the effects of alcohol use in pregnancy, they discovered that they simply could not find a safe level of use. So strong is the evidence that the National Foundation of the March of Dimes recommends, "If you are pregnant, don't drink. If you drink heavily, don't become pregnant."

The same guide for intervention in birth can be applied to any drug use in pregnancy: Avoid use unless the benefits outweigh the risks. For example, a pregnant woman may need to continue medication for epilepsy to prevent seizures.

Earlier in her pregnancy Kathy had taken a relaxation class. As her pregnancy progressed, she tried to practice relaxation half an hour before bedtime. The evenings when she practiced were followed by a better night's sleep than those evenings when she skipped practicing. Now well into her eighth month, she noticed that sometimes her stomach became firm to the touch and she became conscious of the heaviness of her abdomen. After a few days she realized that these sensations were the uterine contractions of late pregnancy. She was thrilled at her discovery. She decided that whenever she experienced these very mild contractions, she would practice her relaxation—as a sort of conditioning to respond with relaxation whenever she felt a contraction. Her days seemed very full because she needed to move more slowly and she tired very easily. Some days she could hardly make it through her teaching job, often going directly to bed when she got home from work.

Early in her pregnancy her doctor had referred her to his nurse to discuss a good diet. Gaining weight rather than trying to hold the line was emphasized. So Kathy was astonished to find that some women in her childbirth education class had recently begun dieting because they had "gained enough weight," according to them.

Years ago mothers were cautioned to limit how much weight they gained during their pregnancy. Since then research has accumulated to show that having a healthy baby of normal birth weight is linked to the woman's prepregnancy weight, and to whether or not she has gained enough during pregnancy. To have a normal-birth-weight baby, women who were underweight at the beginning of pregnancy needed to gain more than women who were not underweight to start with. An average weight gain in normal pregnancies of twenty-four to twenty-eight pounds was established. However, the "average" often became the "ideal," just as average labor curves became the standard for what was normal or abnormal labor. Too many mothers who had gained the "average" twenty-four to twenty-eight pounds by the seventh or eighth month of pregnancy felt that they should gain no more. In 1980, childbirth educators in four geographic areas of the United States assisted Madeleine Shearer, editor of *Birth*, in surveying 250 women on their nutrition and weight gain in pregnancy. Many women, ranging from 25 to 80 percent of the childbirth education classes, were dieting to hold the line at their seventh-month weight gains. The end of pregnancy is not only the time when the baby has a huge growth spurt, doubling his weight from four to eight pounds, but it is also a time of rapid growth of his brain cells.

"Even mild degrees of maternal undernutrition in the last few weeks can interfere with the normal growth and development of the normal fetal brain," says Dr. John Dobbing, British research professor, quoted by Gail Brewer in *What Every Pregnant Woman Should Know, The Truth About Diets and Drugs in Pregnancy*. Written in consultation with her husband, Tom Brewer, M.D., an ob/gyn, this book advises women:

- Don't worry so much about weight gain; eat according to your appetite.
- Make good nutrition your primary concern.
- Don't restrict salt intake.
- Be very careful about drugs, especially diuretics, which are dangerous to women and their unborn babies.

The Brewers' advice resulted from Dr. Brewer's research on toxemia, a metabolic disease of pregnancy. For years, doctors prescribed weight control and salt restriction, together with diuretics (water pills) to prevent toxemia. The Brewers explain, however, that these prescriptions contribute to low-birth-weight and brain damaged babies, and may actually trigger toxemia by promoting malnutrition in the pregnant woman.

In normal pregnancy the woman's circulating blood volume expands by more than 40 percent to take care of the nutritional needs of the woman and her growing baby. The expanded blood volume is determined and maintained by adequate salt intake. If you have ever tasted your own blood, you know it is very salty. The crucial need for salt is the reason that salt should *not* be restricted in pregnant women, the Brewers say.

Given the American passion for being skinny, it's not easy for a woman pregnant for the first time to watch her body contours change, to see her waistline go, her stomach begin to protrude, and her body put on fat where she never had it before. So it's important for you to realize that you'll gain the right amount of weight for you if you eat when you are hungry, taking in nutritious foods and avoiding empty calories. Underweight women will need to make special efforts to eat enough to gain regularly.

It's hard to cut out cakes, pies, cookies, candy, and fried foods, which have a lot of calories and few nutrients; but it's also important to get all the nutrients you and your baby need each day by concentrating on milk products, fruits, vegetables, whole grain cereals, breads, fish, poultry, and lean meat. However, you need not be a meat eater to get the high-protein nutrition essential in a healthy pregnancy if you carefully combine grains and vegetables to form the complete proteins your body needs. *Diet for a Small Planet* gives an excellent explanation of ways to combine foods to get complete proteins, without eating meat.

Kathy had arranged to stop working late in her eighth month of pregnancy. By then her baby's movements reminded her of its presence many times a day. She began to turn away from outside interests and to turn inward. She decided not to fight it, but to go with her feelings. At least once a day, but especially when she was changing clothes and could see her nude body, she would put her hands on her stomach and talk to her baby. The uterine contractions of late pregnancy—which some experience and some don't—came a little more often. Wherever she was, she used them as an opportunity to practice her relaxation, letting calmness flow through her body.

Kathy had tried to take a walk every day during her pregnancy. Now that she was no longer working, she had more time for walking. Every day she looked forward to getting out to walk a mile or two.

Pregnant women need regular exercise to stay fit.

> Walking, swimming, and bicycling are enjoyable activities that not only provide excellent general exercise but bring you into the fresh air and sunshine. Done regularly, they combine many of the desirable features of prenatal exercise planning: to strengthen muscles, build up endurance, improve circulation and respiration, adapt to increasing weight and changing balance.
>
> —Elizabeth Noble, R.P.T.,
> *Essential Exercises for*
> *the Childbearing Year*

Women who have been inactive prior to becoming pregnant need to ease slowly into exercise. Strenuous exercise that leaves a pregnant woman gasping and exhausted, either right after exercising or later, is not good, for her or her baby. Easy does it. Exercise, done regularly, in a way that causes you to breathe deeper and faster, helps you to be physically fit and better able to cope with physical and mental stress.

Another benefit of regular exercise while pregnant may be an increased secretion of endorphins in labor. Endorphins, the "well-being" hormones we mentioned earlier, are linked to your pleasure in the birth process. Daniel B. Carr, M.D., et al., reporting in 1981 in the *New England Journal of Medicine* demonstrated an increased endorphin response in women exercising regularly. Exercise increases the blood levels of endorphins and conditioning enhances that effect. Women who exercise regularly have higher levels of endorphins when they are exercising than women who exercise irregularly. Although we know of no such research on pregnant women, it may be that by conditioning in pregnancy, a woman may increase her endorphin levels when she is in labor and her uterus is working strenuously.

Even if it's late in your pregnancy, you still have time to do one exercise more important to you for your health than any other. The pelvic floor (made up of the pubococcygeous or Kegel muscle) supports your expanding uterus which holds your baby. Exercising your Kegel muscle makes your perineum stronger, yet more "stretchy," more resilient in the pushing stage of labor. Relaxing the pelvic floor while pushing with the abdominal muscles eases your baby's way out and helps prevent tears and episiotomies.

You exercise this muscle by contracting or tightening and then releasing. To find the Kegel muscle, try stopping your flow of urine. The muscle that tightens at that moment is your Kegel muscle.

Elizabeth Noble, R.P.T., describes the Kegel exercise:

Remember: Quality is more important than quantity. Slowly contract the muscles as you would in making a hard fist, not just closing your fingers but clenching to bring in every muscle fiber. About 5 in a series, holding each contraction for about 5 seconds. . . . Always end with a contraction. . . . Fifty a day, at least, during pregnancy and postpartum. Fifty a day, at least, *for the rest of your life.*

Kathy especially enjoyed her contacts with other pregnant women and nursing mothers in her childbirth preparation class and in La Leche League meetings. There was a common bond of excitement, anticipation, and fear that these women instantly understood. Women who already had their babies talked about how helpful friends had been before, during, and after birth. Kathy realized a few weeks before her baby was born that having other women with her during her birth was not just a preference, it was a really strong need. She was glad her husband's mother, Maria, who had four children, would be there because she was experienced in giving birth, was a loving, calm person, and was the grandmother-to-be. She was also a supportive friend to her daughter-in-law Kathy. She was especially glad that her friend Julie, who had a three-year-old son, had agreed to be there. Kathy wanted Julie to handle any questions or problems there might be with the hospital staff, so that Kathy and Tim could concentrate on the labor.

As we discussed in Chapter 11, a laboring woman needs to have another woman or women with her. In many other cultures the grandmother-to-be, midwife, or another experienced-in-birth woman is always present with a laboring woman. Most of the time their reassuring message is unspoken but understood: "You will give birth; you can stand the pain; you can find your own way to labor; I have done it and I am here to let you know you can do it too. Your body is made to give birth, and all will be well." Women learn about giving birth and breast-feeding from other women. They instinctively trust other women.

When Kathy's due date came and went, she was not too depressed because half the women in her childbirth class still had not delivered. By the forty-second week of her pregnancy, however, she was tired of lugging around thirty-five extra pounds. She felt very discouraged to learn at her routine prenatal visit that the baby's head was not yet engaged in the pelvis, and her cervix showed no signs of effacing (softening—an early sign of labor). Her friend Julie had arranged to call her every day so that Kathy would know where she would be and could reach her. This time when she called, Kathy wept and said, "I'm so tired of being pregnant." Julie said all the right things. She even correctly anticipated Kathy's unspoken thought that maybe—just maybe—she'd accept induction just to get the pregnancy over. Kathy felt better after talking with Julie. She returned to her acceptance of the truism that the baby would come when it was ready, and not a moment sooner. But it felt good just to know that someone else could empathize with her impatience.

For those last five days all Kathy thought of was the baby. It seemed to her that her brain had turned to mush, and that she must be the most uninteresting conversation partner. All she wanted to talk about was the baby. Concentrating on anything else seemed impossible. One morning in the grocery store where she always shopped, she became very frustrated when she couldn't find half the things on her list. She just felt weird. When she got home from the grocery store, she had some gentle contractions, not any different from before, and automatically relaxed through each one. When she had four contractions in an hour, however, a feeling came to her that maybe this was the real thing. She called her husband, Tim, and asked if he could take off work for the rest of the day. "Are you in labor?" he asked. "I don't know, but I need you," said Kathy.

Almost all women know when they are in true labor that will soon lead to the birth of their baby. The problem comes from thinking and worrying about being in labor when you are not. Everyone, women and their birth attendants, has "difficulty in accurately timing the onset of labor," said Gordon C. Gunn, M.D., of the Department of Obstetrics and Gynecology, University of California, Los Angeles and Torrance. "This problem is especially true in primigravidas where regular uterine contractions may not result in cervical dilatation and where cervical effacement [thinning of the cervix] usually precedes the onset of true labor." True labor consists of regular uterine contractions resulting in a progressive opening of the cervix. Early labor, when the cervix gradually thins, can precede true labor by many hours or days. If you are near term and are having regular contractions, you may be in early labor. The contractions could go on for several days, perhaps alternating hours of regular contractions with periods of rest (when you should!).

What's the rush to get to the hospital? If you are in the one percent of women who have a very rapid labor and birth (an hour or two) you may end up among the tiny number of women who have a baby in the car on the way. In her review of all available data, Doris Haire, D.M.S., reported at the 1981 La Leche League International conference in Chicago that infants born in cars have the lowest infant mortality of any group. Everyone else may be anxious, but mothers and babies do fine. "Nature unaided will usually conduct a successful delivery," said Gregory White,

M.D., home-birth attendant to over 1,000 women during thirty years of practice, and author of *Emergency Childbirth*. "Childbirth is not nearly so dangerous as a wild ride in an automobile."

Dr. White says to stop the car for the birth. "The mother, sitting in a slumped down position in the back seat, can deliver the baby over the edge of the seat into the hands of the attendant; or she may lie across the seat. As soon as the baby has been born and is breathing freely, it may be placed between the mother's legs and the trip to the hospital continued; it is not necessary to deal with the cord or wait for the afterbirth."

Stay home until you feel sure you are in well-established labor and will deliver soon. If you are feeling very uncertain, consider having a vaginal examination to establish dilatation. If it is during a weekday you can go to your doctor's office. Call his secretary first, of course, to alert him you are coming in. Set this up ahead of time with him, so you can be taken right in for a quick check, rather than a possible long wait in the waiting room. If it is outside office hours, go to the hospital emergency room for a dilatation check. If you are not at least 4-5 cm. dilated, you will not have checked into the hospital, and you can return home without upsetting hospital routine.

For nine hours, from ten in the morning until seven in the evening, the contractions continued, never too close together, never really regular, but always there. As each one came Kathy stopped what she was doing and allowed a wave of relaxation to pass over her body, at the same time breathing slowly and deeply. She wasn't interested in regular meals, but did become hungry during the day and had a small snack three or four times. Between six and seven o'clock in the evening the contractions were so light she was hardly aware of them. She felt very sleepy because she had missed her nap that day, so she decided to go to sleep. Because he felt he might be up later for the real thing, Tim got in bed with her, put his arms around her, and the two of them fell asleep.

Two hours later Kathy woke up because she felt she had to have a bowel movement. A half hour later she had another bowel movement, and a half hour later another one. The contractions had come back, about every twenty minutes now, and seemed stronger than she had ever felt before. Suddenly Tim laughed and said, "You know what, I think the baby's moving down and you have labor diarrhea." Kathy wasn't at all sure of anything at this point, except that she knew that she felt a little hungry again and wanted to take a shower. So first she snacked, and then she stood under a warm shower. She found that the water not only helped her to relax during the contraction, but the sensuous feeling of the water on her skin seemed to help her tune into her body better. She decided she wanted Maria and Julie to come. After Tim called them, it seemed only minutes before they arrived. Kathy was surprised at how relieved she felt just to have them there.

Supported and cared for in a safe, quiet place, a woman can turn inward and listen to what her emotions tell her to do in labor and birth. Such a philosophy of care is used by Michel Odent, M.D., and the six midwives with him in practice in Pithiviers, France. "What we try to do at Pithiviers is to rehabilitate the instinctive brain, the emotional brain, the brain which is close to the body, in a world that generally just knows and takes into account the other brain, the rational brain," said Dr. Odent at a 1982 conference, "Birth, Interaction and Attachment" moderated by Marshall Klaus, M.D., and John Kennell, M.D. "Michel Odent has put together clinically much of what is known from recent research to be of value in human childbirth," said Klaus and Kennell.

Odent, author of *Birth Reborn,* directs the obstetric unit at Centre Hospitalier in Pithiviers. In a 1983 interview, he told us that his unit is in a public hospital giving all maternity care for the local population, without selection, including immigrants and women with complications (for example, previous cesarean delivery). Induction, amniotomy, oxytocin to speed labor, and analgesia or anesthesia (unless for cesareans) are not used. Episiotomies are rare. The cesarean rate is 6 percent.

The emphasis is on providing a milieu, a setting for the woman "to forget what is cultural and to reach a level of consciousness in which she listens to the instinctive, emotional brain, to find for herself positions for labor and birth," said Odent in the journal *Birth.*

The change in level of consciousness, the regression of a woman to the more primitive, feeling level of awareness results in a safer, smoother, faster, and less painful labor and birth in the thousands of women who have given birth at Pithiviers. The average primipara labors 5 hours from 2 cm. to 10 cm. dilation, less than half the average labor reported for American primiparas. Yet, a short labor is not a goal of the birth attendants. When we asked Odent how long he's willing to wait for a birth, he said, "As long as it takes. We have no clocks anywhere in the birth rooms."

During pregnancy, couples can attend weekly group meetings (with the midwives) which emphasize the excitement, happiness, and normal nature of childbirth. Group singing is included to enhance familiarity with the midwives and to reduce women's inhibitions. Odent described five needs during labor affecting the woman's ability to tune into her emotional, instinctive brain.

The human factor. The midwife acts as a substitute for the laboring woman's mother, expressing love, support and giving skin to skin contact in preference to talking, which is kept simple and to a minimum.

The setting. The birth room where the woman labors and gives birth is like a living room with a large comfortable platform with soft cushions. To avoid the suggestion of the "right" place to labor or give birth, there is no bed. There is a wooden birthing chair.

Reduced sensory stimulation. Absence of noise, talking as little as possible, reduced lighting even to the point of semidarkness help the laboring woman tune out the world and turn inward.

Warm water in labor. "The efficiency of water during the first stage is mysterious," said Odent. "We observe many times that a good bath in warm water with semidarkness is the best way to reach a high level of relaxation." Some women prefer to shower. Some immerse in the small pool in the unit. Women are encouraged to use the pool if their labor has stalled at 5 cm. "It is common that within an hour the woman is fully dilated," Odent told us. Sometimes the women have felt so comfortable they have stayed in the pool and given birth there, very quickly. "Our purpose is never to have a baby born under water," said Odent. "But it is important to know that it happens. It has happened 38 times to me." All had excellent outcomes for mother and baby.

Positions for labor and birth. There is no confrontation at Pithiviers, no telling a woman what she must do or not do. Women search for the position of most comfort. Many women kneel, bending forward during a contraction. Odent has observed that this particular posture oftens helps a woman forget what is cultural, turn inward and regress from logic to feeling. (It also helps the rotation of the baby's head in the pelvis, as in a posterior presentation of the baby.) But there are no "best" postures. Some few women deliver in the birthing chair, some lying on the platform. The most common position sought out for births is a "standing-squat": the woman's knees are bent as if she were seated, but spread apart. Her full weight is supported by someone standing behind her, holding her. "When the mother is at risk, or the baby is at risk, as in twin or breech deliveries, for example, the standing-squat position for delivery is imperative," says Odent.

After delivery, the mother, usually in a sitting position, is active (rather than prone and passive), and ready to hold and caress her baby. The naked mother and baby, comfortable in a birth room warmed for them, have easy touching access to each other. Cradled against the mother's breast in a natural nursing position, most newborns find the mother's nipple and begin nursing with no effort on the mother's part.

From his experience at Pithiviers, Odent believes the optimum level of consciousness in birth is reached in a safe, quiet and supportive environment, and is accompanied by optimum secretion of oxytocin by the mother, and, very likely, a secretion of endorphins that protect both mother and infant against pain. "It is easy to understand that any drug given to the woman in labor can disturb the system of endorphins," says Odent. "More generally speaking, one cannot study protection against pain without studying at the same time the capacity to have pleasure and a sense of well-being."

Kathy found she was most comfortable either sitting on the floor cross-legged or slowly walking. With each contraction she would automatically relax and breathe deeply. In between contractions she felt nothing at all. Though she was concentrating on the present moment, she suddenly realized she was really getting very good at what she was doing. The long labor gave her a chance many, many times to use her relaxation with each contraction. About two o'clock in the morning she found that she was no longer comfortable relaxing and breathing through a contraction. She had to stop and lean against a chair, or the wall, or Tim, for the contraction to stay manageable. She felt somewhat irritable at one point when Tim laughed nervously in response to her abrupt command to stop walking. She said, "If you think it's so funny, why don't you try this for five minutes?" Then they both laughed, and Kathy said, "You know what, I want to go to the hospital."

Tim called the doctor's answering service to let them know they were coming in, and also called the nurse they had hired to be with Kathy. Maria, Julie, Kathy and Tim all went in one car for the fifteen-minute drive. Kathy did not feel comfortable sitting in the car. When one contraction came during the trip, she asked Tim to pull over and stop because she couldn't relax as they bumped over the road. After she arrived at the hospital, Kathy realized that she was most comfortable if she just kept walking, so she walked in a little circle in the labor room. She undressed, making a trail of clothes behind her. The hospital admitting nurse examined Kathy and told her she was 5 centimeters dilated. She was disappointed, until her cheering section reminded her that "you're halfway there." The monitrice arrived half an hour after Kathy, and began the procedure she would carry out every fifteen minutes during labor. She listened for the baby's heart tones for thirty seconds immediately after a contraction. She pronounced the baby doing "just fine." She drew a little flower on Kathy's stomach in the place that was easiest to hear the baby's heart tones.

Kathy was finding the contractions more difficult to handle and felt there must be something she should do. Then she remembered what another friend had told her. "You don't have to do anything, just relax and let your uterus open up your cervix." She thought of this often, and it helped her to let go and allow her body to work. She even tried visualizing the uterus and cervix working together with each contraction.

Contractions are the means by which a woman's body labors and gives birth. In her book *Preparation for Childbirth*, Donna Ewy, Ed.D., explains contractions:

> Probably one of the greatest fears a woman has concerning child-birth is how can a baby pass through such an obviously small opening without excruciating pain. The whole function of "labor" is to allow the contractions of the uterus to open the cervix (the lower part of the uterus) to about 4 inches, the diameter of the baby's head. After the cervix has opened the baby passes through the birth canal. The tissues of the vagina are extremely elastic, and once the cervix opens, the baby passes through with relative ease.

The woman's response is different for the two stages of labor, the first, the opening of the cervix, and the second, when the baby passes through the birth canal.

Relaxation is the first and most important response of the mother to first-stage labor. You don't have to *do* anything. Contractions are involuntary. Let the body work. In her book, *Exercises for True Natural Childbirth*, Rhondda Hartman says:

> The only help you can give the uterus with its work in the first stage is to "let it be." To do this requires great concentration on relaxing . . . just remember any part of your body in tension is going to add tension to the uterine contraction. It also detracts from the uterus's efficiency. Stay out of the way and let the uterus do its work. . . .

Controlled breathing is another helpful technique in labor. The primary purpose of controlled breathing is as a distraction, however, and if carried out over a long labor can be very tiring. The easiest and least tiring breathing to accompany relaxation is the effacement breathing, or relaxed-chest breathing, of the Lamaze method; or the abdominal breathing of the Bradley method.

A woman's response to second-stage labor is very different from the first stage. Rhondda Hartman describes it like this:

Second stage is a time for strenuous activity and total involvement with the work going on inside you. Rather than trying to keep out of the way of the working uterus, as in first stage, now you will make your strong pushes coincide with the effort of the uterus, so second stage will be as efficient as possible.

The nature of the contractions change, the time between them is longer. Contractions are still involuntary, but a woman can now effectively use her abdominal muscles to assist the contractions in pushing her baby out.

Kathy continued her slow walking with Tim right beside her, his arm around her upper back, partially supporting her. When a contraction came, she leaned her full weight against him to relax. When the contraction was over, she complained of the pain and suggested that she must not be doing very well. Her childbirth education class had given her the impression that if she relaxed and breathed correctly she wouldn't have any pain. Her monitrice explained that even though she was relaxing and breathing very well, the intensity of the contractions was stretching her cervix open. That's something some women simply feel to be more painful than do others. But Kathy was reassured that they would all help her get through it.

As they discussed the intensity of the experience, Kathy's mother-in-law, Maria, said that, of her four births, three had been without drugs or anesthesia. She had a mixture of experiences with those three, she said: with one labor and delivery there was no pain at all; with another, there was a kind of searing pain at the peak of contractions; the last birth, a five-hour labor, hurt most of the time. Sometimes she felt like she just couldn't stand the pain anymore, but the people she had with her got her through. They were going to do that for Kathy, too.

Maria mentioned one thing that had helped her was to yawn and stretch between contractions. It seemed to help get rid of extra tension. Kathy tried it, and it did seem to help her relax fully between contractions. As the morning rolled in, more suggestions were offered. If what was suggested felt right to her, she would try it. More often than not, everything she tried worked for awhile. But then the pain would build again during a contraction, and she would feel overwhelmed. She tried several different positions, but for her, on her feet supported by her helpers or sitting on the bed cross-legged with pillows supporting her back and arms so that she was quite upright, were the two positions in which she felt the least pain.

Tim could see she was getting very tired and very hot, and he suggested they take a shower together. Kathy was so involved with her contractions that she couldn't think of things to do and the idea of a shower right then sounded like a clever idea. (Tim had brought his bathing suit to the hospital just in case Kathy wanted to shower during labor.) It was slow going because, although Kathy had a good three minutes between contractions, she walked slowly. Before she got from bed to shower she had two more contractions. While she waited them out, she stood with her arms draped around Tim, who supported her weight.

The shower cooled, refreshed, and relaxed Kathy, and once more she felt she was going to make it. In fact, there were moments when Kathy could almost laugh at herself. As the labor went on, she felt not only her body but her mind was opening up. She felt free to express whatever it was she was feeling—early in labor, her pleasure and excitement that the baby was almost there, and now, later in labor, her pain and despair at ever getting through it. She felt that those around her gave her permission to do whatever it was she needed to do, and that was probably the best help of all.

When things frequently got tense, Julie's job seemed to be to remind everyone that the baby was just fine. The monitrice was continuing her regular monitoring, and the baby's heart rate was strong. Tim drew strength from his mother and from Julie, both of whom praised him for the way he was helping Kathy. Sometimes he was uncertain that he was being helpful, because of Kathy's irritability. But Julie and Maria reassured him by saying things like, "Oh, I know that feels good to Kathy." They could see that Kathy was responding to his touch. Tim opened up, too, as the labor went on, and felt free to kiss, touch, and hold Kathy, to express his love and support for her. Tim noticed that sometimes when they were kissing, Kathy's mouth was tense and she was feeling a lot of pain. He suggested she might be tightening up her bottom. They discovered that smooching a lot helped to keep her mouth and her bottom much more relaxed. There seemed to be a connection between the two.

About seven o'clock in the morning, after five hours in the hospital, and about twenty hours since labor had started, Kathy no longer wanted to move around on her feet but wanted to stay in the upright, supported sitting position. It didn't seem possible that the contractions could hurt more, but they did. Kathy was flushed and sweaty. She felt confused because now she felt she had no time to recover between contractions. The monitrice told Kathy she had all the signs of being in transition, and she was going to alert Kathy's doctor. When he arrived he agreed Kathy was in transition, and there was no need for a vaginal check. He did suggest that they might move labor along now if they broke the bag of waters. Julie reminded him how strongly Kathy felt about not artificially breaking the bag of waters. He said yes, he had remembered that, and it was fine.

Kathy was in transition for two hours. It was the worst time for her. Her pain, discomfort, and confusion were at their height, and she needed very strong assistance from those around her.

The intensity of pain experienced in childbirth is often unexpected by prepared women, who assume that if they just relax and breathe well enough, there will be no pain. It is difficult to predict ahead of time which women will have pain and how intense it will be. The childbirth literature suggests that about 5 percent of women have painless labors and births. So clearly, most women do have pain in labor and delivery.

In our culture, pain is considered abnormal, either due to disease or injury, and a symptom to be avoided or medicated. Aidan Macfarlane, author of *The Psychology of Childbirth,* suggests that pain serves a useful purpose to keep mothers alert during labor and in the period immediately following delivery. "Many mothers and babies who have gone through a normal labor and delivery without drugs also experience an hour or two of extreme alertness following delivery," she says. Obstetricians see the relief of pain as an obligation. It goes against their training to see a woman suffering in labor, and many feel the woman is a martyr, a little crazy, or both, to refuse analgesia or anesthesia. Mothers who have had painful labors and deliveries without drugs, but with caring and supportive birth attendants, family, and friends there, describe the pain as in a sense enhancing the whole experience for them by creating a need to reach out strongly to those around them. In addition, many of these mothers remark on the tremendous euphoria immediately following birth. They feel that pain and pleasure can sometimes be linked in the same experience. They have found that the exquisite pain of labor if responded to by caring birth attendants is followed by the most exquisite pleasure following birth.

Kathy had not felt hungry all night and had only felt the need for occasional sips of water or apple juice. However, during the transition, she was aware that she was tremendously thirsty and, over a two-hour period, drank about six full glasses of apple juice that Tim had brought in a thermos to the hospital. About every hour, the monitrice reminded Kathy to get to the bathroom and try to urinate, "so a full bladder won't be in the way of the baby."

The last two hours of labor were truly the hardest work that Kathy had ever done in her life. She frequently felt overwhelmed and at one point during a contraction started to pant the words, "Help, help, help, help." Julie picked up on the word and repeated it with her over and over, then put her hands on Kathy's shoulders, looked into her eyes,

*and said, "Now breathe with me, Kathy." And slowly Kathy got back in
the rhythm of breathing and relaxing with the contraction. Julie's eyes
never wavered from Kathy's during the contractions of those last hours,
and to Kathy it was a lifeline.*

Author Donna Ewy, Ed.D., includes many comforting techniques in
her book *Guide to Family Centered Childbirth.* She summarizes them by
saying, "Three key methods that will help you get her back in control
are eye contact, firm voice, and a secure touch."

A nurse discusses the power of eye contact with a laboring woman:

> One of the many useful ideas discussed in *Spiritual Midwifery* is
> the technique of "catching eyes" with the woman during those parts
> of her labor when she feels like she is disintegrating or losing her
> perspective. The transference of power and feeling between two peo-
> ple whose gaze is fixed on each other and who are breathing in
> rhythm during a very intense moment in their lives is so charged
> with energy that it makes one stand back in awe. The power is
> tremendous. The problem is that, as a culture, we are not comfort-
> able with prolonged eye contact. It is something that people need
> to be taught. However, in my experience in the hospital, it has been
> worth the effort to try. When a woman suddenly looks lost or
> desperate, I say, "Open your eyes and *look* at me, I'll breathe with
> you." If she'll do it, if she will allow herself to trust you enough
> to maintain eye contact, you can get her through almost any kind
> of a contraction just by the power of being there and experienc-
> ing it with her on a level that is difficult to appreciate unless you
> have been there yourself.
>
> —Peggy Vincent, R.N.,
> *Birth,* Summer 1977

*Tim was sitting next to Kathy, massaging her thighs where she seemed
to be feeling a lot of tension, lightly stroking her face, kissing her
between contractions, and telling her she was "almost there" and doing
great. Gradually, over the space of about three contractions, Kathy
started grunting at the end of each one. The monitrice felt she was
probably fully dilated, did a vaginal check, and found that Kathy was
indeed 10 centimeters dilated.*

*The contractions seemed to change. There was much more time in
between and Kathy felt like pushing with each one. The monitrice
notified Kathy's doctor, who was waiting in the doctor's lounge. He
checked Kathy and confirmed that the baby's head was well engaged,
that she was fully dilated, and that she could go ahead and push. Kathy
felt like she wanted to stand and lean against Tim. He stood behind
her, supported her under her arms, and held her full weight during each
contraction as she pushed whenever she felt like it. Marie remarked that*

it was a good thing that her son had been a football player, and the laughter broke some of the tension.

Kathy had planned to deliver in the birthing room. But she reconsidered that decision because she knew that one delivery room had a birthing chair, and after about forty-five minutes of pushing, with contractions coming about every three minutes, she said she thought she would be most comfortable delivering in the birthing chair. Kathy and her party of helpers transferred her to the delivery room with the birthing chair. The doctor took his place to assist her in delivery.

Historically, the most common position for birth in various cultures was some form of the upright position. Today, a modern "birthing chair" is being used in several hundred hospital delivery rooms. The birthing chair is adjustable and can be raised, lowered, or tilted, as necessary. A 1981 report from Lenox Hill Hospital, New York City, showed that for first-time deliveries, which normally have a longer second stage, the upright position provided by the birthing chair shortens second-stage labor. Contractions are stronger and more regular, and the woman seems to be able to relax more completely between contractions. Women seem able to push more effectively because of the assist from gravity in the upright position.

Late in pregnancy try out several positions for birth, so you are familiar with how they feel.

- Sit on the toilet, upright, with back support, hands on your knees to simulate the birth chair. Better yet, try out the one your local hospital may have.
- Lie on your side curled up.
- Kneel on the floor, then lean forward, on all fours, or with your upper body leaning on the couch.
- Stand, bend and spread your knees as if to sit in a chair, and have your partner hold you under your arms from behind, supporting your full weight.
- Squat (avoid this position if you have bad knees).
- Sit with your back supported and your legs comfortably spread apart, knees flexed.
- To get a feel for the "uphill" lithotomy position we hope you can avoid: Lie on your back on the floor with your bottom close to the couch. Bend your legs so your calves rest on the seat of the couch.

In each position, practice your Kegel exercise, so you are familiar with the feeling of releasing your pelvic floor in a delivery position.

"Okay," said the doctor, *"now here's what I want you to do. When a contraction begins, take two deep breaths, in and out. Take a third breath and slowly release it as you push for just as long as you want. You will be making some kind of a sound as you push. Relax your bottom while you are pushing. Whenever you need another breath, inhale slowly and then slowly release your breath as you push. When a contraction is over, take a deep breath and relax."*

Julie, who was standing next to Kathy and who had her hand on Kathy's arm, felt her tense when the doctor was telling her what to do. "Hey, you don't have to remember those instructions, Kathy," said Julie, "because your doctor is going to talk you through each contraction until it's old hat for you. You don't have to worry about anything—you just have to keep your bottom relaxed." Julie could feel Kathy's arm relax. With each contraction the doctor gave his instructions. Soon Kathy picked up her own natural pushing rhythm. It felt good to make "uhhhhhh," grunting sounds, letting out her breath while she was pushing for about five or six seconds with each breath. Her doctor told her to bear down only when she felt the need to push, without trying to hold her breath or prolong a push. He told her that by pushing this way she was getting lots of oxygen to her baby. For several of the contractions the monitrice placed her hand on Kathy's perineum. It helped two ways. The monitrice could feel when Kathy's perineum was tense or when it was relaxed and she could tell Kathy. It also helped Kathy because by having a firm hand on her perineum she could visualize better where she needed to relax.

Kathy pushed whenever she felt the urge; then, suddenly, the bag of waters burst. Kathy felt a warm jet of water between her legs. She was astonished at how much water it felt like her body was putting out. Soon a few centimeters of her baby's head could be seen at the vaginal opening. The monitrice, who sensed that Kathy was tiring, took Kathy's hand and guided it down to touch her baby's head. "You see, Kathy, there is your baby's head; it's almost here." Touching the top of the baby's head with the baby still inside her thrilled Kathy. She felt renewed energy. Slowly the head stretched the perineum until it bulged so large it looked ready to burst. But the slow stretching was doing its job. It looked as if the doctor could avoid doing an episiotomy. Kathy felt better when she was pushing. When, suddenly, the doctor told her to stop pushing so he could ease the baby's head out, the sensation of stretching and pain was tremendous. As the head emerged, Kathy screamed in pain. She felt that she might rip up the front, but there was no tearing. There was another short wait before Kathy felt the next pushing contraction. When it came, Kathy's baby was born with one push. Immediately the doctor gave the baby to Kathy to hold. Her eight-pound, one-ounce baby boy was born just before eleven in the morning, twenty-five hours after she started early labor the previous morning.

Kathy was laughing and crying at the same time and all sensations of pain were gone. She felt only enormous pleasure. About ten minutes later the doctor clamped the cord on the baby's side, but allowed the cord on the mother's side to bleed freely into a bowl. During her pregnancy Kathy had taken a medical article to him showing that when the cord was left unclamped on the mother's side, it shortens the third stage of labor (the delivery of the placenta) and blood loss is greatly reduced. There was close to a half cup of blood in the bowl when Kathy felt a mild contraction, then felt the soft placenta fill her vagina. She pushed and expelled it easily.

Kathy loved the feeling of her wet, warm newborn lying against her breast, the two of them covered with a blanket. Tim put his hand under the blanket on his son's back. Kathy's love for her husband and baby seemed to expand moment by moment until she felt her love radiating out to include the whole world. The words that kept passing through her mind were "miracle—it's a miracle."

SUMMARY: HOW TO HAVE A NORMAL VAGINAL BIRTH AND AVOID AN UNNECESSARY CESAREAN

Pregnancy

1. Choose a place of birth where there is the least intervention, or a hospital with very flexible routines.
2. Choose a midwife, a doctor with a midwife philosophy, or a doctor with whom you can negotiate for your preferences.
3. Decide what is important for your birth, write up a birth plan, and ask your doctor to sign it.
4. *Gain* weight, using nutritious foods and liquids.
5. Do not smoke or use alcohol.
6. Avoid any drug use unless the benefits outweigh the risks. Avoid aspirin, which has been found to cause bleeding in mothers and babies even when taken days before birth.
7. Learn deep relaxation, slow deep breathing, and other breathing techniques which you may use in labor.

Labor

1. If you have premature rupture of membranes, stay home and wait for labor (it may be days), unless you have active genital herpes.
2. If you are near term (within three weeks of due date), stay home in labor until you feel you must go to the hospital. Return home if you are not at least 4 to 5 centimeters dilated. (Particularly important for first labors, which tend to be longer.)
3. Eat and drink as you desire.
4. Urinate frequently.
5. Avoid efforts to intervene in a normal labor.
6. Hire a monitrice to monitor your labor and your baby's heart rate, especially if that is the only way you can avoid a fetal monitor.
7. Walk, stay upright, or in a side-lying position unless your labor is going very fast, and you are more comfortable in another position. Try different positions to find the one most comfortable for you.
8. Alternate resting and walking for a long labor.
9. Have at least one woman you know and like with you—your doula—in addition to your husband.
10. Use warm water, a soaking bath (if your bag of waters is intact), or a shower, to help you relax and open up.

Delivery

1. Use almost any position but on your back with your legs in stirrups. Upright positions allow gravity to help—especially important for first-time mothers whose deliveries tend to take longer.
2. To avoid depriving your baby of oxygen and to allow time for the perineum to stretch slowly (and avoid an episiotomy) use exhale-pushing, also known as gentle or physiological pushing:
- Push only when you feel the need.
- Release your breath very slowly when you push.
- Push no more than five to six seconds at a time. Take another breath when you still feel the need to push.
- Take a deep breath when each contraction is over.

13 ▪ YOUR HELP ON THE INSIDE—THE NURSE

> Before the baby was born, I read many books and talked with my friends. All the time I was focusing on the birth process itself. Then, there I was, in the hospital. I was dealing with hospital bureaucracy and I'd never been in a hospital before. I was flabbergasted. I was on my back and all my defenses were down. I found out that nurses can be either condescending or helpful. Nurses make *all* the difference. The nurses really count. They're the ones on the line. They're there all the time.
>
> —New York mother

If you're like most pregnant women, you're narrowing your focus. You're thinking of your changing body and how different your life will be in a few months. While you may have carefully scrutinized your physician and the options available at your hospital, you're not likely to have given much thought to the nurses who will be almost your entire contact in the hospital. Perhaps no one has told you that how you're treated during your stay depends mostly on the nurses. As important as your doctors are, you'll spend more than 95 percent of your in-hospital time with the nursing staff. So that you'll have more control over your hospital stay, we'll describe what you can expect from nurses, and why they do what they do.

Nurses' Training

Nurses, 98 percent of whom are female, are the largest group of health professionals in the world. The typical nurse is a hard-working woman who wants to help others. All nurses, regardless of education, pass the same state exam after graduating from an approved program. Programs vary in length, cost, and intensity. Of the three training programs, the one producing two thirds of all hospital staff nurses is the three-year hospital school. Associate degree and university-based programs make up the other third.

Although all of these graduates are trained to work in hospitals, the emphasis in the programs varies. Nurses who receive their training in hospital schools are the likeliest to care for you. The training of these nurses emphasizes good bedside care—which is to your advantage. But they are also trained to meet the needs of the hospital, and consequently, the physician, first—which may be to your disadvantage. Most of the hospital-school graduates are not as consumer oriented as the collegiate nurses are.

How does that affect your hospital care? Be reasonable with your expectations. Don't expect the nurses to automatically ask you what you want. They will, however, want to cooperate with you if you are clear and persistent about the options you want, just as you have been with your physician.

The changes over the years in nurses' education have brought mixed blessings to the consumer. On the one hand, nurses teach better and listen more. They don't just tell patients what to do. On the other hand, Florence Nightingale might not recognize her sisters today. Although nurses are still the "hands on" practitioners of the health care profession, they, too, have been caught up in technology. Most nursing schools, for example, don't teach nurses how to listen for fetal heart tones with a stethoscope. They are taught to use a fetal monitor instead. The focus for nurses—as for doctors—has become more exotic. Knowledge of new medications and emergency procedures takes precedence over knowing how to help the normal laboring woman with breathing techniques or with relaxation.

The Demand For (And Shortage of) Nurses— And How That Affects The Care You Receive

A nurse can get a job wherever she goes. Indeed, many hospitals actively recruit her. At least 80 percent of health care institutions report available positions. So nurses need not worry about being employed. In 1982 the typical nurse earned more than $18,000 a year. Although this salary is a big improvement over the past, the typical nurse's salary is still only one fourth of what the typical physician makes in a year.

The demand for nurses exceeds the available supply. Though 250,000 new nurses entered the work force between 1977 and 1980, there are still 100,000 budgeted nursing vacancies in the U.S. today, with shortages expected to get worse. This contrasts with the growing oversupply of physicians, predicted to be a serious glut by the end of this decade.

Although a nurse can *always* get a hospital job, when she does she often assumes enormous responsibilities. And, while working rotating shifts and holidays—times when hospital floors are traditionally understaffed—she may also be expected to assume housekeeping tasks. A common complaint for many nurses is that they can't spend enough time with patients and give quality care. This directly affects you, the consumer.

WHAT MOMS SAY THEY WANT FROM NURSES

Nurses were consistently gracious, overextending and involved in my care and excitement over childbirth. The best way to describe it is that I felt loved and "mothered" by the nursing staff! Much appreciation and thanks.

I would like to comment on one nurse in particular—I don't know her name. She tried in every way possible to make my stay as uncomfortable as she could—even after my daughter was born. She came into my room and gave me this long lecture on how bad and childish I had acted during my labor. It was extremely *painful for me and I did the best I knew how to keep in control while in labor. When the pain got really bad, she came in and said to me, "You're not having any pain yet. You just wait. It'll get* much *worse"—instead of a word of encouragement. And on the day I was discharged, she gave the information to me for postpartum care and then said to me, "Now this is your responsibility for eighteen years and don't forget it!" I am glad now to have a chance to let someone know what I went through during my stay, and hope no other woman will have to put up with this woman's bitterness.*

These two mothers had their babies in the same hospital at about the same time. Your care, too, can vary that much in the same institution. We've read hundreds of comments from mothers regarding the nursing staff and find that most comments, however, fall somewhere between the two quotes above. The care most mothers receive is neither perfect, nor perfectly horrible.

During the Labor and Birth

The theme throughout all the comments from mothers is that they want help, not hindrance; respect, not tolerance. They crave information.

My labor nurse only seemed to know how to offer me drugs when I was uncomfortable. I know she wanted to help me, but it wasn't the right kind of help. I wanted her to encourage me and show me what to do with my breathing.

And when mothers got that support they were indeed grateful.

Without the labor nurse at Community Hospital I would have folded. My comfort was her main concern. That labor nurse was super!

Breastfeeding

In the three surveys, as well as in many other comments from mothers, the emphasis for infant feeding is on breast-feeding, not bottle-feeding. That may be because no special help is usually needed for bottle-feeding mothers. Nurses are trained well to show you how to hold both your baby and the bottle, as well as when and how to burp your infant.

In both the Boulder and the Wenatchee surveys, mothers rated nurses, physicians, childbirth instructors, La Leche League leaders, husbands, and family for help in breastfeeding. Who was helpful? Nurses help more than doctors, but nurses were not as uniformly helpful as were LLL leaders and childbirth educators. Husbands and friends fared well in giving breastfeeding support, too.

Incidentally, the higher the breastfeeding rate in your town, the better the help from the nurses and doctors will probably be. The staff, like anyone else, does best what it usually does on a regular basis.

I was told by the nurse not to nurse before my milk came in because the colostrum was "useless"; told not to let him breastfeed for more than five minutes every three hours or I would get engorged; told if I nursed while lying down I might suffocate the baby and told never to sleep with my baby; told it was very odd not to send my baby to the nursery at all and that perhaps I was "too attached" to my infant.

Only a minority of women found nurses' advice with breastfeeding as shockingly inaccurate as the above. But when they did, they often reacted angrily. New mothers expect nurses to be as competent with their infant feeding advice as they are with blood pressure checks or the use of drugs. Is this a reasonable expectation? Yes. The nursing mother is no longer an occasional patient. She's the majority.

However, the nurses who are on duty when you're in the hospital may not have had access to current information in breastfeeding, or they may have no personal experience with breastfeeding their own children. And then there's resistance to change. In 1982 Lawrence Gartner, M.D., of the Pritzker School of Medicine at the University of Chicago stated:

> I agree that both hospital practices and the support available for the majority of mothers who are breastfeeding are quite inadequate.
> A lot of bad advice is handed out about breastfeeding, even within

good hospitals. . . . You do, in fact, have to go through a formal retraining of groups of nurses, some of whom in fact are resentful about the mother who wants to breastfeed.

Breastfeeding Counselors

Paula J. Adams Hillard, M.D., an obstetrician herself, wrote of her own childbirth experience in *The Female Patient:*

> The person who meant the most to me was a breastfeeding counselor; I now feel that every postpartum floor in the hospital should have someone available to encourage women to breastfeed their babies. Even though I had relatively few problems with breastfeeding, it meant a great deal to have my questions answered and to be able to read the excellent material I was provided.

Regardless of how helpful the surveyed mothers found the nurses to be with breastfeeding, almost unanimously they thought the hospital should hire a person especially trained to help breastfeeding mothers. It's more than information these mothers want. They want support from someone who understands that breastfeeding is a complex giving and receiving between mother and baby. It's a feminine art, not simply a method of feeding.

During my hospital stay, all the nurses and nurses' aides seemed to have their own fixed ideas about the care of my baby. I was trying to nurse and all they seemed to care about was getting Bridgette to drink the glucose solution they provided.

The best breastfeeding counselor is a woman personally experienced with nursing her own child or children and who thinks breastfeeding can work for nearly any woman. She does not perceive breastfeeding as a problem, and does not think it is messy or inappropriate in our culture. This breastfeeding counselor freely mothers the mother, and she knows that no one knows the baby better than its mother. She conveys the pleasure of breastfeeding and helps the mother feel good about her choice.

If you have a doula who fits the description of breastfeeding counselor, you need not look further. But if you don't, we recommend that you contact La Leche League or your childbirth educator. A few breastfeeding counselors are hired by hospitals, in Arizona, California, and elsewhere, and some hospitals have a group of volunteer counselors (nearly all of them LLL leaders). An ongoing service like this is rare. But that's changing. In 1983, LLL announced its Professional Lactation Consultant Program. For more information, see p. 295.

Ask at the nursing station for the local LLL number. Better yet, find out about LLL while you're still pregnant. Women who attend LLL meetings even before the baby is born feel more confident about breastfeeding, have fewer problems and feel more successful. Many childbirth educators, nearly all of whom have been breastfeeding mothers, also help their own students with nursing.

And *Please!* No Criticism

> One time when the nurse came in the room, I said to her: "Isn't it incredible how patient Kathy is with this labor? She has this machine hooked up to her, she is in a strange environment, and she's really tired. You are not letting her eat or drink. And she puts up with all of it, is so patient, and she allows her body to labor." The nurse said, "Yes, she's doing so well. We are proud of her, but we wish she'd hurry up her piddly labor. We'd hate to have to do a cesarean just because she's so slow."
>
> —Doula

That negative comment strikes fear in mothers. It certainly doesn't enhance a laboring mother's belief in herself. And she won't forget that comment either—not if she's like other women we've spoken to. Nor will her labor go faster because of the threat. It may only serve to convince the mom that she's a failure. She can't even get a baby born on time.

But wait a minute! Whose time are we talking about? Why did the nurse say that? Perhaps because most nurses are incorrectly taught in school that normal labors should progress one centimeter an hour. Or perhaps, as we've been told by nurses, that particular nurse is just having a bad day. Frankly, we think birth is too important for our caretakers to have bad days, difficult as that may be to control.

Being criticized about your "noisy" behavior during labor or being taken to task because your baby "only" gained half an ounce after a feeding is *never* helpful. If there's a better way for you to do something, there's also a helpful, encouraging way to tell you.

You wouldn't want your mate in the throes of lovemaking to whisper in your ear: "Darling, you're wonderful, but *GEE* you're so slow (or noisy or quiet)." Comparisons that suggest you're somehow not up to snuff are just as inappropriate when you are giving birth or nursing a baby.

As a laboring woman and new mother, you'll thrive on praise and support. Insulate yourself with the affectionate bubble of family and friends. Have your husband and doula with you. Protect yourself from demeaning comments by nurses, unintentional as they may be. Although all of you will not be subjected to these remarks, many of you will. Anticipating them in advance may deflect their sting.

HOW NURSES SEE THEIR ROLE ON THE MATERNITY FLOOR

Labor and Delivery

Maternity floors can be a tranquil oasis in a hospital filled with the sick and dying. Birth, after all, is not an illness. It's a celebration. But there's the other side of the picture, too. "Most people don't recognize that the maternity floor is also an extremely stressful and high-tension area," said one ob nurse. Even though it may not happen often, a nurse never knows who the next emergency patient will be. Just like the doctors she works with, her eye is trained to look for problems.

The emphasis in nurses' training is on what to do when nature can't seem to manage by itself. Nurses are taught how to put an IV in your arm, and, at a doctor's direction, how to measure the appropriate amount of Pitocin to get your labor started or speeded, and when to give you drugs for pain relief.

For some nurses, childbirth is nothing new. They've seen hundreds before. And when they report to the nursing station that they have "five in early labor," you may be seen as just part of their job on that particular shift. It's very exhausting for nurses to get emotionally involved with each birth. Many nurses learn early to keep themselves at arm's length. In addition, patients are not a nurse's only responsibility. There's paperwork to be done and, above all, she must do whatever the physicians tell her. The nurse's role is not an easy one. She has enormous responsibility, but often little authority.

Other nurses, though, still see each birth as sacred, not routine. Each birth for them is new and exciting. They get involved with the couple during labor and enthusiastically make personalized arrangements for the parents whenever possible. They don't talk loudly and laugh in the halls with other nurses. And they keep their voices hushed in a room with a laboring woman. They avoid examining her during a contraction, because they know that can be painful. And they tell her what to expect next in her labor. They believe the mother's needs are paramount.

Maybe you'll be fortunate enough to have one of these enthusiastic, helpful nurses. Are there very many? Not enough. Not because nurses don't want to give you the best of care—they do. But there may not be enough staff on the floor to permit your nurse to spend much time with you. Or her training or lack of experience with prepared childbirth gets in the way.

The View From the Nursery

> You know in England they don't use the nursery in the hospitals anymore; they just store things in them. They know the baby belongs with the parents and not in the nursery. Ultimately we'll get around to that here [in the United States].
>
> —John Moyer, M.D.

Although hospital planners still usually include large nurseries in the blueprints for new ob units in the United States, the concept of nurseries—a place to keep babies away from their mothers—is under fire. We humans are the only species that routinely separates mothers and babies. Forty years ago, when nearly all mothers were totally unconscious by the time they gave birth in hospitals, it might have been logical to appoint someone else (the nursery nurse) to be the infant's caretaker. Although hospital nurseries may become the health-system dinosaur of the future, if you're pregnant now, you'll probably still have to cope with nurseries during your hospital stay.

Sandra Gardner, Pediatric Nurse Practitioner, addressed her health-care colleagues in *Keeping Abreast, Journal of Human Nurturing*. But the message she sends is for the consumer, too. It's a good description of the view from many hospital nurseries:

> Terri Martin delivered her first infant by c-section three days ago. She has eagerly been breastfeeding her infant for the last two days. This morning she spiked a temperature of 101 degrees. While her physician was making rounds he . . . found no signs of infection. The physican wrote orders for the nursery nurses that the "Baby may come to the mother's room to be breastfed; breastfeeding is not to be discontinued. . . ."
>
> As the nurse enters the [mother's] room she states, "Well, I just want you to know that I do not approve of bringing this baby out to breastfeed. You realize that you have a temperature, and you don't care any more than that about your baby's health." The nurse reaches into the crib and produces a surgical mask. Handing it to the mother she states, "You *will* wear this while this baby is in this room." The mother replies, "The doctor told me that he could not find any reason for my elevated temperature and most likely it was because my milk was coming in. He did not say anything about wearing a mask while I breastfeed the baby." The nurse says, "I don't

care what the doctor said or didn't say; it's not *his* nursery, it's *my* nursery. As long as I'm in there you *will* wear this mask while this baby is in this room."

"Far fetched?!"

"Unlikely?!"

"It couldn't happen here!"

"Not us!"

. . . This "real life" incident and many others happened in community and teaching hospitals in this country.

You, too, may find yourself wondering, "Whose baby is it—the hospital's or mine?" And that's true whether you're breastfeeding or bottlefeeding. Nurses who choose to work in the nursery lavish love on their small charges. That's the good news. Gardner describes the bad news: "Neonatal nurses may, in fact, treat their small patients as their own children and irrationally block, deny, and compete with the biological mother for time with the new baby."

For many nurses the definition of a "good" patient is a woman who is quiet, uncomplaining, and totally passive. Why? Because passive mothers make the nurse's job easier. Gardner quotes nurses who say, "The families don't stay in the hospital very long, and it would be chaotic to try to meet everyone's needs. The hospital order must be maintained and as soon as they go home, they can do what they want to do."

I suppose that in order to be a good nurse, there has to be some part of your brain that says, "I love routine." Because every time I have ever been in the hospital, the smallest bit of change in routine seems to be a threat to the nurses.

Are all nursery nurses threatened by mothers who want to break the routine? No, of course not. But enough are that if you're forewarned, you're forearmed. You can turn that nurse's devotion to your baby into a benefit for both you and your baby.

Or maybe you'll be fortunate enough to have nursery nurses like the ones recently described to us:

> I stayed in the hospital two days. The nurses were so helpful. They brought Brenda every two hours, and made sure I knew how to get her started at the breast. They told me to let the baby nurse as long as she wanted. They told me Brenda didn't need water; she just needed me. Over and over they told me how well the baby and I did together. I'm so thankful to those nurses.
>
> —Colorado mother

Following is a letter Sandy Gardner quoted from a mother who also was grateful to the nursery nurses:

> When I was in the hospital, I developed a fever [101 degrees]. They thought it was from my breast engorgement, but they would not take any chances. They kept the baby away from me for two days. They wouldn't even let me in the nursery area. When he came back, he would not take the breast. They told me to use a nipple shield halfway through, then try. He screamed like someone was killing him. So in the hospital, I just used the shields, and I was going to break him when I got home. On the second night home, he screamed all night. As you probably know, a baby has to work *very hard* to get any milk out of the shield. So, I put him on the bottle. I cried for two days straight. I wanted to breastfeed *so* bad.
>
> But one thing for sure I know that he got excellent care in the nursery.

This mother's experience was full of disappointment and frustration. How can you avoid that yourself? Don't take potluck with the nurses who will be helping you with your new baby in the hospital. You can have some control, but you'll need to tell your nurse what's helpful. And you'll get much-needed assistance in that area from both your husband and your doula—the people who care the most for you.

The mother above, while frustrated and sad, was also grateful to the nursing staff for taking care of her baby. All new mothers are generally grateful to both doctors and nurses, no matter how they were treated. After all, regardless of what happened in the hospital, most mothers get their desired baby. But there's another reason, too. We do want to trust the people who have so much control over our lives—even if it is for only a few days. They are crucial days. And we want to believe that they did what was best for us.

HOW TO GET YOUR NURSE TO BE A HELP, NOT A HINDRANCE

Some of the nurses were really mean, but I was dependent on them. Had there been an emergency, I wanted them to be on my side. I was afraid that if I was a difficult patient, the nurses might take forty-five minutes to answer the bell—just when I needed them the most.

The Role Fear Plays—Getting Past It

You're flat on your back and feeling helpless. You know doctors and nurses don't like "troublesome" patients. (Translated, "troublesome" refers to patients who make requests outside the routine.) And, yes, hospitals *are* intimidating.

Your best guarantee of getting what you want, of not having to cope with unpleasant personnel, of having your stay be the best it can be, is to have your husband and/or doula with you all the time. All of us, including nurses, are on better behavior when there are witnesses present. A deliberately long delay in answering a bell is impossible if you have someone with you who can go out to the nurses' station and get a nurse in person.

Nothing terrible will happen simply because you are persistent. You have everything to gain by letting your wishes be known. You are dealing with people who want to be helpful. But understanding that it's possible for some nurses to be unpleasant, you can protect yourself with your family and friends. And if you should run across a truly nasty nurse, tell the head nurse or your doctor. One of them can arrange to have other nurses care for you.

Getting What You Want

Communicate your preferences clearly, frequently, and repeatedly to get what you want. If you don't, no one will read your mind—not doctors, not nurses. Be specific. Most misunderstandings occur when the nurse is confused about what you want. You've had an opportunity to develop a relationship with your doctor over many months. You'll have only minutes, or maybe hours, with any one nurse.

There is a nursing hierarchy that's usually not clear to patients because the nurses all wear uniforms; therefore, they all look alike. LPNs (licensed practical nurses) and nurses' aides are paid less and have fewer months/years of training than RNs and BSNs (college-trained nurses). The range of duties for LPNs and aides is more limited, and they are always under the supervision of an RN or BSN. A glance at the name tag of any nurse will tell you what category she is in and who's the boss. If you're not sure who to talk to about a request you have, ask for the head nurse.

We've heard many comments from mothers who didn't get what they wanted in the hospital. But you can, if you're prepared to do the following:

1. *Negotiate in advance* with your doctor for any option that is important to you.

When the nurse says to you, "We never do that here," or "It's against hospital policy," or "I've been working here for ten years and I know Dr.

X won't allow that"—or any other statement that doesn't get you what you want—tell her, *"Dr. X said I can* (walk around during labor, keeping both my husband and friend with me, have my other children visit me, etc.)" or *"Dr. X said I don't have to* accept (an enema, drugs during labor, or sugar water for my baby, etc.)."

Plan on someone saying it for you more than once, however. Shifts change, nurses sometimes rotate patients. If your husband and doula are there, you won't have to do the talking.

2. *What to do if you didn't negotiate in advance.* What if something you never anticipated happens and there was no prior negotiation with either your doctor or the hospital? Don't panic. Be clear and specific.

Example: With your first two births you were not "prepped" in the labor room. So it didn't occur to you to talk to your current doctor about that. But you're no sooner in your hospital room with this baby than the nurse comes in with her shaving kit. You could say, "I know you're just doing what you're supposed to do, but I don't get prepped during my labors. If you have any questions about that, please talk to Dr. X."

Now, if it's that simple, why would most mothers in that situation submit to the procedure? Because they are caught by surprise, and feeling so vulnerable, the nurse really seems to be the boss in charge. The mother feels helpless. If you are all alone, the struggle to disagree with the nurse might seem overwhelming. Don't be alone.

Reasonableness and persistence are the key. You don't have to submit to any procedure that you don't want. You are entitled to a full explanation of everything the staff wants to do to you. You are not obligated to participate in *their* routine.

THE MOST TROUBLESOME AREAS OF CONFLICT BETWEEN NURSES AND NEW MOTHERS

Rooming-In

Even though you may have arranged in advance with your pediatrician to have your baby with you as much as you wanted, this option is often the most difficult to obtain *smoothly.*

Part of the problem is in the definition of "rooming-in." For many mothers, either breastfeeding or bottlefeeding, it means keeping your baby with you as much as you want—up to twenty-four hours a day. But that's not the common hospital definition for rooming-in. At one place, it means the babies come out during the day. At another place, it means the babies can be with the mothers all day and once at night (except, of course, during visiting hours). It's not often that hospitals intend for you to have your baby all the time.

If your experience is like that of many other mothers, you will have to remind at least one nurse on every shift that you've made different arrangements for your baby. When a nurse comes to take your baby to the nursery after the birth or after a feeding, you can explain to her that you've made arrangements for the baby always to stay with you, unless you decide differently. You'll probably have to tell every nurse you see that you're keeping your baby with you. You may have to get a private room to arrange for rooming-in, and you may have to forgo visitors. Each hospital's rules differ in that regard, too.

Feeding Your Baby on Demand

Another common arrangement that mothers make that often doesn't go smoothly is "demand feeding." With "demand feeding," your baby mostly stays in the nursery, but comes to you when she or he wakes up. But sometimes this doesn't happen—nurses forget or they get too busy.

When you want your baby and he's not available, the worst thing you can do is to do nothing. Hospitals are busy places and it's easy for the staff to be occupied with other duties, or simply to forget that you want your baby more than other postpartum mothers.

What can you do? We know many mothers who walked down to the nursery and got their babies every two hours or so. If you're not up to walking there, have your husband or your doula go down to the nursery and get your baby for you. That's acceptable in nearly all hospitals. If it's not possible for you or anyone else to go to the nursery in person, just keep asking for your baby. Persist.

Breastfeeding

Though help for breastfeeding mothers is better than it was twenty years ago in hospitals, there are still many mothers in the 80s who have experiences like the following:

> When I was in the hospital, the nursery nurses told me it was hospital policy that all babies, even my breastfed son, get two bottles of formula for a PKU test. They also told me that my baby, like all the others, gets sugar water between feedings because new mothers like me can't produce enough milk. When my breasts got engorged on the third day, the nurses showed me how to use a nipple

shield so that the baby could suck more easily. Now that my baby is a week old, I'm wondering what's the matter with my milk. My baby doesn't seem satisfied and fusses at my breast even though I know he's hungry.

—Colorado mother

Although the nurses who cared for this mother wanted to be helpful, their standard routine for breastfeeding mothers guarantees that many, if not most, new mothers will find that breastfeeding is not going well a week after the birth.

What went wrong? The number one interference with successful breastfeeding in the hospital is not getting your baby as much as you want or need. Next on the "no-no" list are: formula in the nursery, sugar water or "Baby Coca-Cola" as some nurses label it (or even plain water), and nipple shields.

A test for PKU (phenylketonuria), a rare genetic disease, can be done on a completely breastfed baby just as well when the mother's milk comes in. Many surveyed breastfeeding mothers didn't want their babies getting bottles of any kind in the hospital—but especially bottles of formula. Some babies become allergic to cow's milk (one of the most common allergens) with even the briefest contact with formula in their early days. Others get confused with trying to suck from two different nipples—the mother's and a rubber substitute.

And still other babies who drink anything from a bottle in the hospital may become too tired to vigorously nurse at the breast. There's another reason to avoid bottles in the hospital. The delicate balance between supply and demand of breast milk can only be maintained when the baby nurses frequently at his mother's breast. The more he or she nurses, the more milk the mother produces. This frequent feeding is also the key to managing newborn jaundice, which is discussed in the next chapter.

There are two kinds of shields associated with breastfeeding. One is helpful—the breast shield. The other is not—the nipple shield. The nipple shield, which is worn over the mother's nipple while the baby sucks, draws the nipple out so that the baby can grasp it. Theoretically, it might seem helpful. In practice, it's not. The breast shield is worn inside the mother's bra during the last months of pregnancy or in the early weeks after birth to draw out an inverted nipple. If you have true inverted nipples, buy breast shields (*not* nipple shields) and wear them before the baby is born.

Nurses often recommend the use of the nipple shield to relieve temporary engorgement when your breast feels hard. However, there are better solutions to that problem than wearing a nipple shield. Very frequent nursing will prevent or later alleviate engorgement. Or hand expression just before nursing relieves pressure and softens the nipple area so the baby can latch on.

With the inappropriate use of rubber nipples, a nipple shield, and supplements of either formula and/or water that this Denver mother experienced, it's not unlikely that by day seven when she's home with her baby she's wondering what went wrong. Can this mother's problem be solved? Sure, with good help and support. But without help, like many mothers in that situation, she will wean earlier than she wants and probably always believe her body just didn't work right.

What can you do to avoid formula for your baby in the hospital? Arrange in advance with your pediatrician that your baby's chart indicate that she or he's not to get formula for any reason. Discuss with him that you want your baby's PKU test given after your milk comes in.

Remind the nurses that your baby doesn't get formula. Many mothers tell us that nurses automatically bring in bottles of sugar water periodically during the day. You don't have to give those bottles to your baby, especially if you've discussed that, too, with your baby's doctor. "No sugar water" can be put on the infant's chart, also. (Or pin a note to your baby's shirt if he goes back to the nursery—"No bottles, please.") (What about extra water if your baby has jaundice? See Chapter 14).

A rule of thumb to use when you are in any hospital situation is: *Don't plan on getting everything you want without effort on your part.* That's especially true with breastfeeding. You, your husband, or your doula will have to remind nearly every nurse you see—on every shift—that your breastfed baby doesn't get bottles. Or that you want your baby now. Get help from those who care for you during your hospital stay, and that alone will improve the care that the nurses give you with rooming-in, demand feeding, and breastfeeding.

Despite our criticism of some nurses, there are ob nurses who are not only extraordinarily helpful to mothers, but courageous as well. An increasing number of nurses refuse to give medications to mothers when they believe these drugs will be harmful. And many bend the rules as much as they can to accommodate patients' preferences. There are others who spend endless hours trying to change hospital policies from the inside to meet the needs of consumers. Nurses do make all the difference in your hospital stay. Work with them, so that you can have a good and safe birth and hospital stay for you and your baby.

14 ▪ YOUR BABY DOCTOR

> We pediatricians know that 75 percent of our patients
> get better without us. That knowledge keeps us humble.
>
> —Charles Taylor, M.D.,
> pediatrician in private
> practice for more than twenty years

Just as other doctors do, the pediatrician-to-be spends most of his residency learning how to treat sickness, especially rare diseases in children. The emphasis in most pediatric training programs is certainly not on normal processes, although the bulk of any pediatrician's private practice is taken up with earaches, diaper rash, sore throats, colds—and anxious mothers. But pediatricians know that children usually get well no matter what the doctor does or doesn't do.

SPECIAL INFLUENCES ON A PEDIATRICIAN'S PRACTICE

Eight out of ten American women choose an obstetrician for their pregnancy and birth, but not nearly that many women choose a specialist, a pediatrician, for their child. A pediatrician's income depends on a regular influx of new patients. Even though an increasing number of his patients are adolescents, a lion's share of a pediatrician's caseload is still younger children. Pediatricians care for more children in the birth-to-two-year range than do family doctors. As children get older, family doctors take a bigger share of the market. A pediatrician's income is doomed without newborns.

Not only are pediatricians competing against family practitioners and non-physician specialists (like pediatric nurse practitioners and physician assistants), pediatricians more than ever compete against each other. R. Don Blim, M.D., past president of the American Academy of Pediatrics, stated in 1982: "There are approximately 20,000 pediatricians in this country today, but by 1990 it is estimated that we will have approximately 40,000."

Dependence on Obstetricians for New Patients

New mothers usually base their choice of a baby doctor on either their friends' suggestions or their obstetrician's recommendation. A pediatrician, who doesn't have the advantage of an already established relationship with you or your family, depends on having a "good word" put in by obstetricians. Most are well aware that they can't "rock the boat" with obstetricians if they expect to get referrals.

For instance, pediatricians know not to fuss at hospital meetings about the effects routine obstetrical interventions may have on babies. For example, pediatricians are usually present at scheduled cesareans, but they generally do not consider it appropriate to suggest that the obstetrician wait until the mother's labor starts first—thereby reducing the chance of prematurity for the baby, a primary concern for pediatricians. In the medical pecking order, obstetricians are near the top in income (because they're surgeons) and pediatricians are usually at the bottom (because they use the least technology). Obstetricians don't have to listen to pediatricians.

When pregnant patients ask about a baby doctor, some obstetricians may refer them to the new pediatricians in town. That gives the new doctor a chance to build up his practice. But the newcomer will only get the referrals if he shares similar philosophies with the obstetricians and, in some cases, knows his place. Pediatricians are keenly aware of the need to get along with obstetricians. Economic reprisals are real. Peer pressure is intense among doctors, and the urgency to conform to whatever the local medical norms are is relentless.

Formula Companies

Formula companies pursue pediatricians and family practice doctors as earnestly as drug companies pursue all physicians. These manufacturers sponsor seminars, medical research, and help underwrite pediatric journals through advertising. Formula companies pay for some worthwhile projects that would never happen without their financial support. But medicine today has—at best—a tainted marriage with these companies. Much of a physician's information on formula comes directly from the manufacturers. There's seldom an objective, third-party source of information. Even many mothers get breastfeeding information from formula companies in free pamphlets.

Short-term breastfeeding is good for these companies. Formula sales have gone up as breastfeeding rates have increased, paradoxical as that might sound. The reason, according to one formula company representative, is that women who breastfeed are likelier to wean to a formula during the first year of the baby's life, rather than to regular milk. (Most nursing babies are weaned to a bottle by the age of three months.)

If you plan to breastfeed at all, the influence of the formula companies can be insidious. Most mothers take home one of the ubiquitous new mother hospital packs, which always contain some sample formula. A Canadian study shows that mothers who do take these packs home wean to a bottle and start solids in a matter of a few weeks—much earlier than mothers who don't take the free samples home.

And if you plan to bottle-feed your baby, the influence of the formula companies can be misleading. Naturally, each company promotes its own product as the best one, But, as one former salesman for a leading formula company said to us, "There's not a dime's bit of difference between Similac and Enfamil." Infant formula is an enormously profitable, $700 million plus business annually. The supporters of breastfeeding—consumers, and even the American Academy of Pediatrics—don't have the money to provide the information blitz that's standard in big business marketing.

Obviously, there's a place for formula companies and their products. There will always be baby bottles and parents who need them. But you as the parent, with adequate information, can make your own decision about what and when to feed your baby. The more you make your own decisions for your baby, the more self-confident you'll feel as a parent.

HOW TO FIND DR. RIGHT FOR YOUR BABY

The Dr. Right who cares for your baby serves you best when he observes the child's health and development, and equally important, reinforces your ability as a parent to make decisions about your own child. Taking your baby to a doctor who intimidates you will only delay your self-confidence, use of your own common sense, and your growing maturity as a parent. Your doctor's flexibility and willingness to listen to you are as important as his knowledge.

Review Chapter 5 in which we describe the steps for finding the right doctor for your pregnancy and birth. Here, we'll describe those unique parts of the search process for finding Dr. Right for your baby. Just as in looking for your doctor, check with the nurses who work on hospital ob floors, childbirth educators, and La Leche League leaders. Nurses can tell you which doctors are likeliest to have patients who room-in with their babies or who are helpful and enthusiastic about breastfeeding (if you choose to breastfeed). Nurses know which doctors are willing to arrange for your other children to visit even if it's not hospital policy, or which doctors will examine your baby in your room with you present instead of doing daily exams only in the nursery.

The Prenatal Interview

We suggest you interview doctors for your baby's care before your baby's birth—even though most parents don't. If you currently have a family practitioner caring for you, you'll be able to ask him the appropriate questions about your baby's care as you see him through your pregnancy.

There are many mothers and fathers who meet their baby's doctor for the first time after he's already examined their baby in the hospital. Some mothers find they don't like this doctor once they meet him, but are extraordinarily reluctant to change doctors once they've gone that far. ("At this point," they say to themselves, "what difference does it really make?") Somehow, it all seems so final and official. (It's quite similar to, but not as intense as, the feeling that many women have once they've allowed a doctor to examine their bodies.) Yes, of course, you can switch doctors at this point. But it's easier to interview them in advance of the birth and decide then.

The First Questions

Your own list of questions will depend on the particular options you want in the hospital after the baby's born, and your philosophy of child-rearing. What's really important to you? If you think babies should be raised on a schedule—whether it's feeding, weaning, or bedtime—then you should look for a doctor who agrees with you. If, on the other hand, you prefer fewer rules or feel confident you don't need or want frequent consultation with a physician, you can find that out, too, in advance. Many of the following questions can be answered by phone.

1. *How much are your hospital charges and fees for office visits?* In most places, all pediatricians charge a similar fee. Family practitioners and other health care providers may charge somewhat less. However, that varies from town to town.

2. *Do you charge for phone calls?* Many pediatricians spend six hours or more a week on the phone with parents, according to Edward J. Saltzman, M.D., speaking for the Academy of Pediatrics. Most physicians do not charge for these phone calls, but some do. Typically, most parents of first-born children call frequently.

3. *Do you return the call of every parent who calls?* Some pediatricians make every "call-back." Some have trained personnel, usually nurses or nurse practitioners, return the calls. Some parents find that these trained personnel are very helpful. Occasionally, the person who

handles your phone call may not share the same attitude about the issue in question as you or your doctor does.

For instance, in one city many breastfeeding mothers chose one doctor in particular because she not only had breastfed her own children, but was most helpful with any problems the mothers had with nursing. However, the people who answered some of her office phone calls were not as knowledgeable and supportive of breastfeeding as the doctor was. In another instance, one mother chose her doctor because his philosophy of mothering was similar to hers. However, the nurse who took some of his calls had a different attitude. What the mother and doctor called "meeting the baby's needs" the office nurse labeled "spoiling."

If you find that the person who's handling your phone call is not on your wavelength, you can request that the doctor call you back instead. That's your privilege.

4. *What is the scheduled length of your appointments?* The closer his appointments are (ten to fifteen minutes apart, rather than twenty or thirty, for instance), the more likely it is you'll do some waiting, as well as be rushed through your appointment when you do see him. Most doctors allow more time for complete physicals, and therefore charge more for them than they do for routine office visits.

5. *How often do you want to see the baby in the first year? Why?* Pediatricians more than family practitioners will schedule several "well-child" visits for your child. Pediatricians believe this to be a form of preventive care and an opportunity for parent education. Feel free to discuss in advance with your doctor the purpose of these "well-child" visits, so that you can decide in consultation with your doctor what's appropriate for *your* child's care. We all need encouragement as mothers, but you decide if it's always worth an office-visit fee ($25 or $30) to find out how much your baby weighs and the fact that your doctor thinks your baby is doing well.

6. *Do you have a "sick-child" waiting room?* Some doctors try to avoid mixing the well children and the sick children in the same reception area. Young children are very susceptible to contagious diseases.

7. *If you share a practice, will I always see you?* Not likely, unless your doctor has no partners and never takes a day off. If you are scheduling an exam well in advance, it's easy to ask for a day that your doctor will be in the office. However, if you have a sick child and are calling up on short notice, you'll get whomever is in the office or on call. The same is true of night and weekend emergencies. As a matter of

fact, your doctor and his partners may share their "on call" times with another group of doctors. Just as with obstetricians, what this means for you is that you may have a doctor you've never seen before caring for your child in an emergency. If it's important to you, arrange to meet all the doctors who might cover for your baby's doctor in an emergency, or when you're in the hospital.

8. *Do you have evening or Saturday hours?* Although nine-to-five office hours are still the rule for many doctors' offices, there is a growing number who are accommodating working moms and dads.

How Your Doctor Can (Unwittingly) Sabotage You and Your Baby . . . And What You Can Do About It

In the last chapter we described three areas in which mothers and nurses sometimes clash: rooming-in, feeding your baby—when your baby wants to eat—regardless of the clock (demand feeding)—and breastfeeding.

You may have areas of conflict with your baby's doctor, too. True, you will spend most of your time in the hospital with nurses. But the doctor who cares for your baby has the power to make "good care" better and "bad care" worse. Understanding that, you'll have a much better chance of your baby doctor giving you the help you need in the hospital with bonding (including rooming in and delayed newborn eyedrops), breastfeeding, and the care for newborn jaundice.

BONDING

In the not-so-long-ago past, as new mothers, we were told that our infants couldn't see for days, couldn't smile for weeks. Now there's an explosion of information that describes almost endless sensory abilities of newborns. Much of the best-known research supporting the need for parents and infants to be together soon and often from birth comes from pediatric researchers, Marshall Klaus, M.D., and John Kennell, M.D.

Child abuse stimulated their early studies. They found that welcoming mothers into the nurseries and encouraging frequent contact between mothers and newborns reduced the incidence of battering. But as many consumers and professionals now know, early, frequent contact benefits all babies, all parents, not just those at risk of child abuse.

In 1982, William A. Cook, M.D., obstetrician and author, had this to say about bonding:

I may be wrong, but the significance of the 'maternal sensitive period' and bonding, if it exists at all in the human seems to me over-emphasized. It is an interesting idea and I have nothing against its exploration. But it is only an idea, a postulate, an unproven formulation, and should not be accepted uncritically or taken to be revealed doctrine as it has been.

Many doctors still view bonding as a consumer fad. Some doctors not only don't read their own pediatric research, they don't really believe it. What they learned in their medical training is the last word.

Eager to get on the bandwagon of new trends and keep their maternity beds full, though, many hospitals advertise "bonding time" and "bonding rooms." That hospitals even recognize the benefit of parents and infants being together is wonderful. It's a good start. But that's all. Since many hospital personnel think there's a time limit to bonding, both doctors and nurses may think they've satisfied you and your newborn's needs by giving you your hour. Klaus and Kennell and others never meant to imply that the bonding process was one of glue, a magic sixty minutes at birth.

The idea that gazing into your baby's eyes while holding him lovingly for the first hour will create an attachment for life—at least through those first hard eighteen years—is misleading. That moment is an exhilarating experience for parents, and should be encouraged for that reason alone. But attachment doesn't work like that. Love relationships are much more complicated. The issue really is getting acquainted with your baby, and she or he with you, as easily, as early, as continuously as possible. That takes time—lots of it. And hospitals don't always make that easy.

ROOMING-IN

I want my baby with me at all times. If, however, there is some terrible reason that this could not happen, I would want my baby on request. The set schedule of seeing the baby is the worst possible idea!

I was not pleased with the rooming-in. My baby was taken to the nursery several different times for checkups and I had to complain loudly in order to have her returned to me. It does not take three to four hours for a physical or for a heel stick!

Don't expect doctors and nurses to share your view of bonding or rooming-in. If having your baby with you as much as you want—which is a primary preference of surveyed mothers—is important to you, too, then you'll have to negotiate with both your baby doctor and the hospital.

Be specific. Describe what you want. Your conversation could go something like this:

YOU: *I want to have my baby with me as much as I choose.*

THEY: Yes, you can do that. We believe in rooming-in.

Now don't stop here. We've learned from talking with many mothers that you need to ask more. For instance:

YOU: *Can I keep my baby during visiting hours? Can I keep my baby at night?*

THEY: You can have your baby whenever you want, except during visiting hours (three hours in the afternoon and another three hours in the evening); at night (nearly all mothers find out they don't want their babies at night; besides it's not safe for the baby to be with you when you are asleep); and for an hour in the morning when the pediatricians come in to check the babies in the nursery.

From that answer, it's clear that they expect your baby to be someplace other than with you for two thirds of any given day. If you know that you'll want your baby with you about eight hours a day, then this hospital has what you want. If, however, you want the option of having your baby with you more than that, you have several alternatives:

1. *Talk to both your baby doctor and the hospital in advance.* Ask if you can arrange for a private room. Often patients who get a private room can keep their babies with them during visiting hours. Since the hospital staff may then want you to forgo having visitors yourself (except your husband), you may need to negotiate to have grandparents and/or a doula present, as well as the baby.

You can also tell them that although their experience at the hospital is that most mothers don't want their babies at night, you do. Many satisfied mothers can tell you that the more they roomed-in with their babies, the more self-confident they were when they took the baby home. Rooming-in doesn't necessarily increase your fatigue. Rather, it increases your knowledge of your baby and, therefore, your self-assurance. And if you're nursing, rooming-in almost guarantees a good milk supply because you'll be feeding your baby whenever he or she's hungry.

Many pediatricians are happy to examine your baby in your room with you, but they are seldom asked to do so. If you cannot arrange to have your baby checked in your room, you can go to the nursery while your baby is examined there. Or, if you can't go yourself, your husband or doula can be with the baby in the nursery at all times.

2. *If you cannot negotiate an acceptable compromise on rooming-in, look for another hospital (or a birth center).*

Chances are, you'll find an acceptable alternative within a fifty-mile radius of your home.

Let's say you've found a hospital that offers the rooming-in arrangement you want. Once you've arranged with your baby's doctor to write on your chart that you are rooming-in, the doctor has not done everything he can for you.

If the arrangement doesn't work out the way you want (the nurses don't want to bring the baby at night, or you are receiving criticism from the staff because you want the baby with you all the time), *the next move is yours.* You can let your doctor know that you are not satisfied with the arrangement, and he can talk to the nursing staff. He is in charge of your hospital care. He is the last word on the floor.

He can even remove a nurse from your care, but that's probably not necessary. Or he can remind the staff of your special arrangements. Theoretically, every patient's care is unique, though we know that in practice most patient care is routine. Only you, or someone acting in your behalf (your husband and/or your doula), can get personalized care for you.

Doing your part when you don't get what you want means speaking up, taking action, even if it means calling your baby's doctor at five A.M. If you've arranged to have your baby whenever you want, but the nurses come to get your infant anyway, don't give your baby to the nurse. You have as much power as you choose to have. Tell the nurse if she has any questions about it to discuss it with your doctor (or the head nurse).

You'll only spend a few days in the hospital. But your doctor has to work with the nurses every day. For that reason, he won't be enthusiastic about complaining to the staff—especially if you haven't explained your preferences to the staff yourself. But he will speak up, and you'll make it easier for him if you've already done your part.

NEWBORN EYEDROPS

Putting silver nitrate in all newborns' eyes within minutes after birth to prevent blindness has been a hospital nursery routine for years. Back in the not-so-long-ago past, no one much objected to this procedure because everyone erroneously "knew" babies couldn't see anyway. But much more is known now. Many now question a procedure designed to help a small minority while inflicting an unnecessary burden on 100 percent of all babies and their parents.

Researcher Perry Butterfield in 1983 said:

> Infants with silver nitrate in their eyes do not follow an object or scan around the room. They also are fussier and rarely have their eyes open within the first three or four hours. Infants who have not had silver nitrate or other eye prophylaxis are quiet and alert after birth, able to scan the room and follow faces and objects. And their parents, especially fathers, are more affectionate and involved with their babies.

What Are Your Alternatives?

1. *Let's not assume all mothers have gonorrhea.* Why not test the mother in a routine office check, as some authorities suggest, and avoid eyedrops altogether? E. Shaw pointed out ten years ago in *Pediatrics* that systematic screening of mothers is a better approach.

2. *Postpone the treatment.* If there's no getting around your state law that your baby *must* have the eyedrops within the first twenty-four hours, then negotiate to delay the drops until later in the first day of the baby's life, when the infant is sleeping, rather than give them in the midst of a waking period, which the first hour often is.

3. *Request an alternative.* Tell both your doctor and the baby's doctor that you're willing to pay the extra charge, if there is any, for erythromycin ointment. This ointment, according to the Academy of Pediatrics, is less abrasive to the baby's eyes and has been approved as an acceptable alternative to silver nitrate.

Whom do you negotiate with for a different-than-routine arrangement for these eyedrops? Since the authority for that decision may vary from place to place, talk to both your doctor and your baby's doctor.

BREASTFEEDING

Medical support for breastfeeding has come a long way. When our own teenagers were born, the image of the breastfeeding mother was more bovine than madonna-like. (You can breastfeed, of course, my dear, but you'll lose your shape, perhaps your husband's affection, and eventually all your milk.)

Now more doctors than ever favor Nature's Own. The American Academy of Pediatrics has taken a strong stand, and the Canadian Pediatric Society has joined hands with La Leche League of Canada to provide packets of breastfeeding information which reach 95 percent of all new Canadian mothers. But your baby doctor's help with nursing your infant is more than just his writing "breastfeeding" on your baby's hospital chart. Your pediatrician will not only check your baby every day, but he'll come in and talk with you, too. Much of his advice focuses on infant feeding.

For all the lip service given, many doctors' enthusiasm for breastfeeding still exceeds the amount of helpful advice they offer. Your doctor's "how to" knowledge might be lacking if:

- Accurate breastfeeding information was not part of his training, and is not now a current interest.
- He has not learned what is helpful by observing his patients or his own breastfeeding wife.
- She is a woman, but has not breastfed a baby herself.

How To Find A Doctor Who Is Helpful

How do you know when your doctor's help is "helpful"? Inform yourself in advance. Read the excellent information available for consumers today. Many mothers have successfully breastfed without their doctor's support by learning from other nursing mothers. But why set up obstacles for yourself if you don't have to? Find a doctor who's not only enthusiastic about breastfeeding, but knowledgeable and supportive, too.

When you interview prospective doctors for your baby's care, go beyond asking them if they approve of breastfeeding. Ask if he'll be discussing breastfeeding with you every day that you're in the hospital. According to Warren M. Kleinberg, M.P.H., reporting in the *American Journal of Public Health*, mothers who receive well-informed counseling each day in the hospital have fewer breastfeeding problems later than the mothers who only receive breastfeeding counseling on the day they are discharged.

Ask what percentage of his patients are breastfed at birth. Then ask how many are still breastfeeding at three months or six months. If the number is almost nil (the number will be less than the number breastfeeding at birth), it suggests that he probably isn't very knowledgeable about breastfeeding problems.

How does he handle breastfeeding problems? Ask if he thinks babies should always be weaned if the mother gets a breast infection or sore nipples, or the baby has diarrhea or what growth charts call "slow weight gain?" These are all common problems that can be better managed without weaning the baby from the breast if you get the right information.

You Can Breastfeed and Work

Many of you will be returning to work when your infant is a few months old. Can you still breastfeed? You bet you can. But you'll benefit from information unique to your situation. Thousands of working mothers have found ways to manage both outside jobs and nursing babies.

The doctor you choose probably doesn't know how to help you with the unique management of this style of breastfeeding. Not many health professionals do. What you do need from him is his support for your decision to breastfeed. Many mothers who work feel guilty about the separation, whether bottlefeeding or breastfeeding. The last thing a working mother needs is a doctor who is negatively evaluating her ability as a parent.

If you plan to return to work, mention that to any doctor you interview. You'll know soon enough what his attitude is. He still may not have the information to help you, but perhaps may be able to give you the names of mothers in his practice who have successfully breastfed and worked.

Where do you get help if you plan to be a working and nursing mother? Ask your childbirth educator. These women often know mothers who combine working and nursing. Call La Leche League. Few of these LLL volunteers have any personal experience with working and nursing. If you find that the LLL person you're talking to is not helpful, ask her for the name of a mother who has worked and nursed.

Mothers who've managed to breastfeed and work, like other pioneers, are often quite enthusiastic and willing to share tips with other women. Ask the LLL leader if there's a La Leche "working-and-nursing-mothers group" in your area. (Also, LLL groups that meet in the evening are more likely to have working mothers in attendance.) Or ask if she knows a LLL leader who's knowledgeable about working and breastfeeding. And, whether bottle-feeding or breastfeeding, surround yourself with people who are supportive of your decision to be a working mother.

NEWBORN JAUNDICE AND BILIRUBIN LIGHTS

My baby was two days old when she turned yellow on her face. I'd had a beautiful birth, held her immediately, and felt tied to her closely. I was still riding a wave of excitement over her arrival when the pediatrician came in to tell me there was a problem. It had to do with the jaundice which could in some way go to her brain and make her mentally retarded. I was terrified, and quickly agreed to the treatment with the lights in the nursery. I didn't understand whether or not she was in grave danger at the time, and the next 24 hours were difficult for me and my husband. I was given her for feedings every four hours and carefully looked to see if the jaundice was less noticeable, but she was as yellow as ever. She didn't nurse well as she received water in the nursery frequently to wash out the jaundice. The doctor came in that evening to tell me she needed further treatment. I left the hospital, as we couldn't afford to run up a hospital bill for me. I visited to nurse several times a day but it was difficult with another child at home, and I was very tired. Luckily she was better in 30 hours and came home.

—New mother quoted in *Birth*

The media have frequently broadcast and printed complaints about today's childbirth practices. Obs are criticized from coast to coast, but pediatricians usually are patted on the back. Just as obstetricians have, though, they've made their mistakes, too, often because of inadequate testing of new procedures and products.

PHisoHex, a special soap with the ingredient hexachlorophene, was used in thousands of hospitals before being banned. The number of birth defects in babies born to hospital workers who washed up with PHisoHex was much higher than in the population at large.

Visual impairment in premature babies, called retrolental fibroplasia (RLF) was epidemic in the 1940s and early 1950s. According to William A. Silverman, M.D., in his 1980 book, *Retrolental Fibroplasia: A Modern Parable,* fifty different causes were suggested before researchers found through randomized controlled trials that RLF was caused by hospital staff giving these premature babies what turned out to be too much oxygen. RLF was iatrogenic (doctor-caused)—unintentional, but tragic.

A postscript to RLF. Pediatrician Jerold F. Lucey, M.D., editor-in-chief of *Pediatrics,* stated at the 1982 American Academy of Pediatrics meeting in Honolulu that "excessive oxygen therapy for small, premature infants is not the only major cause of RLF." A second RLF epidemic is occurring, but lack of research impedes progress. "Oxygen can certainly cause RLF," Dr. Lucey said, "but after twenty-five years of knowing this, we are still unable to give effective recommendations for oxygen usage." So the research continues.

Dr. Silverman thinks RLF is more than a tragic mistake—it's a parable, a sign of our times. Careful testing is not always done. In his book, he lists twenty-six therapies used on babies. Only 19 percent of the innovations lead to sounder practice. The newest pediatric treatment on the list is "phototherapy for hyperbilirubinemia." Dr. Silverman places a **?** by this treatment.

Most of the public haven't discovered this new pediatric scandal—the misuse of bilirubin lights for the jaundice of full-term, healthy newborn babies. Jaundice is the most common newborn complication. At least half of all full-term babies and eight out of ten prematures develop some form of this condition. Jaundice is a yellowing of the baby's skin and the whites of eyes. It's caused by excess bilirubin in the blood system. Bilirubin is described as "an orange-yellow pigment, a normal product of the breakdown of hemoglobin contained in red blood cells." Most newborn jaundice is a normal reflection of the baby's adjustment to life outside his mother's body.

The current medical concern about jaundice in the newborn is twofold: It's possible—though it actually happens rarely, and then only to infants who show signs of other illness—that if the level of bilirubin in the blood goes high enough, a condition called kernicterus develops, which can cause brain damage. The second concern, which is at the root of the proliferation of newborns being put under bilirubin lights, is that a certain level of jaundice (and pediatricians don't agree on what this level is) may cause neurological damage in the child.

Three Kinds of Jaundice

The most severe and rarest newborn jaundice is caused by Rh or ABO blood incompatibility. This jaundice is visible at birth or within the first twenty-four hours.

Another rare jaundice is caused by a substance in breast milk that makes the baby moderately jaundiced for several weeks. This jaundice doesn't develop until the baby is several days to a week old or more. At most, 1 in 200 babies might be affected. No brain damage has ever been reported from a case of breast-milk jaundice, although many mothers of affected children have been told to wean either temporarily or permanently.

The most common newborn jaundice is physiologic jaundice, a normal condition. It first appears when the baby is two or three days old.

It's the sometimes casual and cavalier treatment of this jaundice in otherwise healthy, full-term babies with phototherapy (bilirubin lights) that is unnecessarily exposing infants to phototherapy's side effects and increasing the number of babies being separated from their parents soon after birth. *Our criticism is not aimed at the appropriate use of the bilirubin lights for the ten percent of jaundiced babies who are premature or sick full-term infants.*

Bilirubin Lights

Bilirubin lights, or phototherapy, combine bright blue and white fluorescent lights. When exposed to these strong lights, bilirubin in the baby's body decomposes. Certainly babies have benefited from phototherapy, but just as with most other medical interventions, the use of bilirubin lights was designed for a few, and ends up being used on many.

In many hospitals, half of all babies, including the full-term healthy babies, are kept blindfolded and separated from their mothers for most of the day for two or three days at a time while undergoing phototherapy. Although phototherapy has been used for more than twenty years, it is still not clear which babies should be put under the lights, how long they should be there, what wattage the lights should be, how effective the process is, and how extensive the side effects are—especially long term.

How can doctors and hospitals allow the management of normal newborn jaundice to be so unclear, you ask? Easy. Available research is not conclusive. Besides, each doctor believes his evaluation and method of treatment—whatever it is—is right. Hospitals aren't in the business of policing medical procedures. The hospital's job is to keep the beds full, and the use of phototherapy contributes to this. Not only do the babies stay an extra two or three days, but often the mothers do, too. This adds thousands of insurance-paid dollars to the hospital revenue. Though hospitals do not coerce you or your doctor to use phototherapy, they are rewarded by your use of this therapy.

J. H. Drew, and other researchers have shown that some of the very common short-term effects of the use of bilirubin lights are irritability and restlessness, intestinal irritation, lactose intolerance, feeding problems, riboflavin deficiency, water loss, diarrhea, short-term growth retardation, and skin rashes. W. T. Speck, et al., stated that phototherapy "may alter intercellular DNA of human cells and may be a carcinogenic hazard." In

1981 Cathy Hammerman, M.D., et al., reporting in *Pediatrics* added to the list of cautions when they stated: "Since monochromatic blue light in particular has been associated with staff discomfort and vertigo, it is theoretically important not to deliver excessive doses of irradiance." Jerold Lucey, M.D., reflected the opinion of many physicians when he stated in *Medical World News* that the long-term effects of phototherapy still are unknown.

Being blindfolded and deprived of touching, except for a few hours of feeding, for two or three days keeps infants from experiencing normal sensations. Oded Preis, M.D., et al., reported in the *Journal of Pediatrics* that those babies who were not blindfolded, but whose eyes were protected from the lights by a screen, "had behavior patterns more like normal healthy newborn infants, as compared to those with conventional eye pad coverage, who tended to have more frequent periods of restlessness and irritability."

Touching is the most natural thing in the world. Hands hold, feed, and bathe the newborn. Arms rock him or her. His mother's body comforts him. Babies who are kept under the bilirubin lights sometimes spend twenty hours out of every twenty-four just lying there, uncomforted by touch, sight, and the sounds of mother's voice and heartbeat.

Because babies lose water from their bodies when they're under the lights, nurses are instructed to give them extra water. According to researchers Edward F. Bell, M.D., et al., some babies get so hot during phototherapy that they develop a fever. Giving water for dehydration is different, though, from the erroneous belief of most doctors and nurses that giving babies extra water helps "flush out" the bilirubin. Pediatric researcher and expert on neonatal jaundice Lawrence Gartner, M.D., of the Pritzker School of Medicine at the University of Chicago stated in 1982 that: "Water or supplements given to newborns in the first four days do not affect the degree of jaundice." As a matter of fact, giving extra water often interferes with breastfeeding. In some hospitals babies are not removed from the bilirubin lights at all, so that the breastfeeding mother is forced to temporarily (or permanently) wean. Unless a mother is highly motivated, it's often difficult for her to keep nursing.

Certainly no parent or physician wants to have a brain-damaged child, especially when it can be prevented. So doctors sometimes put a child under the bilirubin lights "just in case." But when to use the lights varies from hospital to hospital, doctor to doctor.

In the past, a significant number of infants demonstrated neurological damage when their bilirubin levels exceeded 30. (These were otherwise sick babies showing several signs of disease.) Many doctors, consequently, were taught that, in order for bilirubin levels to remain in a safe range, intervention should occur if the level exceeded 20.*

The "danger" number has dropped drastically, so that today babies with levels as low as 9 are considered at risk. The worry is that if lower levels don't cause kernicterus, they may still negatively affect future intellectual performance. In fact, studies by several researchers, including Gerald Odell, et al., and Rosalyn A. Rubin, et al., show *no* relationship between bilirubin levels up to 23 and I.Q. scores at 5 years. David Stewart, Ph.D., editor of *The Five Standards for Safe Childbearing,* asks the question: "Does this mean that the rates of mental retardation and infant death were higher in the past because of the lack of treatment for normal, physiologic jaundice? There are no data to indicate that this is so."

In some U.S. hospitals, full-term, healthy babies with bilirubin levels of 9 and 10—more often 12 and 13—are considered in danger. In Great Britain, reports Marshall Klaus, M.D., "bilirubin lights tend to be used at a higher level of bilirubin, around 16–17." In 1982 La Leche League International stated: "Some authorities set a limit of 25 in babies with non-Rh jaundice." Information on just what constitutes a dangerous level is sketchy at best. Australian researcher Richard A. Cockington, M.B., in 1979 stated in *Pediatrics,* "Because of the lack of valid data, controversy exists regarding the indications for commencement of phototherapy."

Pediatricians who have been in practice for many years tend to pay more attention to the physical signs of the baby—for instance, is the baby lethargic or not sucking well? Some newer pediatricians pay more attention to the number—the bilirubin level in the blood. "If your baby's bilirubin level reaches 12 [or 10 or 13], we'll have to put the infant under the lights," is a common statement made to parents.

Dr. Gartner stated at a 1982 medical meeting:

> If you start babies' phototherapy when the bilirubin level is at 10 to 13 (sometimes 15), which is where most people will start phototherapy . . . you will find the great majority of these babies, in fact, have already started on the decline of the bilirubin at the time that you started the phototherapy. . . . Ninety to ninety-five percent of those babies really didn't need phototherapy and were about to turn the corner anyway.

*The serum bilirubin level is measured in milligrams of bilirubin per 100 milliliters of blood. This ratio is then expressed as a percentage. A bilirubin level of 20 can also be expressed as "20 mg. percent."

Researcher H.M. Lewis, et al, in *Lancet II*, August 1982, found that jaundice may persist 24 to 48 hours longer if infants are not given phototherapy at these lower levels (13–14), but the level of jaundice itself won't increase. Agreeing with Dr. Gartner, they conclude that the risks of phototherapy outweigh the benefits at these levels.

Iatrogenic (Doctor-Caused) Reasons for Phototherapy

1. *Drugs, especially Pitocin.* Studies show that the use of Pitocin, in particular, but also epidurals and other drugs (like sulfanamids, Valium, some tranquilizers, morphine and vitamin K) increase jaundice in many newborns. According to P. C. Buchan, reporting in the *British Medical Journal,* there are indications that the higher the level of Pitocin in your body, and the longer it's been there, the higher the jaundice level will be in your baby.

There are other researchers who think the problem may not necessarily be Pitocin's chemical effect. If Pitocin is used at all, it can be an indication that the baby would have been born later and is premature, suggests P. Boylan, M.B., writing in the *British Medical Journal.* Researchers Chew and Swann include amniotomy, the breaking of the bag of waters (a routine procedure used with Pitocin), for the same reason.

2. *Increased cesareans.* One of the most frequent complications of cesareans is jaundice in the baby. Now that one in five births is a cesarean, there are more jaundiced babies. We don't know why this is so. Perhaps jaundice is a common complication of cesareans because of drugs used on the mother. Also, delayed breastfeeding, a factor in jaundice, almost always occurs after a cesarean birth.

3. *Fear of malpractice lawsuits.* "Many physicians have been forced to think of their patients as potential lawsuits rather than real people with medical problems," reported the *Journal of Insurance.* According to Donald Blim, M.D., past president of the American Academy of Pediatrics, "Less than one percent of suits filed in a recent year involved pediatricians at all." But when it does happen, the likeliest area to be targeted with malpractice suits is the newborn period. Blim continues:

> We would predict that the most likely situation for possible pediatric vulnerability has to do with pediatric procedures performed at, or very nearly following, birth. For this reason we often have noted pediatricians being named as co-defendants in suits along with obstetricians, anesthesiologists, hospitals, and others who have participated in the birth experience.

Lawsuits for newborn jaundice do occur. Dr. Gartner stated:

> Unfortunately, and perhaps I'm colored by this, I see a fair num-
> ber of lawsuits that I am asked to comment on, where a suit has
> been brought specifically because the bilirubin has gone up and
> the baby has kernicterus and these do occur. It's hard to find them
> in the literature, but they are certainly in the law courts. And they
> are very real.

"If you are going to err," another pediatrician told us, "err on the side of
intervention."

4. *Convenience—phototherapy is handy.* As one pediatrician said a
dozen years ago, "Now that every hospital is getting the bilirubin lights,
for sure we pediatricians are going to diagnose more jaundice." And
they have. Babies don't have to be sent to a high-risk center for
phototherapy. It's as near as the nursery. In fact, in some hospitals even
nurses can order blood tests for bilirubin counts without a physician's
okay.

When a nurse tells a pediatrician that the bilirubin level is 10 or 12, he
may feel he has to do something about it. Not too long ago many of
those babies wouldn't have had blood tests at all. The doctor would
have made an evaluation of the baby by examining him or her. If the
baby wasn't lethargic, if it nursed well and seemed normal, though
jaundiced, the doctor would not have been likely to intervene.

Just as X-ray machines and ultrasound equipment are used more
when doctors have them, phototherapy use increases with availability.
Prior to the bilirubin lights, babies were placed by a sunny window at
home for a few hours or the ultimate treatment for very sick infants was
a blood exchange.

5. *Fear of criticism.* If you're a doctor, using technology means you're
up to date. Some pediatricians we spoke with told us they felt newborn
jaundice was being overtreated. But even so, they sometimes put babies
under the bilirubin lights just to avoid criticism from their peers. The
pressure to be "scientific," to use the available technology, is great.

How to Avoid Unnecessary Phototherapy for Your Baby

1. *Avoid drugs.* Avoid going to the hospital too soon; wait until labor
is well established. If Pitocin is suggested to you because your labor
slows, use the nonmedical techniques described in Chapter 8.

2. *If you breastfeed, do it early and often.* An important key to
preventing or controlling jaundice is to move the bilirubin out of the

baby's body via meconium, the black bowel movement of a newborn. The most effective way to do that is to breastfeed early and often (every two hours or so), especially in the first three days. Colostrum, which is produced by the mother's body until the "true" milk comes in, has a laxative effect and promotes the passage of meconium.

Room-in, if possible. If not, arrange for demand feeding. Protect yourself by finding a breastfeeding counselor, especially if this is your first baby. Go home early if you can, where feeding a baby frequently is easier, because there are no hospital routines to interfere. Nursing infrequently may actually increase your baby's jaundice, Dr. Gartner says, by causing "starvation jaundice." Your baby needs you and your milk. "Supplementation with water or glucose water will worsen the problem," Gartner continues, "or at least won't alleviate the jaundice."

3. *Ask your doctor why your baby needs phototherapy.* Let him know you know there is controversy about when to use phototherapy. Ask him to explain why a normal condition that affects most babies is not normal in your full-term, healthy baby. Ask him to describe the guidelines he uses and why. Ask him to tell you what symptoms your baby exhibits in addition to a certain bilirubin number. Ask him what the risks of treatment are. Ask that the hospital do another blood test (if they haven't already), just to make sure the number is accurate. And if none of this satisfies you, you can always ask for a second opinion. Ask another doctor in your town. If you don't know who to call for a second opinion, call La Leche League or NAPSAC and ask for the names of doctors on their medical advisory boards.

What to Do if Your Baby Does Need Phototherapy

1. *If possible, stay with your baby even if your infant needs to be under the lights.* Ask if the hospital has portable bilirubin lights that can be placed over both you and your baby (though you may find the lights just as uncomfortable as your baby does). Or have the portable bilirubin light unit placed in your hospital room, so that you can at least be with your baby. You will quite naturally be concerned about your baby if the infant needs phototherapy—you will be reassured if you are able to see him or her.

If your baby is treated with phototherapy, there is a valid concern about your baby having adequate liquids. Denver Pediatrician Marianne Neifert, M.D. at the University of Colorado Health Sciences Center, suggests you can express your milk and give that to the baby for extra liquids in addition to nursing her or him frequently. (A breastfeeding counselor will be helpful in showing you how to express your milk.)

2. *Discuss home phototherapy for your baby with your doctor.* Portable bilirubin light units are available at rental agencies. Other doctors, like pediatrician Jay Gordon, M.D., in Los Angeles, have sent home hundreds of jaundiced babies with instructions for sun phototherapy with good results.

Dr. Gordon suggests that you place your naked baby in a direct sunbath for five to ten minutes at a time, two or three times a day. (Use common sense. "July and August in California would be too hot," he adds.) At other times keep the baby in front of the window in indirect light. Leave on all the lights in the house, since any light will help. Dr. Gordon has the parents bring the baby into his office at least once a day during home therapy and asks the parents to call him immediately if there's a change in the quality of the breastfeeding—if the baby slows down or doesn't nurse as vigorously. If the parents are not comfortable with home phototherapy, or if the baby is not doing well and does need to be hospitalized, he suggests that the mother and baby go to a hospital where the mother can stay twenty-four hours a day, and breastfeeding never has to be stopped. It's been Gordon's experience that the vast majority of babies don't need to be hospitalized for phototherapy treatment.

What about vitamin E for a jaundiced baby? Steven J. Gross, M.D., in his Duke University study found that jaundiced premature babies had reduced bilirubin levels when they received 50 milligrams of vitamin E each day for the first three days of life. Premature babies are much more susceptible to the consequences of bilirubin than full-term healthy babies. (He did not study full-term infants.) Some lay midwives have told us that they recommend that mothers give their babies vitamin E once on the first day. Dr. Gordon suggests to mothers that they pierce a capsule of vitamin E (200 or 300 units), spread it on their nipples, and let the baby nurse it off gradually.

Though the hospital staff may tell parents that their baby is in no danger because he's under the lights, most parents are terrified. They often feel a sense of failure or guilt. So instead of feeling warm, loving feelings about their wonderful baby, they may be anxious and worried. Many parents whose infant has been under the bilirubin lights carry lingering doubts for years that there's something permanently wrong with their child.

If your doctor suggests phototherapy for your infant, talk over your feelings with him first. Let him know how important it is to you that your baby stay with you. Since treating newborn jaundice with bilirubin lights might be an everyday occurrence for him, he may not see the situation as the crisis you do. Discussing your baby's situation in detail may also relieve some of your doctor's anxiety about a malpractice suit.

You've got time to talk about this with your doctor if your baby has physiologic, (normal) jaundice or even the rare breastmilk jaundice. (We're not talking here about jaundice caused by blood incompatibility or a premature or sick full-term baby.) With physiologic jaundice, it's not a we-must-do-something-in-the-next-hour emergency, although being in a hospital often makes it seem so.

A San Francisco pediatrician told us that "only a minority of people want the right to make decisions about their child. Many parents don't think they're capable. They forget to depend on themselves." But no one knows or cares about your child more than you do. Do your part . . . so that the care for your child is the best it can be.

Your baby doctor wants to do a good job for you and your child. He wants you to feel good as a parent. He knows any baby has a better chance with self-confident parents. Choose a pediatrician who shares your philosophy, whom you feel comfortable with, and with whom you can build a partnership for the better health of your child.

EPILOGUE

"I feel overwhelmed." "So much to think about!" "I think I'll leave everything up to the doctor." When you reach this point in the book, you might feel a little panic.

We knew some of our information could be scary, and it wasn't until we were well along in writing that we realized how much information has been kept from pregnant women. Maternity care is the most important consumer service we buy. If we are not informed, we don't know what good care is, much less how to get it.

"Okay, so you've informed me; but do I really have to do all those things you say to get what I want? It seems like so much trouble." Yes, it's work. But how many times in your life do you give birth? Isn't it worth the effort to get a good and safe birth?

By working for what you want you are contributing to better maternity care for all women. Thousands of women will read this book. Some will take one step. ("I will get a woman friend to be with my husband and me during my labor and birth.") Others will draw up a detailed birth plan and persist to get many options. Others will decide there are really only two or three things important to them, talk with their doctor and get his agreement. Add up all these individual changes and you have a widespread demand for better maternity care. Yet all you need to do is take one step for yourself.

"What happens if I do all that you suggest and my beautiful birth plan goes awry?" Your satisfaction with the birth will not be based on whether the birth goes according to the plan. It will be based on whether the family is kept together, whether you receive pleasure from the birth, and whether you feel good about yourself afterwards. If you have carefully chosen Dr. Right and the place of birth, and have set up a support system (your husband, one or more doulas, and a nurse for one-to-one care), your satisfaction with the birth is likely to be very high whatever happens. Why? Because the environment and supporters will ensure that even though the birth is different from what you planned, you can open yourself to whatever the experience brings. Dealing with the unexpected, with your supporters' help, you will find an inner strength, a capacity for courage and coping you did not know was within you.

APPENDIX A
HOW TO BE A CHANGEMAKER

So far, this book has focused on helping you get what you want for you and your baby. This last chapter is a guide to help you create improved maternity options in your hospital for all women. Of course, these same steps apply to changing other bureaucracies, too.

Our local hospital administrators never asked for our input. From day one, we offered our opinions totally unsolicited. It's an understatement to say that we were not very popular with them. In spite of our pariah status, we were very successful. When the local hospital announced plans for a new ob unit several years ago, we set out to persuade the hospital administrators to offer women the maternity options they want. All of our original goals were met. The hospital added to its blueprints an alternative birth center; facilities for labor and delivery in the same room in the traditional unit; mostly private postpartum rooms; and more.

If you're thinking, "What changes can I make? What makes me an effective changemaker?" remember, as a childbirth consumer, no one knows better. And you can't get fired. Doctors and nurses who want to make changes always face a threat of peer pressure, even dismissal. But as a consumer (who is buying medical service), we're convinced that you, too, can be successful in making changes.

The strategies that worked for us didn't come to us neatly prepackaged. We learned a lot from trial and error. Other tactics were learned from watching "the big boys" themselves—hospital administrators, doctors, and board directors—or from talking with successful business people.

If you believe that hospital administrators and doctors are all powerful, all knowing, all doing—don't read on. But if you're not sure, take what is helpful to you from our formula for success. If we did it, so can you. We built our confidence and knowledge one step at a time. We didn't always know how we were going to accomplish the next step. We just knew we'd do it. You may not need to use each and every strategy, or you may discover new ones. Use what works.

We've divided the strategies into two sections that are equally important: what worked for us, and what strategies were used against us.

WHAT WORKED FOR US

1. *Choose your partners well.* Look for optimists; avoid naysayers. As Henry Ford said, "If you think you can or you can't, you're always right."

Look for risk takers. Avoid those people who always say, "Yes, but . . ." Beware potential partners who think they have to ask permission from those in authority. Getting approval is unimportant and works against success. Some people will always disapprove of you, no matter what you do—especially when you're questioning the status quo.

Keep the action group very small or energy dissipates when trying to achieve harmony. Rule by consensus is usually a guarantee you'll only have a discussion group. It's better to have a strong leader or two to implement the goals of the group. If you give your group a name, make it positive sounding—not negative. Be *for* something, not against.

2. *Do your homework.*

■ *Set concrete, measurable goals and deadlines.* Don't just say, "Someday we want Hospital X to have more family-centered maternity care." Do say, "Within eighteen months (or twelve, or twenty-four) we want Hospital X to provide a birth room where families can stay together during the birth process, any mother can room-in as much as she wishes, and siblings can visit both the mother and the new baby on the ob floor."

Having established your goal and deadline, then you can make your timetable. Sometimes events outside your control determine your deadline. We had to finish and publish the M.O.M. Survey within nine months because that's when the hospital was going to have the first set of blueprints for the new ob unit available, and we wanted the impact of the survey to come before the blueprints were literally set in concrete.

We established our goals when we saw the M.O.M. Survey results. Since the results from all three surveys (Boulder, Wenatchee, Baltimore) are the same, you are safe in assuming that these goals represent women in your area, too. Or do your own survey. Also, be sure to find out what other hospitals are offering.

■ *Go to experts for help.* Once we decided our goal was to give the hospital input from consumers, we realized the best method was a survey. We consulted with a local university sociology professor, who counseled us on the appropriate way to do the survey and to train the telephone surveyors.

When asking experts for help, remember that you don't always have to do what they suggest. Use your own common sense, too. One of the doctors we asked to review our survey results before they were published was aghast that not only did one in five women want a home birth, but that we actually intended to print that information. Yes, we did want his input. But we didn't agree with him on deleting the data on home-birth preferences.

■ *Know what's in it for the hospital to change.* Your success in change-making will come as a result of a partnership with the hospital. When hospitals change their policies to offer the maternity care women prefer, hospitals benefit, too. This collaboration between consumers and hospital becomes a win-win situation.

—It gets the government off the hospital's back. Federal policymakers want hospital care to be more consumer oriented.

—It will get women off the hospital's back, too. Fewer complaints from consumers.

—But most of all, these changes make money for the hospital. Administrators need healthy financial statements. Offering women what they want means more mothers use the facilities. And families who come to hospitals to have babies tend to return when they need hospitalization again.

If your town has more than one hospital with a maternity unit, you're in luck. Since the hospitals compete with each other for the same patients, they'll be especially interested when you tell them women will use the hospital that offers these options.

—The hospital's prestige will increase. Hospitals like to make money *and* be progressive. You'll give them that chance.

3. *Decide it's your battle.* You've done your homework. You've thought through your goals, established a timetable, selected your partners, found your experts, and come to understand what's in it for the hospital to change. You're probably riding the high from your initial enthusiasm and zeal, but somewhere along in the process you'll have to decide that it is indeed *your* battle—or that it's not.

Do you have the persistence to hang in for several years? Is this issue of maternity change paramount with you? If you feel you only have two or three months to devote to this project, you're not likely to accomplish your goals—unless your partners pick up the slack.

Persistence is the key. If you persist, you can find a way to succeed. But none of us can fight every battle that beckons. If you decide that this project *is* your battle, form a network of supporters. Feel free to call us.

4. *Go with what is,* not what you wish were true. It's counter-productive to insist otherwise. Let's say you've got your heart set on an out-of-hospital birth center. But your state's health department laws prevent such an establishment. You could work through the legislature to change the laws, but maybe you want more immediate results. So then you go to your local hospital and suggest they construct a birth center in the hospital down the hall from the traditional ob department. Don't expect to find any building funds budgeted for your project. But you don't need new wallpaper or colorful bedspreads to have a birth center.

When hospitals say they can't do what you want, ask what they *can* do. Remind them of the need for the facility. Back your requests up with some numbers. If the hospital is unwilling to make a long-term commitment, discuss a short-term pilot project. Compromise is inevitable. It's a necessary part of changemaking.

5. *Go to the top.* In a hospital, the top is the board of directors. When we first published our survey, we were ignored. But we didn't allow that to go on for long (three weeks), and you can't be ignored, either, if you go to the top.

To make sure that our hospital's board of directors knew about us, we sent a letter to the chairman. We also sent copies to the homes of all of the other members. The letter described briefly what women wanted, based on our survey, and what specific changes the hospital would need to make to provide those options. The list of changes the hospital would have to make was what we called our "fat minimum." (That's more than we absolutely had to have, but allowed space for compromise.) The list of changes was also concrete and clear. Telling hospital administrators that women want "family-centered maternity care" is too vague. Telling them women want their other children to visit them in their hospital rooms, for instance, is specific.

You'll increase your chance of getting what you want by offering solutions, not just problems. That thoroughness separates you from those who "just want to complain."

Although hospital boards of directors are supposed to represent the community, they seldom hear directly from the public. These boards are predominantly male and are often composed of bankers, businessmen, and university administrators. You cannot expect them to know much about childbirth if you don't educate them.

6. *Work on all levels, cover all flanks.* We kept contact with all levels— other consumers, childbirth educators, hospital administrators, doctors, nurses, the board of directors, even a government agency (the Health Systems Agencies, Inc.) that would eventually review the hospital plan to renovate and expand the maternity unit. We encouraged and helped organize public meetings with panel discussions on maternity options.

We didn't keep secrets. We sent copies of our letters to all, to let everyone know what we were doing. You cannot be ignored if you're obviously and persistently visible—by phone, mail, or in person.

7. *Use the power of groups.* Well-known Canadian obstetrician Murray Enkin, M.D., once said that "one couple is weird, two are a committee, and 1,000 are a movement." Swell your ranks, broaden your support by forming alliances with others. In union there is strength."

At about the same time we began our M.O.M. project, a new group, the Boulder Perinatal Council, began to meet at the hospital. This group was established as an information exchange, not as an action group. But because it did exist, we asked for and received support from many of the member agencies for our project.

The hospital increasingly recognized this group as the "official" consumer voice. Having this group support accelerated our progress. If you're not already part of such a group, contact other organizations with perinatal interests and form your own. The local director for the March of Dimes, Becky Messina, was the key organizer for the Boulder Perinatal Council.

But don't just look for support from other health organizations. The hospital received support letters for changing maternity options—at our urging—from women's political groups, the YWCA, and other organizations that don't exclusively focus on health.

8. *Look for insiders.* When Woodward and Bernstein exposed the Watergate scandal, one of their sources was an unidentified White House insider labeled "Deep Throat." Do you know of a doctor or nurse who's on the staff who may be a "closet" supporter of your goals? He or she is likely to be a doctor who is more progressive than the others, or a nurse who wants the hospital to make their policies more consumer oriented. Do you know a member of the board of directors who will let you know what discussion, if any, is made of your project at board meetings? Will this board member put the topic of maternity options on the board meeting agenda? Do you have a

relative, neighbor, friend, or member of your social group who has inside knowledge? For example, among our "bridges" was Roberta's husband, who as a doctor, was a member of the hospital's staff and privy to many medical meetings.

These "bridges" can keep you apprised of the temperature inside the institution. Remember, you don't need their agreement with your project, just some interest.

9. *Use outside connections.* Outsiders can be influential. Sometimes, there is nothing like a name. If they don't influence the hospital policymakers themselves directly, these outsiders can certainly make you—the change-maker—feel better.

In the early months after we published the survey, we got a lot of negative feedback. We heard complaints about our survey methods or criticism that we were butting into other people's business. Then along came a letter from internationally known pediatric researcher Marshall Klaus, M.D. (we had sent him a copy of our survey results), telling us: "You've done an excellent survey." It certainly reassured us that we were on the right track.

At about the same time we asked fifteen or twenty medical professionals, both state and nationally known figures, for letters of support for our M.O.M. project in our attempt to get more funding. We didn't get the funding, but we got the letters. Those letters increased our confidence. Don't overlook politicians and other public officials. They are potential sources of strong support for you.

10. *Use publicity.* Get attention. No matter how much the other side wants to ignore you, getting publicity forces them to recognize you. It keeps the pressure on and prevents the hospital from sweeping your project under the rug. In a magazine interview, John Kenneth Galbraith commented that women at Harvard made inroads in getting equal treatment only when they presented a "mood of menace." This mood, he said, "must be strong enough so that it can induce a certain measure of alarm. That alarm is mostly achieved by uninhibited public criticism, which is something the people resisting women don't want to hear." We gave a copy of our survey to a newspaper reporter and invited an interview. The resulting article was the first of nearly 100 nationwide about the M.O.M. Survey and maternity care in Boulder.

You, too, can make maternity care in your town a public issue. Following are steps that worked for us:

■ *Keep media journalists informed about your project.* The likeliest person to contact at a newspaper is the one who covers the women's page. The best contact person at radio and TV stations is the public affairs director. At cable TV companies, it's the local access director. Reporters are always looking for news, but that doesn't mean that they'll necessarily be interested in supporting your pet project. It's up to you to find the appropriate person and let her or him know that maternity care in your community is not just a local, isolated issue, but a national issue. Meet her or him in person. Give that person background information to read. A media release, hand delivered, is helpful for newspapers, radio, or TV. It should describe what women want locally and what changes the hospital would have to make.

Most reporters do not have the luxury of a lot of time to research issues. By giving them background material, whether it's newspaper clippings or surveys like ours, you're expanding their available information. But that doesn't mean they necessarily will write the story the way you want, or that they'll do a story at all.

If a reporter does write anything on your project, thank that person afterward. Reporters seldom get anything but negative feedback. Get others to write or phone, too. Although women reporters may have a lot of empathy for your project, especially if they're mothers themselves, we found there are male reporters who are very interested in this issue also.

■ *Encourage letters to the editor.* The letters to the editor mirror current concerns of the community. They are an ideal place for you and your allies to go public. But it's often tough to get people to actually write the letters and send them in. Make it as easy for them as possible, though, because these published letters can be *so* effective. They can create a bandwagon effect.

It's very discouraging to send in a letter to the newspaper and then discover it's not printed. It's a fact of life that newspapers don't publish all the letters they receive. Call or go in and talk with the publisher (that's going to the top) and/or the person responsible for that section of the newspaper. Tell that person of your project and ask if he or she will run all letters that come in on that issue. That person may agree. If so, you're that much ahead.

Give potential letter writers ideas for letters (or even rough drafts). Know the rules for letters to the editor. Do they have to be typed double-spaced? Do they have to include an address? Does it help if the letters are hand delivered? (It often does, especially if you bring a baby with you.) Give your letter writers all the information you can.

■ *Consider petitions.* Getting petition signatures is a form of publicity, as well as a means to rally public support. It's a concrete way to acquaint the population with your specific requests. Petitions with dozens (hopefully hundreds) of signatures not only make a strong statement to a hospital, but they may also interest the media even more to cover the story of maternity care in your town.

11. *Act like an equal at meetings.* Eighty percent of the message you convey is in your body language, even when you're talking. You may be uneasy, but you want to appear calm.

■ *Dress like you mean business.* No jeans or casual clothes when you're in three-piece-suit territory. That's going with what is. You want them to listen to you, not judge you "unlistenable" because of what you're wearing. You'll feel more successful and powerful if you look as though you belong there. Even if you feel anxious and insecure you can become what you pretend to be by dressing for the part. At least one of you should wear a "color of authority" if you have it—navy blue, gray, or beige.

Yes, you can dress like you mean business with a baby in tow. As a matter of fact, having a baby along can be to your advantage. It's a definite visual reminder of the issue at hand, and we found that administrators and doctors were disarmed with a baby present. That's a disadvantage for them that can work for you. Roberta's infant daughter, Amanda, accompanied us for about a year after she was born. By sitting next to one of the administrators or doctors, Amanda seemed to calm and humanize him. Roberta was sometimes distracted caring for Amanda, but Diana took up the slack. Besides, distractions gave us time to think.

Be on time for meetings. It's appropriate, and it will make you feel more secure. You don't want to apologize for being late. You don't want to apologize for anything.

■ *Be prepared.* Know exactly what you want to accomplish. If you've done your homework, you'll feel more competent, tactful, and dignified. When we had meetings with hospital administrators, we knew what our "fat minimum" was before we went into the meeting. We expressed it to ourselves this way: "Today we'll find out their timetable for approval of the blueprints." Or, "Today we'll find out what the next step is in changing the policy on allowing siblings to visit their moms."

If you decide your goal in advance for any particular meeting, it's easier for you to say, as the time draws near for the end of the meeting, "We've covered many items in our discussion today, but I promised the others I wouldn't leave until I found out X."

■ *Keep your cool.* You can often set the tone of any meeting by your own behavior. Avoid showing anger during the meeting. Ventilate that anger before the meeting or afterward—not during. Save that for your "autopsy" meeting. (That's when you discuss later what you did right, where you went wrong, and how you can fix it the next time.)

Don't burn your bridges with these people. An enemy today may be a helper tomorrow. The people you will be meeting with are just doing their jobs. If they don't want to give you what you want, if they disagree with your whole premise, it's nothing personal. It's just business.

They may get angry and holler at you. (That's "saber rattling," a common technique to intimidate people.) Or they may think that once you're there, they'll tell you what's what. (That's known as the "king holding court.") But you can't be intimidated or made to feel inferior if you decide you won't be.

■ *Keep your expectations reasonable.* Part of being prepared is knowing what's reasonable to expect. We knew when we arranged a meeting with one influential pediatrician that we could expect that for most of one hour he would tell us all the things wrong with our project. And he did. He certainly met our expectations. However, we did squeeze in an explanation of our project from our point of view.

As it turned out, this particular doctor was helpful later in making some of the very changes we had suggested. No, it's not always going to work out that way. But it's important to remember that the people you are trying to persuade are looking at the issues from a different perspective. Don't take your marbles and go home just because they disagree with you. There are always areas of disagreement.

■ *Don't go alone to any meeting.* Pad your delegation. If possible, have more people on your side than they have on theirs. Presidents of big companies travel with a regular entourage of people. You can do the same. You'll automatically be perceived as more important. Have all members prepared—if only to remain silent observers.

■ *Know their deadlines* (and use them to your advantage). Before the hospital here could begin construction on their new maternity unit, they had to get an okay from the state. Consequently, we knew the hospital's deadline was the final state hearing. Because we were invited to testify at that hearing, it was important to the hospital that we be in agreement with them on the plans. When we next met with the administrators, they had to make concessions to us. They were up against the clock, and we gave the impression we had all the time in the world.

■ *Go on the offensive in meetings.* Bring up your own issues, your own agenda. For instance, if you want to talk about special arrangements for cesarean mothers, say so. Don't expect them to say, "Now, what's on your mind?" They'll be busy bringing up their own issues instead.

■ *Be a good saleswoman,* not an apologizer. Present your project in the best light. If you're convinced that women want maternity options your hospital doesn't now offer, be enthusiastic. Be unafraid to represent all women. All women do want individualized care. A hospital that offers women alternatives meets the needs of all women.

■ *Use the "broken record" technique* if it helps you get where you're going. Sometimes it's clear that the administrators don't want you to give them the facts. Their minds are made up, and they don't want to be confused with the facts. Then use the "broken record" technique. When they tell you that they can't change the hospital policy to allow fathers in the cesarean operating room, just keep repeating the same phrase, "It's very important to cesarean mothers that their husbands be present at the birth." They may tell you that the anesthesiologists refuse or that the obstetricians refuse. You just keep repeating your original sentence. It's not your problem that the administrator might have some difficulty in making this policy change. That's his problem. He's paid to solve problems.

12. *Develop staying power.* Changemaking is a process, not a single event. To be successful, you must let them know that the issue will not go away. Send regular reports to people at every level. Schedule meetings. Tell the other side you look forward to continued review of this project with them.

Part of staying power is follow-up. One West Coast hospital gathered a full day's worth of speakers to discuss what hospital-maternity-care options women wanted. However, for all the talk that day, no changes were made. A follow-up would have indicated a meeting with administrators to discuss *which* options would be added and *when.*

How long do you have to last? Your timetable may be different from ours, but two years passed from our first conversation about doing a survey until the hospital policies and blueprints contained all the major preferences of women.

No, you don't have to work on this project all the time, every day. But you must keep abreast of the issues. Do take care of yourselves, too. Because you're dealing with a serious issue, you'll find you need a balance—time to laugh and have some fun. Keep in touch with your network of supporters. Don't lose heart. There will be pitfalls. You'll make mistakes. You'll be criticized. That's okay. Develop a watchdog committee to monitor the hospital after changes are made, or the hospital will lapse back to former policies. Above all, persevere.

STRATEGIES TO GUARD AGAINST

Bureaucracies don't like outsiders trying to rock the boat. That's understandable. If you were in their shoes, you wouldn't like it either. So what the hospital will do in response is what most anyone in a position of power will try. You may find that not all of these steps are used against you, but if some are, you'll be forewarned and forearmed, so that they won't deflect you from your goals.

Hospital administrators, doctors, nurses, and board directors aren't bent on frustrating you, so don't take it personally. They're just doing the job they're hired to do. And they do it very well. Here's what they'll do—how they sock it to you:

1. *They'll ignore you.* An effective technique, guaranteed to weed out the faint of heart. You'll write a letter and get no response. Your phone calls won't be returned. You'll present a proposal and they'll smile and say, "Thank you, the committee will consider it." Months will go by before you find out from a friend who's on the staff that it never came before the committee. Or it was voted down in the last two and a half minutes of the November meeting. We circulated 125 copies of our survey to every doctor, health care agency, hospital administrator, and nurse having anything to do with birth or babies in our community and asked each for a response. Out of 125 copies circulated, we got zero responses. Frankly, being ignored makes you feel like a balloon that just got stuck with a pin. We thought we had finished the job by circulating the survey, but we were wrong. Oh, you faint of heart. It was just the beginning.

You do the obvious then. Refuse to be ignored. Contact people. We decided who the opinion leaders were (one obstetrician, one pediatrician, one hospital administrator) and arranged to meet with them individually. When it seemed the information still wasn't going places, we went to the top. We wrote a letter to the chairman of the board summarizing in one page what women wanted. We asked other agencies to send a similar letter, using ours as a model. Many did, which forced the hospital to realize we were determined to be visible. So, keep plugging. Make phone calls. Write letters. Solicit support from others. Do not accept silence as the final response. Never go away.

2. *You'll be told, "Don't call us, we'll call you."* When we first began our survey, we kept the original hospital administrator we worked with informed of what was happening—not to ask permission, remember, just to keep him informed. We had not been invited to do this project, but we were always open to talking about it. As a matter of fact, in the first conversation, he told

us we didn't need to go to "all that trouble." "You and some of the girls could come in, and we could all just sit down and chat about it," he said. We thanked him kindly for his suggestion and went on with the survey.

Later, when we discussed the questionnaire with him, he complained about some of the questions asked. He said we had no business asking women questions about procedures that only doctors should decide.

Incidentally, in other cities when groups (such as childbirth educators) begin to make noises about wanting changes at the hospital, more than one group has been called in for a meeting, usually 7:30 A.M.—good for doctors, not so good for mothers with young children—and has been told, "Don't call us, we'll call you" (which translates to "when it's too late for your input to matter" or "never").

Remember, when you accept their timetable, you have totally given away yours.

3. *They'll find flaws.* When our survey was hot off the press and we had found a way to get them to talk to us about it, we were told we had gone about it all wrong. "You only interviewed mountain hippies," one doctor said. Another told us the survey was heavily biased. Disappointed, we could have accepted their verdict. We could have nit-picked details, whined a little, and said, "Well, we did the best we could." But the issue (always remember your goal) was not defending *how* we did the survey. The issue was what options do women want. We said, "You may not have confidence in our methods, but are you saying that you don't think this is what women want?" Now what could they say? No one else had ever asked women what they wanted, so how could our detractors know? Doctors told us that their patients didn't tell them that they wanted these options. But women often don't tell their doctors what they like or don't like.

When your "fatal flaws" are pointed out, remember, it's a sign of success. You're getting somewhere. It's usually the next step after being ignored. If you've done your homework well, and your project is well thought out, you're not likely to have a genuine "fatal flaw." Stick to the real business at hand—your goals.

4. *They'll placate you, even excite you, with their interpretation of what you want.* They'll use words like "homelike delivery" or "birth room" and you'll think it's music to your ears. What's homelike to many hospital personnel (who live in a world of rules and regulations and gray-green paint) may be just a splash of color, a rug on the floor, a comfortable chair, and, the ultimate ruse, a cheerful bedspread. Is that what you really wanted when you said you wanted a "homelike delivery?"

Specify exactly what changes you want a hospital to make. Follow up with a letter. Be specific and definite. State: "Most postpartum rooms need to be private, so that women may more easily have their babies with them," *not* "Women want more contact with their babies." State: "Based on survey results, two of the four planned delivery rooms should have the flexibility of labor and delivery in the same bed," *not* "Women want an alternative birth situation." Vagueness allows the hospital to interpret as they wish.

5. *They'll appeal to your logic.* They'll say . . . "The doctors won't use a

birth center, no sense in putting one in" . . . "You may want to do that, but it's not safe" . . . "It's not financially possible" . . . "It's not structurally possible" . . . "It's just not reasonable; be logical." In a world where books of rules and regulations are inches thick and numerous enough to line a wall, it's easy to pull a book out, open to almost any page, and find a reason why you can't do something. Keep repeating what you want. Stick to your goals. Don't let their version of logic sidetrack you.

6. *They'll refuse you access to the facts,* and then tell you your information isn't good enough. When we questioned an administrator about a government procedure, he said, "Well, it's so complicated, you wouldn't understand." The initial refusal to disclose facts is often just that—the first response. Keep asking. If you're still refused, try something else. Ask, "If you can't help me, who can?" You are signaling to them that you can't be put off. (We finally contacted the government agency ourselves for the information.)

We were refused the use of patient names from hospital records for our survey. We found another source (all the while keeping the administration informed). Naturally, they told us our results would not be valid. Remember, they'll find flaws.

7. *They'll keep you an "outsider."* They won't let you into the system, because they know that you will disrupt their comfortable routine. That's fair. It's their football, and if you don't play the game they want to play, they can take their ball home. They don't have to let you serve on the hospital obstetrics committee, for example. It's composed of eight men and only one woman—and it's in the business of providing health care for women. But it certainly isn't discrimination: nine out of ten doctors are men.

So go with what is. Make sure that you contact individual members of this committee and tell them what women say they want. Do not always rely on hospital-appointed go-betweens to keep committee members informed.

8. *They'll appoint someone to listen to you, raise your hopes, and they'll make sure that person is powerless.* Now this is really dirty pool. They'll send a head nurse on the maternity floor, or the director of public relations. Yes, you finally get someone to listen to you, and though he or she will write reports or whatever, there will still be no change.

A group on the West Coast was told to take their requests to the head nurse. They did. Months passed, nothing happened. Finally, they asked the nurse, "What's going to happen?" "Nothing," was the reply. The head nurse this group spoke to had no power to change anything.

Don't quit talking to nurses, though. They're key to getting the maternity care women want. Nurses are on the front line. They can either help wonderfully or sabotage changes thoroughly every day they're at work on the floor. But don't stop with nurses. Make an appointment with the hospital administrator. Always start at the top. If you're denied access, try again. Use another tactic. Call a member of the board of directors, explain who you are, what you want to do. Board members represent the public—that's you. Once you have the board's ear, the administrator will probably be available, too.

9. *They'll act like they're playing along.* Ah, this is so effective. This is not

usually immediately obvious. One changemaking group had drawn up their own list of needed maternity options. Then came one of those 7:30-in-the-morning meetings with doctors. Told "Thanks for coming, meeting with us, and giving us input. We'll take care of it," the women went home excited about their "partnership" meeting. Nine months later, there were no changes in sight.

Another example is one of our own. Our group was told that our input on the kind of bed used in the birth center would be welcomed. However, only a short time later we discovered that the budget for the hospital—which is established six to twelve months in advance—already had another kind of bed planned-for and ordered. And it sure wasn't the one we wanted. We goofed! When making requests for certain kinds of equipment, ask what the status of the budget is. How much money is allocated for equipment, when could it be bought, what is the timetable for purchase?

10. *They'll get frustrated and start retaliating.* Name-calling and sabotage are the two most popular ways to retaliate. Be ready to grow a thick skin for name-calling. You need to respond swiftly to sabotage. Nurses can be skilled at sabotage, and it doesn't always have to be intentional. In one hospital, the nursing staff reluctantly followed a new policy that allowed siblings to visit their moms on the maternity floor. But in complying with the new policy, they sabotaged an old one that permitted mom to keep her baby during visiting hours if she had no visitors herself. Here's where you changemakers need to stay on top of things. This contradiction was pointed out right away to the director of nursing, who showed the staff a way to include both policies and prevent neither.

Another obvious retaliation is plain old lying, missed deadlines, or statements like, "Gee, didn't I tell you about that?"

11. *They'll try to make you feel guilty.* This can easily come from an ally. As a matter of fact, men have never intentionally or unintentionally used this strategy with us. It's always been other women.

An up-to-then-supportive board member accused us of "ruining the whole project and making mothers suffer yet another summer in that sweat-box of a hospital" because our testimony at a preliminary government agency hearing might have delayed the project.

Another time a fellow worker in the Perinatal Council told us that we were causing trouble for people like her, who worked regularly with the hospital. She didn't feel as welcome there as she used to and suggested it was all our fault.

Your first response might be an anxious, "Who me?" Accept that momentary twinge of anxiety and realize that this tactic is used on all persons who try to change the system. Remember, it gets easier with practice to accept the grievance for what it is, one person's opinion.

You may not have all these tactics used against you. But when any one of these is used, pat yourself and your fellow changemakers on the back. You are right on schedule.

What's in it for you to be a changemaker? You'll use up your own resources—money, time, and emotion. But you'll also feel a sense of accomplishment. It will be one of the hardest, best jobs you've ever done. You'll develop your creative powers to a new level. You'll permanently share mutual respect with "the other side." You'll be able to get what you want in other areas in the future.

And the ultimate success? If you've done your job well, the "other side" will take credit for it when the project is completed.

Nobel peace laureate Betty Williams, told us, "It is within the power of any individual to fight for what is right and to change the course of events." She was talking about achieving peace. But the fight for humane maternity care is just as important—perhaps the beginning of all other issues. And change doesn't happen just because the cause is right. Families are the backbone of every culture. Why not become a changemaker yourself and give families the best of starts by getting maternity care that women want for good and safe births.

APPENDIX B
READER QUESTIONNAIRE

Readers are invited to complete this questionnaire, or use it for their own local surveys. You may wish to photocopy this or simply answer on a fresh sheet with reference to the question number.

1. Rate your satisfaction with your most recent birth experience. (Circle One)
Completely satisfied   Mostly satisfied   Satisfied   Unsatisified
Mostly unsatisfied   Completely unsatisfied

2. What would you have changed about your prenatal care, your labor, your birth, or your hospital postpartum stay?

3. Where was your baby born? (Circle One)
Traditional hospital unit   Birth room
ABC (Alternative birth center in the hospital)
Out-of-hospital birth center   Home   Other (Describe)

4. Who was your primary birth attendant? (Circle One)
Obstetrician   Family practitioner   Nurse-midwife
Lay midwife   Other (Describe)

5. Who is the doctor for your baby? (Circle One)
Pediatrician   Family practitioner   Other (Describe)

6. What interventions were used in your birth?

7. What complications did you have?

8. What complications did your baby have?

9. If your baby had to stay in the hospital or be rehospitalized, please explain.

10. Did you have a doula or monitrice present during your labor? (Please circle which one) Was this person helpful?
Doula   Monitrice

11. Did you attend childbirth preparation classes? _____Yes _____No
If you did, were they helpful? _____Yes _____No

If you did, what kind of class was it? (Lamaze, Bradley, etc.)

Who sponsored the class? (Circle One)
My doctor   My hospital   The childbirth teacher   Don't know
Other (Describe)

Do you wish you had been given any additional information?
If so, what?

12. Circle which of the following were helpful to you with breastfeeding:
Friends   Hospital nurses   La Leche League   Childbirth educator
Family   Obstetrician   Pediatrician   Family practitioner
Books/Publications   Other (Describe)

Circle which of the following were *not* helpful to you with breastfeeding:
Friends   Hospital nurses   La Leche League   Childbirth educator
Family   Obstetrician   Pediatrician   Family practitioner
Books/Publications   Other (Describe)

13. Did you attend La Leche League meetings or have personal or phone contact with a LLL leader? (Circle which one)
Meetings   Phone
Do you wish you had been given any additional information?
_____Yes   _____No If so, what?

14. What information in this book helped you the most?

15. What information in this book was not helpful?

16. What information was missing in this book?

17. Anything else you'd like to tell us? (Birth stories are welcome.)

18. Please give your name, address, and phone number in case we decide to ask for additional information. (Omit if you prefer.) Send to: Diana Korte and Roberta Scaer; %Bantam Books, 666 Fifth Avenue, New York, New York 10103

APPENDIX C
THE THREE SURVEYS

The three surveys of American women, asking what options they wanted in their hospital maternity care, were conducted in Boulder, Colorado, in 1976; in Wenatchee, Washington, in 1978; and in Baltimore, Maryland, in 1979. The first, the Boulder survey, was the impetus and model for the others.

The M.O.M. Survey; Boulder, Colorado

Boulder is an attractive college town of 85,000, in the foothills of the Rocky Mountains, 30 miles northwest of Denver. Many residents are highly educated, white-collar workers. The city is home to high-technology government research programs and private business. Most of the citizens think of Boulder as a progressive place. For example, 84 percent of new mothers breastfeed their babies (many of them in public).

The survey started with our concern that women weren't being asked for input into plans for the local hospital's new maternity wing. We didn't know what a radical idea that was; it seemed logical to us. And so the M.O.M. (Maternity Options for Mothers) Survey was developed, with a network of women friends and health professionals.

We are long-time leaders in the worldwide breastfeeding organization, La Leche League. We knew from our many years of working with mothers that many women were frustrated about the care given to them when their babies were born. So we knew there were things that hospitals could and should be doing differently. We were also mothers ourselves, so we had some ideas on how things could have been different for us.

We got together a proposal and the assistance of forty-two volunteers, and applied to the Northern Colorado Chapter of the March of Dimes for a grant to cover the costs of computer-assisted analysis of data and publication of survey results. With the grant approved, over a period of four weeks, we were able to contact and survey 694 women from a master list of 906 names. Three groups of women were surveyed: nearly 100 percent of the Boulder Area La Leche League Women (240 women), a sample of women attending childbirth classes (205 women), and a random sample taken from newspaper birth announcements over a one-year period (210 women). All three groups totaled 694 women surveyed by means of a telephone interview. Only 24 women refused to participate. The survey took about fifteen minutes, but some women stayed on the line another half hour or more. Once started, they wanted to talk more about their birth experience.

The women were asked to indicate their preferences ("strongly agree, agree, disagree, strongly disagree") on thirty-eight maternity care options.

We were greeted with great enthusiasm from the moms, and a willingness to cooperate. One of our surveyors said: "This is an experience many women feel strongly about, but have no convenient way to get their opinions to the proper people." When the results of the survey were published early in 1977, it was a first—not only for Boulder, but for the nation, and for the American health-care system. Never had health consumers been so approached.

The Mothers' Survey; Wenatchee, Washington

Wenatchee is another attractive city, with a population of nearly 20,000. It is located in the rolling hills of apple-growing country in eastern Washington State. Wenatchee residents are mostly blue-collar workers, with high-school educations.

The Mothers' Survey in Wenatchee was the result of the "radicalization" of one woman. Here's her story:

"I was angry!" says Shannon Pope of Wenatchee, in reply to why she was the first person to duplicate the M.O.M. Survey. "When I was pregnant with my first child, I knew just what I wanted, and I kept telling my ob what I wanted at each visit, as he was rushing out the door. I knew the risks of anesthesia to the baby, and I wanted a natural childbirth. When I got to the hospital in labor, I found out that my doctor wasn't on call. I had to argue all over again for everything I wanted. I thought everything went well, until I got my bill and discovered I had been charged for a pudendal block. I had been given this without being asked. I hadn't wanted it, and didn't need it. The doctor had exposed my unborn baby to anesthesia completely against my wishes. I was still upset months later when I came across an article in *McCall's* about the M.O.M. Survey and knew I had to do something."

Shannon went directly to the top and made an appointment with the hospital administrator. He suggested that the M.O.M. Survey only represented women in Boulder, and asked her to do a similar survey and present the information to the doctors. After getting a copy of the M.O.M. Survey and consulting with Roberta Scaer by phone, Shannon did the second maternity-options survey. Central Washington Hospital of Wenatchee contributed money and staff time for the study. In a random sample of 173 women who were mailed questionnaires, 68 replied. As in Boulder, they expressed definite opinions about what they wanted in maternity care.

Committee on Maternal Alternatives; Baltimore, Maryland

Baltimore, with 1,600,000 people, is one of the oldest cities in America. It is a port city famed for its Chesapeake Bay seafood, its rich immigrant culture traditions, its professional sporting teams, and its famed Johns Hopkins Hospital. In the fall of 1978, just as the Wenatchee survey was being completed on the other side of the country, Bobbie Seabolt and her committee were hard at work putting the finishing touches on the third and most extensive questionnaire of women's preferences in maternity care ever done. Bobbie, too, had read of the M.O.M. Survey in *McCall's*. She wrote us for a copy of the survey results and the M.O.M. questionnaire and passed it around her group of volunteers (who call themselves the Committee on Maternal Alternatives or COMA). Bobbie, like Shannon Pope, consulted with Roberta Scaer before doing the survey. Her group received some funds from the Baltimore Childbirth Education Association and the March of Dimes, but, as in Boulder, it was a huge volunteer effort that enabled them to get the job done. A total of 6,000 questionnaires was distributed by the Nu-Dy-Per Baby Service to all women using their diaper service in the greater Baltimore area. Responses came in from 1,345 women, who told of their preferences in their birthing experience. In addition, they replied to a whole new section asking what kinds of medical interventions were used in their births, and what their opinions of those interventions were. A complete report, first published in the fall of 1979 by the Committee on Maternal Alternatives, is available for $14.00 from Bobbi Seabolt; 1822 Notre Dame Avenue; Lutherville, Maryland 21093.

APPENDIX D
YOUR LIST OF HELPERS

For an impressively complete listing of childbirth organizations, books, and resources, see the 300-page, oversized *Whole Birth Catalog: A Sourcebook for Choices in Childbirth* by Janet Ashford (Crossing Press, Trumansburg, New York, 14886, 1983. $14.95.)

In requesting information from the following organizations, please send a stamped, self-addressed envelope.

Childbirth Organizations (General)

AMERICAN FOUNDATION FOR MATERNAL AND CHILD HEALTH
Doris Haire, President
30 Beekman Place
New York, New York 10022
(212) 759-5510

Promotes unmedicated, normal childbirth by sponsoring research and seminars, publishing literature, and by exerting pressures on national and state legislators and agencies.

INTERNATIONAL CHILDBIRTH EDUCATION ASSOCIATION
P.O. Box 20048
Minneapolis, Minnesota 55420

Gathers together parents and professionals interested in family-centered maternity care. Publications and films.

NATIONAL ASSOCIATION OF PARENTS AND PROFESSIONALS FOR
SAFE ALTERNATIVES (NAPSAC)
Dave and Lee Stewart, Directors
P.O. Box 267
Marble Hill, Missouri 63764
(314) 238-2010

Promotes education about all childbirth alternatives. Newsletter, books, and other publications. Active in legislative reform and political action. *Directory of Alternative Birth Services and Consumer Guide* ($5.95) has 4,500 listings, but NAPSAC reminds readers that these listings are not verified as accurate.

Cesarean Birth

CESAREAN BIRTH COUNCIL INTERNATIONAL, INC.
P.O. Box 6081
San Jose, California 95150
(415) 343-4044

Provides prenatal classes, phone counseling, rap groups, newsletter.

CESAREAN CONNECTION
P.O. Box 11
Westmont, Illinois 60559
(312) 968-8877

Provides a referral service for individuals looking for a Cesarean support group. Their list of groups covers the U.S. as well as some in Canada. Newsletter.

CESAREAN PREVENTION MOVEMENT
Esther Zorn, President
P.O. Box 152
Syracuse, New York 13210
(315) 424-1942

Information on cesarean prevention and VBAC. Book: *Silent Knife* Newsletter: *Cesarean Prevention Clarion*

CESAREAN/SUPPORT, EDUCATION, AND CONCERN, INC.
22 Forest Road
Framingham, Massachusetts 01701
(617) 877-8266

Provides information on many aspects of cesarean birth in order to make couples more aware of what the procedure involves and what options may be available to them.

CONSCIOUS CHILDBEARING
Lynn Baptisti Richards   (516-627-1636)
10 Summit Drive
Manhasset, New York 11030
Other counselors: Barbara Brownhill   (516) 593-7556 and
Nancy Wainer Cohen (617) 449-2490

Information, childbirth classes and hot line for avoiding cesareans and having a VBAC in hospital or at home. Call them if you're advised that you need a cesarean. Please do not call after 9 P.M. Eastern time unless it's an emergency or you are in labor. Send $15 for information packet on Vaginal Birth After Cesarean (VBAC).

COUNCIL FOR CESAREAN AWARENESS
5520 S.W. 92nd Avenue
Miami, Florida 33165
(205) 596-2699

Provides information and support for cesarean births and VBACS.

Childbirth Education

AMERICAN ACADEMY OF HUSBAND-COACHED CHILDBIRTH
(AAHCC)
Jay and Marjie Hathaway, Directors
P.O. Box 5224
Sherman Oaks, California 91413
(213) 788-6662

Certifies and trains instructors in Bradley method. Publications and films.

AMERICAN SOCIETY FOR PSYCHOPROPHYLAXSIS IN OBSTETRICS
(ASPO)
1411 "K" Street N.W. Suite 200
Washington, D.C. 20005
(202) 783-7050

Certifies and trains instructors in Lamaze method. Publications and films.

CHILDBIRTH WITHOUT PAIN EDUCATION ASSOCIATION
20134 Snowden
Detroit, Michigan 48235

Certifies and trains instructors in the Lamaze method. Publications and films.

MIDWEST PARENTCRAFT CENTER
627 Beaver Road
Glenview, Illinois 60025

Teaches techniques of Grantly Dick-Read. Numerous groups in the greater Chicago area hold childbirth classes for parents-to-be. Publications.

NATIONAL ASSOCIATION OF CHILDBIRTH EDUCATORS (NACE)
3940 Eleventh Street
Riverside, California 92501

Certifies and trains childbirth educators in Lamaze method. Publications and films.

READ NATURAL CHILDBIRTH FOUNDATION, INC.
1300 South Eliseo Drive, Suite 102
Greenbrae, California 94904
(415) 461-2277 or 456-3143

Teaches techniques of Dick-Read for parents in Marin County, California. Publications and film.

Home Birth

THE ALTERNATIVE BIRTH CRISIS COALITION
P.O. Box 48371
Chicago, Illinois 60648
(312) 625-4054

Provides a referral service for consumers and professionals who are sued because of home birth participation. Newsletter.

AMERICAN COLLEGE OF HOME OBSTETRICS
P.O. Box 25
River Forest, Illinois 60305

Provides information for physicians who cooperate with couples choosing a home birth.

ASSOCIATION FOR CHILDBIRTH AT HOME
P.O. Box 39498
Los Angeles, Calif. 90039
(213) 667-0839

Trains and certifies home-birth teachers and attendants; publications.

BIRTH DAY
P.O. Box 388
Cambridge, Massachusetts 02138
(617) 354-2385

Provides referrals, classes, discussion groups, publications.

THE BIRTHING CIRCLE
303 East Main Street
Burkittsville, Maryland 21718
Robyn Molloy: (301) 834-7325
Patricia Gentry: (301) 898-7890
Rose Gerstner: (301) 473-4900

HOME ORIENTED MATERNITY EXPERIENCE (HOME)
511 New York Avenue
Takoma Park, Maryland 20912
(202) 726-4664

Provides international support group for couples planning a home birth through certified HOME leaders who hold monthly meetings. Newsletter.

INFORMED HOMEBIRTH
Box 788
Boulder, Colorado 80306
(303) 449-4181

Trains and certifies home-birth teachers and attendants, as well as offers classes for couples planning home births. Newsletter, books, educational cassettes available.

Midwives

AMERICAN COLLEGE OF NURSE-MIDWIFERY
15 K Street, NW Suite 1120
Washington, DC 20005
(202) 628-4642

Certifies nurse-midwives and provides referrals for consumers. Publications.

THE FARM
Ina May Gaskin, Head Midwife
156 Drakes Lane
Summertown, Tennessee 38483
(615) 964-3574

Provides information on midwifery, natural childbirth, and vegetarian nutrition. Publications, including newsletter.

MIDWIVES ALLIANCE OF NORTH AMERICA (MANA)
30 South Main
Concord, New Hampshire 03301
(603) 225-9586

Is a national organization in support of all midwives.

NATIONAL MIDWIVES ASSOCIATION
1620 Howze Street
El Paso, Texas 79903
(915) 533-8142

Provides referrals for consumers looking for midwives. Newsletter.

Monitrice Service

MONITRICES OF MARYLAND (MOM)
Patricia Curran, R.N. Codirector
307 Dunkirk Road
Baltimore, Maryland 21212
(301) 377-5958

Provides private-day obstetrical nursing service in metropolitan Baltimore.

Breastfeeding

LA LECHE LEAGUE, INTERNATIONAL
9616 Minneapolis Avenue
Franklin Park, Illinois 60131
(312) 455-7730

Provides mother-to-mother breastfeeding information worldwide to one million mothers annually. It also has dozens of information sheets (including medical) and books. Send a stamped, self-addressed envelope to LLL for the name of the group nearest you. Contact also for information about the newly-formed Professional Lactation Consultant Program.

Resources for the Postpartum Period

FULL CYCLE PARENTS NETWORK
P.O. Box 685
Capitola, California 95010
(408) 475-6866

Provides help to families after birth of a new baby with household chores and other necessities. Workshops and publications.

POSTPARTUM EDUCATION FOR PARENTS
% Jane Honikman
927 North Kellogg Avenue
Santa Barbara, California 93111

Provides postpartum support, classes and publications.

COPE (COPING WITH THE OVERALL PREGNANCY/PARENTING EXPERIENCE)
37 Clarendon Street
Boston, Massachusetts 02116
(617) 357-5588

Provides counseling and support groups.

THE MOTHERS' CENTER
% United Methodist Church
Old Country Road and Nelson Avenue
Hicksville, New York 11801
(516) 822-4539

Provides support groups and information.

THE PEOPLE PLACE
1465 Massachusetts Avenue
Arlington, Massachusetts 02174
(617) 643-8630

Provides counseling for individuals and groups.

Other Organizations

CHILDREN IN HOSPITALS, INC.
31 Wilshire Park
Needham, Massachusetts 02190

Provides information about the need for ample contact between children and parents when either is hospitalized. Encourages hospitals to adopt flexible visiting and living-in policies. Publications.

COMMITTEE ON PATIENT'S RIGHTS
Box 1900
New York, New York 10001

Mail a stamped, self-addressed envelope for a copy of the Pregnant Patient's Bill of Rights.

COUPLE TO COUPLE LEAGUE
3621 Glenmore Avenue
P.O. Box 11084
Cincinnati, Ohio 45311
(513) 661-7612

Offers couples help with the practice of natural family planning. CCL teaches ecological breastfeeding and the full sympto-thermal method. Publications.

HOPING (Helping Other Parents in Normal Grieving)
%Edward W. Sparrow Hospital
1215 East Michigan
P.O. Box 30480
Lansing, Michigan 48909

THE NATIONAL FOUNDATION—MARCH OF DIMES
1275 Mamaroneck Avenue
White Plains, New York 10605
(914) 428-7100

Provides information on the prevention of birth defects and any life-threatening condition in the newborn. March of Dimes supports a network of research, education, and medical service programs. Publications.

PARENTS CONCERNED FOR HOSPITALIZED CHILDREN, INC.
176 North Villa Avenue
Villa Park, Illinois 60181

Encourages health care facilities to develop family-oriented pediatric care. Services include support of families and education of parents as to effects of hospitalization on children, and appropriate measures to prevent or lessen trauma.

NATIONAL FOUNDATION FOR SUDDEN INFANT DEATH
1501 Broadway
New York, New York 10036
(212) 563-4630

Provides information to parents and professionals on the sudden infant death syndrome (SIDS). Publications.

SHARE
% Sister Jane Marie Lamo
800 East Carpenter Street
Springfield, Illinois 62702
(217) 544-6464

Provides information and support for parents who experience miscarriage, stillbirth, or loss of newborn baby. Newsletter.

Journals and Periodicals

BIRTH JOURNAL
Madeleine H. Shearer, Editor
110 El Camino Real
Berkeley, California 94705

MOTHERING
Mothering Publications, Inc.
P.O. Box 2208
Albuquerque, New Mexico 87103

THE NEW NATIVITY
Marilyn Moran
4010 West 9th Street
Prairie Village, Kansas 66207

Spokeswoman for do-it-yourself home birth.

THE PEOPLE'S DOCTOR NEWSLETTER
P.O. Box 982
Evanston, ILL 60204

THE PRACTICING MIDWIFE
156 Drakes Lane
Summertown, Tennessee 38483

WOMEN & HEALTH
Biological Sciences Program
SUNY/College at Old Westbury
Old Westbury, New York 11568
(516) 876-3040

Mail Order Bookstores

BIRTH AND LIFE BOOKSTORE, INC.
Lynn Moen
P.O. Box 70625
Seattle, Washington 98107
(206) 789-4444

Sells full range of birth, childcare, and health books.

CHILD BIRTH EDUCATION SUPPLY CENTER
10 Sol Drive
Carmel, New York 10512
(914) 225-7763 and 4809.

Sells full range of birth and childcare books. Free catalog.

EDUCATIONAL GRAPHIC AIDS
1315 Norwood Avenue
Boulder, Colorado 80302
(303) 443-6874

Sells books, publications, films, slides.

ICEA BOOKCENTER
P.O. Box 20048
Minneapolis, Minnesota 55420
(612) 854-8660

Sells full range of birth, child care, and health books.

NAPSAC MAIL ORDER BOOK STORE
P.O. Box 428
Marble Hill, Missouri 63764
(314) 238-2010

Sells full range of books on safe alternatives in childbirth.

THE PENNYPRESS, INC.
1100 23rd Avenue East
Seattle, Washington 98112

Sells material on childbearing and parenting.

APPENDIX E
BIBLIOGRAPHIC REFERENCES
(By Chapter)

Introduction

Brackbill, Yvonne, Ph.D. "Lasting Behavioral Effects of Obstetric Medication on Children," testimony before the U.S. Senate Subcommittee on Health and Scientific Research, April 17, 1978, reprinted in *Compulsory Hospitalization or Freedom of Choice in Childbirth?* Vol. 1, David Stewart, Ph.D., and Lee Stewart, C.C.E., eds., Marble Hill, Mo.: NAPSAC Reproductions, 1979

Clein, Richard, National Center for Health Statistics, Division of Vital Statistics. Phone interview, September, 1983

"Medical Education in the U.S.," *American Medical Association News Release*, December 24, 1982

Smith, Dian G. "Viewpoint," *Glamour*, November 1979

"Women Still Look First to the Doctor for Information About Medications," *American Medical Association News Release*, December 24, 1982

1■ What Women Want

Anderson, Sandra F., R.N., M.S., and Leta J. Brown, R.N., C.C.E. "A Scientific Survey of Siblings at Birth," *Compulsory Hospitalization or Freedom of Choice in Childbirth?* Vol. 3, David Stewart, Ph.D. and Lee Stewart, C.C.E., eds., Marble Hill, Mo.: NAPSAC Reproductions, 1979

Eisenstein, Mayer, M.D. "Homebirth and the Physician," *Safe Alternative in Childbirth*, David Stewart, Ph.D. and Lee Stewart, C.C.E., eds., Chapel Hill, N.C.: NAPSAC, 1976

Ericson, Avis J., Pharm.D., ed. *Medications Used During Labor and Birth*, Milwaukee: ICEA, 1977

Hathaway, Marjie and Jay, AAHCC, and Kids. *Children at Birth*, Sherman Oaks, Ca.: Academy Publications, 1978

Klaus, Marshall, M.D., et al. "Maternal Attachment," *The New England Journal of Medicine*, 286:9:460–463, 1972

——, and John H. Kennell, M.D. *Parent-Infant Bonding*, St. Louis: C.V. Mosby Co., 1982

Kennell, John, M.D. "Are We in the Midst of a Revolution?" *Am. J. Dis. Child*, Vol. 134, March 1980

La Leche League. *The Womanly Art of Breast-feeding*, Franklin Park, Ill.: La Leche League International, 1981

Montagu, Ashley, Ph.D. *Touching*, New York and London: Columbia University Press, 1971

Newton, Niles, Ph.D. "Trebly Sensuous Woman," *Psychology Today*, July 1971

——, and Michael Newton, M.D. "Psychologic Aspects of Lactation," *The New England Journal of Medicine*, 277:22:1179–1188, 1967

Phillips, Celeste R. Nagel, R.N., B.S.N., M.S. "Neonatal Heat Loss in Heated Cribs vs. Mothers' Arms," *JOGN Nursing*, Vol. 3, No. 6, Nov.–Dec. 1974

Pitt, Jane, M.D. Phone interview, November 14, 1979

Pittenger, James E. and Jane G. "The Perinatal Period: Breeding Ground for Marital and Parental Maladjustment," *Keeping Abreast Journal*, 1:18–29, 1977

"Regionals Can Prolong Labor," *Medical World News,* October 15, 1971

Sander, Louis W., M.D., et al. "Early Mother-Infant Interaction and 24-Hour Patterns of Activity and Sleep," *Journal of the American Academy of Child Psychiatry,* 9:103–123, 1970

Sugarman, Muriel, M.D. "Review of Maternal-Infant Attachment Literature," presented at ICEA Eastern-Southeastern Regional Conference, 1977

Tanzer, Deborah, Ph.D. "Natural Childbirth: Pain or Peak Experience?" *Psychology Today,* October 1968

Thoman, Mark, M.D. Personal interviews, July and November 1979

Wernick, Robert, and the Editors of Time-Life Books, *The Family,* New York: Time-Life Books, 1974

2■ The Pleasure Principle

Baldwin, Rahima. "The New Homebirth," *Informed Homebirth Newsletter,* September 1978

Bing, Elisabeth and Libby Colman. *Making Love During Pregnancy,* New York: Bantam, 1977

Cherry, Lawrence. "The Doctor Within Us All," *New York Times Magazine,* November 23, 1980

Cogan, Rosemary, Ph.D., and Evelyn P. Edmunds. "The Unkindest Cut?" *Contemporary Ob/Gyn,* April 1977

Dieffenbach, Al. "Researchers Find Hope in the Body's 'Happiness Hormone'," *Seattle Times,* August 12, 1979

Haney, Daniel Q. "Runner's High Has Chemical Basis, Research Shows," Boulder *Daily Camera,* September 3, 1981

Hartman, Rhondda Evans, R.N., M.A. Interview, January 1983

Huston, Barbara. "Seattle Obstetrician Advocates Return to Nature's Painkiller," *Seattle Post-Intelligencer,* February 8, 1981

Masters, William, M.D. and Virginia Johnson, D.Sc. *Human Sexual Response,* Boston: Little, Brown, 1966

————and Virginia Johnson-Masters, D.Sc. Interview, July 1979

Newton, Niles, Ph.D. "Psychologic Factors in Birth and Breastfeeding," LLLI Northwest Area Conference, Seattle, Wash., September 28, 1979

————. *Maternal Emotions,* New York: Paul B. Hoeber, Inc., 1955

————. "Trebly Sensuous Woman," *Psychology Today,* July 1971

————. "Interrelationships between Sexual Responsiveness, Birth, and Breastfeeding," *Contemporary Sexual Behavior, Critical Issues For the 1970s,* J. Zubin and John Money, eds., Baltimore: Johns Hopkins University Press, 1973

————. "The Role of the Oxytocin Reflexes in the Three Interpersonal Reproductive Acts: Coitus, Birth, and Breastfeeding," a paper given at Serono Symposia, Siena, Italy, December 2, 3, and 4, 1976

Pert, Agu. "The Body's Own Tranquilizers," *Psychology Today,* September 1981

Sherfey, Mary Jane, M.D. *The Nature and Evolution of Female Sexuality,* New York: Random House, Vintage Books, 1973

Tanzer, Deborah, Ph.D. "Natural Childbirth: Pain or Peak Experience?" *Psychology Today,* October 1968

3■ If You Don't Know Your Options, You Don't Have Any

Adamson, G. David, M.D., and Douglas J. Gare, M.D. "Home or Hospital Births," *JAMA,* 243:17:1732–1737, May 2, 1980

Ballard, Roberta, M.D., F.A.A.P., et al. "Safety of a Hospital-Based Alternative Birth Center (ABC)," American Academy of Pediatrics Plenary Session, undated

"Barbara Brennan's Modern Midwives Deliver Personal and Professional Care, as well as 650 Babies a Year," *People,* February 8, 1982

Bennetts, Anita B., C.N.M., Ph.D., and Ruth Watson Lubic, C.N.M., Ed. D. "The Free-Standing Birth Centre," *Lancet,* 1:8268:378–380, February 13, 1982

Berman, Vic, M.D. Letter with NACHIS statistics, December 3, 1981, and update on first 1,000 births, September 25, 1982

"Birth Rooms," *Nurture,* 1:3, The Borning Corporation, June 1980

Bond, Enriqueta, Ph.D., research scientist, National Academy of Science. Phone interviews, July and August 1982

"Boulder Country Board of Health Study Session on Midwifery," Record of Proceedings, February 25, 1980

Brand, Margaret Stamm, R.N., M.H.A., and Leslie Z. Wirn, M.H.A. *Birthing Centers: Alternative in Obstetric Services in Indiana,* Pragmatics, Inc., December 1978

Burnett, Claude A. III, M.D., M.P.H., et al. "Home Delivery and Neonatal Mortality in North Carolina," *JAMA,* 244:24:2741–2745, December 19, 1980

"Can Midwives and Doctors Ever Be Colleagues?" *Ms.,* November 1981

Clark, Linda, C.N.M., in group practice with Richard B. Stewart, M.D. Phone interview, October 6, 1982

Cranch, Gene, C.N.M., Ph.D., Maternity Center Association, NYC. Phone interview, January 1982

de Courcy Hinds, Michael. "Midwife Births Gaining Wider Acceptance," *The New York Times,* January 24, 1981

Denver Birth Center. Open house, November 1977

Devitt, Neal. "The Transition from Home to Hospital Birth in the United States, 1930–1960," *Birth,* 4:2;47–58, Summer 1977

———. "Hospital Births versus Home Birth: The Scientific Facts, Past and Present," *Compulsory Hospitalization or Freedom of Choice in Childbirth,* Vol. 2, David Stewart, Ph.D., and Lee Stewart, C.C.E. eds., Marble Hill, Mo.: NAPSAC Reproductions, 1979

Editors of Heron House. *The Odds,* New York: G.P. Putnam's Sons, 1980

Eshelman, Michael, M.D. Personal Interview, January 1980

Faison, Jere B., M.D., et al. "The Childbearing Center, An Alternative Birth Setting," *Obstetrics and Gynecology,* 54:4:527–532, October 1979

Family-Centered Maternity/Newborn Care in Hospitals, Interprofessional Task Force on Health Care of Women and Children, June 1978

Feldman, Silvia, Ph.D. *Choices in Childbirth,* New York: Bantam, 1980

Franklin, John, M.D. "Homelike Deliveries in the Hospital," *Birth,* 5:4:235–238, Winter 1978

Gaeddert, Beth. "Use of Nurse-Midwives Resisted by Some Doctors," *Rocky Mountain News,* December 16, 1979

Gaskin, Ina May. "The Farm: A Living Example of the Five Standards," *The Five Standards for Safe Childbearing,* David Stewart, Ph.D., ed., Marble Hill, Mo.: NAPSAC International, 1981

Goodlin, Robert C. "Low Risk Obstetric Care for Low Risk Mothers," *Lancet,* I (8176):1017–1019, May 10, 1980

Goodman, Linda M., R.N., C.N.M., and Richard B. Stewart, M.D., F.A.C.O.G. "The Douglas Childbearing Center," *News from H.O.M.E.,* Spring 1977

Health Science Center, ob/gyn department, Denver. Phone interview, November 1981

"Home-birth Practitioners Defy Medical Profession," (UPI) *Denver Post,* September 28, 1981

"Homelike Birth Advised if Risks are Low," *Ob. Gyn. News,* January 1, 1980

Hosford, Betty, R.N., C.N.M., and Ruth Watson Lubic, C.N.M., Ed.D. "Childbearing and Maternity Centers—Alternatives to Homebirth and Hospital," *Safe Alternatives in Childbirth,* David Stewart, Ph.D. and Lee Stewart, C.C.E., eds., Chapel Hill, N.C.: NAPSAC, 1976

"Hospital Birth Center Held Safe for Low-Risk Women," *Ob. Gyn. News,* July 15, 1980

"Infant Mortality Study Issued: Supervised Home Births Found Safest," Boulder *Daily Camera,* December 18, 1980

Iritani, Evelyn. "A mid-Wife on the Hospital Staff," *Seattle Post-Intelligencer,* February 10, 1980

Ivory, Loretta, C.N.M., Director, Denver Birth Center. Personal interview, November 6, 1981

Kerner, John, M.D., F.A.C.O.G., and Carolyn Bailey Ferris, R.N. "An Alternative Birth Center in a Community Teaching Hospital," *Obstetrics and Gynecology,* 51:3:371–373, March 1978

Klass, Kay, B.S.N., and Kay Capps, R.N. "Nine Years' Experience with Family-Centered Maternity Care in a Community Hospital," *Birth,* 7:3:175–180, Fall 1980

Korte, Diana. "Birth Once Again a Family Affair," Boulder *Daily Camera, Focus,* November 26, 1978

Levy, Barry S., M.P.H., et al. "Reducing Neonatal Mortality Rate With Nurse-Midwives," *American Journal of Obstetrics and Gynecology,* 109:1:50–58, January 1, 1971

Lubic, Ruth Watson, C.N.M., Ed.D. "Midwifery: An Extended Role in Nursing Practice," Maternity Center Association, undated

———, and Eunice K.M. Ernst, C.N.M. "The Childbearing Center: An Alternative to Conventional Care," *Nursing Outlook,* 26:12:754–760, December 1978

Mehl, Lewis E., M.D., Ph.D. "Home Delivery Research Today: A Review," presented at the annual meeting of the American Foundation for Maternal and Infant Health, New York City, November 15, 1976

Melrose, Frances. "Women Choosing Midwifery Because of Personalized Care," *Denver Post,* July 27, 1981

Moran, Marilyn. *Birth and the Dialogue of Love,* Leawood, Ka.: New Nativity Press, 1981

Nelson, Linda P., M.Ed.N., B.Sc., S.C.M. (London). "Results of the First 124 Deliveries in the Birth Room at Roosevelt Hospital in New York City," *Birth,* 6:2:97–102, Summer 1979

"New Program Supports Development of Low-Cost Birth Alternatives," *NAPSAC News,* Vol. 6, No. 3, Fall 1981

"No Place of Birth Like Home," *The Times* magazine, London, July 9, 1978

"Nurse-Midwives Complain of Conspiracy by Doctors," (UPI) Boulder *Daily Camera,* December 19, 1980

"Nurse-Midwives See Growing Role in U.S. Care System," *American Medical News,* February 26, 1982

Petty, Roy. *Home Birth,* Chicago and New York: Domus Books, 1979

Poppema, Suzanne, M.D. Interview, January 1980

Porter, Gail. "Research Needs Described for Evaluating Birth Settings," summary of *Research Issues in the Assessment of Birth Settings,* communication dated January 5, 1983

"Review of Practice Shows 'Surprising' rise in Cesareans," *Ob. Gyn. News,* May 15, 1979

Rice, Patricia. "Birthing Rooms: Delivery in a Family Way," *St. Louis Post Dispatch,* May 18, 1980

Richard, Ralph M., M.D. "Is There a Scientific Basis for Repeat Cesarean?" *Contemporary Ob/Gyn,* January 1982

"Safety-Rating Nurse-Midwife Deliveries," *Self,* February 1982

Schmidt, Judith, R.N., M.S. "The First Year of Stanford University's Family Birth Room," *Birth*, 7:3:169–174, Fall 1980

Shearer, Madeleine H. "Editor's Reply," *Birth*, 6:3:205, Fall 1979

Sheehy, Gail. *Passages*, New York: E.P. Dutton & Co., Inc., 1976

Stewart, David, Ph.D. "The Philosophy of Proponents of Home Birth," paper given at District IV Conference, The Nurses Association and Junior Fellow Division of ACOG, November 9, 1977

————. "Skillful Midwifery: The Highest and Safest Standard," *The Five Standards for Safe Childbearing*, David Stewart, Ph.D., ed. Marble Hill, Mo.: NAPSAC International, 1981

————, and Lee Stewart, C.C.E. Phone interview, September 23, 1982

Stewart, Richard B., M.D., F.A.C.O.G., in group practice with four midwives. Phone interview, October 8, 1982

————, and Linda Clark, C.N.M., M.N. "Nurse-Midwifery Practice in an In-Hospital Birthing Center: 2050 Births," *Journal of Nurse-Midwifery*, 27:3:21–26, May/June 1982

————, Asher Galloway, M.D., and Linda Goodman, C.N.M., "An In-Hospital Birthing Room: One Year's Experience," *Compulsory Hospitalization or Freedom of Choice in Childbirth,* Vol. 1, David Stewart, Ph.D., and Lee Stewart C.C.E., eds., Marble Hill, Mo: NAPSAC Reproductions, 1979

Sumner, Philip E., M.D., F.A.C.O.G., and Celeste R. Phillips, R.N., M.S. *Birthing Rooms, Concept and Reality,* St. Louis, Toronto and London: The C.V. Mosby Co., 1981

"Testimony Before New Jersey Board of Medical Examiners Public Hearing," *NAPSAC News,* Summer 1980

"Testimony of American College of Nurse-Midwives Before the Subcommittee on Oversight and Investigation of the House Interstate and Foreign Commerce Committee," Record of Testimony, December 18, 1980

Torrington, Judy L., R.N., and James R. Dingfelder, M.D. "Recent Surveys of Parental Attitudes and Preferences in Childbirth," paper presented at NAPSAC conference, Atlanta, May 1978

Ward, Charlotte and Fred. *The Home Birth Book,* Garden City, N.Y.: Doubleday and Co. Inc., Dolphin Books, 1977

"What Is Family Centered Care and What Are Its Goals?" ICEA, 1971

Wilf, Ruth, C.N.M., Ph.D. "Alternatives: Booth Maternity Center in Philadelphia," Booth Maternity Center, March 1977

————. "Fulfilling the Needs of Families in a Hospital Setting: Can It Be Done?" *21st Century Obstetrics Now!* Vol. 1, David Stewart, Ph.D., and Lee Stewart, C.C.E., eds., Chapel Hill, N.C.: NAPSAC, Inc., 1977

Wilner, Susan, M.S., M.P.H., et al. "Comparison of the Quality of Maternity Care Between a Health Maintenance Organization and Fee-For-Service Practices," *New England Journal of Medicine,* 304:13:784–787, March 26, 1981

Youcha, Geraldine, and Sharon Youcha. "Where Should Baby Be Born? A Guide to Today's Options in Childbirth," *Woman's Day,* April 7, 1981

4■ Understanding Doctors

"Annual Report—Board of Obstetrics and Gynecology, Inc.," submitted by James A. Merrill, M.D., Secretary, *Bulletin of the American College of Surgeons,* December 1980

Barber, Hugh R.K., M.D. "Editorial: The Hospital—Our Alma Mater," *The Female Patient,* 6:10, October 1981

Beck, Joan. "Medical Profession Must Police Itself," Boulder *Daily Camera,* November 26, 1977

"Bendectin Production Ends," *Science News,* 123:25, June 18, 1983

Boone, Richard W., J.D., Michael D. Roth, J.D., and John W. Scanlon, M.D. "What Every Perinatologist Should Know About Medicolegal Problems," *Contemporary Ob/Gyn,* Vol. 18, October 1981

Bronson, Gail. "Checking Your Medical Policy's Health," *Money,* September 1982

Brown, Stephen W., Ph.D. "How Physicians See Themselves," *Medical Marketing & Media,* 17:2, February 1982

Chapman, Carleton B., M.D. "On the Definition and Teaching of the Medical Ethic," *New England Journal of Medicine,* September 20, 1979

Cousins, Norman. "Internship: Preparation or Hazing?" *JAMA,* 245:4, January 23–30, 1981

————. "Malpractice Backlash," *Saturday Review,* May 1980

————. "The Malpractice Crisis—Winner: The Lawyer, Loser: The Patient," *The Female Patient,* 6:8, August 1981

Donnelly, Julie C., Ed.D. "Management Report: Understanding Physicians: Stresses of Internship Can Have Adverse Effects on Doctors," *Hospital Management Quarterly,* Fall 1981/Winter 1982

Drummond, Hugh, M.D. "Playing Doctor," *Mother Jones,* July 1980

Eichna, Ludwig W., M.D. "Medical-School Education, 1975–1979," Special Article, *The New England Journal of Medicine,* 303:31, September 25, 1980

"80th Annual Report in Medical Education," *JAMA,* December 26, 1980

Emerson, Ralph S., M.D. "Trends in Professional Liability," *Bulletin of the American College of Surgeons,* March 1981

Eshelman, Michael, M.D. Interview, January 1980

"Excess Marks the Spot—The FDA Blows the Whistle on Abuses in New-Drug Ads," *Time,* September 27, 1982

"Fee Survey," *Medical Economics,* October 13, 1980

Freeman, Jonathan L. *Happy People: What Happiness Is, Who Has It and Why,* New York: Harcourt Brace Jovanovich, Inc., 1978

Fuchs, Victor R., Ph.D. "Who Shall Live?" *Rochester Review,* Spring 1978

Glandon, Gerald L., and Roberta J. Shapiro, eds., Department of Economic Research. "Profile of Medical Practice—1981," Center for Health Research and Development, American Medical Association

"GMENAC Predicts Physician Surplus," *Health Resources Administration,* Department of Health and Human Services, November 1980

Goodman, Ellen. "Doctors Take the Rap for Public Uncertainties," Boulder *Daily Camera,* January 5, 1979

Gurtner, William. "The Changing Relationship Between Hospitals and Surgeons," *Bulletin of the American College of Surgeons,* April 1982

Harrison, Michelle, M.D. *A Woman In Residence,* New York: Random House, 1982

"Health Expenses Rise 15.2 Percent," Boulder *Daily Camera,* October 31, 1981 (from *Health Care Financing Review,* Department of Health and Human Services, September 1981)

"High Incidence of Suicide, Alcoholism Among Physicians," *The U.S. Journal,* January 1980

"Impairment Among Residents is Often Unnoticed," *Ob. Gyn. News,* January 15, 1979

"Interview with Richard Selzer, M.D.," *East West Journal,* November 1980

Kirchner, Merian. "Doctor Surplus—What 1990 Will Look Like," *Medical Economics,* September 29, 1980

————. "Non-Surgical Practice: What's The Key to Higher Earnings," *Medical Economics,* February 16, 1981

Lander, Louise, J.D. "Why Some People Seek Revenge Against Doctors," *Psychology Today*, July 1978

"Loyalty—Why More Patients Are Switching," *Medical Economics*, November 29, 1976

Marieskind, Helen I., Dr.P.H. "An Evaluation of Cesarean Section in the United States," report for Department of Health, Education and Welfare, June 1979

Mawardi, Betty Hosmer, Ph.D. "Satisfactions, Dissatisfactions, and Causes of Stress in Medical Practice," *JAMA*, 241:14, April 6, 1979

"M.D.'s Seek to Stifle Competition," *ABCC News* (Alternative Birth Crisis Coalition), Vol. 1, November 1981

"Medicine: Business or Charity? A Los Angeles M.D. Stirs Debate," *American Medical News*, October 5, 1979

Moore, Francis D., M.D., and Susan M. Lang, B.S. "Board-Certified Physicians in the U.S. —Specialty Distribution and Policy Implications of Trends During the Past Decade," *New England Journal of Medicine*, April 30, 1981

Moyer, Linda, M.A. "What Obstetrical Journal Advertising Tells About Doctors and Women," *Birth*, 2:4, Fall-Winter 1975–76

Obstetrician-gynecologist, anonymous. Interview, January 1983

Owens, Arthur. "Who are the High-Fee Doctors?" *Medical Economics*, June 9, 1980

———. "Doctors' Earnings: A Brighter Picture This Time," *Medical Economics*, September 15, 1980

Pagliuso, James J., J.D. "Situations to Avoid If You Don't Want to Be Sued," *Contemporary Ob/Gyn*, March 1982

"Phone Calls That Are Shortening My Career," *Medical Economics*, February 16, 1981

"Physicians Miseducated, Hearing Told," *The U.S. Journal*, January 1980

Queenan, John T., M.D. "Foreword to the Technology 82 Issue," *Contemporary Ob/Gyn*, Vol. 18, October 1981

Sanders, Lawrence. *The Sixth Commandment*, New York: Granada, 1979

Schiefelbein, Susan. "The Female Patient—Heeded? Hustled? Healed?" *Saturday Review*, March 29, 1980

Schwartz, William B., M.D., Joseph P. Newhouse, Ph.D., Bruce W. Bennett, Ph.D., and Albert P. Williams, Ph.D. "The Changing Geographic Distribution of Board-Certified Physicians," *New England Journal of Medicine*, October 30, 1980

Scully, Diana. *Men Who Control Women's Health: The Miseducation of Obstetricians-Gynecologists*, Boston: Houghton-Mifflin, 1980

Shearer, Madeleine H. "The Effects of Regionalization of Perinatal Care on Hospital Services for Normal Childbirth," *Birth*, 4:4, Winter 1977

Smith, Cynthia. *Doctor's Wives—The Truth About Medical Marriages*, New York: Harper & Row, Seaview Books, 1981

"Study Indicates M.D.'s Tend to be Victims of Emotional Problems," *Medical World News*, October 29, 1971

"Talkative Doctors Avoid Suits," *Moneysworth*, August 1, 1977

"This Is What You Thought About Doctors' Attitudes," *Glamour*, October 1981

"Why Are Cesarean Rates So High," *Contemporary Ob/Gyn*, December 1981

"Why More Doctors Won't Mean Lower Bills," *Business Week*, May 11, 1981

5■ Finding Dr. Right

Barber, Hugh R.K., M.D. "High-Risk Pregnancy—Part 1," *The Female Patient*, 7:7, July 1982

Benzaia, Diana. "Your Doctor/Patient Confidence Score," *Self*, May 1981

Dilanni, Denisce. "Ultrasound," *Mothering*, Summer 1982

"Doctors, Lawyers, Birth Rooms, Courts," *NAPSAC News*, 7:1, Spring 1982

Freeman, Roger K., M.D., and Susan Pescar. *Safe Delivery: Protecting Your Baby During Pregnancy*, New York: Facts on File, Inc., 1982

Hobbins, John C., M.D. "Ultrasound Can Diagnose Fetal Malformations," *Contemporary Ob/Gyn*, March 1982

"Long Term Safety of Ultrasound on Fetus Still Unresolved," *American Medical Association News Release*, April 23, 1982

McCormack, Patricia, UPI Health Editor. "Do American Obstetrical Practices Harm Babies?" Boulder *Daily Camera*, February 17, 1980

McElhinney, Susan, J.D., and Stuart McElhinney. "The Legal Rights of Parents," *ABCC News* (Alternative Birth Crisis Coalition), undated

"Medical Schools Facing Possible Retrenchments," *American Medical Association News Release*, December 26, 1980

"New York Law Requires Disclosure Risks of OB Drugs," *NAPSAC News*, September 1979

"The Pregnant Patient's Bill of Rights," *Journal of Nurse-Midwifery*, Vol. 20, No. 4, Winter 1975

"The Pregnant Patient's Responsibilities," International Childbirth Education Association, Inc., undated.

Yoder, Marilyn. "Finding Out Your Hospital Options," *Leaders Line* (a La Leche League area newsletter), September 1980

6■ Obstetricians' Beliefs About a "Safe Birth"

"ACOG Offers Family Physician Larger Share of OB Practice If They'll Join in Fight Against Midwives," *NAPSAC News*, Vol. 5, No. 3, Fall 1980

"AGOG Official: Home Delivery 'Maternal Trauma, Child Abuse,' " *Ob./Gyn. News*, October 1, 1977

Alderman, Mary M., Editor. "Childbirth at Home? U.S. experts: Safety vs. Sentiment," *Patient Care*, November 15, 1977

Anderson, Sandra F., R.N. M.S. "Childbirth as a Pathological Process: An American Perspective," *The American Journal of Maternal Child Nursing*, July/August 1977

Aubry, Richard, M.D. "The American College of Obstetrician and Gynecologists (ACOG): Standards for Safe Childbearing," *21st Century Obstetrics Now!* Volume 1, Lee Stewart, C.C.E. and David Stewart, Ph.D., eds., Chapel Hill, N.C.: NAPSAC, 1977

Beard, Richard. "Childbirth at Home? Mother's Wishes vs. Doctor's Duties," *Patient Care*, November 15, 1977

Cardwell, Jewell. "Doctor Decries Trend Toward At Home Delivery of Babies," Boulder *Daily Camera*, August 26, 1982

Chalmers, Iain and Martin Richards. "Intervention and Causal Inference in Obstetric Practice," *Benefits and Hazards of the New Obstetrics*, Tim Chard and Martin Richards, eds., London: William Heinemann Medical Books; Philadelphia: J. B. Lippincott Co., 1977

Chard, Tim and Martin Richards, eds. *Benefits and Hazards of the New Obstetrics*, London: William Heinemann Medical Books; Philadelphia: J. B. Lippincott Co., 1977

Clein, Richard, National Center for Health Statistics, Division of Vital Statistics. Phone Interview, September 1983

Corea, Gena. *The Hidden Malpractice*, New York: Jove Publications, 1977

Devitt, Neal. "Hospital Birth Versus Home Birth: The Scientific Facts, Past and Present," from *Compulsory Hospitalization or Freedom of Choice in Childbirth?*, Vol. 2, David Stewart, Ph.D. and Lee Stewart, C.C.E., eds., Marble Hill, Mo.: NAPSAC Reproductions, 1979

"Do Most Obstetricians Really Care About Family Centered Programs," *NAPSAC News*, Vol. 3, No. 1, Winter 1978

Erickson, J. David, Ph.D., and Tor Bjerkedal, M.D. "Fetal and Infant Mortality in Norway and the United States," *Journal of the American Medical Association*, 247:7:987–1028, February 19, 1982

Garvey, J. "Infant Respiratory Distress Syndrome," *American Journal of Nursing*, 75 (4):614–7, April 1975, abstract from *Birth*, Vol. 2:3, Summer 1975

Goldenberg, R. L., et al. "Iatrogenic Respiratory Distress Syndrome: An Analysis of Obstetric Events Preceding Delivery of Infants Who Develop Respiratory Distress Syndrome," *American Journal of Obstetrics and Gynecology*, 6:617–20, November 15, 1975, abstract from *Birth*, Vol. 3:2, Summer 1976

Guyer, Bernard, M.D., M.P.H., et al. "Birth-Weight Standardized Neonatal Mortality Rates and the Prevention of Low Birth Weight: How Does Massachusetts Compare with Sweden?" *The New England Journal of Medicine*, 306:20:1230–1233, May 20, 1982

Haire, Doris, D.M.S. "Maternity Practices Around the World: How Do We Measure Up?" *Safe Alternatives in Childbirth*, David Stewart, Ph.D., and Lee Stewart, C.C.E., eds., Chapel Hill, N.C.: NAPSAC, 1976

Hellman, Louis M., and Jack A. Pritchard. *Williams Obstetrics*, 14th edition, New York: Appleton-Century-Crofts, 1971

Knox, G. Eric, M.D., et al. "Management of Prolonged Pregnancy: Results of a Prospective Randomized Trial," *American Journal of Obstetrics and Gynecology*, 134:4:376–384, June 15, 1979

Lake, Alice. "Childbirth in America," *McCall's*, January 1976

Lee, Kwang-Sun, M.D., et al. "Neonatal Mortality: An Analysis of the Recent Improvement in the United States," *American Journal of Public Health*, 70:1:15–21, January 1980

McCoy, Jan. "County Officials Troubled by CU Hospital Limitations," Boulder *Daily Camera*, August 12, 1982

" 'Natural' Childbirth Decried; High Mortality Rates Cited," *Convention Reporter*, Vol. 11, No. 30, November 1981, reprinted in *NAPSAC News*, Vol. 7, No. 1, Spring 1982

Obstetrical Practices in the United States, U.S. Senate Subcommittee on Health, 95th Congress, 2nd Session, April 17, 1978

Paneth, Nigel, M.D., M.P.H., et al. "Newborn Intensive Care and Neonatal Mortality in Low-Birth-Weight Infants, *The New England Journal of Medicine*, 307:3:149–155, July 15, 1982

Pearse, Warren, M.D. "Home Birth Crisis," *ACOG Newsletter*, July 1977

Poppema, Suzanne, M.D. Personal interview, January 1980

"Quarter of New Moms Don't Get Prenatal Care," Boulder *Daily Camera*, October 10, 1981

Ratner, Herbert, M.D. "History of the Dehumanization of American Obstetrical Practice," *21st Century Obstetrics Now!* Vol. 1, David Stewart, Ph.D., and Lee Stewart, C.C.E., eds., Chapel Hill, N.C.: NAPSAC, 1977

Shearer, Madeleine H. "The Effects of Regionalization of Perinatal Care on Hospital Services for Normal Childbirth," *Birth*, 4:4:139–151, Winter 1977

Statistical Resources Branch of the Division of Vital Statistics, National Center for Health Statistics, U.S. Department of Health and Human Services, 301-436-8980. Phone inquiries, September 3, 1982 and October 12, 1982.

Steward, Marsh, M.D., ed. "Consumerism and the Malpractice Problem," *CAOG Newsletter*, Vol. 3, No. 3, November 1981, reprinted in *NAPSAC News*, Vol. 7, No. 1, Spring 1982

Stone, Martin, M.D. "Presidential Address," *ACOG Newsletter*, May 1979

"The Heavy Burden of Low Birth Weight Babies," American Medical Association news release, February 19, 1982

"U.S. Infant Mortality Falls to Lowest Level," (AP) Boulder *Daily Camera*, June 19, 1983

7■ The Obstetrician's Black Bag of Interventions

"A New Delivery Position—It's More Comfortable," "Medical Bulletin," *Self,* April 1979

Banta, H. David, M.D., M.P.H., and Stephen B. Thacker, M.D. *Costs and Benefits of Electronic Fetal Monitoring: A Review of the Literature,* National Center for Health Services Research (NCHSR), Research Report Series, DHEW Publication No. (PHS) 79-3245, April 1979

Beard, Richard W. "Mother's Wishes Versus Doctor's Duties," *Patient Care,* November 15, 1977

Brackbill, Yvonne, Ph.D. "Lasting Behavioral Effects of Obstetric Medication on Children," testimony before the U.S. Senate Subcommittee on Health and Scientific Research, April 17, 1978, reprinted in *Compulsory Hospitalization or Freedom of Choice in Childbirth?* Vol. 1. David Stewart, Ph.D., and Lee Stewart, C.C.E., eds., Marble Hill, Mo.: NAPSAC Reproductions, 1979

Brazelton, T. Berry, M.D. "Psychophysiologic Reaction in the Neonate, II. Effect of Maternal Medication on the Neonate and His Behavior," *Pediatrics,* 58:4:513–518, April 1961

———. "What Childbirth Drugs Can Do to Your Child," *Redbook,* February 1971

Caldeyro-Barcia, Roberto, M.D. "Some Consequences of Obstetrical Interference," *Birth,* 2:2:34–38, Spring 1975

———. "The Influence of Maternal Position on Time of Spontaneous Rupture of the Membranes, Progress of Labor and Fetal Head Compression," *Birth,* 6:1:7–15, Spring 1979

Carr, Katherine Camacho, C.N.M., M.S. "Obstetric Practices Which Protect Against Neonatal Morbidity: Focus on Maternal Position in Labor and Birth," *Birth,* 7:4:249–254, Winter 1980

Chalmers, Iain and Martin Richards. "Intervention and Causal Inference in Obstetric Practice," *Benefits and Hazards of the New Obstetrics,* Tim Chard and Martin Richards, eds., London: Wm. Heinemann Medical Books; Philadelphia: J. B. Lippincott Co., 1977

Cogan, Rosemary, Ph.D., and Evelyn P. Edmunds. "The Unkindest Cut?" reprint from author, undated.

"Consequences of Epidural Anesthesia for the Behavior of Newborns and Their Mothers," *Child Development,* February 14, 1980

Conway, Esther and Yvonne Brackbill. "Delivery Medication and Infant Outcome: An Empirical Study," *The Effects of Obstetrical Medication on Fetus and Infant,* by Watson A. Bower, Jr., et al., Monographs of the Society for Research in Child Development, Serial No. 137, Vol. 35, No. 4, June 1970

"Criticism of Certain Treatment Decisions," *USA Today: Your Health* section, February 1980

Davis, Flora. "Who's Having the Baby—You or the Doctor?" *Woman's Day,* March 1976

"DGH Birth Surge 'Courts Disaster,' " *The Denver Post,* April 27, 1978

Doering, Susan G., Ph.D. "Unnecessary Cesareans: Doctor's Choice, Parent's Dilemma," *Compulsory Hospitalization or Freedom of Choice in Childbirth?* Vol. 1, David Stewart, Ph.D., and Lee Stewart, C.C.E., eds., Marble Hill, Mo.: NAPSAC Reproductions, 1979

Dunn, P. "Obstetric Delivery Today: For Better or For Worse?" *Lancet,* 7963:790–793, April 19, 1976, abstract from *Birth,* 3:3:141, 1976

"Electronic Fetal Monitoring: How Necessary?" *Journal of the American Medical Association,* 241:17:1772–1774, April 27, 1979

"Electronic Fetal Monitoring Takes More Professional Time, Not Less," *NAPSAC News,* Vol. 6, No. 3, Fall 1981

"Episiotomy Use Questioned," Boulder *Daily Camera,* June 15, 1981

Ericson, Avis J., Pharm. D. *Medications Used During Labor and Birth,* Milwaukee, Wisconsin: International Childbirth Education Association, Inc., First Edition, January 1977

Ettner, Frederic M., M.D. "Comparative Study of Obstetrics," *Safe Alternatives in Childbirth,* David Stewart, Ph.D., and Lee Stewart, C.C.E., eds., Chapel Hill, N.C.: NAPSAC, Inc., 1977

———. "Hospital Obstetrics: Do the Benefits Outweigh the Risks?" *21st Century Obstetrics Now!,* Volume 1, David Stewart, Ph.D., and Lee Stewart, C.C.E., eds., Chapel Hill, N.C.: NAPSAC, 1977

"Expectant U.S. Mothers 'Shortchanged,'" *The Denver Post,* April 25, 1972

Flanagan, Tracy. "New Findings About Induced Labor," *Ms.,* July 1980

Flynn, A.M., et al. "Ambulation in Labor," *Br. Med. J.,* 2(6137):591–3, August 26, 1978, abstract from *Birth,* 6:1:73, Spring 1979

Gaskin, Ina May. *Spiritual Midwifery,* Summertown, Tn.: The Book Publishing Company, 1978

Glassman, Judith. "The Changing World of Childbirth," *Cosmopolitan,* April 1981

Gold, Marion. "Dissent, Debate Mark Fetal Monitor Verdict," *Medical Tribune,* September 5, 1979

Gray, Ann. "FDA Reviews Brackbill–Broman Research on OB Drugs," *NAPSAC News,* Vol. 4:2, 1979

Haire, Doris, D.M.S., *The Cultural Warping of Childbirth,* International Childbirth Education Association, 1972

———. "Maternity Practices Around the World: How Do We Measure Up?" *Safe Alternatives in Childbirth,* David Steward, Ph.D., and Lee Stewart, C.C.E., eds., Chapel Hill, N.C.: NAPSAC, 1976

———. "Safety of Drugs—How Safe is 'Safe'?" American Foundation for Maternal and Child Health, 30 Beckman Pl., N.Y.C., undated

———. Testimony before Senate Health Subcommittee on April 17, 1978

Havercamp, Albert, M.D., et al. "A Controlled Trial of the Differential Effects of Intrapartum Fetal Monitoring," *American Journal of Obstetrics and Gynecology,* 134:4:399–412, June 15, 1979

———. "The Evaluation of Continuous Fetal Heart Rate Monitoring in High-Risk Pregnancy," *Am. J. Obstet. Gynecol.,* 125:3:310–317, June 1, 1976

Hellman, Louis M. and Jack A. Pritchard, *Williams Obstetrics,* 14th Edition, New York: Appleton-Century-Crofts, 1971

Hess, Orvan W., M.D. "Impact of Electronic Fetal Monitoring on Obstetric Management," *Journal of the American Medical Association,* 244:7:682–686, August 15, 1980

Hughes, Richard. "Infant Brain Damage Linked to Delivery Drugs—Study's Author Charges U.S. Delaying Release," *Valley News,* January 14, 1979

Jonas, Gerald and Candace B. Pert, Ph.D. "What Your Obstetrician Doesn't Know May Hurt You or Your Baby," *Family Circle,* September 20, 1977

Kolata, Gina Bari. "Childbirth Drugs May Affect Newborn's Behavior," *Washington Post,* reprinted in Boulder *Daily Camera,* December 13, 1978

Lake, Alice. "Childbirth in America," *McCall's,* January 1976

Lumley, Judith, Ph.D. "The Irresistible Rise of Electronic Fetal Monitoring," *Birth,* 9:3:150–152, Fall 1982

Martell, M., et al., "Blood Acid-Base at Birth in Neonates from Labors with Early and Late Rupture of Membranes," *Journal of Pediatrics,* 6:963–7, December 1976 abstract in *Birth,* 4:2:87, Summer 1977

Mehl, Lewis E., M.D., Ph.D. "Home Delivery Research Today: A Review," paper from author presented at the annual meeting of the American Foundation for Maternal and Infant Health, NYC, N.Y., November 15, 1976

———. Research on Obstetric Procedures and Neonatal Outcome reported in *The Five Standards for Safe Childbearing* by David Stewart, Ph.D., Marble Hill, Mo.: NAPSAC, Int'l, 1981

Minkoff, Howard L., M.D., and Richard H. Schwarz, M.D. "The Rising Cesarean Section Rate: Can It Safely Be Reversed?" *Obstetrics and Gynecology*, 56:2:135–145, August 1980

Moore, W.M.O. "The Conduct of the Second Stage," *Benefits and Hazards of the New Obstetrics*, Tim Chard and Martin Richards, eds., London: Wm. Heinemann Medical Books; Philadelphia: J. B. Lippincott Co., 1977

Neutra, Raymond R., M.D., Dr. Ph., et al. "Effect of Fetal Monitoring on Neonatal Death Rates," *The New England Journal of Medicine*, 299:7:324–326, August 17, 1978

"New York Law Requires Disclosure Risks of OB Drugs," *NAPSAC News*, Vol. 4, No. 1, Spring 1979

"The Nurses' Role in Electronic Fetal Monitoring," *NAACOG Technical Bulletin*, No. 7, July 1980

O'Connor, Michael C., et al. "Is the Fetus 'Scalped' in Labor?" *The Lancet*, pp. 947, November 3, 1979

"Patching Up Post-Lumbar Headaches," *Medical World News*, November 7, 1969

Read, John A., Lt. Col., M.C., U.S.A., et al. "Randomized Trial of Ambulation Versus Oxytocin for Labor Enhancement: A Preliminary Report," *American Journal of Obstetrics and Gynecology*, 139:6:669–672, March 15, 1981

"Regionals Can Prolong Labor," *Medical World News*, October 15, 1971

A Review of Research Literature and Federal Involvement Relating to Selected Obstetric Practices, United States General Accounting Office, September 24, 1979

Richards, M.P.M. and J. F. Bernal, "Effects of Obstetric Medication on Mother-Infant Interaction and Infant Development," *Psychosomatic Medicine in Obstetrics and Gynecology*, pp. 303–307, 3rd Int. Congr., London, 1971

"Shave Prior to Surgery Criticized," Boulder *Daily Camera*, October 20, 1977

Shearer, Madeleine H., R.P.T. "Auscultation is Acceptable in Low Risk Women," editorial, *Birth*, 6:1:3–5, Spring 1979

———. "Fetal Monitoring: For Better or Worse?" *Compulsory Hospitalization, Freedom of Choice in Childbirth*, Vol. 1, David Stewart, Ph.D. and Lee Stewart, C.C.E., eds., Marble Hill, Mo.: NAPSAC Reproductions, 1979

"Signs of Uterine Rupture Not Apparent in Many Patients," *Ob. Gyn. News*, January 15, 1979

"Stilbestrol and Adenocarcinoma of the Vagina," *Pediatrics*, 51:2:297–299, February 1973

Stimeling, Gary. "Will Common Delivery Techniques Soon Become Malpractice" *The Journal of Legal Medicine*, May 1975

"Subgaleal Hematoma, A Complication of Instrumental Delivery," *JAMA*, 244:14:1597–98, October 3, 1980

Thoman, Mark, M.D. Personal Interviews, July and November, 1979

Wood, C., et al. "A Controlled Trial of Fetal Heart Rate Monitoring in a Low Risk Obstetric Population," *Am. J. Obstet. Gynecol.*, 141(5):527, November 1, 1981, abstract from *Birth*, 9:3:211, Fall 1982

Wunderlich, Cherry. "Predictors for Fetal Distress Identified," *ICEA News*, 18:3:4, 1979

8■ The Cesarean Epidemic

Banta, H. David, M.D., M.P.H., and Stephen Thacker, M.D. *Costs and Benefits of Electronic Fetal Monitoring: A Review of the Literature*, Washington DC: DHEW Publications No. (PHS) 79–3245, April 1979

Boehm, Frank H., M.D., et al. "Management of Genital Herpes Simplex Virus Infection Occurring During Pregnancy," *American Journal of Obstetrics and Gynecology*, 141:7:735–740, December 1, 1981

Bottoms, Sidney F., M.D., et al. "The Increase in the Cesarean Birthrate," *The New England Journal of Medicine*, 302:10:559–563, March 6, 1980

Brice, John E. H., and Colin H. M. Walker. "Changing Pattern of Respiratory Distress in Newborns," *Lancet*, 2:8041:752–754, October 8, 1977

Clein, Richard, National Center for Health Statistics, Division of Vital Statistics. Phone Interview, September 1983

Burkhard, Nancy. "Group Advocates Birth at Home," *Denver Post*, January 19, 1979

Carrow, Levin A., M.D., F.A.C.S. "Gynecology and Obstetrics," *Bulletin of the American College of Surgeons*, January 1982

Cesarean Childbirth, Consensus Development Conference, Bethesda, Md.: NIH Publication No. 82–2067, October 1981

"Cesareans," Documentary, KMGH-TV Channel 7, Denver, October 30, 1981

"Cesareans Increasing But Few Study Related Maternal Deaths," *Ob/Gyn News*, July 1, 1980

Chalmers, Iain and Martin Richards, "Intervention and Causal Inference in Obstetric Practice," *Benefits and Hazards of the New Obstetrics*, Tim Chard and Martin Richards, eds., London: William Heinemann Medical Books; Philadelphia, J. B. Lippincott Co., 1977

Cohen, Wayne R., M.D. "Influence of the Duration of Second Stage Labor on Perinatal Outcome and Puerperal Morbidity," *Obstetrics and Gynecology*, 49:3:266–269, March 1977

Collea, Joseph V., M.D., et al. "The Randomized Management of Term Frank Breech Presentations: A Study of 208 Cases," *American Journal of Obstetrics and Gynecology*, 137:2:235–244, May 15, 1980

Cooke, Cynthia W., M.D., and Susan Dworkin. "Tough Talk About Unnecessary Surgery," *Ms.*, October 1981

Cook, William A., M.D. *Natural Childbirth: Fact and Fallacy*, Chicago: Nelson Hall, 1982

Corea, Gena. "The Cesarean Epidemic; Who's Having This Baby, Anyway— You or the Doctor?" *Mother Jones*, July 1980

Corey, Lawrence, M.D. "The Diagnosis and Treatment of Genital Herpes," *JAMA*, 248:9:1041–1050, September 3, 1982

"Correcting a Breech Presentation," *Informed Homebirth Newsletter*, January– February 1978

Doering, Susan G., Ph.D. "Unnecessary Cesareans: Doctor's Choice, Parent's Dilemma," *Compulsory Hospitalization or Freedom of Choice in Childbirth*, Vol. 1, David Stewart, Ph.D., and Lee Stewart, C.C.E., eds., Marble Hill, Mo.: NAPSAC Reproductions, 1979

Enkin, Murray W., M.D. "Having a Section is Having a Baby," *Birth*, 4:3:99–102, Fall 1977

Evrard, John R., M.D., M.P.H., F.A.C.O.G., and Edwin M. Gold, M.D., F.A.C.O.G. "Cesarean Section and Maternal Mortality in Rhode Island, Incidence and Risk Factors, 1965–1975," *Obstetrics and Gynecology*, 50:5:594–597, November 1977

Feldman, Silvia, Ph.D. "Cesarean Deliveries/When and Why are They Justified," *Self*, May 1979

———. *Choices in Childbirth*, New York: Bantam, 1980

Frechette, Alfred L., M.D., M.P.H., and Pearl K. Russo. "A Comparison of the Quality of Maternity Care Between a Health Maintenance Organization and Fee-For-Service Practices," *The New England Journal of Medicine*, 304:13:784–787, March 26, 1981

Gibbs, C.E., M.D. "Planned Vaginal Delivery Following Cesarean Section," *Clinical Obstetrics and Gynecology*, 23:2:507–515, June 1980

Gluck, Lewis, M.D. Quoted from "current issue" of *Hospital Practice* in *Tallahassee Democrat*, April 7, 1977

Goldenberg, R. L., M.D., et al. "Iatrogenic Respiratory Distress Syndrome: An Analysis of Obstetric Events Preceding Delivery of Infants Who Develop Respiratory Distress Syndrome," *Am. J. Obstet. Gynecol.*, 6:617–20, November 15, 1975, abstract in *Birth*, 3:2:93, 1976

Gottlieb, Bill. "Great Moments in Medicine—That Backfired," *Prevention*, September 1978

Graves, William, M.D., F.A.C.O.G. "Breech Delivery in Twenty Years of Practice," *American Journal of Obstetrics and Gynecology*, 137:2:229–234, May 15, 1980

Havercamp, Albert, M.D., F.A.C.O.G. "A controlled Trial of the Differential Effects of Intrapartum Fetal Monitoring," *American Journal of Obstetrics and Gynecology*, 134:4:399–408.

————. "Does Anyone Need Fetal Monitors," testimony before the U.S. Senate Sub-Committee on Health, April 17, 1978, reprinted in *Compulsory Hospitalization or Freedom of Choice in Childbirth*, Vol. 1, David Stewart, Ph.D., and Lee Stewart, C.C.E., eds., Marble Hill, Mo.: NAPSAC Reproductions, 1979

Heilman, Jean Rattner. "Breaking the Cesarean Cycle," *New York Times Magazine*, September 7, 1980

Hellegers, Andre E., M.D. "Fetal Monitoring and Neonatal Death Rates," editorial, *New England Journal of Medicine*, 299:7:357–8, August 17, 1978

Hellman, Louis M. and Jack A. Pritchard. *Williams Obstetrics*, 14th edition, New York: Appleton-Century-Crofts, 1971

Janov, Arthur. *The Feeling Child*, New York: Simon and Schuster, 1973

Johnson, John W. C., M.D., et al. "Premature Rupture of the Membranes and Prolonged Latency," *Obstetrics and Gynecology*, 57:5:547–556, May 1981

Jones, M. Douglas Jr., et al. "Failure of Association of Premature Rupture of Membranes with Respiratory-Distress Syndrome," *New England Journal of Medicine*, 292:24:1253–1292, June 12, 1975

Kappy, Kenneth A., M.D., et al. "Premature Rupture of the Membranes: A Conservative Approach," *American Journal of Obstetrics and Gynecology*, 134:6:655–661, July 15, 1979

Kaye, Edward M., M.D., and Elizabeth C. Dooling, M.D. "Neonatal Herpes Simplex Meningoencephalitis Associated With Fetal Monitor Scalp Electrodes," *Neurology*, 31:1045–1047, August 1981

Larned, Deborah. "Cesarean Births: Why They Are Up 100 Percent," *Ms.*, October 1978

Marieskind, Helen A., Dr. P.H. *An Evaluation of Cesarean Section in the United States*, Washington D.C.: Department of Health, Education and Welfare, June 1979

McQuaig, Linda. "Doctor's Choice, Mother's Trauma," *Macleans*, July 28, 1980

Montagu, Ashley, Ph.D. *Touching*, New York and London: Columbia University Press, 1971

"More Attacks on Cesarean Deliveries," *Science News*, May 30, 1981

"The New Scarlet Letter," *Time*, August 2, 1982

Pines, Maya. "How Old is Too Old to Have a Baby?" *McCall's*, June 1980

Pitkin, Roy, M.D. "Breech Delivery—Some Thoughts on a Continuing Predicament," *Contemporary Ob/Gyn*, March 1982

Placek, Paul J., Ph.D., and Selma M. Taffel. "The Frequency of Complications in Cesarean and Noncesarean Deliveries, 1970–1978," *Public Health Reports*, 98:4:396–400, July-August 1983

————, and Selma M. Taffel. "One-Sixth of 1980 U.S. Births by Cesarean Section," prepublication release for *Public Health Reports*, March–April 1982

————, and Selma Taffel. "Trends in Cesarean Section Rates for the United States, 1970–78," *Public Health Reports*, 95:6:540–548, November–December 1980

————, Selma Taffel and Joel C. Kleinman, Ph.D. "Trends and Variations in Cesarean Section Delivery," *United States Health,* PHS 81–1232, U.S. Department of Health and Human Services, 1980

Randal, Judith. "Doctors: First Cesarean Section Needn't Start Pattern," *New York Daily News,* reprinted in Boulder *Daily Camera,* February 25, 1982

Reeves, Billy D., M.D., and Ernest R. Anderson. "Perinatal Mortality Rate at a Community Hospital, 1956 to 1975," *American Journal of Obstetrics and Gynecology,* 128:6:677–683, July 15, 1977

"Review of Practice Shows 'Surprising' Rise in Cesareans," *Ob./Gyn. News,* May 15, 1979

Richart, Ralph M., M.D., ed. "Is there a scientific basis for repeat cesarean?" *Contemporary Ob/Gyn,* January 1982

————. "Turn a Breech and Prevent a Cesarean," *Contemporary Ob/Gyn,* March 1982

Rubin, George, M.D., et al. "The Risk of Childbearing Re-Evaluated," *American Journal of Public Health,* 71:7:712–716, July 1981

Shearer, Madeleine H., R.P.T. "Complications of Cesarean to Infant," *Birth,* 4:3:105, Fall 1977

————. "Complications of Cesarean to Mothers," *Birth,* 4:3:103–104, Fall 1977

————. "Not Identifying the Sources of the Recent Decline in Perinatal Mortality Rates," *Birth,* 10:1:33–37, Spring 1983

Sumner, Philip E., M.D., and Celeste R. Phillips, R.N., M.S., *Birthing Rooms,* St. Louis, Toronto, London: The C.V. Mosby Co., 1981

Taffel, Selma M. and Paul J. Placek, Ph.D. "Postpartum Sterilization in Cesarean Section and Non-Cesarean Section Deliveries: 1970–1975, United States," *Working Paper Series,* No. 2, U.S. Department of Health and Human Services, October 1980

Varner, Michael W., M.D., and Rudolph P. Galask, M.D. "Conservative Management of Premature Rupture of the Membranes," *American Journal of Obstetrics and Gynecology,* 140:1:39–45, May 1, 1981

Williams, Ronald L., Ph.D., and Peter M. Chen, B.A. "Identifying the Sources of the Recent Decline in Perinatal Mortality Rates in California," *The New England Journal of Medicine,* Special Article, 306:4:207–214, January 28, 1982

"Why are Cesarean Rates So High?" *Contemporary Ob/Gyn,* December 1981

Young, Diony, "Cesareans in the United States: A Sobering Situation," *ICEA News,* 18:41:1, 1979

————, and Charles Mahan, M.D. *Unnecessary Cesareans,* ICEA, Minneapolis, 1980

Yudkin, Patricia, M.A., Diana Pettitti, M.D., Ronald L. Williams, Ph.D. and Peter M. Chen, B.A. "Identifying the Sources of the Recent Decline in Perinatal Mortality Rates in California," *Birth,* 10:1:39–45, Spring 1983

9■ Having a Cesarean Is Having a Baby

Botlos, Kate. "Birth Dis-Illusions," *Mothering,* Summer 1979

Brorup-Watson, Marianne. "Vaginal Birth After Two Cesareans: How to Have Your Cake and Eat It, Too," *ICEA Communications Canada,* Vol. 2, No. 1, 1982

Cohen, Nancy. Interview, September 18, 1982

Heilman, Joan Rattner. "Breaking the Cesarean Cycle," *The New York Times Magazine,* September 7, 1980

Klaus, Marshall H., and John H. Kennell. *Parent-Infant Bonding,* St. Louis: C.V. Mosby Co., 1982

Larned, Deborah. "Cesarean Births: Why They Are Up 100 Per Cent," *Ms.,* October 1978

Meier, Paul R., M.D. and Richard P. Porreco, M.D. "Trial of labor following cesarian section: A two-year experience," *American Journal of Obstetrics and Gynecology,* 144:6:671–678, November 15, 1982

Porreco, Richard P., M.D. Phone Interview, October 1983

"Ob. Gyns. Concerned Over Continuing Rise in C–Section Rate—'Once Section, Always Section' An Anachronistic Concept," *Ob. Gyn. News*, November 1, 1979

Randal, Judith. "Doctor: First Cesarean Section Needn't Start Pattern," Boulder *Daily Camera*, February 25, 1982

Reisner, Laurence S., M.D. "Anesthesia for Cesarean Section," *Clinical Obstetrics and Gynecology*, 23:2:517–523, June 1980

Richart, Ralph M., M.D., ed. "Is There a Scientific Basis for Repeat Cesarean?" *Contemporary Ob/Gyn*, January 1982

Shearer, Elizabeth Conner, M.Ed., M.P.H. "Education for Vaginal Birth After Cesarean," *Birth*, 9:1:31–34, Spring 1982

10■ Understanding Your Feelings

Adams, Virginia. "Pain and Pleasure in Childbirth," *Psychology Today*, March 1983

Affonso, Dyanne D., R.N., M.S. "Missing Pieces, A Study of Postpartum Feelings," *Birth*, 4:4, Winter 1977

Frate, Dennis A., Ph.D. "Most Women Show Some Postpartum Depression," *Ob. Gyn News*, January 15, 1979

Halas, Celia, Ph.D., and Roberta Matteson, Ph.D. *I've Done So Well—Why Do I Feel So Bad?* New York: Macmillan, 1978; London: Collier Macmillan, 1978

Kitzsinger, Sheila. "Brief Encounters: Effects of Induction on the Mother-Baby Relationship," *Practitioner*, 1976.

Lang, Raven. "Delivery In the Home," *Maternal Attachment and Mothering Disorders: A Round Table*, Marshall H. Klaus, M.D., Treville Leger, and Mary Ann Trause, Ph.D., eds., Johnson & Johnson, 1975

Loftus, Elizabeth. *Memory—Surprising New Insights Into How We Remember And Why We Forget*, Reading, Massachusetts: Addison-Wesley, 1980

Lozoff, Betsy, M.D. "Birth in Non-Industrial Societies," *Birth, Interaction and Attachment: Exploring the Foundations for Modern Perinatal Care*, Marshall Klaus, M.D. and Martha Oschrin Robertson, eds, Johnson & Johnson, 1982

Newton, Niles, Ph.D. Address reported in *News From H.O.M.E. (Home Oriented Maternity Experience)*, 1977

———. *Maternal Emotions*, New York: Paul B. Hoeber, Inc., 1955

Oakley, Ann. *Women Confined: Towards A Sociology of Childbirth*, New York: Schocken, 1980

Peterson, Gayle. *Birthing Normally: A Personal Growth Approach to Childbirth*, Berkeley, California: Mindbody Press, 1981

Rothman, Barbara Katz. *In Labor: Women & Power In the Birthplace*, New York: W. W. Norton and Company, 1982

Sanz, Luis E., M.D., and James A Patterson, M.D. "How to Tell When Your Patient Has Postpartum Depression," *Contemporary Ob/Gyn*, Volume 18, October 1981

Scarf, Maggie. *Unfinished Business: Pressure Points in The Lives of Women*, Garden City, New York: Doubleday, 1980

Stewart, David, Ph.D., ed. *Five Standards for Safe Childbearing*, Marble Hill, Mo.: NAPSAC Reproductions, 1981

Sumner, Philip E., M.D., and Celeste R. Phillips. *Birthing Rooms-Concept and Reality*, St. Louis: C.V. Mosby, 1981

Yarrow, Leah. "When My Baby Was Born," *Parents*, August 1982

11■ Your Supporters

Bradley, Robert, M.D. *Husband-Coached Childbirth,* New York: Harper & Row, 1981

Curran, Patricia, R.N., co-director of Monitrices of Maryland. Interview and correspondence, July, August, December, 1982

Dick-Read, Grantly, M.D. *Childbirth Without Fear: The Principles and Practices of Natural Childbirth,* New York: Harper & Row, 1974

Karmel, Marjorie. *Thank You, Dr. Lamaze: A Mother's Experience in Painless Childbirth,* New York: Doubleday, 1965

Kennell, John H., M.D. "Are We In the Midst of a Revolution?" *Am. J. Dis. Child,* Vol. 134, March 1980

————. "The Physiologic Effects of a Supportive Companion (Doula) During Labor," *Birth, Interaction and Attachment: Exploring the Foundations for Modern Perinatal Care,* Marshall Klaus, M.D., and Martha Oschrin Robertson, eds., Johnson & Johnson, 1982

Klaus, Marshall H., M.D., and John H. Kennell, M.D. *Parent–Infant Bonding,* St. Louis: C.V. Mosby Company, 1982

Kuehn, William L., Ph.D., then Director of Communications for the American Nurses Association. Interview and correspondence, March 1982

Lozoff, Betsy, M.D. "Birth in Non-Industrial Societies," *Birth, Interaction and Attachment: Exploring the Foundations for Modern Perinatal Care,* Marshall Klaus, M.D., and Martha Oschrin Robertson, eds., Johnson & Johnson, 1982

McNatt, Nona L., R.N., C.N.M. "A Lesson in Empathy," *Obstetrics and Gynecology,* 56:1, July 1980

Memery, Marsha, R.N., Manchester Monitrices. Phone Interview, December 1982

"Nursing Staff Shortage," *Hospital Administration,* Second Quarter Investors Report, Abbott Laboratories, October 1981

Pryor, Karen. *Lads Before the Wind,* New York: Harper & Row, 1975

Raphael, Dana, Ph.D. *The Tender Gift,* Englewood Cliffs, New Jersey: Prentice-Hall, 1973

Simkin, Penny, R.P.T. "The Childbirth Educator: Certified to Represent the Hospital or the Parents?" *Birth,* Vol. 7:3, Fall 1980

————. Interview, December 1982

Sosa, Roberto, M.D., John Kennell, M.D., Marshall Klaus, M.D., and Juan Urrutia, M.D. "The Effect of a Supportive Woman on Mothering Behavior and the Duration and Complications of Labor, Abstracted," *Pediatr Res,* 13:338, 1979

————, John Kennell, M.D., Marshall Klaus, M.D., Steven Robertson, Ph.D., and Juan Urrutia, M.D. "The Effect of a Supportive Companion on Perinatal Problems, Length of Labor, and Mother-Infant Interaction," *The New England Journal of Medicine,* 303:11, September 11, 1980

Sumner, Philip E., M.D., and Celeste R. Phillips, R.N. *Birthing Rooms: Concept and Reality,* St. Louis: C.V. Mosby Company, 1981

Tanzer, Deborah, Ph.D. "Natural Childbirth: Pain or Peak Experience?" *Psychology Today,* October 1968

Waletzky, Lucy R., M.D. "Husbands' Problems with Breastfeeding," *Amer. J. Orthopsychiat.,* 49(2), April 1979

Yarrow, Leah. "Fathers Who Deliver," *Parents,* June 1981

12■ How to Have a Normal Vaginal Birth

"Aspirin Causes Unusual Bleeding in Mothers and Their Newborns," Boulder *Daily Camera,* October 7, 1982

Berman, Salee, C.N.M. "How Mothers' Smoking Affects Her Child," NACHIS, undated

Berry, Karen. "Childbirth—Letting Gravity Help," *Ms.,* February 1982

"Birthing Chair Cuts Labor Time," *New Woman*, September–October 1981

Brewer, Gail Sforza, with Tom Brewer, M.D. *What Every Pregnant Woman Should Know*, New York: Random House, 1977

Brown, J.E., M.P.H., Ph.D., et al. "Influence of Pregnancy Weight Gain on the Size of Infants Born to Underweight Women," *Obstetrics and Gynecology*, 57:1:13–17, January 1981

Brozan, Nadine. "Childbirth is Eased in a Chair," *New York Times*, February 2, 1981

Burchell, R. Clay, M.D. "The Negotiated Medical Contract," *The Female Patient*, August 1981

Carr, Daniel B., M.D., et al. "Physical Conditioning Facilitates the Exercise– Induced Secretion of Beta–Endorphins and Beta–Lipotropin in Women," *New England Journal of Medicine*, 305:10:560–562, September 3, 1981

Cassel, Eric J., M.D. "The Nature of Suffering and the Goals of Medicine," *New England Journal of Medicine*, Special Article, 306:11:639–645, March 18, 1982

"Clinic Finds Squatting Eases Birth," *Seattle Post Intelligencer*, June 9, 1980

Cogan, Rosemary. "Comfort During Prepared Childbirth as a Function of Parity, Reported by Four Classes of Participant Observers," *Journal of Psychosomatic Research*, Vol. 19, pp. 37–39, 1975

Enkin, M. W., M.D., "Changing Attitudes Toward Childbirth Need Not Create Patient-Physician Conflict," brief, *Postgraduate Medicine*, Vol. 71, No. 1, January 1982

Ewy, Donna and Rodger. *Guide to Family Centered Childbirth*, New York: E. P. Dutton, 1981

———. *Preparation for Childbirth: A Lamaze Guide*, Boulder, Colo.: Pruett, 1970

Gamper, Margaret, R.N. *Preparations for the Heir Minded*, Chicago, self-published, 1971

Gander, Rosemary. "Spontaneous Second Stage Rationale," *Communications Canada*, Vol. 1, No. 2, 1981

Gaskin, Ina May. *Spiritual Midwifery*, Summertown, Tenn.: The Book Publishing Co., 1978

Gillett, Jane. "Childbirth in Pithiviers, France," *Lancet*, 2:8148:894–896, October 27, 1979

Gunn, Gordon C., M.D. "Premature Rupture of the Fetal Membranes," *American Journal of Obstetrics and Gynecology*, 106:3:469–483, 1970

Haire, Doris, D.M.S. Comments at La Leche League International Conference, Chicago, July 1981

Hartman, Rhondda Evans, R.N. *Exercises for True Natural Childbirth*, New York: Harper and Row, 1975

Klaus, Marshall, M.D., and Martha Oschrin Robertson, eds., *Birth, Interaction and Attachment*, Johnson and Johnson Baby Products, 1982

Lappe, Frances Moore. *Diet for a Small Planet*, New York: A Friends of the Earth/Ballantine Book, 1971

Macfarlane, Aidan. *The Psychology of Childbirth*, Cambridge, Mass.: Harvard Press, 1977

McNeal, Chuck, O.C., and Ramona McNeal. "The Neurophysiology of Letting Go," *Special Delivery*, Spring 1980

"Motherly Advice; Don't Drink While Pregnant," *Time*, August 3, 1981

Noble, Elizabeth, R.P.T. *Essential Exercises for the Child Bearing Year*, Boston: Houghton Mifflin Co., 1982

Norton, Mary. "Study Explains How Smoking Affects Fetal Growth," *Denver Post*, April 26, 1979

Odent, Michel, M.D. *Birth Reborn*, New York: Pantheon, 1984

———. "The Evolution of Obstetrics at Pithiviers," *Birth*, 8:1:7–15, Spring 1981

————. "The Milieu and Obstetrical Positions During Labor. A New Approach From France," reprint from Marshall Klaus, M.D., undated

Pomerance, Jeffrey, M.D., M.P.H., et al. "Attitudes Toward Weight Gain in Pregnancy," *The Western Journal of Medicine*, 133:4:289–291, October 1980

"Pregnancy, Alcohol Don't Mix: Report," Boulder *Daily Camera*, July 16, 1981

Shearer, Madeleine H., R.P.T. "Malnutrition in Middle Class Pregnant Women," *Birth*, 7:1:27–35, Spring 1980

"Smoking Termed 'National Tragedy,' " Boulder *Daily Camera*, January 11, 1979

"Study Shows Smoking Increases Fetal and Maternal Risks," *Genesis*, Dec./Jan. 1981

Tanzer, Deborah, Ph.D. "Natural Childbirth: Pain or Peak Experience?," *Psychology Today*, October 1968

"Unborn Baby is the Loser When Woman Smokes, Drinks," *Everett Herald*, January 9, 1980

"Unclamped Cord Seen as Mother's Helper," *Medical World News*, March 14, 1969

Vincent, Peggy, R.N. Review of *Spiritual Midwifery*, *Birth*, 4:2:81–82, Summer 1977

"When You Drink, Your UNBORN BABY Does, Too!" The National Foundation/ March of Dimes, undated

White, Gregory, M.D. *Emergency Childbirth*, Franklin Park, Ill.: Police Training Foundation, 1958

13■ The Nurse

Barclay, Delores. "American Salary Oddities, Outrages," *Rocky Mountain News*, June 3, 1980

Culley, Phyllis, Pamela Milan, Claudia Roginski, John Waterhouse, and Ben Wood, "Are Breast-Fed Babies Still Getting a Raw Deal?" *British Medical Journal*, Vol. 2, January 1979

Fenwick, Loel, M.D. "Letter from the Executive Editor," *The Cybele Report*, quoting John Moyer, M.D., "Effecting Change in Maternity Care," 1:3, Spring 1980

Gardner, Sandra L., P.N.P. "Mothering: The Unconscious Conflict Between Nurses and New Mothers," *Keeping Abreast, Journal of Human Nurturing*, 3:3, July– September 1978

Gartner, Lawrence M., M.D. "Facts And Fantasies About Neonatal Jaundice," address, 10th Annual Seminar for Physicians on Breastfeeding, La Leche League International, Las Vegas, July 15 and 16, 1982

Hillard, Paula J. Adams, M.D. "When an Obstetrician Has a Baby," *The Female Patient*, 6:8, August 1981

Johnson, Walter L., Ph.D., "Supply and Demand For Registered Nurses: Some Observations on the Current Picture and Prospects to 1985," Part I and Part II, *Nursing & Health Care*, September 1980

Klass, Kay, B.S.N., and Kay Capps, R.N. "Nine Years' Experience With Family-Centered Maternity Care in A Community Hospital," *Birth*, 7:3, Fall 1980

Kuehn, William L., Ph.D., then American Nurses' Association Director of Communication. Correspondence, 1981 and 1982

Meara, Hanna, Ph.D. "A Key to Successful Breastfeeding in a Non-Supportive Culture," *Journal of Nurse Midwivery*, Vol. XXI:1, Spring 1976

Moses, Evelyn and Aleda Roth, "What Do Statistics Reveal About the Nation's Nurses," *American Journal of Nursing*, October 1979

"Nursing Staff Shortage," *Hospital Administration*, Second Quarter Investors Report, Abbott Laboratories, October 1981

"Perinatal Center: Serving High-Risk Mothers and Babies," *News Rounds*, Rush-Presbyterian-St. Luke's Medical Center, Chicago, December 1981

Tompson, Marian. "The Effectiveness of Mother-To-Mother Help—Research on the La Leche League International Program," *Birth*, 3:4, 1976

14■ Your Baby Doctor

Bedell, Richard, M.D. Interview, October 1982

Bell, Edward F., M.D., et al. "Combined Effect of Radiant Warmer and Phototherapy on Insensible Water Loss in Low-Birth-Weight Infants," *Journal of Pediatrics*, 94:5, May 1979

Bergevin, Y., M. Kramer, C. Dougherty, "Do Infant Formula Samples Affect the Duration of Breastfeeding?" abstract presented at Annual Meeting of Ambulatory Pediatric Association, May 1981

"Birth Defects from PHisoHex Higher Than First Expected," Boulder *Daily Camera*, June 28, 1978

Blim, R. Don, M.D. "The President's Column—The 51st Year," *News and Comments*, 31:11, American Academy of Pediatrics, November 1980

———. "The President's Column," *News & Comments*, September 1981

Boylan, P., M.B. "Oxytocin and Neonatal Jaundice," *British Medical Journal*, September 4, 1976

Brown, Stephen W., Ph.D. "Survey Results: How Physicians See Themselves— And Their Image," *Medical Marketing Media*, 17:2, February 1982

Buchan, Peter C. "Pathogenesis of Neonatal Hyperbilirubinaemia After Induction of Labour with Oxytocin," *British Medical Journal*, 2(6200)1255–57, November 17, 1979

Butterfield, Perry M., et al. "Effects of Silver Nitrate on Initial Visual Behavior," *Am. J. Dis. Child*, 132:426, April 1978

———. Phone Interview, October 1983

Campbell, Neil, M.B., et al. "Increased Frequency of Neonatal Jaundice in a Maternity Hospital," *British Medical Journal*, June 7, 1975

Campbell, Priscilla, Academy of Pediatrics spokeswoman. Communication, quoting Edward J. Santzman, M.D., Hollywood, Florida pediatrician who is Chairman of the Provisional Committee on Practice and Ambulatory Medicine for the Academy of Pediatrics

"Canadian LLL," *News*, La Leche League, January–February 1981

Chew, W.C., and I.L. Swann, "Influence of Simultaneous Low Amniotomy and Oxytocin Infusion and Other Maternal Factors on Neonatal Jaundice: A Prospective Study," *British Medical Journal*, January 8, 1977

Cockington, Richard A., M.B., B.S., F.R.A.C.P. "A Guide to the Use of Phototherapy in the Management of Neonatal Hyperbilirubinemia," *Pediatrics*, 95:2, August 1979

Committee on Drugs, Committee on Fetus and Newborn, Committee on Infectious Diseases, "Prophylaxis and Treatment of Neonatal Gonococcal Infections," *Pediatrics*, 65:5, May 1980

Committee on Nutrition, "Encouraging Breastfeeding," *Pediatrics*, 65:3, March 1980

Cook, William A., M.D. *Natural Childbirth: Fact and Fallacy*, Chicago: Nelson-Hall, 1982

Costich, Timothy, M.D. Correspondance, 1981

Countryman, Betty Ann, R.N., M.S. "Breastfeeding and Jaundice," Information Sheet No. 10, La Leche League International, June 1978

Daystar, Paula, C.N.P. "Jaundice," Denver Birth Center, *News*, 2:3, Fall 1981

Dharamraj, Claude, M.D., Concepcion G. Sia, M.D., Catherine M. P. Kierney, M.B., Ch.B., and Aruna Parekh. "Observations on Maternal Preference for Rooming-in Facilities," *Pediatrics*, 67:5, May 1981

Drew, J. H., K. J. Marriage, V. V. Boyle, E. Bajraszewski, and J. M. McNamara, "Short and Long-Term Complications," *Archives of Disease in Childhood*, 51: 454, 1976

"Editor's Note: A Jaundiced Baby," *News,* La Leche League, November–December 1982

Fishbane, Marsha, M.D., Sc.M., and Barbara Starfield, M.D., M.P.H. "Child Health Care in the United States—A Comparison of Pediatricians and General Practitioners," *The New England Journal of Medicine,* 305:10, September 3, 1981

Gartner, Lawrence M., M.D. "Facts and Fantasies About Neonatal Jaundice," address, 10th annual Seminar for Physicians on Breastfeeding, sponsored by La Leche League International, Las Vegas, July 15 and 16, 1982

————. "Hospital Policies, Breastfeeding, and Neonatal Jaundice," *Breastfeeding Abstracts,* 2:4, La Leche League International, Spring 1983

Gordon, Jay, M.D. Phone Interview, October 1982

Graham, Bruce D., M.D. "The President's Column—Why Change Pediatrics?" *News and Comment,* 31:7, American Academy of Pediatrics, July 1980

Gross, Steven J., M.D. "Vitamin E and Neonatal Bilirubinemia," *Pediatrics,* 64:3, September 1979

Hammerman, Cathy, M.D., Arthur I. Eidelman, M.D., Kwang-Sun Lee, M.D., and Lawrence M. Gartner, M.D. "Comparative Measurements of Phototherapy: A Practical Guide," *Pediatrics,* 67:3, March 1981

Klaus, Marshall, M.D. Correspondence, March 1982

————, and John Kennell, M.D. *Parent-Infant Bonding,* St. Louis: C.V. Mosby, 1982

Kleinberg, Warren M., M.D., M.P.H. "Counseling Mothers in the Hospital Postpartum Period: A Comparison of Techniques," *Public Health Briefs,* 67:7, July 1977

"Lawsuit Fever," *The Journal of Insurance,* 39:5, September/October 1978

Lewis, H. M., et al. "Use or Abuse of Phototherapy for Physiological Jaundice of Newborn Infants," *Lancet II,* 8295:408, 21 August 1982

Lozoff, Betsy, M.D. "Birth in Non-Industrial Societies," *Birth, Interaction and Attachment—Exploring the Foundations of Modern Perinatal Care,* Marshall H. Klaus, M.D., and Martha Oschrin Robertson, eds., Johnson & Johnson, 1982

Mawardi, Betty Hosmer, Ph.D. "Satisfactions, Dissatisfactions, and Causes of Stress in Medical Practice," *JAMA,* 241:14, April 6, 1979

Mendelsohn, Robert, M.D. "Effects of Bilirubin Lights Questioned," 'People's Doctor,' Boulder *Daily Camera,* June 13, 1980

Neifert, Marianne, M.D. Interview, March 1982

Nutrition Committee of the Canadian Pediatric Society and the Committee on Nutrition of the American Academy of Pediatrics, "Breastfeeding," a commentary in Celebration of the International Year of the Child, 1979, *Pediatrics,* 62:4, October 1978

O'Connell, Patricia, March of Dimes Director of Media. Phone Interview, August 1982

O'Connor, Susan, M.D., Peter M. Vietze, Ph.D., Kathryn B. Sherrod, Ph.D., Howard M. Sandler, Ph.D., and William A. Altemeier III, M.D., "Reduced Incidence of Parenting Inadequacy Following Rooming-in," *Pediatrics,* 66:2, August 1980

Odell, Gerard B., et al. "Studies in Kernicterus, III. The Saturation of Serum Proteins with Bilirubin During Neonatal Life and Its Relationship to Brain Damage at Five Years," *Pediatrics,* 76:1, January 1970

"Old Assumptions About Preventing Infants' Eye Disease Are Incorrect, Physician Says," *News Release,* American Academy of Pediatrics, March 22, 1982

Pittard, William B., III, M.D., and Mandel de Carvalho, M.D. "Letters," *Birth,* 9:2, Summer 1982

Preis, Oded, M.D., and Nathan Rudolph, M.B.B.Ch. "Abdominal Distension in Newborn Infants on Phototherapy—the Role of Eye Occulsion," *Journal of Pediatrics,* 94:5, May 1979

"Professional Pharmaceutical and Nutritional Products," Abbott Laboratories Annual Report, 1981

Ramer, Cyril, M.D. Interview, October 1982

Rosta, J., et al. "Delayed Meconium Passage and Hyperbilirubinemia," *Lancet,* 2:1138, 23 November 1968

Rubin, Rosalyn A., et al. "Neonatal Serum Bilirubin Levels Related to Cogitive Development at Ages 4 Through 7 Years," *Pediatrics,* 94:4, April 1979

Scheidt, P.C., et al. "Toxicity to Bilirubin in Neonates: Infant Development During First Year in Relation to Maximum Neonatal Serum Bilirubin Concentration," *Journal of Pediatrics,* 91:2, August 1977

Shaw, E.B. "Gonorrhea Opthalmia Neonatorium," *Pediatrics,* 52:281–282, 1973

Silverman, William A., M.D. *Retrolental Fibroplasia: A Modern Parable,* New York: Grune and Stratton, 1980, review in *Birth,* 8:3, Judith Lumley, Ph.D., Fall 1981

Simkin, Penny, R.P.T. and Margot Edwards, R.N., M.S. "When Your Baby Has Jaundice," Seattle: the pennypress, 1979

Simkin, P., P. A. Simkin, and Margot Edwards. "Neonatal Jaundice," *Birth,* 6:1, Spring 1979

Speck, W. T., C. C. Chen, and H. S. Rosenkranz. "In Vitro Studies of Effects of Light and Riboflavin on DNA and HeLa Cells," *Pediatr. Res.,* 9:150, 1975

Stewart, David, Ph.D., ed., *The Five Standards for Safe Childbearing,* Marble Hill, Mo.: NAPSAC Productions, 1981

Taylor, Charles, M.D. Interview, January, 1980

Whittaker, Nancy. "A Short Course on Neonatal Jaundice," *Mothering,* Summer 1982

Winfield, C. R., and R. MacFaul. "Clinical Study of Prolonged Jaundice in Breast- and Bottle-fed Babies," *Archives of Disease in Childhood,* 53, 1978

The Womanly Art of Breastfeeding, La Leche League International, Franklin Park, Illinois, 1981

Appendix A
References

Cohen, Herb. *You Can Negotiate Anything,* New York: Bantam, 1982

Enkin, Murray, M.D. La Leche League International Conference, Toronto, 1977

O'Reilly, Jane. "Breakfast with John Kenneth Galbraith—A Man of Influence Offers Advice on Becoming a Woman of Influence," *Savvy,* July 1981

INDEX

ABOUT THE AUTHORS

Diana Korte has won 15 awards for medical journalism in both print and radio, including the 1978 American Academy of Pediatrics Award. She hosts two public radio programs which focus on women's health, and she is a frequent workshop leader and lecturer on health issues. A La Leche League leader for 20 years, she also served as a director of La Leche League's International Board. She has been a maternity care consultant to doctors, hospitals and consumers, and served on local and state health-related boards of directors. She lives in Boulder, Colorado with her husband and four children, and is currently working on another book and a radio documentary about women's health.

Roberta Scaer is a maternity care advocate, breastfeeding counselor, lecturer and workshop leader who has helped women as a La Leche League leader for 18 years. A Phi Beta Kappa graduate of the University of Rochester with a master's degree in social work, she initiated and co-authored the first survey of women's preferences in maternity care. Of her four children, three were born in hospital (two with the Bradley method), and one child was born at home with siblings present. She lives in Boulder, Colorado with her husband, a physician whose specialties are neurology and rehabilitation.